Strength for the Fight

LIBRARY OF RELIGIOUS BIOGRAPHY

Mark A. Noll, Kathryn Gin Lum, and Heath W. Carter, series editors

Long overlooked by historians, religion has emerged in recent years as a key factor in understanding the past. From politics to popular culture, from social struggles to the rhythms of family life, religion shapes every story. Religious biographies open a window to the sometimes surprising influence of religion on the lives of influential people and the worlds they inhabited.

The Library of Religious Biography is a series that brings to life important figures in United States history and beyond. Grounded in careful research, these volumes link the lives of their subjects to the broader cultural contexts and religious issues that surrounded them. The authors are respected historians and recognized authorities in the historical period in which their subject lived and worked.

Marked by careful scholarship yet free of academic jargon, the books in this series are well-written narratives meant to be read and enjoyed as well as studied.

Titles include:

*Her Heart Can See: The Life and Hymns of **Fanny J. Crosby***
by Edith L. Blumhofer

*The Religious Journey of **Dwight D. Eisenhower**: Duty, God, and Country*
by Jack M. Holl

*One Soul at a Time: The Story of **Billy Graham***
by Grant Wacker

***Thomas Merton** and the Monastic Vision*
by Lawrence S. Cunningham

***Howard Thurman** and the Disinherited: A Religious Biography*
by Paul Harvey

For a complete list of published volumes, see the back of this volume.

Strength for the Fight

The Life and Faith of Jackie Robinson

Gary Scott Smith

WILLIAM B. EERDMANS PUBLISHING COMPANY

GRAND RAPIDS, MICHIGAN

Wm. B. Eerdmans Publishing Co.
4035 Park East Court SE, Grand Rapids, Michigan 49546
www.eerdmans.com

28 27 26 25 24 23 22   1 2 3 4 5 6 7

ISBN 978-0-8028-7942-4

Library of Congress Cataloging-in-Publication Data

Names: Smith, Gary Scott, 1950– author.
Title: Strength for the fight : the life and faith of Jackie Robinson / Gary Scott
    Smith.
Description: Grand Rapids, Michigan : William B. Eerdmans Publishing
    Company, 2022. | Series: Library of religious biography | Includes bibli-
    ographical references and index. | Summary: "A religious biography of
    Jackie Robinson that describes how his faith sustained him during his
    struggle to integrate Major League Baseball and later throughout his civil
    rights activism"—Provided by publisher.
Identifiers: LCCN 2022001188 | ISBN 9780802879424 (hardcover)
Subjects: LCSH: Robinson, Jackie, 1919–1972. | Robinson, Jackie, 1919–
    1972—Religion. | Baseball players—United States—Biography. | African
    American baseball players—Biography. | Christian biography—United
    States. | BISAC: BIOGRAPHY & AUTOBIOGRAPHY / Cultural, Ethnic &
    Regional / African American & Black | HISTORY / African American &
    Black
Classification: LCC GV865.R6 S636 2022 | DDC 796.357092 [B]—dc23/
    eng/20220209
LC record available at https://lccn.loc.gov/2022001188

To the members of the 1962 Rockland Little League team:
Tom, Sam, Dave, Jim, Butch, Rolla, Tom, Chuck, Wayne, and Harry.
Like Jackie Robinson, we were baseball pioneers.

Contents

CONTENTS

Preface

Between March and June 1947, three dramatic events changed the course of world history—Harry Truman proclaimed the doctrine that helped save Europe from communism, Congress adopted the Marshall Plan to restore Europe's economy, and Jackie Robinson broke the racial barrier in Major League Baseball (MLB).[1] It may seem strange to place the actions of a baseball player on the same level of significance as events on the grand stage of world politics. But understanding Jackie Robinson's life in the complete context of the United States' noxious history of racism justifies the comparison.

Robinson's gripping story has been told many times. He himself wrote five books, and many biographers, most notably Arnold Rampersad, have described his trials, tribulations, and triumphs. Yet in popular American culture, Robinson is often portrayed as more a monument than a man, more a mythical figure than a human being. To grasp his significance, we must understand the toxic, systemic racism against which Robinson battled his entire life. To him, "one irreducible truth" transcended his remarkable Hall of Fame baseball career and makes his story much more than a tale of athletic prowess. As he declared in his 1972 autobiography, "I was a black man in a white world. *I never had it made.*"[2] In that candid book, as well as in numerous magazine articles and scores of newspaper columns, Robinson vividly described the challenges of being a black American during the middle decades of the twentieth century. We never tire of Robinson's heroic tale because it combines "two American obsessions: sports and freedom."[3]

Despite the many scholarly accounts of Robinson's athletic career and his important role in the expansion of American freedom, Robinson's Christian faith has received far less attention than it deserves. It played a significant role in Robinson's life and achievements, including the integration of MLB. Robinson talked openly about his faith in three of his autobiographies and more fully in an unpublished manuscript titled "My Greatest Day." As he succinctly stated in 1952, "my faith in God . . . sustained me in my fight."[4]

Robinson's style of faith was different from that of evangelical Protestants like Olympic decathlete Rafer Johnson, MLB pitcher Clayton Kershaw, or former National Football League quarterback Tim Tebow, all of whom accentuated their personal relationship with Jesus and exhorted others to commit their lives to Christ as their Savior and Lord. Although frequently acknowledging God's assistance as he battled discrimination in baseball and the larger society, Robinson focused more on the Bible's teaching on social justice than on personal spirituality. Despite this difference, Robinson's faith was deep and meaningful and a powerful force in his life. It clearly played an integral role in shaping his worldview and convictions, which, in turn, undergirded his amazing transformative work as a black athlete and a civil rights activist.

To their credit, three authors have recently highlighted how Robinson's faith inspired him to embrace his excruciatingly difficult role as MLB's first African American player and supported him during his darkest moments. Their books published in 2017—Michael G. Long and Chris Lamb's *Jackie Robinson: A Spiritual Biography; The Faith of a Boundary-Breaking Hero* and Ed Henry's *42 Faith: The Rest of the Jackie Robinson Story*—accentuate Robinson's religious convictions. Long, a religious studies professor, and Lamb, a journalism professor, contend that Robinson's faith supplied him with "inspiration and motivation, comfort and strength, wisdom and direction." They maintain that although his faith was deeply private, Robinson could not have accomplished what he did in baseball or civil rights without it.[5] It enabled him to overcome his childhood poverty and racial discrimination, cope with being court-martialed by the army for refusing to move to the back of a military bus, and endure brutal racism as a baseball player.[6] Henry, a journalist who has worked for CNN and Fox News, insists that Robinson "leaned on the Bible and his personal faith to get him through" his ordeals.[7] Many biographers of Branch Rickey, the Brooklyn Dodgers' general manager who signed Robinson to a contract in 1945, discuss Rickey's strong Christian commitment and religious motives for integrating baseball, but they treat Robinson's faith as secondary.

This book reverses the priorities of most books about Robinson. It situates his faith and life journey, along with the story of the integration of MLB, within broader religious and sociopolitical contexts and in the context of the role of sports in American life more generally. Along with highlighting Robinson's faith, I argue that his breaking of the color barrier in baseball was such a pivotal event not only because of baseball's popularity and significance in American society but also because it helped inspire the civil rights movement of the 1950s and 1960s. I also feature Robinson's own exemplary activism. Both during his baseball career and after his retirement, he strove energetically to end racial discrimination in the United States and to improve the life circumstances and prospects of people of color. By denouncing discrimination in dozens of interviews and hundreds of articles and speeches, supporting numerous civil rights organizations, exhorting presidents to promote equal rights, campaigning for various politicians, creating businesses, and befriending civil rights leaders, Robinson used his platform to uplift all black Americans. Arguably, Robinson did more to benefit American society than any other baseball player and perhaps any other professional sports figure.

Acknowledgments

I n researching and writing this book, I am greatly indebted to many individuals. Historians Mark Noll and Heath Carter, two of the editors of Eerdmans' Library of Religious Biography series, provided much beneficial advice and guidance in revising my manuscript. So did three anonymous readers they solicited to review my book. Christopher Evans, professor of history of Christianity and Methodist studies at Boston University; Michael G. Long, coauthor of *Jackie Robinson: A Spiritual Biography; The Faith of a Boundary-Breaking Hero* (2017); and Michael Stevens, professor of English at Cornerstone University, who blogs regularly about baseball and researches Negro league baseball, all read my manuscript. They provided numerous excellent suggestions for revision and helped prevent interpretive and factual errors. My cousin Tom Smith, who knows as much about baseball as anyone on Earth, and my son Greg Smith read parts of my manuscript and provided valuable feedback. My wife, Jane, helped me with various aspects of my research. Sue McCaffray, a retired history professor at the University of North Carolina Wilmington, procured books for me from the UNCW library during the pandemic. Bruce Kirby, a reference librarian at the Library of Congress, sent me many important primary documents from the Jackie Robinson Papers. Andrew Kloes, an applied researcher at the United States Holocaust Museum, obtained many newspaper articles for me. Bruce Barron once again greatly improved the readability of my manuscript and raised many insightful and helpful questions about my assertions and arguments. Many thanks also go to Tom Raabe for his meticulous copyediting. Both men helped make my book more factually accurate and improved its style and formatting. I am very grateful to all these people.

Introduction

Jackie Robinson—a Trailblazer and a Man of Faith

I n 1947, a man whose grandparents had been enslaved became the catalyst for decisively changing baseball. And by opening the doors of baseball to racial minorities and through his activities after his retirement from the game, Jackie Robinson helped open other fields to racial minorities, including other sports, broadcasting, banking, insurance, and construction. A star athlete at UCLA, a World War II veteran, a baseball Hall of Famer, an outspoken newspaper columnist, a prominent businessman, and a resolute civil rights activist, Robinson played a pivotal role in integrating baseball and combating discrimination. He was a trailblazer, hero, symbol, and man of principle and faith.

Bearing the weight of his race on his shoulders, Robinson faced substantial animosity, extensive verbal abuse, and numerous threats to his life as he demolished the color line in Major League Baseball (MLB). Resolute, assertive, and fearless, he stood up to taunts, insults, beanballs, and flying spikes. Robinson endured spectators flinging watermelons and putting shoe-shine kits outside the Dodgers' dugout; fans of opposing teams likened him to animals and denigrated his family.[1] These obstacles, contends Dodgers' announcer Red Barber, required Robinson to fight harder to succeed than any other baseball player in history.[2] In doing so, he became baseball's biggest attraction since Babe Ruth.

Robinson's integration of MLB in 1947 "is arguably the most significant event in the history of modern American sport," partly because no other sport has the symbolic importance of baseball.[3] The desegregation of baseball

---

1

was much more "public and spectacular than the integration of almost any other aspect of American life."[4] Negro league star Buck O'Neil, later MLB's first African American coach, emphasized that before Martin Luther King Jr. became a civil rights leader, the Supreme Court issued *Brown v. Board of Education*, Rosa Parks initiated the Montgomery bus boycott, and Thurgood Marshall became a Supreme Court justice, Robinson integrated baseball. King called Robinson the true founder of the civil rights movement; Barack Obama insisted that "there is a straight line from what Jackie did to me being elected the first African-American president." Robinson's quest to integrate MLB in 1946 and 1947 attracted more sustained public attention than any other episode in the history of employment discrimination in America.[5]

Robinson's dazzling performance on the baseball diamond had enormous implications. From 1945 to 1949, he and other black players altered the nation's consciousness and produced a new, although still troubled, pattern of race relations.[6] Robinson represented the new black American: proud of his heritage, articulate, bold, and insistent on equal rights.[7] For many African Americans of his generation, "baseball began and lived through one person: Jackie Robinson. He was the game incarnate."[8] He helped many African Americans achieve what poet Langston Hughes called "the dream deferred."[9]

Robinson understood that his performance as a baseball player was not just a personal triumph; it also helped many white Americans who had been prejudiced against darker-skinned people experience "a breakthrough in their own thinking."[10] Before the civil rights movement gained momentum in the mid-1950s, many black persons viewed Robinson "as their standard-bearer leading the onslaught against segregation." Following his lead, numerous African Americans soon excelled in MLB, and by the late 1960s, they starred in the National Football League and dominated the National Basketball Association.[11] Black athletes have inspired millions of minorities to battle for social equality and pursue their dreams in many areas of society, and sports have helped to increase racial understanding. And yet Robinson's story is not one of complete victory, given the continued persistence of racism in American society.[12]

After 1900, many African American physicians, lawyers, scientists, intellectuals, and entertainers attacked racial discrimination and helped elevate the reputation of their race. Educator Booker T. Washington, professor and author W. E. B. Du Bois, editor and businessman Monroe Trotter, attorney Thurgood Marshall, minister Vernon Johns, labor union leader A. Philip Randolph, scientist and inventor George Washington Carver, college founder and president Mary McLeod Bethune, contralto Marian Anderson, trumpeter and composer Louis Armstrong, composer and orchestra leader Duke Ellington, singer and pianist Nat King Cole, author Richard Wright, poets Paul Laurence Dunbar and Langston Hughes, and actors Paul Robeson and Lena Horne helped lead these efforts. However, the contribution of black athletes was arguably even more impactful.[13]

Several black sports stars captured the public imagination before Jackie Robinson, most notably bicyclist Major Taylor, boxers Jack Johnson and Joe Louis, and track star Jesse Owens. Taylor won the world cycling championship in 1899 and the American sprint championship in 1900 and established numerous track cycling records. Johnson was the world heavyweight boxing champion from 1908 to 1915, and Louis held the same title from 1937 to 1949, the longest tenure in the history of any weight division in boxing. In 1935, Owens broke five world records and equaled a sixth in track and field, and the next year he won four gold medals at the Berlin Olympics. Although all four black athletes endured racial taunts and discrimination, none of them faced as much verbal abuse and as many threats as Robinson or did as much to advance black civil rights.

Robinson's cracking of the long-standing color barrier in baseball, writes Scott Simon, does not rank as high in Americana as Revolutionary troops wintering in Valley Forge, Harriet Tubman's daring rescues, Yankees and Confederates fighting at Gettysburg, or Abraham Lincoln's Civil War ordeal, but his story "testifies to the power of pure personal courage to turn history and transform adversaries into admirers." It is the tale of a man who had the audacity and verve to unflinchingly resist ridicule, smash line drives after being knocked down by beanballs, and steal home to the delight of thousands of fans. America already had black heroes, but Robinson's audacity and accomplishments dramatized the kind of courage African Americans needed to secure their rights.[14]

A Complicated History

In popular culture, the tale of the desegregation of baseball is simple and straightforward: Jackie Robinson singlehandedly integrated the game in

April 1947. The actual story is much more complicated, because it also involves Native Americans, Latinos, and Asians, not just whites and blacks. Robinson's historic role is "part of a larger, longer, and more complex process whose significance" has been incorrectly buried "beneath a black-white narrative" that portrays "the contributions of Latinos as inconsequential to the story of race in organized baseball."[15] In the 1880s about twenty-five blacks participated in white professional leagues, with brothers Moses Fleetwood Walker and Weldy Walker playing for the major league Toledo franchise in 1884.[16] Several Native Americans, including Louis Sockalexis, Charles Albert Bender, John T. Meyers, and Jim Thorpe, broke into MLB in the late nineteenth or early twentieth century.[17] Thorpe is the best-known Native American ballplayer, but Bender is a Hall of Fame pitcher who compiled an impressive 212–127 record. Professional baseball's color line was never officially stated and was not legally binding; only an informal "gentleman's agreement" kept baseball executives from signing blacks. Whether a player with darker skin would be accepted in MLB depended on how his teammates, his opponents, the fans, and the press treated him. Before 1947, MLB officials used "racial ambiguity and plausible deniability" as a basis for signing about fifty players from Latin America, thirty of whom made their debut between 1935 and 1945. Washington Senators' owner Clark Griffith, who signed about one-quarter of these players, contended that the Cubans who played for his team were not black but rather individuals born to "Spanish" parents. These lighter-skinned, Spanish-speaking players served "as test subjects in a battle over the color line's exclusionary point" in the almost fifty years prior to baseball's "great experiment" with Robinson.[18] Thirteen of MLB's sixteen teams had at least one Latino player before 1947. Cuban Adolfo Luque, for example, pitched for four National League teams from 1914 to 1935, winning 194 games while losing 179. Moreover, during the 1930s and 1940s, teams composed of white MLB players, Latinos from Central and South America and the Caribbean islands, and Negro league stars competed against each other in hundreds of fall and winter games throughout the southern United States and Latin America, as many blacks, whites, and Cubans had done earlier.

During the first half of the twentieth century, baseball players, like leaders in other sectors of American life, "created, revised, re-created, nullified, negotiated, and invented racial categories to serve their interests or to create group identities."[19] Baseball executives' desire to expand their markets, attract more fans, increase profits, hire players inexpensively, and control their "employees" pitted owners against each other, owners against players, players against each other, and whites against racial minorities. In this context, Latinos, with their ambiguously perceived racial status as neither white nor black, could be permitted to play without eroding the color line. Moreover, as Rickey did later with Robinson, owners who signed Latinos, who were typically designated as persons having Spanish or Iberian ancestry, put other executives in the awkward position of having to protest the inclusion of a group of players. Despite the arduous efforts of MLB executives to define Latino players in suitable ways, however, their status as nonwhite limited their participation and subjected them to constant scrutiny and harassment. As a result, between 1905 and 1947, more than 80 percent of Latinos played in the Negro leagues (where they represented 10 to 15 percent of all players) rather than in MLB. Latinos nevertheless helped challenge and weaken racial barriers, thereby beginning to crack the door open for other people of color. On the other hand, only after Robinson broke the color barrier could Latinos acknowledge their racial identity openly. Between 1947 and 1959, about thirty-five Latinos who self-identified as black entered the majors.[20]

The Importance of Jackie Robinson

African American journalist Carl Rowan correctly predicted in 1960 that future generations would remember Jackie Robinson as a "proud crusader against pompous bigots and timid sentinels of the status quo."[21] Nevertheless, between his retirement from baseball in 1956 and his death in 1972, although Robinson remained personally popular and even revered in some black circles and was courted by numerous black leaders and organizations and by both Republican and Democratic politicians, the story of his remarkable achievement under incredible duress and its importance for American sports and society were seldom emphasized. Robinson's 1972 autobiography attracted significant attention, and when other athletes broke racial barriers, they were often identified as the Jackie Robinson of their sport. His widow, Rachel, worked strenuously to keep her husband's legacy alive. Nevertheless, the baseball star's saga and accomplishments were underappreciated until 1997.

Beginning with the celebration of the fiftieth anniversary of his trailblazing year, however, Robinson's reputation has been rejuvenated. The drama and significance of his life story have been extensively portrayed and discussed, lifting him to almost legendary status. Countless scholarly and popular-level publications, dozens of children's books, a number of novels, hundreds of sermons, and several movies (most notably *42* in 2013) have extolled his achievements. Communities have named baseball fields, parks, playgrounds, schools, streets, and scholarships in his honor. Postage stamps (in 1982, Robinson became the first MLB player to appear on a stamp), T-shirts, coins, collectible dolls, and statues all display his image. In 1997, MLB retired number 42, prohibiting any team from using it; he was the first professional athlete in any sport to be honored in this way. There is one exception per year: since 2004, April 15 has been celebrated as Jackie Robinson Day and everyone—all players, coaches, managers, and umpires throughout MLB—wears number 42 in tribute.

When Commissioner Bud Selig announced the MLB-wide retirement of Robinson's number in 1997, he declared, "No single person is bigger than the game of baseball . . . except Jackie Robinson."[22] Fifteen years later, Selig proclaimed that Robinson "transcended the sport he loved and helped change our country in the most powerful way imaginable."[23] Robinson's entry into MLB, opined the *Los Angeles Daily News*, was "the sport's most powerful moment," with a great impact not only on baseball but on society.[24] Without using mass marches, governmental aid, or judicial intervention, baseball, more than any other entity, cracked racial barriers in the late 1940s and 1950s. Not only was Robinson the first African American to play MLB since the 1880s, but during his playing career and for the remainder of his life, he "personified blacks in baseball" and through his actions and personality "probed and expanded the boundaries of the 'noble experiment.'"[25]

Perhaps no MLB player contributed more to American society after his playing days ended than Jackie Robinson. He gave speeches throughout the nation, and hundreds of his newspaper columns denounced discrimination. He raised money for civil rights causes, created businesses to employ blacks and improve their lives, urged presidents to make civil rights a higher priority, and campaigned for several candidates, especially New

York governor and Republican presidential candidate Nelson Rockefeller. He wrote several books and pressured MLB to hire African American executives, managers, and coaches. More than any athlete in any sport, Robinson articulated and advanced the cause of black civil rights both during and after his playing career.[26]

Beyond all this, Robinson was perhaps the most versatile athlete in American history. He is the first person to letter in four sports at UCLA. He was the Pacific Coast Conference's leading scorer in basketball for two consecutive years, averaged twelve yards a carry in football as a junior, and won the NCAA long jump championship in 1940. He is the only person to have been inducted into both the Baseball Hall of Fame and the College Football Hall of Fame.

Robinson's Christian faith was a significant factor in the decision by Dodgers' general manager Branch Rickey to choose him as the man to integrate baseball. His faith helped Robinson cope with the challenges he faced in this endeavor and promote civil rights after his retirement. Robinson was not outspoken about his relationship with God and rarely described his faith in detail, but his relationship with God was very meaningful and inspiring to him. Presbyterian pastor Richard Stoll Armstrong, who helped found the Fellowship of Christian Athletes in 1954, was "tremendously impressed by Jackie Robinson's spiritual depth and theological maturity."[27] Powerfully influenced by three Methodists—his devout mother, Mallie, pastor Karl Downs, and Rickey—Robinson relied on prayer to guide him and sustain him during his trials. Mallie nurtured Jackie spiritually and required him to attend Scott Methodist Church in Pasadena. Downs rescued Robinson from gang life, helped him develop a personal relationship with God, and persuaded him to participate in many church activities, including teaching Sunday school. Rickey's Christian commitment helped motivate him to integrate MLB and to sign Robinson, who believed that God had endowed him with the athletic ability to demonstrate that African Americans could excel in baseball.

Robinson's faith is best understood in the context of black churches, Methodism, and the Social Gospel movement in America from 1880 to 1925. Although Christianity was the religion of their oppressors, many enslaved and free blacks espoused it, beginning in the First Great Awakening in the 1740s. Their understanding of Christianity, however, differed substantially from that of whites. During the eras of slavery and Jim Crow, Christianity provided many African Americans with a sense of personal dignity and worth, spiritual resources to deal with debasement and subjugation, and the promise of a better life in heaven—and hopefully someday on earth. Although characterized by regional, theological, and liturgical differences, black congregations, whether they belonged to black Baptist, Methodist, or Pentecostal denominations or predominantly white denominations, or were independent, have long been a source of inspiration, hope, solidarity, identity, belonging, moral language, and transcendent meaning for countless African Americans.

After emancipation, black congregations, most notably those that were part of the African Methodist Episcopal Church, the African Methodist Episcopal Zion Church, the National Baptist Convention, or the Church of God in Christ, became the center of African American life, furnishing not only spiritual but also social, economic, and educational programs and assistance. In a hostile world, black churches provided a haven where members could express themselves and experience spiritual nourishment and nurture. Literary associations, social clubs, insurance companies, newspapers, and educational organizations were important in the lives of millions of black Americans, but churches were the central black institution. They sponsored schools, promoted economic development, produced leaders, and provided forums for discussing black problems. Almost all black Protestant churches exhorted their parishioners to walk closely with God, view the Bible as God's inspired and authoritative word, pray and read Scripture daily, witness to others, and live morally upright lives.

Since their founding in England by John Wesley in the 1740s, Methodists have stressed intimacy with God, prayer, study of the Bible, and personal holiness. Members of one of America's largest religious communions during the first half of the twentieth century, Methodists strongly emphasized both individual salvation and social amelioration. During these years, many members of the predominantly white Methodist Episcopal Church (MEC) (renamed the Methodist Church after its merger with the Methodist Episcopal Church, South and the Methodist Protestant Church in 1939) worked diligently to shape the nation's moral norms and social practices. MEC minister William H. Brooks helped found the NAACP (National Association for the Advancement of Colored People) in 1909. Numerous Methodists embraced the Social Gospel, whose adherents strove during the Progressive Era to alleviate social ills, reform American society, and bring the kingdom of God on earth. The MEC created the Methodist Federation for Social Service (later Social Action) in 1907 to further these aims, and many prominent Methodist leaders still actively participated in it in the 1930s, including Francis McConnell, Franklin Harris Rall, Georgia Harkness, Ernest Fremont Tittle, and G. Bromley Oxnam. During the 1920s, the fundamentalist-modernist controversy produced theological division among Methodists (although not as great as Presbyterians and Baptists experienced). In 1946 the Methodist Church had about forty thousand congregations and more than 8 million members.[28] Harkness's *Understanding the Christian Faith* (1947) expressed mainstream Methodist Church views at midcentury, to which Karl Downs, Robinson's pastor at Scott Methodist Church, subscribed. Harkness argued that faith entailed "confident trust, courageous adventure," the "inflowing of God-given power," and "insight that lights the way toward truth." She insisted that "any act or attitude is sinful that runs counter to the nature and the righteous will of God." Harkness asserted that "there are sinful attitudes and acts" as well as "social sins such as racial prejudice, economic injustice, tyranny, persecution and war."[29] Through his preaching, social activism, and personal friendship with Robinson, Karl Downs modeled the motto of Scott Methodist Church, a Methodist Church congregation: "A crusading body seeking to establish a divine society."

From the 1920s to the present, the Methodist Church has been one of America's mainline white Protestant denominations. So named because of their numerical strength, social status, and cultural influence, mainline denominations have also included major Congregationalist, American Baptist, Presbyterian, Lutheran, and Episcopal communions. Although these denominations contained some fundamentalists and liberals, most of their members were theological moderates. As described in more detail in the concluding chapter, these communions emphasized both individual salvation and social activism. Robinson was a part of mainline Protestant congregations during his childhood and young adult years in Pasadena, his baseball career with the Dodgers, and his postbaseball life.

From 1880 to 1925, many black congregations, like their white counterparts, became advocates of the Social Gospel and supplied a wide range of educational, economic, and social services to their parishioners and communities. Reverdy Ransom, Adam Clayton Powell Sr., Henry Hugh Proctor, Francis Grimke, and Richard Robert Wright Jr. spearheaded African American efforts to apply the social teachings of Jesus to society and to combat racial discrimination. Black Christian women, led by Helen Burroughs and Mary McLeod Bethune, worked tirelessly to provide better social conditions, education, and opportunities for African Americans.[30]

Robinson's sermons, speeches, and opinion pieces resonate with the language of black Christians, Methodists, and Social Gospelers. He attacked the same social ills they did while seeking to enhance the dignity and opportunities of his compatriots, who were still second-class citizens. Convictions derived from the black church, Methodists, and the Social Gospel inspired Robinson throughout his adult life and helped empower him to integrate MLB and promote racial equality.[31]

The National Pastime

Since the mid-nineteenth century, baseball has been a major feature of American life and has often been called America's pastime. "Whoever wants to know the heart and mind of America," claimed cultural critic Jacques Barzun, must learn "the rules and realities" of baseball. The sport, he insisted, "expresses the powers of the nation's mind and body" and is "the most active, agile, varied, articulate, and brainy of all group games."[32]

Historian John Thorn declares that baseball "reflects who we have been, who we are, and who we might, with the grace of God, become."[33] The sport has been seen as "a symbol for all that is noble, virtuous and unique about the American experience."[34] In *Take Time for Paradise: Americans and Their Games* (1989), MLB commissioner Bart Giamatti argues that "Baseball fulfills the promise America made itself to cherish the individual while recognizing the overarching claims of the group."[35] Baseball is a mirror of American experiences, reflecting our national successes and failures, but also a projection of the best aspects of our national identity and democratic ideology. It has "served as a metaphor" for America's "highest hopes and best dreams."[36] Baseball also became a cultural battleground over the issues of citizenship, social respectability, and racial equality.[37]

No other sport has embedded itself so deeply in the national psyche or generated such a large body of important literature, from Ring Lardner's

"You Know Me Al" stories in the 1910s through Bernard Malamud's *The Natural* (1952), Mark Harris's *Bang the Drum Slowly* (1956), W. P. Kinsella's *Shoeless Joe* (1982—the basis for the 1989 movie *Field of Dreams*), Doris Kearns Goodwin's *Wait Till Next Year* (2009), and John Grisham's *Calico Joe* (2012). Sportswriters such as Roger Kahn in *The Boys of Summer* (1972) and former New York University president John Sexton in *Baseball as a Road to God* (2014) have analyzed baseball from historical, religious, and philosophical perspectives and celebrated its contributions to American society.[38] "Casey at the Bat" and "Take Me Out to the Ball Game" are among the most recognizable American sports motifs.

Although baseball has complex origins, its invention is popularly credited to Abner Doubleday in 1839. Baseball became well known thanks in large part to Alexander Cartwright, a bank teller and volunteer fireman in New York City, who codified a set of rules for his baseball club, the Knicker-bockers, at midcentury. It was first promoted by members of the Excelsior Club of Brooklyn, who traveled by train through the East in 1860 and played games before large crowds. By the Civil War, hundreds of baseball clubs were competing, and many soldiers played games during their free time.

During the Gilded Age, baseball captured the imagination of millions of Americans.[39] Journalist Henry Chadwick edited the first baseball guides and penned the first expert analysis of the sport in 1868, earning the title "father of baseball." Convinced that baseball provided valuable "physical exercise and healthful outdoor recreation," Chadwick preached that baseball could become "a national sport for Americans."[40] When the National League was created in 1876, other professional sports—boxing, billiards, and horse racing—were widely associated with ignoble aspects of American society, especially gambling and drunkenness. Baseball would deal with moral issues as well—players throwing games, the scheduling of games on Sundays, the selling of alcoholic beverages, and deciding whether owners or players would control the sport. It handled these challenges and "became the undisputed national game" by presenting itself as the sport that best promoted the "popular sentiments of Victorian middle-class maleness." In addition, it embodied hard work, teamwork, and fair competition, virtues allegedly peculiar to America.[41]

From 1890 to 1920, baseball was a "microcosm of America," reflecting the nation's increasing urbanism, professionalism, and commercialism that accompanied the growth of industrial capitalism.[42] During these years, baseball was closely intertwined with the contentious issues of immigration, social control, and social mobility.[43] Baseball thrived because large numbers of people concluded that playing or watching the sport was "the quintessential American experience."[44] In *America's National Game* (1911), Albert Spalding, perhaps baseball's greatest promoter, argued that the game embodied, more than any other sport, America's primary values, including courage, discipline, energy, enthusiasm, pluck, sagacity, and virility.[45]

Since its creation, baseball has loomed large in the nation's consciousness and identity; it has been closely connected with America's principal ideals and mission. Prominent Social Gospel proponents Washington Gladden and Shailer Mathews extolled the value of baseball, arguing that it accentuated the importance of teamwork and demanded individual discipline and perseverance. To them, baseball was an outpost of the kingdom of God they sought to build in America. Sadly, however, baseball, like the nation itself, often failed to fulfill its allegedly divine mandate by "succumbing to racism, sexism, capitalist exploitation of workers, and commercial interests."[46]

During some of our darkest moments, Americans have turned to MLB to bring healing, hope, and a sense of normalcy to everyday life.[47] Fans have flocked to ballparks during two world wars and numerous other crises, in part because attending baseball games provided a bond that helped unify the country.[48] In 1918, the World Series was held after a regular season reduced by about twenty-five games due to World War I. That September, the Boston Red Sox, led by the pitching of Babe Ruth, defeated the Chicago Cubs in the World Series. During game five of this series, the US Navy band played "The Star-Spangled Banner" during the seventh-inning stretch. It was played again before the beginning of the climactic sixth game; during subsequent seasons, many teams played the song on holidays and special occasions, and the Red Sox featured it before all their home games. Fueled in part by its popularity in ballparks, "The Star-Spangled Banner" was made the national anthem by Congress in 1931.[49]

Baseball was by far the nation's dominant spectator sport in the 1940s. Most American males had played baseball in some setting, and many "cherished heroic World Series fantasies."[50] After the Japanese bombed Pearl Harbor on December 7, 1941, President Franklin D. Roosevelt insisted in a letter to major league commissioner Kenesaw Mountain Landis that "it would be best for the country to keep baseball going."[51] Although many players, including some of its greatest stars, served in the two global conflicts (twenty-seven future Hall of Famers, including Christy Mathewson, Grover Cleveland Alexander, and Ty Cobb, fought in World War I, and more than five hundred major leaguers, including Bob Feller, Ted Williams, Stan Musial, and Joe DiMaggio, participated in World War II), baseball provided a balm during the turmoil and tragedy of war. It was a pleasant diversion on the home front and boosted morale for troops overseas who followed games in tabloids. Before the widespread televising of NFL games in the 1960s, baseball's radio broadcasts and extensive newspaper coverage made it more important in American life from 1920 to 1960 than any other sport has been before or since.

The playing of MLB games one week after the September 11, 2001, attacks helped buoy the spirits of many Americans. Philadelphia Phillies' outfielder Doug Glanville wondered how MLB could justify its resumption. "In the grand scheme of things," he wrote, "we were only playing a game." But "we found that some of what we recaptured *was* essential"—to uplift spirits and restore "our inspiration and our passion for fair competition and gamesmanship."[52] The suspension of the baseball season caused by COVID-19 in 2020 contributed to the angst, boredom, and feeling of deprivation millions of Americans experienced. Anthony Fauci, who led the federal government's battle against COVID-19 as director of the National Institute of Allergy and Infectious Diseases, argued that holding an abbreviated MLB season was crucial to "the country's mental health" and threw out the first pitch when the Washington Nationals, the defending World Series champions, held their 2020 home opener on July 23.[53] Although the NFL and NBA now attract more viewers for individual televised games, baseball provides more television programming than any other sport, and more than four times as many people attend MLB than NFL games each season. In addition, a 2019 poll reported that almost 170 million Americans age twelve or older identified as MLB fans—the highest number in the past twenty-five years.[54]

"I see great things in baseball," wrote journalist and poet Walt Whitman in 1846. "It is our game, the American game. Baseball will . . . relieve us from being a nervous, dyspeptic set, repair those losses and be a blessing to us."[55] Baseball has indeed often been therapeutic, giving Americans teams to cheer for, cities to celebrate, and players to cherish; in many ways, it has mirrored the American experience and been as much a part of the national ethos as apple pie, motherhood, and Chevrolets.[56] Sadly, however, except for a brief period in the Gilded Age, professional baseball was racially segregated until the 1940s. The 1896 *Plessy v. Ferguson* decision ruling that racial segregation was legal under the "separate but equal" doctrine, "the flamboyant personality and his incessant appetite for confrontation and white women" of boxer Jack Johnson, and the growing racism in college sports and other aspects of American society in the early twentieth century all prevented immensely talented black baseball players like Josh Gibson, Oscar Charleston, Cool Papa Bell, and Satchel Paige (until 1948) from playing in MLB.[57]

From its inception, baseball was supposedly a meritocracy where only ability, skill, performance, and hard work mattered and where "the 'male virtues' of intelligence, athleticism, and technical skill" triumphed.[58] In reality, however, it accentuated "the social sins that historically fragmented Americans along lines of race, class, ethnicity, and gender."[59] Branch Rickey, Jackie Robinson, and other pioneers believed that integrating the national pastime could serve as a model for other aspects of American society. While protesting that MLB still discriminated in some ways against players of color, Robinson argued in 1963 that the integration of baseball had "proved that all Americans can live together in peaceful competition." Similar integration, he insisted, could "be achieved in every corner of the land."[60] As we will see, Robinson himself—inspired by his Christian faith—helped smash racial barriers not only on the baseball diamond but also in politics, business, religion, and society.

1

"God Will Have to Keep His Eye on You": From Birth to the Negro League

1919–1945

Jackie Roosevelt Robinson was born on January 31, 1919, outside Cairo, Georgia, near the Florida state line. He entered a troubled world ten weeks after the armistice that ended World War I and in the midst of a deadly influenza pandemic that infected about one-third of the world's population and killed at least fifty million people, two and one-half times more than the deaths caused by the Great War. During 1919, racial disturbances and riots rocked the country, including a Chicago clash in July that killed twenty-three blacks and fifteen whites. The same year, the Boston Red Sox traded Babe Ruth to the Yankees (inaugurating "the Curse of the Bambino"), and the Black Sox cheating scandal shook the baseball world.

The grandson of enslaved Americans, chattel who "could be bought and sold," Jackie was the fifth and final child born to Jerry and Mallie Robinson.[1] Mallie chose his middle name to honor Theodore Roosevelt, who had died earlier that month. The twenty-sixth president had condemned lynching, attacked the peonage system that sought to reduce southern African Americans to a new form of slavery, appointed several black men to significant political offices, hosted Booker T. Washington for dinner at the White House, and sought unsuccessfully to develop a political coalition of southern whites and blacks. After Jackie was born, his mother, cradling him in her arms and looking at their impoverished home, declared, "For you to survive all this, God will have to keep His eye on you."[2]

Mallie Robinson

Mallie was born in 1889 to Washington and Edna McGriff, who had begun their lives in slavery; she was the seventh of their fourteen children. After obtaining their freedom, the McGriffs raised their children on a small farm near Cairo. As with most African Americans in southern Georgia, family, church, and the land were paramount. The McGriffs raised livestock and grew cotton, corn, sugarcane, peanuts, and vegetables. They prospered more than most of their black neighbors, but they still suffered under Jim Crow laws that rigidly separated blacks and whites and prevented most African Americans from voting and adequately providing for their financial needs. Acts of mob violence and lynchings were frequent, and poverty, crime, disease, cynicism, and despair were prevalent.

Mallie went to school through sixth grade (receiving more education than most of her black peers) and faithfully attended the Rocky Hill African Methodist Episcopal Church. At age ten, she taught her father to read, enabling him to achieve his goal of studying the Bible.[3] Mallie developed a strong faith in God, believing that family relationships and faith provided the primary defense against "the evils of the unjust world into which she had been born as a black in the Deep South."[4]

Much to her parents' dismay, at age fourteen Mallie began dating handsome, charming Jerry Robinson, four years her senior, and they married six years later in 1909. Jerry, probably the oldest of eleven children born to Tony Robinson, could neither write nor read. He worked on a plantation just south of Cairo owned by James Madison Sasser, a white county commissioner and an enterprising farmer. Jerry made a mere twelve dollars a month, barely enough to supply his and Mallie's basic needs. Mired in debt and upset by how badly the workers on the Sasser plantation were treated, Mallie devised a plan to lift them out of poverty. She counseled Jerry to warn Sasser that he would move off the plantation unless he was permitted to keep half the crops he produced. Not wanting to lose a valuable worker, Sasser reluctantly agreed, and Jerry began sharecropping. Sasser supplied a house, land for growing crops, fertilizer, and seed in exchange for half of the Robinsons' harvest.

"Without belief that God was watching over her," Jackie declared about his mother, "I don't see how she could have made it through the difficult times she had in life." Explaining Mallie's sharecropping plan, Jackie wrote, "She had faith and trust in God, and she believed that God wants human beings to work and speak for the freedom and equality which is rightfully theirs, even if they must suffer because they do this." He added, "My mother's faith paid off." After Jerry began sharecropping, their family had more food, clothes, and respect. Her faith, Jackie wrote, helped change "my father from a slave worker into a man of pride."[5]

The Robinson family, consisting of Edgar (born in 1910), Frank (1911), Mack (1914), Willa Mae (1916), and Jackie (1919), still struggled financially because of Jerry's periodic laziness, which forced Mallie and her older children to help with the farming. Their marriage was unstable because of Jerry's philandering, and they separated several times. Jerry's erratic love and commitment prompted Mallie to rely even more strongly on God. She declared, "I always lived so close to God till he would tell me things, what would happen." She believed that God spoke to her through her prayers and dreams and insisted God had warned her that Jerry would leave. In July 1919, Jerry deserted his family, traveling to Florida on a train with a female partner.[6]

Blaming Mallie for the loss of one of his best farmers, Sasser evicted her family from their house and forced them to occupy a dilapidated shack. He soon evicted her from that property as well, telling her she would have to move into a house at the sawmill with several men. Not willing to raise her children in that overcrowded, filthy environment, Mallie instead left the Sasser plantation, even though the family lost a sizable amount of food and hogs. As she later explained, "I put my trust in God and moved." Despite the resulting uncertainty and instability, she felt "exhilarated and empowered,"[7] believing that she had escaped the clutches of the devil.[8] Mallie worked briefly as a domestic for affluent whites in Cairo, but her family's living conditions were very meager.

Facing poverty and humiliation and troubled by the widespread racial violence in Georgia and other southern states (125 lynchings occurred in Georgia alone between 1909 and 1918), Mallie decided to leave the South. Her half brother Burton Thomas extolled the wonders of the West and encouraged her to join him there. He told her if she wanted "to get closer to heaven," she should come to California.[9] Jerry, who had returned to the area, asked the police to prevent Mallie and their children from leaving, but the police decided not to stop them. On May 21, 1920, Mallie, her five children, and seven other members of her extended family boarded a train for their journey to Pasadena. The future baseball star, then sixteen months old, was thus transported across the country, moving from a potential "life of sharecropping to the promise of Pasadena by a determined single mother."[10] Jackie later marveled at his mother's courage and faith in moving to California, "even though she was penniless and had no guarantee" she could provide for her family on the West Coast. Thankfully, Mallie had not been afraid to leave "a land of hopelessness" and go to a place where her family had better opportunities.[11] When they arrived in Pasadena, the six Robinsons shared a two-bedroom house that had no hot water with nine other relatives.

Family members, friends, and biographers agree that Mallie was a devout Christian whose faith directed her life and empowered her to improve her family's circumstances. Through her personal example, teaching them at home, and taking them to church, Mallie sought to instill her faith in her children. "My mother is a religious woman," Jackie wrote in 1964, who "struggled and sacrificed so unselfishly for us" and had the courage to defend her beliefs.[12] She believed that "God will look out" for those who stand up for their rights.[13] "I often wonder what would have happened to me and the rest of our family," Jackie asserted, "if it hadn't been for her faith."[14] "She indoctrinated us with the importance of family unity, religion, and kindness toward others." Mallie, Jackie declared after her death, "was a simple, understanding, loving, and courageous woman who gave me both tools and weapons to help in living my life."[15] Robinson thanked "God for having a mother" who taught him "right from wrong" and guided him to a good wife.[16] "I grew up in a home," he added, "where we loved and respected our mother."[17]

Other family members testified to Mallie's faith. Jackie's older sister, Willa Mae, declared, "As my mother always said, the Lord took care of us."[18] Much of her mother-in-law's "determination came from her religious beliefs," Rachel Robinson asserted. She believed that "the Lord was watching over her and He would see that she got what she needed."[19] Jackie, Rachel insisted, "derived his sense of himself—his life mission, and the courage to carry it out—from his mother. She was an extraordinary woman—courageous, determined, extremely religious, and self-reliant."[20]

Outsiders provided a similar appraisal. *Time* magazine described Mallie in 1947 as "a fervent Methodist who can be volubly graphic on the subject of hell."[21] Mallie, Jules Tygiel claims, had an "indomitable spirit and strong sense of Methodist moralism."[22] "Family was vital to Mallie," asserts Arthur Rampersad, "but God was supreme." She insisted that faith must be sustained by daily prayer, Sunday worship, and continual awareness of God's power; people should seek "to carry out the divine will as set out in the Bible" and constantly "appeal to Heaven for aid, comfort, and guidance." Mallie's resolute religious commitment and surrender of her life helped produce "in Jackie the rare and attractive quality of piety untainted by piousness."[23] "The Lord will provide," Mallie repeatedly reassured her children.[24]

Mallie taught Jackie that God created all people free and equal, exhorted him to pray and trust God, and encouraged him to develop a strong work ethic and get a good education; she made many sacrifices to assist him, modeling courage, strength, resolve, hope, and perseverance.[25] She also instructed her children to respect others and themselves. Mallie sought to instill racial pride in them, arguing that blackness was a divinely created, positive attribute. In her fictitious version of the Adam and Eve story, humans were originally black but became pale after eating the forbidden fruit in the garden of Eden. Adam and Eve subsequently had two sons, a black one and a white one. The black child's color, Mallie declared, embodied God's original design for humanity.[26] Mallie's stories and instruction helped make Jackie proud of his racial heritage.

Mallie exhorted her children to live by biblical principles as she understood them. "Take one step toward God, and he'll take two toward you," she often told them.[27] Mallie frequently warned her children: "God watches you whatever you do" and "You must reap what you sow, so sow well."[28] As they struggled to feed and clothe themselves, she promised that life would get better. His mother, Jackie recalled, "always believed the Lord would take care of us," which "I never stopped believing."[29] In dealing with bigotry and injustice, Mallie "tried to overcome the hatred of others with love and kindness."[30] Followers of Jesus, she insisted, must be generous and kind and help others.

In addition to instructing her children in the Christian faith at home, Mallie required them to attend Sunday school and worship services every week at Scott Methodist Church, a black congregation in Pasadena that was part of the predominantly white Methodist Episcopal Church. Jackie claimed that as a youth he attended church "all the time."[31] Mallie thought it was sinful for twelve-year-old Jackie to play baseball on Sundays while the pews at Scott Methodist Church were half empty. "The devil is sending the people to watch you play," she warned him, "and he's also sending you to play."[32] As a teenager, Jackie did not like going to church; he argued that he could be a moral person without doing so. Mallie strongly disagreed: "If you plant a crop and don't cultivate it, nothing grows," she avowed. Similarly, religion "dries up if you don't tend it." When the pastor of Scott Methodist Church wanted the teenage Jackie to be baptized, Mallie objected, arguing that "he's got to understand what this means and believe in it" before being baptized.[33]

Intruders in Pasadena

When the Robinsons moved to Pasadena in 1920, African Americans represented only 1 percent of California's population.[34] Three days after they arrived, Mallie began working as a domestic for an affluent white family, but this family soon moved away. The city's welfare department supplied the desperate family with food and clothes, and shortly thereafter Mallie took a domestic position with another white family, the Dodges, for whom she worked for the next twenty-seven years. Her income, coupled with continued welfare assistance and shrewd budgeting, enabled Mallie to save enough money during her first two years in Pasadena to buy a house on Pepper Street with five bedrooms, two bathrooms, and a spacious yard.

"Pasadena regarded us as intruders," Jackie later explained. Their presence upset many of the Robinsons' white, working-class neighbors. Segregation was rampant in Pasadena, and blacks were second-class citizens. No African Americans served on the Pasadena police force. Among other restrictions, black persons could swim in the public pool only on Tuesdays, after which it was drained and refilled. They watched movies from segregated theater balconies. Jackie and his brothers participated in many fights that began because of racial slurs. "Restaurant doors were slammed in our faces," Jackie reported. "In certain respects, Pasadenans were less understanding than Southerners and even more openly hostile."[35]

After their neighbors tried but failed to buy out the Robinsons, some of them burned a cross on the Robinsons' front lawn, but Mallie adamantly refused to move. The neighbors tried to convince a widow who lived next door to the Robinsons to help buy her house, but she declared at a community meeting that the Robinsons were the best neighbors she had ever had, and the scheme collapsed.[36] Despite this hostility, Mallie was convinced that God wanted her family to live on Pepper Street.[37] She eventually gained the friendship of many of her neighbors by sharing food and drinks that a local bakery and milkman gave to her family.[38]

The three older Robinson children were already attending school, so when Willa Mae began kindergarten at Cleveland Elementary School and three-year-old Jackie had nowhere else to go, she took him along, and he played all day in the sandbox outside the school. They sometimes went to school so hungry they could hardly stand up, much less think about their lessons, Willa Mae later reported. Two kindhearted teachers regularly shared their lunches with the children.[39] Using a baseball analogy, Jackie asserted that "every child born into poverty has one or two strikes on him before he starts the game."[40] During his own years in elementary school, Jackie often went hungry, disliked the classroom, and lacked interesting activities to do at home.[41]

At about age eight, Jackie had his first memorable encounter with racial discrimination. As he swept the sidewalk in front of his house, a young neighbor girl shouted, "Nigger, nigger, nigger" at him. Aware that "cracker" was the most insulting name one could call a white person in the South, he responded with this epithet. This prompted a rock-throwing fight with the girl's father that lasted for several minutes until the girl's mother broke it up.[42]

Although African Americans were discriminated against in almost every other aspect of Pasadena's life, they were permitted to play sports with whites in schools and community leagues, which had a tremendous impact on Robinson's life. In elementary school, Jackie's phenomenal athletic ability was first displayed in soccer, as his teams frequently defeated ones composed of players from older grades.[43]

Influenced by Mallie, Jackie's oldest brother, Edgar, had a great interest in and knowledge of the Bible. He retold biblical stories in his own words, enthralling his younger siblings at bedtime.

All the Robinson children had great athletic ability. Edgar excelled at speed skating and bicycling; Frank, the second oldest, was a fast runner and good basketball player; Willa Mae starred in track, basketball, and soccer. Mack, the middle of the five children, set the junior college long jump record and starred in track at the University of Oregon. Mack tied the Olympic record for the 200 meters in the semifinals at Berlin in 1936; in the finals, he finished second behind Jesse Owens. Jackie testified that Mack was always his "idol," but Mack lived much of his adult life in Jackie's shadow.[44]

While at the 1936 Olympics, Mack lost his maintenance job with the city of Pasadena when city officials dismissed all African American munic-ipal employees, in retaliation after black residents obtained access to the community swimming pool several days a week instead of just one. Thus an Olympic silver medalist returned home not to civic recognition but to unemployment.[45] Thereafter, despite his college degree, Mack worked as a ditch digger, machinist, street sweeper, gas station attendant, chauffeur for comedian Lou Costello, and custodian at Warner Brothers' Hollywood studio; he became progressively disillusioned as Jackie upstaged him.[46]

Jackie's High School Years

Growing up, Jackie sometimes felt bitter toward his father for deserting their family, especially when he saw his mother "bone-weary from scrub-bing floors and ironing clothes all day to earn money."[47] He contributed to the family's income by shining shoes, mowing lawns, running errands, selling newspapers, collecting and peddling junk, and hawking hot dogs at the Rose Bowl and other venues.[48]

As a young teen, Jackie joined the Pepper Street Gang. Consisting of Af-rican American, Hispanic, white, and Asian American youth, the gang was rowdy and mischievous but not violent. Discrimination, boredom, and ca-maraderie brought its members together. They threw dirt patties at passing cars, stole fruit from street vendors and grocery stores, and resold golf balls scavenged from the rough of the local course.[49] Gang members also en-gaged in various pranks, sometimes to retaliate against racist community residents. After they spread black tar on the lawn of a bigoted neighbor, Mallie forced them to remove it by cutting blades of grass with scissors and scrubbing the tar off with kerosene.[50] Despite her arduous efforts, Mallie was unable to get Jackie to quit the gang. "Jackie admired the bravado and swagger of the young outlaws" and enjoyed the social support and security it provided as they controlled the streets of their neighborhood.[51]

Their delinquent acts often got gang members in trouble with the police. They were frequently arrested and detained at the Pasadena police station where Captain Hugh Morgan, the head of the force's youth division, strove to reform their behavior. Robinson was arrested several times for minor infractions, but his success in high school sports helped him avoid serious legal problems. Robinson often credited Morgan, car mechanic Carl Anderson, and pastor Karl Downs with helping him avoid more serious problems with the law. Anderson, who worked near where the Pepper Street Gang loitered, had a positive effect on the youth. Robinson said, "[He] made me see . . . that if I continued with the gang it would hurt my mother as well as myself. . . . He said it didn't take guts to follow the crowd, that courage and intelligence lay in willing to be different. I was too ashamed to tell Carl how right he was, but what he said got to me."[52]

Robinson excelled at sports at Pasadena's integrated John Muir Technical High School, but, like other African Americans, he was barred from joining the YMCA and discriminated against by movie theaters, restaurants, and other businesses. White Pasadenans cheered his exploits in athletics but refused to share public facilities with him. To cope with these injustices, Jackie followed the example of his older brother Mack and channeled his energy and anger into sports.[53] He scrupulously avoided alcohol and tobacco not because he "was a model of morality" but to enhance his athletic performance.[54] Sometimes, during games or meets, fans of other teams would claim that a Robinson family member had called with an emergency, trying to get him to leave. In addition, competitors used racial slurs or underhanded tactics to try to provoke him to fight.[55]

Karl Downs to the Rescue

In January 1938, Karl Downs, only seven years older than Robinson, began his ministry at Scott Methodist Church. Downs, the son of a Methodist pastor and Methodist district superintendent (a supervisor of a geographical division), had earned a BA at Samuel Huston College in Austin, Texas, in 1933, a BD degree at Gammon Theological Seminary in Atlanta in 1936, and a master's of sacred theology at Boston University in 1937. Before coming to Pasadena, he had traveled throughout the country to recruit college youth for the Methodist Board of Foreign Missions. Downs, who combined evangelical theology with social progressivism, changed Robinson's life by befriending him, leading him to Christ, nurturing the faith he relied on heavily for the rest of his life, counseling him, and influencing his view of racial issues.[56] Downs made Scott Church a haven where members could develop their strength and power to confront discrimination, which helped equip Robinson for the battles that lay ahead.[57]

Shortly after arriving in Pasadena, Downs went looking for Robinson. Finding a group of his friends loitering on a street corner, he asked them to tell Robinson to come to church. Soon thereafter, Robinson showed up at Scott Church and began a ten-year relationship that transformed his life.[58] Downs became the father and mentor for whom Robinson longed; he convinced the athlete to leave gang life and strongly influenced his worldview, perspective on people, and response to discrimination. Robinson came to recognize that as a child of God he had immense dignity and worth that no experience, no matter how deplorable or dehumanizing, could destroy. Robinson's friend Ray Bartlett declared, "I'm not sure what would have happened to Jack if he had never met Reverend Downs."[59] Rachel wrote that Downs's intervention, which Jackie called a "rescue," "changed the course of his life." Downs's spiritual mentoring strengthened "his ability to cope with all the challenges he would face in his life." "Like Mallie," Rachel maintained, "Jack felt God's presence in the most personal way." Jackie experienced "a spiritual awakening" and gained "a sense of direction."[60] "He kept saying," Rachel added, "that Karl changed his life."[61]

Downs helped Robinson develop a close relationship with Christ and recruited him to teach Sunday school. Attracted both to Downs's personality and his position on racial matters, Robinson began to spend more time at Scott Church. Participation in church services and Sunday school, which his mother had mandated, soon "became a pleasure instead of a duty." After his grueling Saturday football games, Robinson wanted to stay in bed on Sunday morning. But, he explained, "no matter how terrible I felt, I had to get up. It was impossible to shirk duty when Karl Downs was involved." He could communicate with a person spiritually and still be "fun to be with." Robinson said, "He participated with us in our sports. Most importantly, he knew how to listen. Often when I was deeply concerned about personal crises, I went to him." Robinson added, "We had a good many long talks which affected me deeply."[62]

Robinson did not have a distinctive conversion experience, but through Downs's ministry, as a young adult, he fully accepted "Mallie's message of religion and hope." Robinson developed a spirituality he never previously had, and his faith in God began to direct his life.[63] He thanked Downs for giving him "the most precious gift" possible—the ability to believe in God and, therefore, in himself.[64]

Downs connected with Robinson and other gang members through the personal relationships he developed, playing sports with them, relating biblical stories to real-life events, and creating church programs and activities they enjoyed. Downs, a good athlete himself, and Robinson often played golf together (though Downs never won). As Downs interacted with neighborhood youth by playing golf or badminton and attending their dances, he constantly found "a way to apply something that happened to the Bible." Youth respected him, Robinson asserted, because "he was right in there with you, competing, beating you, getting beat, and proving all the while that the Christian life doesn't have to be dull or colorless." Downs "didn't preach and he didn't talk down like so many adults or view you from some holy distance."[65] Downs, Rachel explained, participated in youth games and outings "like a big brother, but he never lost his focus on religious and ethical teachings or his standing as their spiritual advisor."[66]

For Robinson and many of his friends, church became "an alternative to hanging out on street corners."[67] To attract youth, Scott Methodist Church sponsored dances and installed a badminton court, a basketball court, and a skating rink.[68] It opened a day-care center, started a social service ministry, and lent books and toys to children. It also hosted a celebrity night that featured prominent black and white leaders, including US congressman Adam Clayton Powell Jr. and physicist Linus Pauling. In addition, Downs helped organize a monthly forum for prominent black and white speakers. The pastor persuaded Pepper Street Gang members to participate in building a youth center at the church, and he provided financial aid for their families and toys for indigent community children.[69] Downs immediately began to build the self-esteem of gang members and "made a place for them in the church."[70] Under Downs's leadership, the church thrived as new families began attending; the church's income increased substantially, enabling it to operate on a sound financial basis.[71]

Robinson described Downs as "a militant Christian who diplomatically induced others to do what he wanted them to do by his powers of persuasion."[72] By word and deed, by his "friendship and companionship," Downs taught Robinson how to develop his abilities to their fullest extent; to avoid evil and do good; and "to help others without expecting anything in return."[73] Like Mallie, Downs emphasized racial pride; he told his parishioners that "to be born black is more than to be persecuted; it is to be privileged."[74] Downs helped Robinson become "proud of his skin color" and taught him that Christians must not simply pray; they must also work to better themselves, advance justice, and improve society. Downs also taught Robinson how to appropriately express his anger.[75] To Mallie, Downs was "the personification of God's goodness and charity on earth"; "the disciple of Christ" comforted her during many "troublesome hours." Mallie had long dreamed that Jackie might enter the ministry, and she was delighted by Downs's great spiritual influence on her son.[76]

About a month after arriving at Scott Methodist Church, Downs journeyed to Chicago to address four thousand attendees at a Methodist conference on issues pertaining to youth, held at the Stevens Hotel. Although the Methodist Church claimed it would not meet at venues that discriminated against blacks, the hotel refused to allow him and the other three hundred black delegates to stay there. Worse yet, a white Methodist leader censured Downs in front of the hotel staff for complaining about his exclusion. Although upset and offended, the young pastor decided not to mention the incident in his speech. After the conference, however, Downs published an article in *Zion's Herald*, a Methodist periodical, protesting that as a conference speaker "whom God had willed to make a Negro," he was not permitted to stay at the hotel. He also blasted the denomination for responding so feebly to racial injustice.[77]

Downs's experience in Chicago captured newspaper and magazine headlines across the nation; an article in *Time* lauded his response to the injustice.[78] One more combative black newspaper editor contended that "it might have been more effective if the Rev. Downs had exploded" and openly accused the white Christians of hypocrisy.[79] On the other hand, after Downs gave a talk titled "Wanted, Revolutionists" at the NAACP's annual meeting in November 1938, the same newspaper noted that since the incident, Downs had often been "hailed as the most promising and potent young minister today."[80] Robinson undoubtedly heard about this incident from Downs and may have concluded that African Americans must sometimes bear their cross in the short run to achieve their long-term racial goals.[81]

Downs's *Zion's Herald* article was not his first attack on racial injustice. As a student at Gammon Theological Seminary, he wrote an article for the *Crisis*, the mouthpiece of the NAACP, deploring the timidity of black students in attacking racial discrimination. Progress had come through African Americans who had been "born of courage, steeped in conviction," and who had acted fearlessly. Black people would progress, Downs argued, only if they shook "from their shoulders the shackles of timidity." He exhorted black students to challenge lynchings in the South and other racial injustices.[82]

In 1943, at age thirty, Downs left Scott Methodist Church to become the president of Methodist-related Samuel Huston College (now Huston-Tillotson College) in Austin, Texas. During his four and a half years there, the college's enrollment tripled, its annual budget grew each year, and the number of buildings doubled.[83] That year, Downs also published *Meet the Negro*, in which he argued that sports helped advance black pride and promote Christian ideals. Among its biographical vignettes were stories about African American sports stars Jesse Owens, Joe Louis, and Satchel Paige.

Downs continued to denounce racism and to work to end discrimination. In 1946, he encouraged Heman Sweatt to enroll in the University of Texas Law School. Sweatt's denial of admission on the grounds that the Texas state constitution prohibited integrated education led to the Supreme Court case of *Sweatt v. Painter* (1950), which prepared the way for *Brown v. the Board of Education* four years later. Downs planned the strategy with Thurgood Marshall and Adam Clayton Powell Jr. for the cases preceding the one at the nation's highest court.

In February 1946, Downs flew from Austin to Pasadena to perform Jackie and Rachel's wedding ceremony. During his one season in Montreal and his first year with the Dodgers, Rachel stated, Jackie called Downs "more than any other person. He trusted Karl."[84] Downs helped shape Robinson's view that African Americans could overcome racism through sports.[85]

Robinson Dazzles the Collegiate Sports World

After graduating from high school in 1937, Robinson attended Pasadena Junior College (PJC), which was free, integrated, and fairly progressive in racial matters. There he excelled in football, basketball, baseball, and track and field. Robinson played quarterback for a football team that won sixteen straight games, was hailed as the nation's best junior college team, and attracted forty-five thousand fans to games at the Rose Bowl. The 1938 team won all its games as Robinson scored 131 points and gained more than one thousand yards from scrimmage.[86] While playing football, Robinson chipped a bone in his left ankle. For the rest of his life, any sudden major change in temperature produced tightness and often pain.[87] In basketball, Robinson averaged nineteen points a game and propelled PJC to the California junior college championship. In his first baseball season, he hit .417 and stole twenty-five bases in twenty-four games; he was named the most valuable junior college player in Southern California after leading his team to the league title.[88] His long jump of 25 feet 6⅓ inches broke his brother Mack's junior college record and was among the ten longest jumps in history at that time.

As in high school, Robinson had a couple of minor run-ins with the local police. But he graduated from PJC in June 1939 and turned down scholarship offers from Oregon and Stanford to enroll at UCLA.

Robinson also participated in four sports at UCLA. His brother Frank, whom he considered his "greatest fan," died in a motorcycle accident shortly after Jackie matriculated at UCLA. Frank, who battled various health problems, had encouraged Jackie from an early age to run, jump, and compete in neighborhood games. Recovering emotionally from his brother's untimely death was a slow and painful process.[89] Robinson majored in physical education and had a C average. Although college grade-point averages were generally much lower in the 1940s than today, Robinson admitted that he was a mediocre student. He concluded that spending long hours studying was "a waste of time" because his brothers and black friends who had excelled in college still ended up working as porters, bell-hops, and taxicab drivers.[90] Robinson was especially close to his basketball coach, Wilbur Johns, and was still communicating regularly with Johns, then UCLA's athletic director, in 1949.[91]

Jackie excelled on the gridiron, the basketball court, and the cinders. During the 1939 football season, he averaged an astonishing 12.2 yards per carry and led the nation with a punt return average of 20.1 yards. In both 1940 and 1941, Robinson led the Southern Division of the Pacific Coast Conference in scoring in basketball, averaging twelve points per game. In 1940, he won the long jump competition at the NCAA men's outdoor track and field championship. Ironically, Robinson did not excel in baseball at UCLA. Despite hitting .417 at Pasadena Junior College and .400 for a Pasadena community team that won the state amateur title, Robinson batted a meager .097 during his one season at UCLA.[92]

The most important event of Jackie's four semesters at UCLA was meeting Rachel Isum. Three and a half years younger than Jackie, Rachel was a freshman in 1940–1941, Jackie's last year at UCLA. Rachel's father, Charles, had been gassed during World War I, producing a chronic heart condition. Health problems forced him to retire in the late 1930s after he had spent twenty-five years as a bookbinder for the *Los Angeles Times*. Rachel's mother, Zellee, created a catering business to supply food for luncheons and dinner parties for affluent families in Bel Air, Beverly Hills, and Hollywood. As a high school student, Rachel assisted her mother with this business, sold food at a concession stand in the public library on Saturdays, and made baby clothes as part of the New Deal's National Youth Administration.[93]

Rachel grew up as a third-generation Southern Californian on the predominately white west side of Los Angeles, where she often confronted racial bigotry. "Within a two-mile radius [of home], I had everything I needed to support my growth," she explained. Bethel African Methodist Episcopal Church, named after the original AME church in Philadelphia established by Richard Allen in 1816, "was central to our social activities." Rachel faithfully attended Sunday school, sang in the church choir, and ate many dinners at the church.[94] She excelled at the city's Manual Arts High School and was awarded a scholarship to enter UCLA's highly competitive five-year nursing program. As of fall 1940, only 5 percent of American women—and less than 2 percent of black women—had completed a college degree.

As a college student, Rachel held various part-time jobs to help pay her expenses. During her senior year, she worked as a riveter at the Lockheed Aircraft factory in Los Angeles, helping to assemble airplanes for the Army Air Corps. After working the night shift, she drove to UCLA, changed her clothes in the parking lot, and headed for class. Despite that schedule, she maintained a 4.0 average, and at graduation, her professors and classmates gave her the Florence Nightingale Award for her outstanding achievement.[95]

Rachel socialized with UCLA's small number of fellow black students in Kerckhoff Hall, where Jackie worked part time as a janitor. It was impossible to miss the physically attractive athletic star, Rachel declared.[96] She had watched Jackie play football at PJC and thought he was cocky and conceited, but as she got to know him, she concluded that he was self-confident rather than arrogant. She was very impressed that Jackie was "comfortable and proud of being a black man," a rare trait in the 1940s when few African Americans carried their "racial identity with such pride." She was also attracted to his sense of dignity and purpose.[97] Soon after a mutual friend introduced them, they began dating. Robinson was captivated by her beauty, charm, and listening skills. Rachel was one of the few people Jackie felt he could confide in. He could tell her anything, and she responded with warmth, understanding, and honesty.[98]

Rampersad argues that Jackie won Zellee Isum's approval in part because she viewed him as "serious and religious." Sharon Robinson claims that Zellee loved Jackie because "he was a clean-cut, well-mannered Christian."[99] Mallie, meanwhile, was impressed that Rachel attended church regularly, did not drink or smoke, was an excellent student, and planned to be a nurse.[100] She viewed Rachel as "a Rock of Ages, a rudder, and anchor" for her son.[101] Her "calm, warm, thoughtful manner complemented Jackie's fiery impetuousness. They formed an enduring bond of mutual love and support" that would enable them to overcome the immense challenges ahead.[102] The AME Church, in which Rachel grew up, emphasized "self-determination, self-sufficiency, and black independence," beliefs that would be central as she and Jackie combated discrimination in baseball and society.[103]

From UCLA to the Great Experiment

Robinson dropped out of UCLA after the basketball season ended in 1941. While playing four sports and pursuing his degree, he had worked as a busboy at a restaurant and a janitor on campus, plus selling candy and hot dogs at the Rose Bowl to cover his and his mother's expenses. Robinson believed that finishing college would be selfish and wanted to help his mother more financially. Downs, his mother, brother Mack, and coaches strove to persuade him not to leave UCLA without graduating and were disappointed when he departed in March.[104]

Robinson accepted a job with the National Youth Administration as an assistant athletic director at California Polytechnic Institute in San Luis Obispo. In this role, he trained youth, many of whom had grown up in poverty and had a record as delinquents. The program enabled underprivileged youth to get off the streets and learn a trade.[105] "No matter what their background or how much trouble they had gotten into," Robinson averred, these youth were starving "for attention, understanding and intelligent discipline."[106] He found the work rewarding, but the likelihood of American participation in World War II led the government, which needed more industrial workers and soldiers, to end the program.

During fall 1941, Robinson played semiprofessional football with the Honolulu Bears. While in Hawaii, he also did construction work near Pearl Harbor; he left just two days before the Japanese bombed the naval base on December 7.[107] Robinson had planned to play on an all-star basketball team when he returned to California,[108] but instead he worked briefly at Lockheed Aircraft near Los Angeles, as he waited, like many other men his age, to be drafted. Like most African Americans, he was deeply troubled by the prospects of being expected to help defeat the Axis Powers while being deprived of full freedom at home. The *Pittsburgh Courier*, a leading black newspaper, called for a "Double V" campaign—victory abroad and over racial discrimination at home. The *Crisis*, the organ of the NAACP, asserted that Americans must fight for "freedom for everyone, everywhere," not only "those under Hitler's heel."[109]

Robinson was drafted into the army on March 23, 1942, and assigned to Fort Riley, Kansas, joining the more than one million African Americans who served in the US military during World War II. He refused to use the fact that his mother depended on him financially or that he suffered from painful bone chips in his ankle to avoid military service.[110] Although he was a proficient marksman and passed the tests for Officer Candidate School (OCS), Robinson was denied admission into the program and instead was assigned to groom horses. He and other black aspirants informed heavyweight champion Joe Louis, whom they met at Fort Riley, that no African American had ever been admitted to OCS. "Louis's carefully manicured image, which conspicuously featured" his Christian faith, made him a hero despite the nation's "virulent anti-black racism."[111] The Bible-toting boxer used his influence with the civilian aide to the secretary of war, African American Truman Gibson, to have this claim investigated, and in early 1943, Robinson and several other blacks were commissioned second lieutenants after completing OCS.

Robinson was appointed as a platoon leader and his unit's morale officer. In the latter role, he protested many of the discriminatory practices at Fort Riley and helped black soldiers receive more seats at the segregated post exchange.[112] On the other hand, Robinson was not permitted to play on the camp's baseball team, which included his future Dodgers' teammate Pete Reiser. He was invited, however, to play on Fort Riley's football team. But when the University of Missouri refused to play Fort Riley if its squad included a black player and the army gave him leave to get him off the base, an irate Robinson quit.[113]

In April 1944, Robinson was transferred to Fort Hood near Waco, Texas, where he joined the segregated 761st "Black Panthers" Tank Battalion. Eleven years before Rosa Parks's defiant act in Montgomery, Alabama, Robinson was court-martialed for a similar act. On July 6, 1944, a civilian bus driver ordered Robinson to move from his seat in the middle to the rear of the bus. Aware of the federal policy that prohibited segregation on army buses, the second lieutenant refused to move. As a result, military police boarded the bus and took him to the police station at the next stop. At the station, Robinson got into a heated argument with army MPs and the assistant marshal provost in response to a racial slur and being denied a chance to defend himself. Robinson was arrested and charged with insubordination, conduct unbecoming an officer, disturbing the peace, and refusing to obey the orders of a superior officer. If convicted at his court-martial, he could be incarcerated in a military prison or dishonorably discharged.

Robinson had valid reasons to be concerned about the outcome of his trial. During World War II, historian Jack Foner asserts, "many black soldiers were unjustly convicted by courts-martial, either because their officers assumed their guilt regardless of the evidence or because they wanted to 'set an example' for other black soldiers."[114]

Robinson and his supporters sought help from the NAACP, Truman Gibson, California's two US senators, and the black press to ensure that his trial received national attention. The NAACP and African American newspapers vigorously defended Robinson's actions, arguing that he had simply stood up for his rights. The case against Robinson was heard by nine men—eight white and one black—with six votes required for acquittal. Sitting in the courtroom with shackles on his hands and legs, Robinson "remained confident" that he would be acquitted "because of his deep faith in God that his mother had instilled in him."[115] Summarizing the army's case against him, Robinson's attorney, Captain William Cline, declared that it rested on a few individuals seeking "to vent their bigotry on a Negro they considered 'uppity' because he had the audacity to seek to exercise rights that belonged to him as an American and as a soldier."[116] On the witness stand, Robinson explained why he became so angry when called a nigger at the police station. "My grandmother was a slave," he declared. "She told me a nigger was a low, uncouth person . . . but I don't consider that I am low and uncouth. I am a Negro, but not a nigger."[117] At his trial, several superior officers (all white), including Lieutenant Colonel Paul Bates, Robinson's commanding officer, testified that he was an exemplary soldier and highly respected by the enlisted men with whom he served.[118] The combination of their witness, Robinson's talented defense counsel, his own articulate testimony, the army's recognition of the widespread interest in the proceedings, and the soundness of the military justice system led the military judges to acquit him of all charges on August 2, 1944.[119] Perhaps most significant was that the conviction of Robinson, a star athlete with a national reputation, might have brought embarrassment to the army.[120]

Robinson's experiences in the army clearly illustrated the problems black persons faced in America and demonstrated his fortitude and racial pride—two qualities that would be essential in demolishing baseball's color line.[121] The mistreatment, discrimination, racial taunts, and the ugly episode that produced his court-martial further raised Robinson's political consciousness and helped prepare him for the battles ahead. The trailblazer later wrote that his acquittal "was a small victory." He went on, "I had learned that I was in two wars, one against the foreign enemy, the other against prejudice at home."[122] Had Robinson been convicted or dishonorably discharged, Branch Rickey, the Dodgers' crafty and morally upright general manager, would never have selected him to integrate Major League Baseball. Conversely, his poise under immense pressure may have strengthened his suitability.

Robinson's composure during his military trial, Rampersad argues, sprang in large part from "his faith in God; he still said his prayers on his knees at night before going to bed, as he would for many years to come." Rachel explained that her husband deeply believed "that God would take care of you. . . . Because God is there, nothing can go wrong with you. . . . An ordeal like the court-martial was a sign to Jack that God was testing him." Jack's "faith in God was not very articulate, but it was real, and it did not allow for much doubt."[123]

By the time the trial ended, Robinson's tank unit had gone to Europe. Its members played a major role in the Battle of the Bulge during December 1944 and January 1945, where they suffered heavy casualties. Not going to Europe enabled Robinson to play in the Negro leagues and become the leading candidate to integrate MLB. After his discharge from the army in November 1944, Robinson was unsure of what to do next, but he believed "that he yet might be destined by God for something great."[124]

Robinson took a job at Samuel Huston College, where Karl Downs had become president two years earlier. He taught physical education and coached the basketball team during the 1944–1945 season. Aided by US congressman Lyndon Johnson, an ardent segregationist who wanted black colleges to succeed, Downs strove diligently to keep the college afloat despite the challenges of World War II.

Robinson then went to spring training with the Kansas City Monarchs, managed by Buck O'Neil and starring Satchel Paige. Robinson had not played baseball since his junior year at UCLA. Robinson disliked black baseball. The schedule was demanding, and the conditions were difficult. Teams traveled hundreds of miles by bus to cities stretching from Kansas City to Newark, New Jersey; often played two games the same day; and, because of discriminatory policies, had trouble finding comfortable places to sleep or good food to eat. Frequently going without baths, nice beds, or hot meals was a shock to him.[125] Robinson criticized owners for failing to furnish players with contracts and "attacked low salaries, sloppy umpiring, and the miserable living conditions."[126]

Robinson was also upset by the heavy drinking and sexual carousing of many black players. His values sometimes produced conflict with his teammates. While playing with the Monarchs, Robinson derided their whiskey drinking and promiscuity, "once tossing a glass of Scotch into a lit fireplace to demonstrate the lethality of liquor."[127] His core values, Rampersad argues, were personal dignity and self-esteem, and "he believed in God and the Bible." Robinson drew a line "between himself and sin, and tried not to cross it." He told Sammie Haynes, with whom he frequently roomed, that he had not had sex with his fiancée Rachel and did not need to do so to know she was the woman for him. An astounded Haynes told him that marrying someone with whom he had not had sex was "crazy!"[128]

Although he played in only forty-one games with the Monarchs, Robinson excelled in the Negro league; he hit .387 and was selected for the east-west all-star game.[129] However, he did not have close relationships with other players; often expressed anger toward teammates, opponents, and umpires; and, unlike most other players, denounced segregation. "Among a group of gifted professionals who had to endure all-night rides on bone-clattering buses and blocked doors at whites-only diners and motels," Scott Simon writes, "Robinson was remembered more for griping about the league's showboating and lack of training and discipline."[130] Unhappy with his experience, Robinson planned to quit the Monarchs at the end of the 1945 season, return to California, marry Rachel, and take a job as a high school coach.

Branch Rickey and God, however, had different plans for him. Black sportswriters Wendell Smith and Sam Lacy insisted that Robinson possessed the traits required to succeed in MLB. The devout Christian was college educated, did not drink or engage in other behaviors that might harm his performance, and had exceptional athletic ability, tremendous poise and confidence, and immense self-respect.[131] Smith provided Rickey with positive appraisals of Robinson's play with the Monarchs.

On August 24, Dodgers' superscout Clyde Sukeforth visited Robinson in Chicago and informed him that Rickey wanted to meet with him in Brooklyn. While talking with Sukeforth, Robinson said to himself, "Maybe that star [which he saw in the sky] is especially bright tonight for you. Maybe Someone is trying to lead you. Maybe He is up there trying to tell you to go see Mr. Rickey."[132] Robinson's life and MLB would soon change dramatically.

2

Robinson and Rickey: The Great Experiment

1945

Brooklyn Dodgers' general manager Branch Rickey, who played a decisive role in the racial integration of baseball, was motivated to do so in significant part by his Christian faith. Of course, numerous other individuals, organizations, and political, economic, and social factors helped pave the way for this momentous event. But too little attention has been paid to the influence of Rickey's staunch commitment to Christianity.

Rickey searched diligently for an ideal candidate to break the color line. After meeting with Robinson in August 1945, he concluded that he had found his best candidate. This chapter chronicles that decision, examines Rickey's numerous motives for signing Robinson, and traces the many and varied reactions to the "great experiment" by religious leaders, the black and white press, the black community, baseball executives, managers, and players, and white America.

Branch Rickey

Named for Englishman John Wesley, the founder of Methodism, Wesley Branch Rickey was born in 1881 in southeastern Ohio, to a family whose ancestors had belonged to the abolitionist wing of the Methodist Church. His middle name, Branch, refers to several biblical passages, including John 15:5, where Jesus says, "I am the vine and you are the branches." His father, Jacob Franklin Rickey, was a pious Christian. Branch's mother,

Emily, taught him Bible stories before he could read, along with many of Wesley's tenets, including this famous one: "Having, First, gained all you can, and, Secondly, saved all you can, Then 'give all you can.'"[1] Unfortunately for the family, Jacob Rickey was not very good at the first part; as a vegetable farmer, he barely provided for the family's needs. Branch later testified that his mother and father instilled a strong belief in Christ and his work on earth, which he never abandoned. He firmly embraced the nineteenth-century Methodist emphasis on God's loving fatherhood and the brotherhood of man made possible by Jesus.[2]

Rickey committed his life to Christ at a young age. He taught at a high school in Turkey Creek, Ohio, for two years to earn enough money to attend college. Rickey's intense religiosity made him stand out from most of his classmates at Ohio Wesleyan University in Delaware, Ohio, although the Methodist institution helped prepare many men for the ministry. Unlike most of his classmates, he was thrilled to attend college chapel services.[3] He took a full load of classes, performed several part-time jobs to pay his expenses, and was a catcher in baseball and a fullback in football. The summer after his sophomore year, Rickey played semiprofessional baseball, making him ineligible for further intercollegiate athletics.

Rickey's MLB playing career included short stints with the St. Louis Browns and the New York Highlanders (soon to be renamed the Yankees) from 1905 to 1907; he batted .239 in 120 games, with three home runs, and he still holds the dubious record for allowing the most stolen bases as a catcher—thirteen—in a nine-inning game. Returning to his alma mater in 1908, Rickey coached baseball, football, and basketball and served as the athletic director. He also took night classes in law at Ohio State University, taught Sunday school, campaigned for Republican presidential candidate William Howard Taft in 1908, and supported the Anti-Saloon League's efforts to curb alcohol sales and drunkenness. Influenced by the Social Gospel's quest to alleviate social, industrial, and racial problems, Rickey invited Jane Addams, the founder of Hull House in Chicago; leading black activist Booker T. Washington; and muckraking photojournalist Jacob Riis to speak at the YMCA he headed in Delaware, Ohio.[4]

From 1909 to 1911, Rickey attended the University of Michigan Law School, completing the three-year program in two years. He coached the university's baseball team from 1910 to 1913; for the last two of those years, it included future Hall of Famer George Sisler. In 1913, MLB's St. Louis Browns hired him as their business manager. Rickey also managed the team briefly in 1913 and then for the entire 1914 and 1915 seasons. During the concluding months of World War I, Rickey served in France, leading a unit that included baseball greats Ty Cobb and Christy Mathewson and provided chemical support for soldiers and tanks on more than 150 missions.[5]

From 1919 to 1925, Rickey managed the St. Louis Cardinals. In ten years as an MLB manager, Rickey accumulated 597 wins and 664 losses; his winning percentage was .437 with the Browns and .486 with the Cardinals. As their general manager, however, Rickey helped make the Cardinals the best team in the National League from the mid-1920s to the mid-1940s. They captured six National League pennants between 1926 and 1942 and won four World Series. In 1942, the Cardinals won an impressive 106 games, the most in their history. They excelled in large part because Rickey created MLB's best farm system. It produced numerous stars, including Frankie Frisch, Dizzy Dean, Joe Medwick, Johnny Mize, Pepper Martin, Enos Slaughter, Rip Collins, Max Lanier, and Stan Musial. In addition to overseeing the signing and seasoning of prospects, Rickey taught them how to play the game more effectively and furnished moral instruction, which, he claimed, made them better people and athletes.[6]

Although the Cardinals defeated the Yankees in 1942 to win the World Series, as a cost-cutting measure St. Louis owner Sam Breadon did not renew Rickey's contract, and the Brooklyn Dodgers hired him to serve as their vice president and general manager. The Cardinals' dismissal of Rickey was arguably one of the worst moves in baseball history. The talented team Rickey had assembled won the National League pennant again three of the next four years and the World Series in 1944 and 1946. Without Rickey to replenish their player pool, however, the Cardinals did not capture the pennant again until 1964, stymied in part by the success of his new team.

Rickey, Arnold Rampersad contends, was "a dedicated, Bible-loving Christian."[7] Believing that Sunday was the Lord's day, Rickey, during his long career as a player, manager, general manager, and team president, did not participate in or attend games on the Sabbath.[8] Several other major leaguers refused to play on Sundays, including famed pitcher Christy

Mathewson early in his career, but Rickey's unwillingness to play caused problems with the executives of the Cincinnati Reds, the team that signed him to his first MLB contract.[9] While playing with the St. Louis Browns, he professed, "I try to be both a consistent ballplayer and a consistent Christian."[10] Rickey saw his career in baseball as "a call from God" similar to that of a minister or missionary.[11]

Rickey's strong Christian commitment and character gained increasingly wide notice over time.[12] After he died, evangelist Billy Graham praised the baseball executive as "a man of deep piety and integrity."[13] Prominent pastor and author Norman Vincent Peale, a fellow Ohio Wesleyan graduate, called his good friend and Rickey's wife "two of the greatest, most lovable human beings" he had ever known.[14]

There is ample evidence from Rickey's career as a baseball executive to confirm Graham's and Peale's descriptions, since he participated actively in church affairs and promoted many Christian causes. He gave dozens of speeches at YMCA events and raised large amounts for the organization. In the mid-1920s, Rickey chaired a debate on Christianity versus atheism between nationally renowned lawyer Clarence Darrow and Methodist bishop Edwin Holt Hughes, another Ohio Wesleyan classmate. Rickey strongly affirmed both the humanity and divinity of Christ, but he avoided the biblical literalism that caused William Jennings Bryan difficulty when Darrow, serving as John T. Scopes's defense attorney at the celebrated Scopes trial in Dayton, Tennessee, in July 1925, examined him on the witness stand. Rickey even considered debating Darrow himself but wisely decided against doing so.[15]

In February 1938, Rickey spoke at a large conference held to celebrate the 200th anniversary of John Wesley's "strange warming of the heart" at Aldersgate Street in London, which soon gave birth to Methodism. Rickey inspired delegates in what the *Chicago Tribune* called his "'Onward, Christian Soldiers' address" and coauthored a document exhorting American youth to help stem the tide of German totalitarianism by regularly reading the Bible, participating in Christian fellowship, and growing spiritually. Karl Downs also spoke at this conference, while the baseball headliner was Cleveland Indians' pitcher Bob Feller.[16]

Rickey participated enthusiastically in churches wherever he lived, including Grace Methodist Episcopal Church in St. Louis and two congregations in New York City. While residing in Queens, Rickey worshiped at the Plymouth Church of the Pilgrims in Brooklyn or Church in the Gardens near his home, occasionally preaching at the latter church. Plymouth Church, located a few blocks from the Dodgers' office, was founded in 1847. Its first pastor was Henry Ward Beecher, one the nation's most influential pulpiteers during the second half of the nineteenth century.

At Church in the Gardens, Rickey served on the church's board of trustees and spoke at numerous church functions.[17] Founded in 1913 by Olivia Sage, the widow of industrialist Russell Sage, this Congregational church included members from various denominational backgrounds who lived primarily in Forest Hills Gardens, a planned community composed of families from different socioeconomic classes. Sage hoped that the church would "always be open to everyone who loves the Lord Jesus Christ and wishes to do His will." In addition to Rickey, its members included Thelma Ritter, a six-time Oscar nominee for best supporting actress, and Dale Carnegie, author of the best-selling classic *How to Win Friends and Influence People* (1936).[18]

Other activities in which he engaged also testify to Rickey's faith. For many years he was very interested in Christian missions, especially to Asia. Dodgers' pitcher Carl Erskine reported that Rickey encouraged his players "to develop a spiritual life, whatever our religion."[19] Rickey helped finance Peale's *Guideposts* magazine and wrote several articles for it; as the Pittsburgh Pirates' general manager in the 1950s, he gave every player a subscription.[20] Rickey also motivated numerous players to follow their faith more devoutly.[21] One in particular was Erskine, who had a 122–78 record during his twelve-year career and coached at Anderson College, a Christian institution in Indiana, after his retirement from baseball. In 1954, Rickey helped found the Fellowship of Christian Athletes, the world's leading organization for nurturing the Christian faith of participants in sports at all levels.[22]

Rickey's consistent, deeply engrained Christian convictions were nowhere more important than in his efforts to integrate baseball. "Without the intelligence, personality, and dedication of a Rickey, it would have been very hard" to accomplish, declared sociologist Dan Dodson, one of his collaborators in the process.[23]

This was only one of the many ways in which Rickey was a baseball innovator. One writer likened Rickey's overall impact to how Henry Ford had shaped the automobile industry.[24] Rickey introduced the batting helmet, batting cages, and pitching machines; used tryout camps to sign players; and invented the farm system.[25] In 1947, *Time* magazine called Rickey "the smartest man in baseball," and in 1960 sportswriter Jack Orr labeled him baseball's "most astute mind."[26] While serving as the Dodgers' general manager, Rickey acquired every player who was crucial to the team's domination of the National League between 1947 and 1956. Although the Pirates remained mired in the National League basement during Rickey's tenure as the team's general manager from 1951 to 1955, he put together the nucleus of the team that won the World Series in 1960, including Roberto Clemente, Dick Groat, Bill Mazeroski, Elroy Face, and Vern Law.

Baseball has had flamboyant personalities, including Casey Stengel, Leo Durocher, George Steinbrenner, Charlie Finley, and Yogi Berra, but no one quite matches Branch Rickey.[27] Respected sportswriter Red Smith marveled at Rickey's numerous roles and multifaceted persona, calling him a "player, manager, executive, lawyer, preacher, horse-trader, spellbinder, innovator, husband and father and grandfather, farmer, logician, obscurantist, reformer, financier, sociologist, crusader . . . father confessor . . . friend and fighter."[28] Rickey, another observer adds, "was a Bible-quoting, tight-fisted Republican, a fierce competitor, and a shrewd negotiator."[29] Jules Tygiel describes the baseball executive as "religious, righteous, and rhetorical," "a strange mixture of moralist and mountebank."[30] *Time* depicted Rickey as a combination of the huckster and self-promoter Phineas T. Barnum and theatrical evangelist and former baseball player Billy Sunday, arguing that Rickey was "prone to talk piously of the larger and higher implications of what he is doing."[31]

Nicknames for Rickey abounded. In 1942, sportswriter Tom Meany labeled him the "Mahatma," mirroring John Gunther's depiction of the Indian leader Mahatma Gandhi as "a combination of God, your father, and [a] Tammany Hall leader."[32] Rickey liked this designation, but to his detractors, it expressed "his overbearing pomposity and insufferable certainty."[33] Another sportswriter, Harold Burr, dubbed Rickey the "Great White Father" and called his office the "Cave of the Winds."[34] Viewing him as an insufferable moralist whose "high-flown locutions overwhelmed most opposition and often obscured or embroidered key facts," other reporters adopted the term.[35] More positively, his many religious references and sermonic speeches prompted sportswriters to call him the "Deacon," and his intelligent and innovative approach to baseball earned him the label of "the brain."

The sobriquet that Rickey most despised was "El Cheapo." Many criticized him for being tightfisted, paying paltry salaries, and controlling players. His detractors, including MLB commissioner Kenesaw Mountain Landis, protested that he professed Christian values but acted as a stingy tyrant. Landis decried Rickey as a "hypocritical Protestant bastard" wrapped in "ministers' robes."[36] St. Louis Cardinals' All-Star Enos Slaughter declared in 1934 that Rickey would "go into the vault to get a nickel change." After negotiating his contract with Rickey in 1945, Dodgers' second baseman Eddie Stanky quipped, undoubtedly speaking for many ballplayers, "I got a million dollars' worth of free advice and a very small raise." Roger Kahn insisted that Rickey "had a Puritan distaste for money in someone else's hands."[37] In addition, cartoonists and critics lampooned Rickey's appearance; he was depicted with "a diving bell silhouette," with "wooly mammoth eyebrows," wearing a Churchillian bow tie and smoking a cigar, and with "a fedora raked back with FDR insouciance."[38]

In a 1947 profile of Rickey in *Sport*, Ed Fitzgerald claimed that the Dodgers' executive possessed "tremendous magnetism": "His personality lights up a whole room."[39] His best qualities were his firm convictions, compassion, and easy facility for developing friendships. Rickey, historian Roger Launius argues, displayed "streaks of petulance, moralism, and autocracy that either infuriated or endeared him to those he encountered."[40] Although often overbearing and sanctimonious, "Rickey inspired a fierce loyalty and a respect bordering on worship from his associates and players," perhaps more from Robinson than anyone else. The energetic, pioneering, penny-pinching businessman typically worked eighteen hours a day.[41]

Rickey had all the qualities necessary to break baseball's color line— imagination, commitment to the cause, passion, and perseverance. His position as a baseball executive gave him the opportunity to accomplish the long-standing objective of black sportswriters, activists, and athletes. To achieve this goal, he was willing to sacrifice his wealth, health, and reputation.[42] Rejecting the negative stereotypes of Rickey, Rachel Robinson insisted that she saw "the total man," not just the "cigar-chewing, funny hat guy" or the Bible-thumper "always giving sermons."[43]

Preparing the Way

Because so many MLB owners, players, and fans opposed integrating base-ball, Rickey's religious convictions were essential to this endeavor. The first African American to play in MLB, Washington Senators' owner Clark Griffith correctly predicted in 1938, "will face caustic comments" and be "the target of cruel, filthy epithets." The man who did this would "become a sort of martyr to the cause."[44]

Christian and Jewish leaders, black sportswriters, Communist Party leaders, labor union members, civil rights advocates, and politicians all helped obliterate MLB's color line. In the 1930s, these groups began working to integrate baseball as part of a broader effort to end discrimination in all segments of society. Activists denounced segregation in the military, strove to pass a federal antilynching law, sought to persuade the government to hire blacks for defense jobs during World War II, and boycotted stores that refused to employ black persons.[45] These groups "published open letters to baseball owners, polled white managers and players (most of whom said that they had no objections to playing with African Americans), brought black players to unscheduled tryouts at spring training camps, picketed at baseball stadiums in New York and Chicago, gathered signatures on petitions, and kept the issue [of racial integration] before the public."[46]

Some clergy called for the integration of baseball. Raymond Campion, a white priest who pastored St. Peter Claver Catholic Church in Brooklyn (the diocese of New York's first parish for African American Catholics) from 1940 to 1952, argued that denying people "the opportunity to earn a decent living because of the dark shade" of their skin was "utterly wrong, unfair, un-American, un-Democratic, [and] un-Christian."[47] Campion met with Dodgers' president Larry MacPhail for almost two hours on September 15, 1942. Also present were New York State assemblyman William T. Andrews, former Negro League commissioner Ferdinand Morton, Fred Turner of the NAACP, Dan Burley of the *Amsterdam News*, and George Hunton of the *Catholic Interracial Review*. Campion complained that Pittsburgh and Cleveland had promised to give black players an opportunity but had failed to do so. MacPhail insisted that "plenty of Negro players are ready for the big leagues" but took no steps to give any of them a tryout.[48] Campion, also the chaplain of the Brooklyn Interracial Committee, declared in 1944 at the first session of the Institute of Interracial Justice that American laws declaring that all citizens had equal rights were "a mockery to Negroes." "Racial segregation," Campion protested, "is a serious injustice," a "violation of the law of charity," and "contrary to the law of God." He argued that communities, like individuals, "can and do commit serious wrong."[49]

Jews, fueled by two major factors—their moral convictions and idealism and their ability to identify with another oppressed group—also played an important role in the desegregation of baseball. During the 1940s, Jews, like African Americans, faced discrimination in education, employment, and housing. Although they "risked intensifying anti-Semitism by embracing the cause of the nation's most despised minority," many Jewish journalists, organizations, and fans strongly supported smashing baseball's color line. Leading Jewish organizations—the American Jewish Committee, the American Jewish Congress, the Anti-Defamation League (ADL), the Jewish Labor Committee, and the Union of American Hebrew Congregations—denounced all forms of racism and bigotry and joined African American groups in aggressively lobbying to improve job and educational opportunities and housing for minorities. Journalists Walter Winchell and Shirley Povich led Jewish efforts to desegregate baseball, winning praise from many black newspapers. Winchell, the nation's most influential newspaper columnist and radio newscaster in the 1940s and a longtime champion of civil rights, frequently denounced baseball's color barrier and gave Robinson emotional support during his rookie year. An estimated fifty million Americans read Winchell's columns (which were syndicated in more than two thousand newspapers) or listened to his Sunday evening radio broadcast every week. Povich, an Orthodox Jew and sports editor of the *Washington Post*, also strongly condemned racial discrimination in baseball and other sports.[50]

The contribution of black journalists was especially important in the quest to integrate baseball. A small group of young, talented black sportswriters, most notably Wendell Smith of the *Pittsburgh Courier*, Sam Lacy of the *Baltimore Afro-American*, Fay Young of the *Chicago Defender*, and Joe Bostic of the *People's Voice* in New York, publicized the controversy over integration.[51] Several white journalists at mainstream newspapers also offered support. Robinson argued that sportswriters were more responsible than any other group for African Americans' admission into MLB; they constantly insisted that as long as baseball "barred any race, creed, or color from the diamond," it "could not be called the American sport."[52]

Incorporated in 1910 by attorney Robert Vann and business tycoon Cumberland Posey Sr., the *Pittsburgh Courier* was one of the nation's most prominent black newspapers during the 1930s and 1940s. It established a national reputation through its crusade for black rights, which included constantly touting the achievements of Joe Louis and Jackie Robinson. The *Courier*'s shrewd promotion of Louis's success in the ring helped its circulation surpass that of the *Chicago Defender*, making it the country's largest black paper in the 1940s. During World War II, the *Courier* promoted a "Double V" campaign. Backed by African American newspapers throughout the nation, the *Courier* insisted that black soldiers risking their lives to preserve democracy and achieve victory abroad should also receive full citizenship rights at home.[53] When Wendell Smith joined the *Courier* in 1937, the Pittsburgh Crawfords and the Homestead Grays, both all-black and two of the greatest baseball teams of all time, played in Pittsburgh. Cumberland Posey Jr., the only person inducted into both the basketball and baseball halls of fame, owned the Grays while Gus Greenlee, a numbers kingpin, owned the Crawfords.[54]

Smith called for the integration of baseball and urged African Americans not to pay to watch a sport that excluded black players. Smith later worked for the *Chicago American*, becoming the first black sportswriter to have a byline with a major daily paper. He was also the first African American invited to join the Baseball Writers' Association. Smith maintained that he worked diligently to prevent his ten-year crusade to integrate baseball from becoming flamboyant or "highly militant."[55]

Smith helped arrange a meeting between members of the black press and former Kentucky governor Happy Chandler, who replaced Landis as MLB commissioner in 1944. Smith spoke frequently with Rickey about Robinson's potential to integrate baseball. Rickey paid Smith fifty dollars a week (the same salary he earned at the *Courier*) to serve as Robinson's companion during spring training in 1946. Smith also arranged accommodations and places to eat on road trips during Robinson's first season with the minor league Montreal Royals, when Robinson was barred from whites-only hotels and restaurants; on some trips, he roomed with the ballplayer.

The *Courier*'s extensive coverage of Robinson's exploits and the athlete's weekly columns (which Smith helped write) contributed to the newspaper attaining its highest-ever circulation, 466,000 copies, in 1946.[56]

Both leading white sportswriters (including Shirley Povich, Lester Rodney, and Jimmy Powers) and their black counterparts (especially Smith, Lacy, and Dan Burley) pointed out that racially ambiguous Latinos were already playing in MLB. They accused MLB executives of racial hypocrisy and insisted that if Latinos could play, blacks should too.[57]

The widespread poverty and privation brought on by the Great Depression made the Communist Party attractive to some Americans. Recognizing that the nation's systemic racism made many blacks open to their message, party leaders strove to enlist them as members. One key strategy for winning their allegiance was working to desegregate MLB. From 1936 to 1945, the *Daily Worker*, the party's principal US mouthpiece, published hundreds of columns and articles denouncing the color barrier.[58] In 1936, the *Daily Worker* created a sports section to highlight racial injustice in professional sports. Lester Rodney, the paper's sports editor, continually prodded baseball owners to sign black players.

In 1941, the *Daily Worker* sent telegrams to all sixteen MLB franchises, urging them to give tryouts to Negro league players.[59] Smith contended that because of the Communist Party's unpopularity, such activities "did more to delay the entrance of the Negroes into Organized Baseball than any other factor."[60] Jules Tygiel disagrees. The efforts of the Communist Party to publicize civil rights grievances, he claims, "far outweighed the negative ramifications of their sponsorship."[61]

To support the integration of baseball, numerous labor unions, joined by civil rights groups, picketed outside stadiums in New York and Chicago during the early 1940s and collected more than a million petition signatures. The Trade Union Athletic Association sponsored an "End Jim Crow in Baseball" demonstration at the New York World's Fair in July 1940.[62] The next year, a delegation representing progressive unions met with Landis to urge MLB to recruit black players.

Numerous politicians, especially in the New York City area, also joined the fight. Left-wing Brooklyn congressman Vito Marcantonio urged the US Commerce Department to investigate the absence of black players in MLB. New York State senator Charles Perry introduced several resolutions in

Albany, censuring baseball for discriminating against African Americans. New York City councilmen Peter Cacchione, who represented Brooklyn, and African American Benjamin Davis Jr., a football star at Amherst College who had earned a law degree at Harvard and represented Harlem, exhorted the city's three major league teams—the Giants, Dodgers, and Yankees—to sign black players. The city council passed several resolutions urging them to do so. Davis also distributed thousands of leaflets displaying the photos of two African Americans—a dead soldier and a baseball player. "Good enough to die for his country," it proclaimed, "but not good enough for organized baseball."[63]

Yet another factor that helped demolish the color line in baseball was the spectacular success of African Americans in other sports. Joe Louis was a national hero; Jesse Owens had triumphed at the Olympics. If Americans cheered their accomplishments, why should they oppose black persons playing baseball?[64] Robinson asserted that Louis's conduct and sportsmanship helped pave the way for a black baseball player. To Rickey, Louis proved that a black athlete could be honored and remain dignified.[65]

Moreover, few major league players strongly opposed integration. Based on a poll he conducted in the late 1930s, Smith claimed that 80 percent of National League managers and players were willing to play with African Americans; many of them had already participated frequently in interracial off-season games.[66] Few players, argues Jules Tygiel, were willing to sacrifice their careers to oppose integration. Spring training in the South, "where integrated competition would violate local laws and customs," posed problems, but baseball had the economic clout to pressure southern cities to allow interracial competition.[67]

During the early 1940s, the Pirates seemed most likely to end the color line. In the 1930s, the incredibly talented Pittsburgh Crawfords and Homestead Grays made Pittsburgh the center of black baseball. The *Pittsburgh Courier* strongly pressured Pirates' owner William Benswanger to sign African American players, and he appeared to favor this idea.[68] In September 1942, the Pirates, the National League's perennial cellar dweller, announced that they would give tryouts to four black players. The *Christian Century*, a leading liberal Protestant journal, applauded this move, insisting that only custom, not rules, had "hitherto kept the major leagues lily white." Noting that many experts believed black players "could more than hold their own with the white big leaguers," the editors predicted that if the Pirates signed African Americans, other teams would surely follow. Testifying to the importance of baseball, they insisted that this "revolutionary" action would make ordinary Americans "more conscious that a new day in race relations is at hand" than a "hundred resolutions on racial good will adopted by church assemblies." If baseball magnates did sign blacks, the editors argued, it would be for economic reasons rather than because of "an awakening of democratic fervor." Regardless of the motive, however, the editors simply wanted to see "the doors of opportunity" opened "to a minority whose present treatment makes a mockery of all our democratic pretensions."[69]

In December 1943, actor Paul Robeson and eight black sportswriters met with Commissioner Landis and owners of MLB to urge integration. Robeson, who dominated the meeting, argued that if a black man could star as Othello on Broadway (which he had just done), then African Americans should be able to play in MLB.[70] Meanwhile, in 1942 and 1943, Bill Veeck attempted to buy the Philadelphia Phillies; he planned to rebuild the struggling franchise with veterans of the Negro league. Veeck believed his innovative and inexpensive strategy would enable the Phillies to win the pennant. He complained that Landis, a strong opponent of integration, orchestrated the sale of the team to another party to thwart his plans.[71]

Until his death in 1944, Landis was a stumbling block to integration. Selected as commissioner in 1921 to restore the game's image—tarnished by the 1919 Black Sox scandal—Landis publicly insisted that no rule prohibited signing black players, but privately he steadfastly opposed desegregating the game. Baseball executives, including ones who privately endorsed segregation, recognized the conflict between the American creed of equal opportunity and racism in their domain. Before Rickey, however, no owner strongly challenged Landis's position, and the ban on black participation "reflected the prevailing attitudes of the baseball hierarchy." Racism as well as economic concerns (namely, fears of losing white fans and the fees paid by Negro league teams to rent their stadiums) prevented most baseball executives from wanting to integrate the sport.[72] Reflecting their prejudice, Yankees' owner and general manager Larry MacPhail argued in a 1945 editorial that most African Americans lacked "the technique, the co-ordination, the competitive aptitude and the discipline usually acquired only after years of training in the smaller leagues."[73] But Happy Chandler maintained that "if African Americans could fight and die on Okinawa, Guadalcanal, [and] in the South Pacific during WWII, they could play ball in America."[74]

In March 1945, the Quinn-Ives Act became law, banning "discrimination because of race, creed, color or national origin" in hiring in New York State and establishing a committee to investigate alleged violations. The Federal Council of Churches, the American Jewish Congress, Catholic archbishop Richard Cushing of Boston, and NAACP attorney Thurgood Marshall all applauded the act. Rickey rejoiced at the news. Recognizing that the law and the courts were on his side, he believed that he now had "both the moral and legal authority to sign black players," and declared that the other owners "can't stop me now."[75] The passage of Quinn-Ives and increasing pressure from political progressives prompted New York City mayor Fiorello La Guardia to create the Mayor's Committee to Integrate Baseball, to which he appointed Rickey, in early August. At the same time, the Committee to End Jim Crow in Baseball, organized by the Trade Union Athletic Association, called on city residents to demonstrate outside the city's three major league ballparks to support the integration of baseball. Scores of prominent Americans joined this committee, and numerous luminaries, including Eleanor Roosevelt and Paul Robeson, endorsed its cause.

Meanwhile, black activists were working throughout the nation to obtain equal rights. Jim Crow segregation, including the prohibition of interracial athletic contests, still plagued the South, and most people in other regions were indifferent to the plight of African Americans. In 1941, Franklin Roosevelt created the Fair Employment Practice Committee in part to prevent a large black march on Washington, DC, organized by A. Philip Randolph. The next year, black and white activists associated with the interfaith Fellowship of Reconciliation established the Congress of Racial Equality to mobilize nonviolent protests to end racial discrimination. Deeply distressed by continued discrimination at home during World War II, civil rights advocates, led by the NAACP, used litigation, legislation, and lobbying to pursue their goals. They also worked to register more African Americans to vote in the South. The campaign for civil rights accelerated after the war ended as many black veterans returned home committed to challenging the nation's racist practices and expecting to receive more employment and educational opportunities. Having fought to defend the Constitution, they demanded to enjoy all its rights, including playing all professional sports. The NAACP petitioned the United Nations to discuss a list of racially discriminatory practices in the United States.[76]

All these developments preceded and facilitated Rickey's signing of Robinson. Rickey later explained that he had feared that his experiment would fail, like the Eighteenth Amendment implementing Prohibition. He worried that it "would over-leap itself," impeding rather than solving the nation's racial problems. To determine whether baseball could feasibly be desegregated, he had examined several scholarly analyses of race, finding Frank Tannenbaum's *Slave and Citizen* (1946) compelling. Tannenbaum, a professor of comparative slavery and race relations at Columbia University and an immigrant from Austria-Hungary, helped European Jews escape from Nazi persecution during the 1930s. Rickey accepted Tannenbaum's argument that closer relations between blacks and whites in Latin American societies, which had permitted social mixing and intermarriage (unlike the United States with its racial barriers), had reduced tension and contributed to social harmony. *Slave and Citizen* bolstered his conviction that he "was doing the right thing and that the consequences would be favorable,"[77] as well as his belief that individuals who worked together to achieve a common goal could overcome their racial prejudices.[78]

Rickey disclosed his plans for integrating baseball with Dan Dodson, a sociology professor at New York University and the executive director of the Mayor's Committee on Unity, who enthusiastically encouraged him. Dodson shared much of Rickey's background; he was the son of poor white sharecroppers in Texas, a graduate of a small Methodist college in Texas, a member of Christ Methodist Church in New York City, and active in YMCA work.[79] Dodson called for creating situations where black and white Americans could collaborate to achieve shared goals.[80]

Rickey also consulted with Dr. John H. Johnson, rector of St. Martin's Episcopal Church in Harlem.[81] Founded as a mission congregation in 1928, St. Martin's had more than three thousand members by the late 1940s. Johnson had starred in basketball at Columbia University while earning a BA and MA in anthropology. While attending two seminaries in Manhattan (Union Theological and General Theological), he played professional basketball to pay his expenses. The civil rights activist created the "Don't buy where you can't work" campaign in the mid-1930s to urge blacks to boycott white-owned businesses in Harlem until they hired black workers. In 1935, Johnson was named the first African American member of New York City's Emergency Relief Bureau, and in 1939 Mayor La Guardia appointed him as the city's first African American police chaplain. Johnson was also the first black person to serve on the Borough President's Advisory Board and as a trustee of the Cathedral of St. John the Divine, the headquarters of the Episcopal Diocese of New York. During the 1940s, he worked diligently with other New Yorkers to integrate MLB. He also served as commissioner of the Negro National League, where he strove to improve conditions for both players and fans. The rector published several books, including a collection of sermons, and counseled prominent Harlem mob figure Ellsworth "Bumpy" Johnson, who would become the subject of two major Hollywood movies—*The Cotton Club* (1984) and *Hoodlum* (1997).[82]

Rickey believed that Brooklyn was the best place to integrate baseball. He rightly surmised that Jews, who composed one-third of the borough's population, would support breaking the color barrier.[83] Most Jews were political liberals and strongly opposed discrimination of any type, having been its victims throughout history and especially during the Holocaust, the horrific details of which were becoming increasingly known in 1945–1946. Rabbi Corey Weiss argued in a 1997 sermon commemorating the fiftieth anniversary of Robinson's entrance into the majors that even Rickey could not have envisioned "the way Jewish fans embraced Jackie Robinson."[84] They viewed Rickey and Robinson as "lamed-vavnicks"—in Jewish tradition, people who quietly made the world a better place. Another rabbi insisted that in the late 1940s many Jews worshiped the pair as heroes.[85] Robinson often stated that the borough's large Jewish population made Brooklyn a great place for him to play. Its Jewish residents, he declared in a published letter, "were very welcoming to me and I made many friends that lasted through the years."[86]

Choosing a Candidate

In his quest to integrate MLB, Rickey looked far and wide, but principles arising from his life of faith always played a major role. He sent scouts to scour the Caribbean islands and looked at numerous Negro league players. Some Cubans were very talented and might have been less threatening to white fans than an African American. Havana Sugar Kings' third baseman Silvio Garcia appeared to be a great candidate, but concerns about his age and lifestyle and the accusation that he had dodged the Cuban military draft led Rickey to reject him. Moreover, signing a darker-skinned Latino like Garcia would not necessarily have opened the door to African Americans.[87]

Many Negro league stars were past their peak performance years by 1945. The Cuban-born Martin Dihigo was forty; Buck Leonard was thirty-eight; Satchel Paige was probably at least forty; Josh Gibson, who had smashed fifty to seventy-five home runs a year for many seasons and had a lifetime average of over .360, was thirty-four but already displaying signs of the emotional problems and alcoholism that would lead to his death in 1947. These men had more experience and name recognition than Robinson, but none seemed as likely to be a good role model for other black players.[88] Nineteen-year-old pitcher Don Newcombe, who could hurl a 100-mile-an-hour fastball and hit with power, was "perhaps the best pure athlete in the Negro leagues," but Rickey believed no one so young could survive the intense emotional pressure of being the first African American in MLB.[89] Rickey was very interested in Roy Campanella and eventually signed him too, but the catcher's love of cards, carousing, and good times made the Dodgers' general manager reluctant to choose him as the pioneer.[90]

On one level, ample evidence indicated that African Americans would succeed in MLB. The low salaries of baseball players had led them since the late nineteenth century to "barnstorm" throughout Latin America and the southern United States during their off-season, playing exhibition games to supplement their income. In the process, teams of white major leaguers often competed against black all-star teams and Cuban teams. In the 1930s, these black teams won more than two-thirds of the 167 games they played against white barnstorming teams.[91] Arguably, Gibson, Leonard, Paige, William "Judy" Jones, James Thomas "Cool Papa" Bell, and Oscar Charleston could have been among the greatest major leaguers ever had they played in their prime as Willie Mays, Henry Aaron, and Frank Robinson did in the next generation. Moreover, the 1930s games that pitted

Paige's teams against those of Cardinals' pitcher Dizzy Dean drew very large crowds, suggesting that the integration of baseball would benefit the owners financially. Paige's well-publicized success against major league stars led many sportswriters, baseball officials, and fans to recognize the potential of black ballplayers.[92]

In addition, before World War II numerous African Americans had participated in football, basketball, baseball, and track and field at major universities. Many black athletes, most notably Paul Robeson of Rutgers, Fritz Pollard of Brown, Eddie Tolan of Michigan, Jesse Owens of Ohio State, Ralph Metcalfe of Marquette, and Kenny Washington and Jackie Robinson of UCLA, starred at nonsouthern schools. Despite their outstanding performances, they had often been derided and poorly treated by their universities and some of their white teammates. Their athletic achievements, character, and response to this mistreatment all suggested that African Americans could succeed in MLB.[93]

After considering all the traits necessary for the first black player in MLB to succeed, Rickey concluded that Robinson was the best candidate. He was an extraordinary athlete, an impressive hitter and fielder, an exceptional base runner, and an outstanding bunter who "excelled in the game's mental aspects."[94] Robinson was articulate, courageous, disciplined, and strong-willed. He had charisma and tremendous self-respect. He had attended college and served as an army officer. Robinson deeply desired to improve the status and opportunities of African Americans.[95] While playing four sports at UCLA, he had interacted effectively with white teammates, opponents, and the media. His Christian faith, consistent church attendance, and biblical morality were especially important to the Dodgers' general manager. Rachel Robinson stated that shared belief in God was a major factor in the partnership between Rickey and her husband.[96]

Rickey later explained that he knew he needed to find an outstanding player who had the proper temperament to act responsibly, along with "exceptional intelligence," "exceptional courage," and "fine character." The first black player needed to be accepted by his teammates—a factor over which Rickey admitted he had no control.[97] If handled poorly, Rickey feared that bringing an African American into MLB might retard the "cause of racial equality a quarter century or more."[98]

Time magazine reported that Rickey's scouts had investigated Robinson so thoroughly that "they knew everything about him but what he dreamed at night." They discovered that he did not smoke or touch liquor and rarely swore. Robinson dealt with the difficulties of interracial athletic competition "not by truculence or bitterness, and not by servility, but by a reserve that no white man really ever penetrated." And very important to Rickey, Robinson was a natural athlete.[99]

The primary question mark regarding Robinson was his temper. MLB's first black player would have to withstand immense pressure and potential abuse and possess "the self-control to avoid reacting to his tormentors without sacrificing his dignity." Robinson's disposition caused many Negro league players to question whether he could endure the attacks he would face in integrating MLB.[100] Rickey feared that choosing an overly sensitive or easily enraged player would produce deplorable racial confrontations on the field or in the stands and give his fellow owners a rationale for maintaining the color line.[101] The first black player, Robinson later explained, had to be able to accept "abuse, name-calling, rejection by fans and sportswriters and by fellow players" and to endure "merciless persecution and not retaliate."[102] "I had to get a man," Rickey avowed, "who would carry the badge of martyrdom" and who would be accepted by other African Americans, his teammates, and the press.[103] After thoroughly investigating Robinson's background, Rickey concluded "he had done nothing wrong" on the playing fields or in the military. Had Robinson been white, he would have been widely admired "as a spirited, aggressive competitor," but because he was black, some white Americans were offended by his actions and incorrectly labeled him a "racial agitator."[104]

A. S. "Doc" Young summarized the situation with a large dose of hyperbole and sarcasm, saying the first African American in MLB would have to be as skilled as any Caucasian but also "college-bred . . . as honest as Jesus . . . as pure as Ivory, as emotionless as the Sphinx, as cool as Sky Blue Water . . . merely to get the chance to play the sport which had before him" accepted "all sorts of people of foreign extraction, rowdies, drunkards, temper tantrum throwers, wastrels, and called them heroes" because of their accomplishments on the diamond.[105] Robinson may not have matched Young's description, but he offered great athletic ability, intelligence, confidence, concentration, and dedication to the cause, strong faith in God, and the capacity to channel his aggression and anger.

A Pair Made in Heaven

On May 8, 1945, Germany surrendered and World War II ended in Europe. The conflict had decimated many nations. Winston Churchill described Europe as "a rubble heap, a charnel house, a breeding ground for pestilence and hate." Shortly after the United States dropped two atomic bombs on Japan (Hiroshima on August 6 and Nagasaki on August 9) and five days before Japan's unconditional surrender, which ended World War II in Asia, Branch Rickey and Jackie Robinson met for three hours at the general manager's office on Montague Street in Brooklyn. Their August 28 meeting would change the course of baseball history. Rickey grilled Robinson about his personal life, strongly encouraged him to marry Rachel, and depicted the difficulties he would face as the first black ballplayer in MLB. Rickey said he wanted to sign Robinson to a Dodgers' contract but warned that this "experiment" would not work if the athlete fought back. Based on the information his scouts had provided, Rickey declared, "I know you're a good ballplayer. What I don't know is whether you have the guts . . . not to fight back."[106]

To reinforce his argument, Rickey took an English translation of Giovanni Papini's *Life of Christ* out of his desk drawer. The Italian journalist, novelist, and professor had been a prominent atheist before his remarkable conversion to Catholicism in 1921, a decade before C. S. Lewis turned from atheism to Anglicanism.[107] Rickey read from Papini's book: "Every man has an obscure respect for courage in others, especially if it is moral courage, the rarest and most difficult sort of bravery. . . . The results of nonresistance, even if they are not always perfect, are certainly superior to those of resistance or flight. . . . To answer blows with blows, evil deeds with evil deeds, is to meet the attacker on his own ground. . . . Only he who has conquered himself can conquer his enemies."[108] Rickey also highlighted a passage from the Sermon on the Mount that Papini called "the most stupefying" of Jesus's "revolutionary teachings": "You have heard that it hath been said, 'An eye for an eye, and a tooth for a tooth': But I say unto you, That ye resist not evil: But whosoever shall smite thee on thy right cheek, turn to him the other also" (Matt. 5:38).[109] Papini argued that enacting revenge accelerated the cycle of violence and flight encouraged opponents to be more violent, but turning the other cheek worked; nonviolence, he insisted, was active, not passive or docile.

Rickey then acted out several scenarios to represent the challenges Robinson would confront. He depicted a white clerk who rudely refused Robinson hotel accommodations, a condescending white waiter in a restaurant, and a ruthless white railroad conductor. Rickey portrayed a vulgar opponent, Robinson recalled, who denounced "my race, my parents, in language that was almost unendurable."[110] The Dodgers' general manager "even swung a fist at his head and evoked a base-runner sliding spikes up to cut Robinson's leg or hand, sneering 'How do you like that, nigger boy?'"[111] "They'll taunt you and goad you," Rickey warned. "They'll try to provoke a race riot in the ball park" to prove that an African American "should not be allowed to play in the major league."[112] He concluded, "Above all you cannot fight back. That's the only way this experiment will succeed, and others will follow in your footsteps."[113]

Rickey then asked Robinson: "Promise me that for the first three years in baseball you will turn the other cheek. Three years—can you do it?"[114] Robinson recognized that given his personality and life experiences, this would be an immense challenge. As he later explained, "All my life back to the age of eight when a little neighbor girl called me a nigger—I had believed in payback, retaliation." Comprehending what was at stake for himself and other African Americans, however, he agreed. "I had to do it . . . for black youth, for my mother, for Rae, for myself . . . and for Branch Rickey."[115] Familiar with Matthew 5:38, he proclaimed, alluding to that verse, "I've got two cheeks."[116] Rickey concluded that Robinson's strong faith would enable him to control his temper.[117] He was confident Robinson could cope with maltreatment because he was a "Christian by inheritance and practice."[118]

In keeping his promise, Rickey later effused, Robinson's actions had been "Christ-like." "It was harder to turn the other cheek and refuse to fight back than it would have been to exercise a normal reaction," Robinson admitted. "But it works, because sooner or later it brings a sense of shame to those who attack you. And that shame is often the beginning of progress."[119] By refusing to fight back against the vicious verbal and physical assaults he faced, "Robinson exemplified redemptive suffering."[120]

In a 1948 *Guideposts* article, Robinson recalled other parts of their conversation. When Rickey explained that he wanted to sign Robinson to play with the Dodgers, the athlete responded, "It sounds like a dream come true—not only for me but for my race. For 70 years there has been racial exclusion in Big League Baseball. There will be trouble ahead—for you, for me, for my people and for baseball." Rickey insisted that they use the "courage God gave us," "study the hazards and build wisely." He added, "God is with us in this, Jackie. You know your Bible. It's good, simple Christianity for us to face realities and to recognize what we're up against. We can't go out and preach and crusade and bust our heads against a wall. We've got to fight out our problems together with tact and common sense."[121]

On October 23, 1945, Robinson signed a contract to play the next season with the Montreal Royals, the Dodgers' affiliate in the International League. Two years before President Harry Truman desegregated the US military, nine years before the US Supreme Court declared racial segregation of public schools to be unconstitutional in *Brown v. Board of Education*, ten years before Rosa Parks refused to move to the back of a bus in Montgomery, Alabama, and nineteen years before the Civil Rights Act of 1964, Rickey and Robinson took the first public step in integrating MLB. When Rickey told his friend broadcaster Lowell Thomas that Robinson's signing would be announced the next day, Thomas warned him that "tomorrow all hell is going to break loose." Rickey responded, "I believe tomorrow all heaven will rejoice."[122]

A Guinea Pig

When asked how he felt about being the first black player to sign an MLB contract, Robinson described himself as "a guinea pig in this noble experiment."[123] In a *Pittsburgh Courier* column, he declared, "I will not forget I am representing a whole race of people who are pulling for me."[124] The pressure Robinson faced was indeed immense. Wendell Smith insisted that "the hopes, aspirations and ambitions of thirteen million black Americans" were "heaped upon his broad, sturdy shoulders."[125] Ludlow Werner, editor of the *New York Age*, a black newspaper, warned that Robinson would "be haunted by the expectations of his race." To the nation's African Americans, he would "symbolize not only their prowess in baseball, but their ability to rise to an opportunity. . . . His private life will be watched, too, because white America will judge the Negro race by everything he does. And Lord help him with his fellow Negroes if he should fail them."[126] Rickey told

Robinson that he "had to be both a Job and a Christ" in their joint crusade, as "the cross of the black race was upon his broad shoulders."[127] Robinson promised to carry the mantle of boxer Joe Louis, who had "done a great job" for black Americans. This was quite a challenge, because as Joseph Bibb argued in the *Courier*, Louis was a genuine hero. No black scholar, scientist, artist, or writer "had received the popular accolades or acclaim" accorded to the heavyweight champion.[128]

The reactions to Robinson's signing were mixed. Some sportswriters doubted Rickey's sincerity and viewed the contract as a publicity stunt.[129] Although few white sportswriters openly criticized the signing, most mainstream newspapers downplayed the event and said little about racial discrimination or what breaking the color barrier meant to blacks or the nation.[130] Some white journalists were favorable, even comparing Rickey's action with Lincoln freeing the slaves.[131]

The black community celebrated the event. African American newspapers put it on the front page and hailed the breakthrough in editorials. Robinson "immediately joined Joe Louis atop the pantheon of black heroes."[132] Dan Burley, sports editor of the *New York Amsterdam News*, praised Rickey for having "the courage and foresight to break" the color line. Smith called Robinson's signing the most "democratic step" baseball had taken in twenty-five years.[133] The *Chicago Defender* argued that if baseball could be integrated, businesses, schools, movie theaters, and swimming pools could be integrated too.[134]

Numerous pundits and players predicted that Robinson would fail. A Durham, North Carolina, journalist warned that the first black player "will be so uncomfortable, embarrassed and out of place that he will soon get out of his own accord."[135] New York sportswriter Joe Williams bluntly claimed, "Negroes have been kept out of big-league ball because they are, as a race, very poor ballplayers." *The Sporting News*, "the Bible of Baseball," argued that Robinson would be competing with many "younger, more skilled and more experienced players. . . . This factor alone appears likely to beat him down."[136] Jimmy Powers of the *New York Daily News* estimated Robinson's chance of success as "1,000 to 1."[137] A March 12, 1946, column in the *Daily News*, presumably penned by Powers, asserted: "We don't believe Jackie Robinson . . . will ever play in the big leagues. We question Branch Rickey's pompous statements that he is another Abraham

Lincoln and that he has a heart as big as a watermelon and he loves all mankind."[138] Cleveland Indians' All-Star pitcher Bob Feller insisted that if Robinson were white, "I doubt they would even consider him big league material."[139] Meanwhile, numerous southern players squawked about Robinson's signing. Retired star Rogers Hornsby, a Texan, declared that Robinson would flop. Other southerners had no objections to integration "as long as there are no Negro players on our club."[140]

Many Negro league players feared that Robinson would fail and hurt their cause. Some of them even suggested that Rickey chose a player with inferior talent to ensure that segregation in baseball would continue. Robinson had batted .387 in the Negro league and been selected for its all-star game, so the derogatory assessment of Robinson's ability may have stemmed primarily from jealousy, his lack of friendships with black players, and his frequent criticism of conditions in the Negro league.[141] On the other hand, Satchel Paige, although deeply disappointed that he would not be the first black to play in MLB, graciously said, "They couldn't have picked a better man."[142]

Other sportswriters were more sanguine about Robinson's chances of success and reception. Dan Parker of the *New York Daily Mirror* maintained that there was no reason "why a good, respectable Negro athlete shouldn't fit in just as well into Organized Ball as he does" into college football and basketball and professional boxing and cricket—all sports with a laudable record of interracial relations.[143] Nat Low of the *Daily Worker* rejoiced that Robinson's signing banished "the scourge of Jim Crow from our great National Pastime." W. N. Cox of Norfolk, Virginia, correctly predicted that if "Robinson hits homers and plays a whale of a game for Montreal . . . the fans soon will lose sight of his color."

An apprehensive Rickey warned Robinson, "We can't fight our way through this. . . . We've got no army. There's virtually nobody on our side. No owners. No umpires. Very few newspapermen. And I'm afraid many fans will be hostile. We'll be in a tough position. We can win only if we convince the world that I'm doing this because you are a great ball player and a fine gentleman."[144] Robinson later claimed that he was not "upset or disturbed" by those who contested the "noble experiment" or thought that it was doomed to fail.[145] Others were more optimistic. No one, proclaimed the *Pittsburgh Courier*, can stop the integration of baseball. Its opponents "may be able to detain it for a little while, but not for too long. The world is moving on and they will move with it, whether they like it or not."[146] Reinforcing this argument, the NFL Rams, who had recently moved from Cleveland to Los Angeles, announced the signing of Robinson's former UCLA teammates Kenny Washington and Woody Strode in March 1946 to be the first African Americans to play since 1933.

Branch Rickey's Motives

Although Rickey had varied motives for integrating baseball, his faith and abhorrence of racial discrimination played a major role. Rickey offered three explanations for his actions: he cared about racial injustice, wanted to attract more black fans, and wanted to win pennants.

Rickey's biographers interpret his actions differently. One claimed that by 1946 "Rickey's reputation as a tightwad" had begun to keep new recruits from signing with the Dodgers. Moreover, Brooklyn's farm system was not providing the new talent the team needed to remain competitive. Rickey viewed "the unused pool of players in the Negro Leagues" as an answer to his team's problems.[147] Tygiel insisted just the opposite, contending that financial considerations had little impact on Rickey's decision to integrate baseball since the Dodgers were already drawing well at the box office.[148]

Rickey sometimes denied that achieving racial justice was his primary motive, but at other times he said it was very important to him. In March 1946, Rickey was interviewed by *Life* magazine. He said, "I couldn't face my God much longer knowing that His black creatures are held separate and distinct from His white creatures" in baseball.[149] Dan Dodson, who worked with Rickey to tear down racial barriers in New York City, insisted that the Dodgers' executive was deeply concerned about discrimination in baseball.[150] One African American newspaper described Rickey as "a deeply religious man with the fire of a crusader burning in his breast."[151]

One aspect of Rickey's history that may substantiate his strong motivation to end racism in baseball was his experience with Charlie Thomas, which the baseball executive described many times. When Rickey was coaching the baseball team as a student at Ohio Wesleyan University, the African American Thomas was the squad's best player. Thomas was treated well by his teammates, but players on opposing teams and their fans sometimes taunted him. When Ohio Wesleyan played against the University of Kentucky in Lexington in 1903, some players and spectators chanted, "Get that nigger off the field!" After Rickey warned Kentucky's coach that his team would not play without Thomas, the taunting ceased. That same season, when Ohio Wesleyan traveled to South Bend, Indiana, to play Notre Dame, the manager at the hotel where the team was staying initially refused to permit Thomas to occupy a room. After some negotiation, the manager agreed to allow Thomas to sleep on a cot in Rickey's room. When the two of them were alone, a deeply disturbed Thomas cried while rubbing his arms. "Black skin, Black skin," he moaned. "If only I could make them white."[152]

Although Rickey cited these experiences with Thomas as part of his rationale for signing Robinson, some question how much they impacted an endeavor he undertook forty years later. "Although based in fact," one scholar writes, the stories about Thomas are "vintage Rickey. The allegory is almost biblical and the sermon-like quality of the tale invites skepticism."[153] "To a devout Christian believer such as Rickey," a sportswriter argues, "the incident resonated with the Bible story of the first Christmas in Bethlehem"—there was no room in the inn.[154] Rickey, "the master storyteller," undoubtedly embellished the hotel episode over the years, but Thomas confirmed the core facts. Rickey "instinctively empathized with Thomas's pain of rejection" and sought to console him by promising him that racial discrimination would end someday.[155]

Black journalist A. S. Young claimed Rickey learned from Thomas's experiences "about the terrible degradation of racial prejudice" and concluded that a person's color "had nothing whatsoever to do with one's ability."[156] Rickey may have divulged the Thomas incident to indicate he had wanted to smash the color barrier long before some sportswriters and activists pushed for it in the 1930s.[157] After signing Robinson in 1945, Rickey told the Associated Press that since his coaching days at Ohio Wesleyan he had frequently thought about the negative impact of racial discrimination.[158] Rickey and Thomas, who worked as a dentist in Albuquerque, New Mexico, remained friends throughout their lives. Thomas made several trips to St. Louis to visit Rickey.[159]

A journalist calls Rickey "baseball's equivalent of Oskar Schindler," the German industrialist who saved 1,200 Jews during World War II by employing them in his enamelware and ammunitions factories in eastern European nations, as memorialized in Steven Spielberg's 1993 movie *Schindler's List*.[160] Rickey "saw a chance to intervene in the moral history of the nation, as Lincoln had done." The dangers Rickey perceived caused him to move cautiously, but he believed correctly that history was on his side.[161]

On the other hand, Rickey sometimes maintained that he signed Robinson not "to solve a sociological problem" but "for one reason: to win the pennant. I'd play an elephant with pink horns if he could [help the Dodgers] win the pennant."[162] Refusing to portray himself as a civil rights crusader, Rickey frequently declared, "All I did was pay a superbly talented athlete to play for Brooklyn and help us win a championship." "My only purpose," he added, "is to be fair to all people and my selfish objective is to win baseball games."[163] According to Robinson, Rickey told the Dodgers' brass when he came to Brooklyn in 1943 that he intended to integrate baseball both to win a pennant and because it was morally right.[164]

Although Rickey had complex motives for integrating baseball, his faith played a significant role. Rickey told Robinson about "the promise he made to God and to himself" back at Ohio Wesleyan, that if he gained enough power, he would work to smash the barriers that kept blacks out of the majors. Rickey wanted to "establish the equality of all men in the sight of God." He hoped that Americans would become more interested in the positive qualities of black ballplayers than in the color of their skin.[165] In a sermon he preached at Church in the Gardens, Rickey asserted that he came to New York "to serve the God to whom he prayed, and the Lord's work called for him to bring the first black player into Major League Baseball."[166] "Surely God was with me," he later declared, "when I picked Jackie Robinson as the first Negro player in the major leagues."[167]

On May 13, 1945, five days after Germany's surrender, L. Wendell Fifield, who pastored Plymouth Church of the Pilgrims from 1941 to 1955, joined a Catholic priest and a Jewish rabbi in leading Dodgers' fans in a day of prayer President Truman had designated to commemorate the end of the war in Europe.[168] Sometime during the next several months, Rickey stopped at Plymouth Church. After praying and pacing for forty-five minutes, Rickey told Fifield that he had "decided to sign Jackie Robinson" to a baseball contract. The decision was "so complex," so potentially "far reaching, fraught with so many pitfalls but filled with so much good," that he needed to discuss it with his minister friend after talking "with God about it" to "be sure what He wanted me to do."[169]

Fifield later told his wife, June, about their conversation, and in 1965 she wrote an account for the church's newsletter. She claimed that his conversation with her husband helped propel Rickey "into the fray where he loved to do battle armed with a strength from his God whom he trusted." Convinced that God was guiding him, Rickey launched Robinson, "who rose to great heights" and took thousands of his black brothers with him. Rickey's signing of Robinson, Fifield argued, was "overwhelmingly a moral decision," made in response to "a modern revelation, as powerful" as the apostle Paul's revelation on the road to Damascus, which changed him from a persecutor of the church to its leading evangelist.[170]

Robinson repeatedly extolled Rickey's "deep faith" in God. "Two of the people who had the greatest influence on my life—Mallie Robinson and Branch Rickey," Robinson avowed, shared a "strong faith in the existence of a Supreme Being," which they practiced every day.[171] Rickey, Robinson asserted, "was always doing something for someone else."[172] Rickey's outspokenness about "his religious convictions" deeply impressed Robinson, and he repudiated the contentions of some of Rickey's detractors that his faith was not sincere.[173]

From their first meeting in 1945 to the present, Robinson wrote in 1959, he had relied on Rickey's support, guidance, and friendship. Robinson insisted that he could not have succeeded without Rickey's advice; Rickey called him many times in Montreal to warn him about potential trouble. They had a "close and warm personal relationship," Robinson explained. Any person who believed in the Golden Rule and went to such great lengths to practice it must "be made of pretty stern stuff," Robinson added.[174] "I am Rickey fan no. 1," Robinson declared the next year.[175]

In the 2013 movie 42, after telling chief scout Clyde Sukeforth that he would sign Robinson, Rickey exclaims, "Robinson's a Methodist. I'm a Methodist. God's a Methodist. We can't go wrong." Rickey probably never said this, but a deep bond did develop between him and Robinson based on their deep personal faith. Both were genuine, "muscular" Christians who cared about other people.[176] Both were motivated by the long-standing commitment of white and black Methodists to strive to carry out God's will in their daily actions. They relied on their personal faith to withstand the invective and threats they confronted while demolishing baseball's color barrier and pressuring both the sport and American society to practice racial equality. Both Rickey and Robinson were moralizers who valued hard work, discipline, obedience, and prayer.[177] Their shared Methodist faith, mutual admiration, and personal friendship greatly aided their partnership. They were "collaborators and conspirators" who respected each other, Rachel Robinson declared.[178] They got along so well, she added, because they had similar temperaments, religious faith, determination, and "unshakable integrity."[179]

Lambasting and Lionizing Rickey

Although Rickey's decision to integrate MLB brought him much praise and helped the Dodgers dominate the National League for a decade, it was also widely criticized and placed new obstacles in his team's way. In 1947, Rickey estimated that he had lost $500,000 that year in gate revenues because other teams' scouts were warning players that if they signed with Brooklyn they would have to play with African Americans.[180] Planning and executing his scheme to smash the color barrier also negatively affected Rickey's health. His grueling work schedule produced light-headedness, and he had a seizure, after which he was diagnosed with Ménière's disease, which typically involves vertigo, nausea, and hearing loss. Ignoring his doctors' advice, the Dodgers' general manager refused to slow down.[181]

Many censured Rickey's efforts to integrate baseball. Numerous journalists questioned his moral scruples and smeared his reputation, but they could not destroy his resolution.[182] Rickey was depicted as simultaneously "pious and devious," rather than a benevolent innovator, as he portrayed himself.[183] Robinson claimed that Rickey was a target for the "bitterness, hate and scorn" of "sick whites who considered him a traitor."[184] In both St. Louis and Brooklyn, Robinson lamented, Rickey had faced ridicule and character assassination; "Happily, he has survived the puny darts of his adversaries."[185] Rickey also received numerous letters denouncing his action. A Shelbyville, Illinois, businessman, for example, warned him that integrating baseball would greatly decrease interest in the sport.[186]

His "fellow baseball moguls," Robinson added, pressured him to abandon his plan.[187] Some of them denounced Rickey's signing of Robinson.

Yankees' owner Larry MacPhail protested that Rickey had "double-crossed his associates for his own personal advantage." He had raided the Negro leagues, taking their players without adequately compensating them. According to MacPhail, Winston Churchill must have been thinking of Rickey's efforts to glorify himself when he declared, "There but for the grace of God goes God."[188]

Most managers said nothing about Rickey's plan to smash the color barrier, but a few openly criticized it. One claimed in a speech at a Baseball Writers' Association meeting that Rickey was ruining the sport. A skit performed at a New York Baseball Writers' Association meeting in early 1946 depicted Rickey as a despicable carpetbagger who was exploiting Robinson (portrayed by an actor wearing blackface) and baseball for his own benefit.[189] The smug Puritan did not attend games on Sundays, some contended, but he had no qualms about listening to these games or earning profits from them.[190]

Rickey claimed too much responsibility for himself in breaking baseball's color barrier. For example, he did not acknowledge the contribution of New York mayor Fiorello La Guardia or other political progressives when he announced Robinson's signing or when the trailblazer played his first MLB game on April 15, 1947. Rickey instead told sportswriters and biographers that he alone had integrated baseball.[191] *Daily Worker* sportswriter Bill Mardo argues that there were two Branch Rickeys—one who was "shamefully silent" for much of his baseball career about the color barrier and one whose "extraordinary business and baseball sense" prompted him to "seize the moment, jump aboard the Freedom Train . . . catch social protest at its apex, and then do just about everything right" after signing Robinson.[192] Similarly, Happy Chandler complained that "Rickey felt he was God Almighty, and that he was somehow the Savior of the black people." The MLB commissioner protested that Rickey tried to take all the credit for breaking baseball's color line and ignored the important role Chandler had played.[193]

The *Christian Century* objected that no person in baseball was more ridiculed "for his alleged religious pretensions" than Rickey. Newspaper sports pages rarely referred to him without disparaging his faithful church involvement and active Christian service. Because he was clearly one of baseball's "most resourceful executives," the press often made cracks about his religious commitments. The "pious" Rickey, however, had courageously defied "one of baseball's oldest and most unjust taboos." If baseball is truly America's national game, the editors averred, it must abolish the unwritten ban that had long kept talented black persons from playing. As other clubs gave black athletes a chance, people should not forget that a "much derided churchman" had taken the "first, decisive step." Perhaps "Rickey's religion is not such a humbug after all."[194] Espousing similar admiration, the Federal Council of Churches honored Rickey in 1948 for ending MLB's racial ban.[195]

Signing Robinson was the easy part. Did the ballplayer have the talent, willpower, and temperament to succeed in the face of the enormous obstacles confronting him? Would he be able to turn the other cheek? Whatever happened to Robinson in 1946, Wendell Smith correctly predicted, would be "historically significant."[196] And Robinson's faith would help him cope with the tremendous challenges that lay ahead.

3

Robinson Smashes the Color Barrier:
The Montreal Royals

1946

S oon after the press conference announcing his signing with the Dodgers, Robinson went on a barnstorming tour of Venezuela to honor a
previous commitment, playing with a team of Negro league stars that
featured Buck Leonard and several future major leaguers including Roy
Campanella. After graduating with a nursing degree from UCLA in June
1945, Rachel moved to New York, where she worked as a hostess at a fancy
Park Avenue restaurant and then as a nurse at Joint Disease Hospital. On
February 10, 1946, after dating for four years, Jackie and Rachel fulfilled
one of Rickey's wishes by marrying at the Independence Church of Christ,
a historic black church in west Los Angeles.

As the Robinsons prepared to travel to spring training, which began
on March 1 in Daytona Beach, Florida, Jackie was confident he could succeed for three reasons. He felt comfortable with white people, having often
played sports against them; he had enormous faith in his athletic ability;
and he believed that God had given him this tremendous opportunity and
would enable him to "emerge victorious" in "the coming ordeal."[1] His
faith helped him cope with demeaning language, racial discrimination,
and disappointment as he joined the Montreal Royals, the Dodgers' top
minor-league affiliate, for the 1946 season.

But the South was a frightening place for black people at that time. Between June 1945 and September 1946, fifty-six African Americans were
murdered, and no perpetrators were punished.[2] In 1946, at least six Af-

rican Americans were lynched in the South. Moreover, throughout the United States, restrictive covenants barred black and Jewish families from purchasing houses in many neighborhoods, while inadequate academic preparation, lack of funds, and discrimination kept the number of African Americans very low at the nation's most prestigious colleges and universities. Only two blacks served in Congress, and no large city had a black mayor.[3]

Spring Training 1946

Branch Rickey selected Daytona Beach as the spring training site for both the Dodgers and the Royals in 1946 because it was more progressive on race relations than most other Florida cities. It was the home of Bethune-Cookman College, whose founder and president, Mary McLeod Bethune, had been an advisor to Eleanor Roosevelt on racial issues; it had a sizable black middle class and some elected black officials. In addition, its minor league stadium, Kelly Field, was in the black section of the city. Rickey assured Daytona Beach officials that the teams would abide by the city's segregation laws.[4]

As depicted at length in the movie 42, the newlyweds' trip from Los Angeles to Daytona Beach, which took more than forty hours, was distressing, demeaning, and full of indignities. They were bumped from their seats on a flight from New Orleans to Daytona Beach and were not allowed to eat in the New Orleans airport's restaurant. When she needed to use a restroom, Rachel defiantly went into the one designated for white women, not the one for "colored women." People glared at her, but no one stopped her. Rachel had engaged in her first act of civil disobedience.[5] After being refused a room in a hotel that catered only to white travelers, the Robinsons instead stayed in a "dirty, dreadful" hotel, as Rachel described it.[6]

Following a twelve-hour delay, they flew to Pensacola, Florida. There the Robinsons were again required to give up their seats, this time supposedly to lighten the weight of the plane as it headed into bad weather. They watched in disgust, however, as white passengers took their places. Jackie and Rachel decided to take a Greyhound bus to complete their journey, fearing that they might be bumped off another flight. At the bus's second stop, the Robinsons, who had been sleeping in comfortable seats near the front, were ordered by the driver, who called Jackie "boy," to sur-render their spots to newly boarding white passengers and move to the back. Infuriated, Jackie considered quitting baseball before he ever got to Daytona Beach. He did not protest this humiliating treatment, however, because of his promise to Branch Rickey and because his commitment to Rickey, his race, and himself prevented him from abandoning the "great experiment."

Describing their ordeal, Jackie wrote, "To be a Negro man in the South—or other parts of our country where such savage discriminations face you—is bad enough. To have to watch the woman you love and respect treated in such an inhuman way, and to know that there is nothing you can do about it—nothing to protect and shield her," was horrible.[7]

Daytona Beach had insufficient facilities to accommodate the hundreds of players the Dodgers invited to spring training. So Rickey moved the Royals forty miles southwest to Sanford, the hometown of Dodger announcer Red Barber. Sanford had a Ku Klux Klan branch, and segregation was overt there. A white man warned Robinson after the rookie's second day of practice that his life would be in danger if he did not leave Sanford by sunset. In response, Rickey directed Robinson and black pitcher Johnny Wright to return to Day-tona Beach. Being forced to leave Sanford, Robinson wrote, "was a humil-iating experience." For the second time he thought about quitting, but he refused to disappoint the millions of people who were counting on him.[8]

Florida's stringent segregation in travel, eating establishments, and recreational facilities, coupled with the various ignominies the Robin-sons suffered and the pressure Jackie felt, made the first month of spring training miserable. "Compelled to endure the indignities of the Jim Crow South, barred by racism from many ball parks, and plagued by a sore arm," Robinson batted poorly.[9] "Coming from California," Rachel explained, "Jack and I had never been to the Deep South and the treatment we re-ceived there was just horrendous."[10] She added, "Jackie couldn't perform well that spring because the pressure was unbearable. . . . He was trying too hard; he was overswinging; he couldn't sleep at night; he had great difficulty concentrating."[11] Rachel saw her role as trying to protect Jackie, to "love him without reservation, share his thoughts and miseries," and most importantly, to "help maintain our fighting spirit." Their marriage was strengthened as they discussed their problems openly.[12] Jackie continued his established practice of praying every night before going to bed.

On Sunday, March 17, the morning of his first game, several black Daytona Beach ministers discussed Robinson in their sermons, and many of their parishioners prayed for him.[13] This pattern would be repeated in Montreal, Brooklyn, and cities that the Royals and Dodgers visited. As Robinson confronted discrimination, death threats, and hostile opponents and fans, thousands of pastors (predominantly but not exclusively black ones), priests, and rabbis emphasized what Robinson's success could do to advance African American civil rights and exhorted their congregants to attend his games and pray for him to excel.[14]

The first spring training game Robinson played in Daytona Beach drew four thousand spectators, the largest crowd ever at City Island Ball Park. Much to his surprise and relief, most of the white fans treated him well. Robinson played several more games that spring before large crowds at this stadium, and no racial incidents occurred on the field or in the stands. No other Florida city, however, allowed Robinson to play. The "ugly, contemptible" experiences of not being permitted to play in Jacksonville, Deland, and Sanford, Rachel insisted, "took their toll on Jack."[15] Newspapers around the country deplored the discrimination Robinson faced in Florida, testifying to the substantial national interest in his performance.[16] Various groups, including Christian congregations, protested his mistreatment. When a local ruling prohibited Robinson and Wright from playing in Jacksonville, the members of a northern Presbyterian church denounced it as "a great injury to democracy and brotherhood" and a violation of "the Gospel of Jesus Christ."[17]

Montreal's manager, Clay Hopper, grew up in Mississippi. His deep-seated racial prejudice reared its ugly head in an incident discussed frequently in accounts of Robinson's first spring training. One day when Robinson made an amazing play on a ground ball, Rickey asked Hopper, "Have you ever seen a human being make a play like that?" "Mr. Rickey," Hopper replied, "do you really think a nigra is a human being?" Rickey was flabbergasted and furious, but he did not respond.[18] At the beginning of April, Robinson began to relax at the plate. His hitting improved daily, and he earned a spot on the Royals' roster.

The Montreal Royals

Montreal was a good setting for Jackie Robinson to begin his baseball career. The city's residents were less racially prejudiced than their counterparts in large US cities, and they were excited about their very talented baseball team and the "great experiment." One contemporary dubbed Montreal after World War II "the paradise of the minorities."[19] "No sports story," wrote Lloyd McGowan in the *Montreal Star*, "has ever caught the sports public [here] with such intense interest and speculation."[20] Robinson continued relying on God to sustain him. As the season progressed, he explained, "I began to accept the fact that Branch Rickey was receiving the kind of help which is above and beyond the understanding of man. . . . When I came to believe that God was working with and guiding Mr. Rickey, I began to also believe that he was guiding me."[21]

Robinson was treated very well in Montreal both on and off the diamond. "Canadians regarded me as a United States citizen who happened to have a colored skin," Robinson averred.[22] "For Jackie Robinson and the city of Montreal," a sportswriter proclaimed, "it was love at first sight."[23] The Robinsons, who sublet an apartment, felt genuinely accepted by their French-Canadian neighbors and enjoyed their warm hospitality.[24] "When we got to Montreal it was like coming out of a nightmare," Rachel avowed. "The atmosphere in Montreal was so positive, we felt it was a good omen for Jack to play well." Our "neighbors were all friendly and protective," she added. After Rachel became pregnant with Jackie Jr., several women helped her make maternity clothes and gave her their rationing tickets so she could buy more meat.[25]

On April 18, 1946, fifty-two thousand boisterous fans, many of them African Americans, crowded into Roosevelt Stadium in Jersey City for Robinson's first regular season game as a member of the Montreal Royals. A Montreal sportswriter called it "another Emancipation Day for the Negro race," a day that would have pleased Abraham Lincoln.[26] Hundreds of opposing fans shouted racial slurs, but many more spectators applauded Robinson. Few players have had a more auspicious debut. Before his first at bat, Robinson later reported, his knees felt like rubber and his palms seemed "too moist to grip the bat."[27] Rachel paced the aisles, too nervous to take a seat. Robinson grounded out to the shortstop, but in his second plate appearance he hit a three-run homer. At home plate, teammate George "Shotgun" Shuba shook his hand, in "the first known photographed moment of black and white players saluting each other on a diamond."[28] Robinson added three more hits, stole two bases, and scored four runs.

No one exceeded Wendell Smith's gushing prose as he described Robinson's "Great Day in Jersey" in the *Pittsburgh Courier*. The "whirlwind from California's gold coast . . . ran the bases like a wild colt from the Western plains," Smith wrote. Robinson "befuddled the pitchers, made them balk" by his antics on the base paths, "and demoralized the entire Jersey City team." The large "crowd gasped in amazement" at this "hitting demon" and "base-running maniac," while "opposing pitchers shook their heads in helpless agony." After the game, a large mob of children drowned "this Pied Piper of the diamond" in "a sea of adolescent enthusiasm." In the dressing room, "bedlam broke loose" as "photographers, reporters, kibitzers and hangers-on" surrounded him. After Jackie left the clubhouse, Rachel "greeted him warmly and kindly. 'You've had quite a day, little man,' she said sweetly. 'Yes,' he said softly and pleasantly, 'God has been good to us today!'"[29]

Writing in the same issue of the *Pittsburgh Courier*, managing editor William Nunn (who later worked as a scout for the Pittsburgh Steelers and was elected to the NFL Hall of Fame) accentuated the faith of both Rickey and Robinson that made the trailblazer's impressive performance possible: "A man whose faith in God and democracy caused him to defy baseball's infamous 'unwritten law,' teamed up with a 27-year-old athlete who also had faith in God and the democratic way." Quoting English poet Robert Browning, Nunn concluded, "God's in His Heaven—All's right with the world."[30]

In May 1946, Robinson took on the first of his many activities beyond baseball to combat racism and improve the lives of African Americans by agreeing to chair the New York State Committee of United Negro and Allied Veterans. The committee, which included New York City councilman Benjamin Davis Jr. and Adam Clayton Powell Jr., a US congressman and pastor at the Abyssinian Baptist Church in Harlem, worked to end discrimination against black veterans.[31]

During the 1946 season, "the magnetism of Robinson's play and personality enchanted" black sportswriters and fans. African American newspapers frequently touted his exploits on their front pages, and Robinson joined Joe Louis as the nation's most photographed black celebrities. Sports sections chronicled Robinson's success and analyzed every aspect of his performance. By June, Robinson's courage, determination, and stellar play had won the respect and support of his teammates.[32] "Like plastics and penicillin," declared *The Montreal Star News*, "Jackie is here to stay."[33] Robinson "bunts better than 90 percent of the big league players and runs better than 75 percent," *Sporting News* declared. "What can't he do but eat at the dining room of the Waldorf?"[34]

Despite the warmth and kindness of the Montreal residents and his outstanding exploits on the field, Robinson struggled emotionally and physically. Still stinging from his racist treatment in the South and dealing with the cruelty he experienced in some cities during the season, Robinson was often unable to sleep or eat and felt nauseated. In Baltimore, Robinson was jeered and his life was threatened. Spectators there, Robinson moaned, "regarded me as an obscenity, a savage little above the level of a jungle beast, and told me so in vile language."[35] In Syracuse, opposing players derided him; one even threw a black cat on the field, calling it Jackie's "cousin."

In August, a physician warned that Robinson was on the verge of a nervous breakdown.[36] Rachel claimed that her husband was still upset over not being able to respond to the racist attacks in Florida, but "after he rested and reclaimed his faculties, he was fine for the rest of the season."[37] Jackie presented a different picture, telling *The Sporting News* in October that "all season I have been under terrific pressure."[38] Robinson later admitted that he did not fully recognize the toll the abuse was taking and had been "overestimating my stamina and underestimating the beating I was taking." Often tired and discouraged, Robinson wondered if he could continue to endure the verbal abuse and physical provocations and keep turning the other cheek. "Rachel's understanding love," Jackie professed, "was a powerful antidote for the poison of being taunted by fans, sneered at by fellow-players, and constantly mistreated because of my blackness."[39] Describing his season in Montreal, Robinson asserted in 1947 that the fans "inspired me and, along with the faith I had in God, who was on my side right from [the] opening day of the season, I had a wonderful year."[40]

On September 6, 1946, President Truman met with a delegation of civil rights leaders. NAACP executive secretary Walter White described the intimidation, torture, lynching, and other horrors southern blacks were experiencing. "My God! I had no idea it was as terrible as that," Truman replied. "We've got to do something." Two months later, he appointed a Committee on Civil Rights to investigate discrimination against African Americans and recommend legislation to remedy it.[41]

Meanwhile, Robinson was completing a spectacular season in Montreal. He led the International League in hitting (.349), runs scored (113), and fielding percentage, stole forty bases, and was named the league's Most Valuable Player. Wherever he played, "attendance soared as blacks and whites came out in droves to see history in the making."[42] The rest of the team was almost as good. The Royals won the International League pennant by nineteen and a half games, with a record of 100-54. They batted almost .300 as a team and averaged more than seven runs per game.[43]

As International League champions, the Royals faced the Louisville Colonels, winner of the American Association, in the Little World Series. During the three playoff games in the southern city, Robinson was loudly booed and frequently insulted. One Colonel player recalled that Robinson was called a "watermelon eater, chicken thief, crap shooter, [and] nigger."[44] Robinson had only one hit during the three games in Louisville, two of which the Royals lost.

But after the teams traveled to Montreal to finish the series, Robinson gained his revenge. He knocked in the winning run in the tenth inning of the first game in Montreal. In the second game in Montreal, he smashed a double and triple and squeezed home a run with a bunt. In the deciding game, Robinson had two of the Royals' six hits in their 2-0 victory. After the game, a raucous crowd of French Canadians hoisted Robinson and manager Clay Hopper onto their shoulders as they paraded around the ballpark singing in French, "He has earned his stripes." Robinson finally broke free from the crowd and got into a cab as adoring fans chased him. Sportswriter Sam Maltin hoped the Louisville fans who had come to Canada for the series would tell other southerners about a Montreal crowd who chased a black man "not because of hate but because of love."[45] Impressed by Robinson's performance and character, Hopper had changed his perspective by the end of the 1946 season. He told his star athlete, "You're a great ballplayer and a fine gentleman. It's been wonderful having you on the team." Robinson insisted that Hopper treated him fairly during his year with the Royals.[46] Hopper called Robinson "the greatest competitor I ever saw," while Robinson avowed that the manager had helped him greatly.[47]

As Jackie led a family gathering in prayer on Thanksgiving with Rachel, her mother and grandmother, and the newly born Jackie Jr., he "felt a substantial debt to God" for how well the 1946 season had gone.[48] But greater challenges lay ahead.

4

Robinson Triumphs over Adversity: "The Year All Hell Broke Loose"

1947

Responding to an Associated Press poll in January 1947, sportswriters identified the number-one sports question of the year as whether a black player could succeed in MLB. It was also, Robinson reported, "the No. 1 question in my mind." "I kept telling myself," he added, that "the good Lord was on your side last year in Montreal—just pray He'll be on your side this year when you try out for the Dodgers."[1]

Some analysts call 1947 the most pivotal year in MLB history. Historian William Marshall dubbed it the "season of fury," while Dodgers' announcer Red Barber described it as the "year all hell broke loose in baseball." One person made 1947 so significant—Jackie Robinson.[2]

Robinson's historic first year in MLB occurred during a momentous time in American and world history. In 1947, the sun was setting on the British Empire, the Cold War was beginning, and the world was grappling with the horrors of the Holocaust, the threat posed by the atomic bomb, and the evils of Stalinism. The United States introduced the Truman Doctrine to contain communism. Hindu-majority India and Muslim-majority Pakistan gained their independence from Britain, and many other colonies of European nations clamored for self-government. Four hundred million people faced starvation because of Asian crop failures the previous year, and famine also stalked parts of Europe. Large areas in Europe and Asia damaged by World War II strove to recover and rebuild, as the United States adopted the $12 billion (equivalent to $145 billion today) Marshall

Plan to assist them. The US workforce needed to absorb twelve million men and women who had served in the war. Atomic energy had been developed, television was in its early stages, computers had been invented, and aviation and rocketry had significantly improved.[3]

As the nation's population shifted from rural areas to the cities and millions of African Americans moved from the South to urban centers in other regions, the belief that all Americans should have the opportunity to pursue the American Dream gained adherents. Nevertheless, racism remained a national cancer, not simply a regional aberration. In 1947, the National Committee on Civil Rights, appointed the previous year, issued thirty-five recommendations to reduce discrimination.[4] Its report called for greater federal efforts to promote racial equality, including removing the poll tax and other impediments to black voting, creating a Civil Rights Division in the Department of Justice, and desegregating the armed forces, interstate transportation, and government jobs.[5]

During 1947, Jackie Robinson, because of his style of play, appealing personality, and skin color, changed MLB and transformed how many Americans thought about racial matters. Beginning the season as "a curiosity," Robinson ended it as "a national phenomenon."[6]

Brooklyn, 1947

Just as Montreal was an excellent setting for Robinson's first year in white professional baseball, Brooklyn was the best venue for his rookie season in MLB. In 1947, Brooklyn was the United States' fourth-largest city. Its almost three million residents lived in thirty discrete neighborhoods, many of which were dominated by a single ethnic group—Italians, Irish, Poles, Swedes, Russians, Syrians, West Indians, or Jews ranging from Orthodox to Reform. Jews were about a third of Brooklyn's population, the highest proportion in any city with a major league team. In addition, during World War II, many southern blacks and Puerto Ricans had migrated to Brooklyn. Its cosmopolitan composition and inclusive atmosphere arguably made it more supportive of a black baseball player than any other American city would have been. Bill Veeck, owner of the Cleveland Indians, called Brooklyn the "ideal place" for Robinson to play because it was more hospitable to African Americans than any other major city.[7] The rookie agreed. He had previously thought that Montreal was the greatest baseball city, but Brooklyn was even better. It was filled with "baseball fanatics" who "live and breathe the Dodgers...night and day." They had been wonderful to him, he reported in May 1947, and had given him "all kinds of encouragement."[8]

Brooklyn was known for its church spires, synagogues, three-story brownstones, rebrick factories, corner saloons, and trolley cars. The latter feature was the source of the Brooklyn baseball team's nickname, because residents joked that people had to be skilled "dodgers" to avoid being hit by the electrified streetcars.

Charles Ebbets was the majority owner and president of the Dodgers for about a quarter-century until his death in 1925. He also played the principal role in the construction of Ebbets Field, where the Dodgers played from 1913 to 1957. "Fans followed and admired the Yankees; they cheered for the Giants; they lived and died with the Dodgers." Ebbets Field (which seated only thirty-two thousand, less than half the capacity of Yankee Stadium, which opened in 1923) was as important to many Brooklynites as their own block, church, or synagogue. Before 1947, despite the passion of their dedicated fans, the Dodgers had been "winsome losers, adorable incompetents, perennial basement dwellers." Brooklyn had won the National League pennant only three times—in 1916, 1920, and 1941.[9] After becoming the Dodgers' general manager in 1943, Rickey proclaimed, "Our aim is to make Brooklyn the baseball capital of America."[10] Although the Yankees remained MLB's premier franchise, the team Rickey assembled soon dominated the National League. During the ten seasons Robinson played, the Dodgers captured the league pennant six times, finished second three times, and won the World Series in 1955.

Spring Training 1947

Although Robinson's experience during spring training in 1947 was not as horrible as that of the previous year, it was still miserable. To avoid Florida's Jim Crow laws, Rickey arranged for both the Dodgers and Royals to practice and play their home exhibition games in Havana. The four black players on Montreal's squad—Robinson, catcher Roy Campanella, and pitchers Don Newcombe and Roy Partlow—were not permitted to room with the white members of their team and instead stayed in a rundown hotel near Havana's slums. Disgusted by these segregated accommodations, Robinson suffered from stomach pain.

During spring training, a survey reported in *The Sporting News* claimed that the Dodgers were "mainly antagonistic" about calling up Robinson.[11] Confirming this, several Dodgers' players penned a petition, declaring that they would quit baseball if Robinson made the Brooklyn roster. The mutiny collapsed, however, when Pete Reiser from Missouri and team captain Pee Wee Reese from Kentucky refused to sign the petition and Rickey and manager Leo Durocher vehemently condemned it. "I saw it. I read it. I refused to sign," Reese declared. Durocher assembled the entire team at midnight in the kitchen of a US Army barracks in Panama, where they were staying as they prepared to play an exhibition game. Known for his salty language, Durocher told the rebels that "they could wipe their ass with the petition" and promised them that Robinson's stellar play would put money in their pockets. "I'd play an elephant," the manager added, "if he could win for me and this Robinson is no elephant. You can't throw him out on the bases and you can't get him out at the plate. This fellow is a great player."[12] Rickey met individually with the rebellious players the next morning, giving them the option of being traded if they did not want to play with Robinson. Only two—outfielder Dixie Walker and catcher Bobby Bragan—opted to be traded.[13] Neither player was traded, and during the season both changed their attitude toward Robinson after watching him play.

Red Barber, the Dodgers' popular announcer, also had reservations about staying with the organization if Robinson made the team. Barber had grown up in a religious home in Sanford, Florida, and had attended church faithfully since his daughter was born in 1937. Barber informed his wife that he could not do his job because he believed that blacks were inferior to whites. However, when he prayed about whether to quit, he remembered the statement in the Episcopal Book of Common Prayer asserting that God "hast opened the eyes of the mind to behold things invisible and unseen." This led him to conclude that he could accurately describe, without prejudice, what black and white players did on the baseball diamond. Accepting Robinson as a Dodger, Barber later explained, increased his tolerance and understanding. He thanked the ballplayer for helping him to follow the commandment to love one's neighbors more faithfully.[14]

As the Royals prepared to play their parent club during spring training, Rickey told Robinson, "I want you to be a whirling demon against the Dodgers." Rickey instructed him to "get on base *by any means necessary*" and then "run wild." Rickey hoped that Robinson would perform so well that Brooklyn fans would demand putting him on the Dodgers' team. Robinson hit .625 and stole seven bases during the seven Royals-Dodgers games, but neither the fans nor Brooklyn players asked for him to be promoted.[15]

Five days before the season began, Rickey announced that Robinson would play with the Dodgers in 1947. The white press gave the event little attention and downplayed its significance. In the *Atlanta Journal*, Ed Danforth called Robinson's entry a "sideshow" to prevent fans "from yawning" during the long season. The *Baltimore Sun* considered the banishment of Durocher, the Dodgers' manager, for one year by MLB commissioner Happy Chandler to be a much bigger story than Robinson's signing with the team. The *New York Daily Mirror* insisted that tearing down the color line would produce "no resumption of the War Between the States."[16] Rickey, by contrast, complained at a press conference as the season began that Robinson had become a "sideshow attraction" rather than a ballplayer. He had already received five thousand invitations to attend various events, and often to speak at them.[17]

"Don't Spoil Jackie's Chances"

Rickey appealed to the black community to help Robinson succeed. He feared that overenthusiasm about and excessive adulation of Robinson by black fans would intensify white racial prejudice and antagonism toward the "great experiment."[18] At a meeting on February 5, 1947, at the Carlton YMCA in Brooklyn with thirty-three of the borough's most distinguished African American civic and religious leaders, Rickey argued that black enthusiasts were "the biggest threat to Robinson's success." He worried that exuberant blacks would strut, hold parades, get drunk, fight, be arrested, and wine and dine Robinson until he was "fat and futile." An inappropriate response by the black community, he warned, could turn a "great milestone in the progress of American race relations" into "a national comedy and an ultimate tragedy."[19]

To avoid this outcome, Brooklyn African Americans created a campaign titled "Don't Spoil Jackie's Chances." The campaign committee, headed by Judge Myles Page, used lectures, pamphlets, editorials, and sermons to exhort black residents to restrain their zeal about Robinson's performance during his rookie season.[20] It sent YMCA executive Herbert Miller to other National League cities to establish similar organizations. The committee also devised a long list of do's and don'ts and insisted that Robinson's deportment in public and private should "be supervised as thoroughly as Princess Elizabeth's."[21] Before the 1947 season began, the *Amsterdam News* published numerous articles instructing black fans how to conduct themselves; black ministers prodded their congregants to behave at ballparks; and bars in black communities displayed signs warning "Don't Spoil Jackie's Chances." Community leaders urged black fans not to respond physically or verbally to white bigots shouting racial slurs at Robinson from the stands.[22] Although this campaign reflected racial stereotypes, its enthusiastic endorsement by many African American leaders conveyed both their great desire to see Robinson succeed and fears that boisterous or belligerent black fans might indeed hamper his opportunity.

An editorial in the NAACP's *Crisis* magazine in May praised Rickey for "shrewdly picking" Robinson in 1945 to integrate baseball and then wisely not announcing his promotion to the Dodgers until five days before the season opener on April 15, 1947. The editors urged black newspapers to provide balanced coverage of all major league teams rather than focusing only on Robinson. They praised Rickey's "judgment and courage" and Robinson's ability and fortitude.[23] Nevertheless, during the season, the black press extensively covered Robinson's exploits. Meanwhile, at horse races, church services, and community baseball games, the universal question was, "How'd Jackie make out today?"[24] Many black businesses strove to identify their products and services with Robinson to increase their sales.

According to Robinson, Rickey understood how important the clergy were in this endeavor and asked several of them to participate in the Brooklyn committee. Robinson argued that black fans were as important to the integration of baseball as he was. Had they "overplayed their enthusiasm" or reacted violently when he was "insulted or spiked or called names," he asserted, "we could have lost a tremendous victory."[25] "Blacks supported me with total loyalty" morally and financially by attending games, he declared.[26] "The Negro minister, North and South," he insisted, "was a true friend and ally to me in my early days in the game."[27] Robinson thanked African American pastors for cutting their sermons short so that their parishioners could get to his games on time. That was "one of the supremist [*sic*] sacrifices" they could make, he joked. "I owe so much to the Negro ministers, and it is a debt I never intend to forget."[28] Clergy also helped by preaching that baseball should express the American principle of racial equality.

Play Ball: The 1947 Season

As the season began, Robinson declared, "I know that dreams do come true." He promised to do his "level best" and asserted that the public wanted to see him "make good."[29] Meanwhile, many stressed that the stakes were stupendous for both Robinson and African Americans. Wendell Smith wrote, "If Robinson fails to make the grade, it will be many years before a Negro makes the grade. This is IT!"[30] Linking Robinson's performance and black advancement, the *Boston Chronicle* proclaimed, "Triumph of Whole Race Seen in Jackie's Debut in Major League Ball."[31] What ten-year-old Colin Powell, a New York Giants' fan living in the Bronx, who would become the first black US secretary of state under President George W. Bush, thought as the season began was in the minds of millions of other African Americans: "We said, 'Oh Lord, don't let him strike out.' The greatest fear was that he wouldn't do well and that would be a mark against all of us."[32] Robinson recognized the huge responsibility he shouldered. He declared, "I also want to prove to those who resent me or other members of my race that we are not bad people at all. I want to prove that God alone has the right to judge a person and He is the one who decides people's fates."[33] "To win the friendship of people everywhere," Rickey advised Robinson, he must be "personable," smile, and make the public think he was not bothered by the treatment he received. During the 1947 season, Robinson faithfully followed Rickey's instructions.[34]

Time magazine argued in September 1947 that Robinson had experienced "the toughest first season any ballplayer has ever faced."[35] The editors of *Sport* magazine insisted that the Dodgers' rookie had been "the most savagely booed, intensively criticized, ruthlessly libeled player" in MLB history. From the Polo Grounds in New York City to County Stadium in Milwaukee, every time he appeared on the field, a storm of jeers, catcalls, and name-calling erupted. Only in Ebbets Field did the applause and shouts of encouragement override the verbal abuse.[36] Robinson received cruel, insulting, and threatening notes and endured verbal invective from rival benches, roughhousing on the base paths, and extrahard tags.[37] Throughout the season, Robinson performed at a superlative level with remarkable poise while "standing up to beanballs and cleats launched into his shins, chest, and chin, and the race-baiting taunts raining down from the stands, along with trash, tomatoes, rocks, watermelon slices, and Sambo dolls."[38] Given the "streams of filth, vicious racial taunts, and other forms of public humiliation" he experienced, it is amazing that he could even play.[39] Performing under burdens borne by no other ballplayer, Robinson responded to demeaning treatment with composure and grace and kept his promise to Rickey not to retaliate.[40]

The first African American to play in twentieth-century MLB "had endured the insults, name-calling, hate-filled looks of opposing players and had suffered in martyred silence," asserted Dan Burley in the *Amsterdam News* during the 1947 World Series. His rivals tried to "make him lose his nerve and will and thus be automatically thumbed out of the big show. But they failed."[41] Unlike other players, Robinson complained, he could not respond to "the thousand little barbs every ballplayer is subjected to in a pennant race: batting slumps, bad days, bad plays, umpires' decisions, accidental spikings, close pitches, [and] the manager's distemper."[42] Off the field, conditions were not much better. Robinson was prohibited from staying in hotels with his team in Philadelphia and St. Louis and, when permitted to room in hotels with other Dodgers, frequently had to eat meals in his room.[43]

As the Dodgers opened the season on April 15, newspapers announced that Rudolf Höss would be hanged the next day for executing three million Jews as the commandant of Auschwitz during World War II. As Robinson took his position as the Dodgers' first baseman on a chilly afternoon at Ebbets Field in Brooklyn, rumors circulated that an assassin was planning to shoot him.[44] Unlike his first game as a Royal, Robinson's major league debut was inauspicious. He went hitless, but Brooklyn defeated the Boston Braves, 5–3. After the game, the rookie told Ward Morehouse of the *New York Sun*, "Before I went to bed [last night] I thanked God for all that's happened" and "for the good fortune that's come my way." "I belong to the

Methodist Church in Pasadena and I used to be a Sunday school teacher at U.C.L.A.; they gave me the bad little boys, and I liked it. . . . I know that a lot of players, particularly the southern boys, won't be able to change their feelings overnight" about "playing ball with a Negro. I have encountered very little antagonism, however; I really expected a great deal more." Robinson recognized that he had a "responsibility" to his race and that "this year is the test." "I'll do my best," he promised.[45]

Black sportswriters covered virtually Robinson's every move during his first game. They reported where he sat in the dugout each inning and with whom. They asked fans at Ebbets Field about the rookie's chances of success and quoted the ballplayer extensively. The *New York Amsterdam News* exulted that Robinson had cracked MLB's "hoary-headed, lily-white tradition." The *Pittsburgh Courier* rejoiced, "An up-standing, clean-living, bright-minded young athlete who happens to be a Negro broke a sixty-year tradition." The *Baltimore Afro-American* celebrated Robinson's debut with seven stories, seven photographs, an editorial, and a cartoon. Its front-page photo showed the rookie going into the Dodgers' clubhouse that had "KEEP OUT" written on the door. A caption stated that a black man could enter "the sacred portals of a major league baseball team's dressing room as a player." Reinforcing Rickey's admonition not to ruin Robinson's chances, the *Chicago Defender* warned black fans, "Any untoward incident precipitated by us will have disastrous results for the new experiment in breaching the color line." In contrast, most white newspapers, viewing Robinson as a passing fad and skeptical that integration would work, paid little attention to his debut. Several major southern dailies did not even mention the "great experiment."[46]

On the field itself, however, a circus-like atmosphere pervaded the Dodgers' first thirty games. Large crowds, including many black fans, wildly cheered his every plate appearance. Newspapers dubbed him the "black meteor," the "sepia speedster," the "stellar Negro," an "ebony Ty Cobb," and "the Bojangles of the Basepaths."[47]

On April 18, 37,546 spectators watched Robinson hit his first home run in the majors, against the Giants at the Polo Grounds. The next day, 52,355 fans, the largest crowd in the stadium's history, saw Robinson smash a double and two singles in four plate appearances. On April 23, his season average was .409.[48]

Bothered by an injury to his right shoulder he sustained playing football at UCLA, Robinson went 0-for-20 between April 24 and April 30, dropping his average to .225 and causing some sports analysts to argue that he should be benched. That week was among the most difficult of Robinson's baseball career, and his face displayed his pain. Jackie slept fitfully and confessed to Rachel that he feared "teammates would lose faith in him" before he had proven he could help them win.[49] Dodgers' reliever Rex Barney recalled that it was obvious that "he was pressing and pushing." Working hard to break out of his slump, Robinson took extra batting practice until his hands blistered. He adamantly refused, Barney declared, to let himself or his race down.[50] Robinson's excellent bunting, electrifying baserunning, and competent fielding enabled him to remain in the Dodgers' lineup while he adjusted to major league pitching, especially curveballs.

During the first half of May, Robinson rebounded with a fourteen-game hitting streak that raised his batting average to .299. On May 9, Rickey, giving Robinson a vote of confidence, sold the Dodgers' backup first baseman, Howie Schultz, to the Phillies. The next day, he announced that he was also abandoning his effort to acquire New York Giants' slugger Johnny Mize to play first base. "We'll be all right," Rickey promised fans. "I don't have the slightest doubt of Robinson's ability." He emphasized that Robinson was becoming more comfortable at first base and "hitting with more confidence."[51]

Despite this good news, May 9 was arguably the worst day of Robinson's entire major league career. Ben Chapman, the Phillies' manager, declared before the Dodgers came to play a four-game series that he and his players would verbally attack the rookie. During his first at bat on May 9, the Phillies' bench unleashed a harsher deluge of abuse than Robinson had previously experienced. They shouted racial slurs, named diseases Dodgers' players would contract if they touched towels Robinson used, and simulated executions by pretending the bats they pointed at Robinson were machine guns.[52] Throughout the game, catcalls and insults flowed from the Phillies' dugout: "Hey, nigger, why don't you go back to the cotton field where you belong?" "They're waiting for you in the jungles, black boy!" "Hey, snowflake, which one of those white boys' wives are you dating tonight?" "We don't want you here, nigger."[53] Human behavior, a sportswriter argued, had "rarely sunk lower" than Chapman and the other Phillies dragged it; they "did everything but light the fiery cross."[54]

Robinson later declared that the Phillies had hurled at him "the worst garbage I ever heard in my whole life," including on the streets and in the army.[55] "To hell with Mr. Rickey's 'noble experiment,'" he thought. "It's clear it won't succeed. . . . My best is not good enough for them. . . . To hell with the image of the patient black freak I was supposed to create." Robinson wanted to throw down his bat, run to the Phillies' dugout, punch one of his mockers with his "despised black fist," and then leave baseball.[56] Resisting this temptation, Robinson had two hits and scored two runs, but the Dodgers lost, 6–5, in eleven innings. Honoring Rickey's "turn-the-other-cheek" strategy, Robinson said little publicly about his horrific treatment.

Dan Parker, sports editor of the *New York Daily Mirror*, praised Robinson's "admirable restraint" in ignoring "the guttersnipe language coming from the Phils dugout."[57] After one of Chapman's most distasteful outbursts, Dodgers' second baseman Eddie Stanky, who had initially opposed integration, denounced the taunters as "yellow-bellied cowards" and dared them to pick on someone who could fight back.[58] By not responding, Rickey argued, Robinson brought many fans and his own teammates to his side. Chapman, he insisted, "made Jackie a real member of the Dodgers."[59] He had "solidified and unified thirty men, not one of whom was willing to sit by and see someone kick around a man who had his hands tied behind his back."[60]

The Sporting News reported that the Phillies received "an avalanche of letters and telephone calls . . . commending Chapman for his fair stand toward Robinson."[61] Most Americans, however, viewed the taunting by Chapman and other Phillies as inappropriate, if not reprehensible. Walter Winchell blasted Chapman's actions on his radio show and in his widely read syndicated newspaper column, which Robinson believed influenced Commissioner Happy Chandler to warn the Phillies to refrain from racial baiting.[62] Chapman defended his actions, declaring that the Phillies would treat Robinson the same way they did other targets of ethnic abuse—Jewish Hank Greenberg of the Pirates, German American Cliff Hartung of the Giants, Italian American Joe Garagiola of the Cardinals, and Irish American Connie Ryan of the Braves—but thereafter they did tone down their smears of Robinson.[63] The Dodgers' rookie reluctantly agreed to pose for a photo with Chapman and him holding a bat together to imply that "all was copacetic." "There were times, after I had bowed to humiliations" like this, Robinson explained, "when deep depression and speculation as to whether it was all worthwhile would seize me." He continued to play, however, because some light shone through the gloom.[64]

The same day as the Phillies' tirade against Robinson, a rumor circulated, reported by Stanley Woodward in the *New York Herald Tribune,* that the St. Louis Cardinals were threatening to boycott their next game against the Dodgers if Robinson played.[65] The rookie feared that if they did it might create "a chain reaction throughout the baseball world—with other players agreeing to unite in a strong bid to keep baseball white."[66] To prevent this outcome, National League president Ford Frick promised to suspend any boycotters. Even if half the players in the league participated, strikers would "encounter quick retribution," Frick promised. "I don't care if it wrecks the National League for five years," he declared. "This is the United States of America," and all citizens had an equal right to play baseball.[67] This ultimatum, Robinson later noted, was "one of the most emphatic, clear-cut, and *uncompromising* mandates ever issued in the history of baseball." Refusing to play against him, he added, "would have been sheer hypocrisy" because for many years, major leaguers had barnstormed across North America playing with and against blacks.[68] Although the Cardinals' threat to strike is a widely accepted part of the saga of Robinson's first season, it is difficult to substantiate and likely never occurred.[69]

On May 9, the Dodgers also informed the press that Robinson had received letters threatening to kill him, harm his wife, and kidnap his infant son, prompting the police to assign two detectives to accompany him home every day. As the season continued, Robinson endured more threats, opposing players tormented him, and some hotels denied him rooms. These physical and verbal assaults against Robinson further cemented his place on the team, and spectators in numerous National League cities increasingly applauded his exploits. Publicly, Robinson downplayed the menacing letters sent to him, arguing that they were written by "scatter brained people" who simply sought to vent their frustrations. He insisted that he had received ten to twenty congratulatory letters for every nasty one.[70] On the other hand, Robinson's sister, Willa Mae Robinson Walker, later told a journalist that Jackie received so much hate mail and so many threats to harm him or his family that he "talked about quitting." Family members feared getting a call "saying Jackie was dead."[71]

A three-game series in mid-May against the Pirates was particularly eventful. In describing the first game, a *Pittsburgh Post-Gazette* article noted that Ralph Kiner slugged two home runs and Billy Cox socked one as the Pirates pounded the Dodgers, 7–3, "but they had to share the applause" with "Jackie Robinson [who batted two-for-five and drove in two runs], a ballplayer who has what it takes."[72] During the second game, Robinson collided with Pirates' first baseman Hank Greenberg and fell to the ground as he tried to reach base on a bunt while Greenberg stretched to catch an errant throw from the pitcher. The ball rolled into right field, and Robinson got up and hustled to second. After reaching first base the next inning, Greenberg asked Robinson if he had hurt him and explained that he had not meant to knock him down. The respected slugger, who had hit fifty-eight homers in 1938 and had served as captain of a B-29 bomber squadron in the China-Burma-India theater during World War II, was the first opposing player who offered encouragement to Robinson after the Phillies' taunting.[73] As a Jew, Greenberg had often been the victim of verbal abuse. Robinson was deeply moved by Greenberg's support, which the African American press effusively lauded. The *Pittsburgh Courier* noted that Greenberg, who had had many "racial epithets" hurled at him from the opposing dugout, definitely "understands Jackie's problems."[74] Greenberg wrote that Robinson had it "tougher than any player." He added, "I had feelings for him because they had treated me the same way. Not as bad, but they made remarks about my being a sheenie and a Jew all the time."[75]

The next day, Pirates' pitcher Fritz Ostermueller nearly beaned Robinson with a fastball, which instead struck the rookie's arm as he raised it to protect his head. His teammates jumped to their feet in the dugout and showered Ostermueller with expletives and threats of physical harm. The Dodgers' response, wrote Wendell Smith, showed that they regarded Robinson "as one of them."[76] During this three-game series with the Pirates, one of the Dodgers' most respected players, pitcher Ralph Branca, called a team meeting, which Robinson did not attend, to rally the squad around the rookie. "We have to get behind Jackie to help him," Branca argued, because of the abuse inflicted on Robinson. "He's here to stay. And he's gonna help us win the pennant."[77]

In late May, an all-white jury in Greenville, South Carolina, acquitted twenty-eight "confessed lynch murderers" accused of torturing a black man to death.[78] But on the baseball field, the tide of racism began to turn. When the Phillies came to Brooklyn in late May, some of their players began to express regret about Chapman's treatment of Robinson. "Robinson was one ballplayer you didn't want to get riled up," declared Phillies' catcher Andy Seminick. If you got certain players angry, "they'd hurt you. Jackie Robinson was definitely one of 'em. He rose to the occasion and clobbered the tar out of us. He beat us everywhere—at bat, on the bases, in the field." Recognizing this, Chapman finally said, "Let's lay off him. It's not doing any good."[79]

On June 5, Secretary of State George Marshall outlined the Marshall Plan to supply financial relief to help reconstruct Europe. Nine days later, Robinson started a twenty-one-game hitting streak during which he batted .377; it ended on July 4, one game short of tying the rookie record. At that point, he was hitting .315 for the season and leading the National League in stolen bases. In a pivotal series during this stretch, Robinson tormented the Cardinals with a home run, double, and four singles in thirteen at bats. On June 24, he stole home for the first time in a game against Pittsburgh; the Dodgers' 4–2 win catapulted them into first place, where they remained for the rest of the season. At the end of June, Wendell Smith declared that Robinson is "definitely now one of the Dodgers. . . . No one on the team seems to resent his presence anymore, and Jackie seems to have won them over simply by being himself."[80] By early July, Robinson said he no longer felt like "a sideshow freak."[81]

In the last twelve days of July, the Dodgers won thirteen games in a row. Meanwhile, on July 29, 1947, the New York Supreme Court ruled that the Stuyvesant Town apartment complex in lower Manhattan could exclude African American families; private developers were permitted to "restrict accommodations on grounds of race, color, creed, or religion." At midseason, Rickey removed his ban on Robinson doing advertisements. Thereafter, his smiling face appeared often in New York and national black newspapers hawking Bond Bread, Turfee Hats, and Old Gold cigarettes, although the rookie did not smoke and, in a *Courier* column in July, advised youth not to smoke, drink, stay out late, or eat nonnutritious food.[82]

Robinson batted .311 in August. That month, with the Dodgers entrenched in first place and Robinson dazzling fans and sportswriters, poet Langston Hughes declared, "Maybe if the Dodgers win the pennant a hundred years from now history will still be grinning."[83]

In mid-August Cardinals' outfielder Enos Slaughter cut a seven-inch gash in the back of Robinson's leg when he ran over him in the fifth inning as the first baseman was stretching to receive a throw. Dodgers' relief pitcher Hugh Casey, "a Southerner who never had much to do with me," Robinson explained, "came off the bench and charged Slaughter." The rookie calmed down his teammates because he "didn't want to be the cause of a riot."[84] Dodgers' starting pitcher Ralph Branca had not yet allowed any base runners in the game. Branca offered to forgo his shot at a perfect game and hit Slaughter with a pitch the next time he came to bat, but Robinson encouraged him not to do this.[85] Slaughter denied that he had intentionally tried to hurt Robinson; neither Robinson, his teammates, sportswriters, nor spectators believed him. One spectator, Douglas Wilder (then age sixteen, later Virginia's first black governor), declared that by getting to his feet and finishing the game despite his intense pain, Robinson taught him that people could "rise over and above" their circumstances.[86] Robinson struggled to control his temper, but, he avowed, when teammates "rushed to my support in white hot anger, it gave me the warmest feeling I've ever felt. At that moment I belonged."[87] Several Dodgers told Robinson, "If they give you the works, give it back to them—and the team will be behind you 100%." *Time* agreed that this incident demonstrated that Robinson had "won his long, patient battle" to be accepted as a Dodger.[88] Impressed by Robinson's performance, a white sportswriter declared in the *Pittsburgh Post-Gazette* in late August that the Dodgers' first baseman was "a gentleman and a credit to the game as well as his race."[89]

Meanwhile, the Fernwood Park race riot, one of the worst in the city's history, erupted in Chicago. The riot was instigated by whites who tried to stop African Americans from moving into the Chicago Housing Authority veterans' housing project in the Fernwood Park neighborhood, because they viewed it as an attempt to racially integrate a white community. The one thousand Chicago police officers ordered to protect Fernwood Park residents did little to stop the rioting, which lasted three days and injured at least thirty-five black persons.

Through September 9, Robinson had fourteen bunts for a hit and twenty-eight sacrifice bunts; only four of his bunts had not achieved his objectives—a phenomenal .913 success rate.[90] On September 11, Cardinals' catcher Joe Garagiola spiked Robinson on the heel, cutting his shoe to pieces. The next inning, when Robinson came to the plate, he complained about the incident and Garagiola responded with a racial insult. Losing his temper for the first time, Robinson went toe to toe with the Cardinals' catcher, prompting the home plate umpire to separate them. That no fisticuffs occurred on the field and no rioting broke out in the stands, *Time* declared, indicated that Robinson "had established himself as a big leaguer" who had earned "the right to squawk."[91] Robinson's outburst underscored his pent-up rage and frustration, but "he submerged his naturally combative instincts and channeled them into his performances."[92] Later that night, he smashed a two-run homer to help the Dodgers win, 4–3. He stroked two hits and scored two runs as the Cardinals won game two of the series, and in game three he delivered three hits and made a spectacular catch of a foul popup as the Dodgers won, 8–7, pushing their lead over the Cardinals to five and a half games and virtually clinching the pennant.

The Dodgers did clinch before their ten-game road trip ended on September 18, with Robinson hitting .408 with three homers and five stolen bases in the ten games. Thousands of excited Brooklyn fans greeted their train when it arrived at Pennsylvania Station the next day, carrying Pee Wee Reese from the train to Seventh Avenue and mobbing a phone booth where Robinson had stopped to call Rachel. The police had to clear a path for baseball's most fleet-footed runner so they could escort him to Brooklyn in a squad car.[93] That same day, the Memphis Censorship Board banned the showing of the children's movie *Curley* because it portrayed black and white children playing together. When informed that the city would not permit the film to be shown because the South did not recognize "social equality between the races, even in children," producer Hal Roach retorted, "Will you ban newspapers that show photographs of the Brooklyn Dodgers?"[94]

On September 23, the Dodgers held "Jackie Robinson Day" at Ebbets Field, funded by contributions from Harlem and other black communities across the country. The baseball star received an estimated $10,000 in merchandise, including a Cadillac sedan, a television set, a $500 gold watch, a gold pen and pencil, an electric broiler, and cutlery. Renowned black actor and singer Bill "Bojangles" Robinson served as host for the festivities. Jackie was delighted that his mother could attend this celebration: "I told Ma her prayers were responsible for our winning the pennant. One time when the Dodgers were in a slump, I wrote her: . . . 'pray for the whole team.' She did."[95]

The 1947 World Series between the Dodgers and the New York Yankees was the first to be televised and one of the most exciting in baseball history, with the Yankees prevailing in seven games. Five games were decided by one or two runs. In game four, the Yankees' Bill Bevans was one out away from pitching the Fall Classic's first no-hitter (although he had given up ten walks) when third baseman Cookie Lavagetto doubled to knock in two runs and win the game for the Dodgers, 3–2. Robinson fielded flawlessly, bedeviled Yankees' pitchers with his baserunning, and hit .259 (well above the Dodgers' team average of .230), with three runs scored and three runs batted in (RBIs).

Assessing the 1947 Season

Throughout the 1947 season, Robinson dealt with numerous death threats and the constant danger of flashing spikes and beanballs by playing with ferocity and running the bases with great skill. Wendell Smith reported that hundreds of fans sent Robinson congratulatory messages, and the sportswriter excerpted some of the more memorable lines. Smith said nothing about the hate mail threatening to kill Robinson, assault Rachel, or kidnap Jackie Jr. Rickey, however, asked the police to investigate these death threats and publicly discussed them. To gain greater support for the "great experiment," Rickey, Jonathan Eig claimed, portrayed the athlete as a "Christ-like figure" who turned the other cheek in the face of savage onslaughts.[96]

During the season, the Robinsons lived in a black neighborhood in Brooklyn, in a modest five-room, second-floor flat.[97] Rachel reported that Jackie felt strongly supported by her love and the "good wishes of our neighbors." They especially bonded with the Covington family, who lived four blocks away: Lacy, a forty-six-year-old bricklayer and part-time minister; his wife, Florence; and her sisters Willette, May, Phyllis, and Julia. The Covingtons introduced the Robinsons to community leaders, babysat for Jackie Jr., hosted them for delicious meals on Sundays, and shared their joys and sorrows.[98] Dodgers' players and their wives, by contrast, made no effort to befriend the Robinsons. They did not invite them to eat dinner, see a movie, or engage in any other social activities. Despite her college degree, middle-class demeanor, personal confidence, and "finishing-school poise," the twenty-three-year-old Rachel was not welcome to shop, dine, or knit with the wives of other Dodgers.[99] Jackie later admitted that during the 1947 season, "I felt as lonely and as out of place as I had felt the previous year at Montreal, where I had almost suffered a nervous breakdown in August."[100] He explained further: "I had to fight hard against loneliness, abuse, and the knowledge that any mistake I made would be magnified because I was the only black man out there."[101]

The 1947 season took a heavy toll on Branch Rickey as well. In his midsixties and suffering from Ménière's disease, the Dodgers' general manager had to cope with numerous barbs from reporters and support Robinson emotionally. Criticism from other baseball executives and a deluge of hate mail increased his stress and worsened his disease. Despite his own problems, Rickey and wife, Jane, frequently had dinner with the Robinsons at their home or picnicked with them.[102] In addition, Rickey wrote numerous letters to Robinson during team road trips to counsel and caution him.

Thousands of supporters promised Robinson in letters and telegrams that they were faithfully praying for him.[103] And every night his rookie season, Rachel reported, her husband knelt in prayer beside his bed to ask God for strength. Robinson insisted that 1947 had brought even greater pressure and higher stakes than his season in Montreal. Would he advance or hinder the progress of his race?[104] "I prayed as I never had before," he declared. Robinson told teammate Ralph Branca, "Many nights I get down on my knees and pray to God for the strength not to fight back."[105] Some of Robinson's teammates perceived that his faith undergirded his success. For example, pitcher Carl Erskine, a fellow Christian, argued that "Athletic ability and determination could take Robinson only so far" and that few understood "how pivotal [his] faith turned out to be."[106]

In addition to excelling on the field during his rookie season, Robinson wrote twenty-five weekly columns for the *Pittsburgh Courier*, from March 29 to September 27. These columns were part of a three-pronged public relations campaign Wendell Smith devised to promote Robinson's exploits and celebrate the integration of baseball. The sportswriter collaborated on these "Jackie Robinson Says" columns, championed the rookie's achievements in his own "Sports Beat" column in the *Courier*, and ghost-wrote *Jackie Robinson: My Own Story*, published in 1948. Through these articles, Robinson shared the story of his first season with almost half a million *Courier* subscribers throughout the nation.[107] His column described key games, commented on the pennant race, and praised black athletes, including Larry Doby (signed by the Cleveland Indians in July), Roy Campanella and pitcher Don Bankhead (both with the Montreal Royals), and NFL halfback Kenny Washington (his UCLA backfield partner).[108]

Neither Robinson nor Smith said much in their columns about the racial prejudice the ballplayer confronted. They presented Robinson as unfazed by discriminatory treatment; the insults and social isolation he experienced appeared to bounce off him like bullets striking Superman. For example, in his May 3 column, Robinson wrote disingenuously that the bench jockeying "really didn't bother me."[109] Their accounts emphasized the harmony among Dodgers teammates and the rabid support from Brooklyn fans, and they usually described Robinson's interactions with opposing players as "nice" or "swell." The rookie declared in May that he had been treated nicely in Pittsburgh, especially by Pirates' infielder Frank Gustine and slugger Hank Greenberg, and in Cincinnati, where MLB commissioner Chandler shook his hand and asked how he was doing; the fans and sportswriters in Boston, he wrote in June, were also very good to him.[110] On September 27, he declared that "it's been a wonderful year in many ways."[111]

Robinson's alleged serenity was, however, an illusion, "a carefully crafted façade to reduce potential causes—real or perceived—of failure, foment, or bad publicity." Although he "was seething within," a sportswriter contends, Robinson's "columns read like the letters that soldiers at the front" sent to their anxious mothers during World War II, avoiding any description of the dangers they faced.[112] Other African American papers quoted freely from the *Courier* and kept beseeching black fans to behave at ballparks, keep their mouths shut, "and give Jackie the chance to PROVE he's major league caliber!"[113] In addition, the *Courier*, the *Chicago Defender*, and other major black newspapers described every Robinson at bat in their accounts of Dodgers' games. Robinson and Smith, by ignoring racial strife and focusing on how smoothly the "great experiment" was proceeding, sacrificed two hallmarks of American journalism—truth and accuracy. Portraying Robinson's rookie year as a trouble-free, unqualified success may, however, have been justified to combat the rampant racism that had long prevented African Americans from playing in white professional leagues.[114]

Rickey instructed Robinson to "wear the armor of humility" during his first season, and he "wore it so effectively, and it seemed to fit so well, that for quite a while no one realized how thick a disguise it was." Behind the scenes, though, Robinson struggled mightily with the abusive treatment he received from fans, opposing players, and initially even some teammates. Rachel was furious that, as one sportswriter complained, "Some pitchers can't resist that Coney Island urge to throw at Robinson." "My blood would boil," she lamented, "at some of the things people yelled at him." "Jack suffered constantly under the playing constraint imposed on him by Mr. Rickey."[115] "Players slid into the base Jackie was covering with their spikes high to draw blood," Rachel declared; "pitchers threw at his head to injure him . . . the bench jockeying crossed the line from insulting repartee" to abusive language, expressing hatred and bitterness, "intended to provoke rage."[116] "No matter what he'd been called, or how sarcastic or bigoted others had been to him," Rachel testified, "he never took it out on any of us."[117]

As noted, Robinson received thousands of letters during the 1947 season. Physicians, pastors, lawyers, blue-collar workers, and students from elementary school to college all wrote to him. Jackie and Rachel spent much of their free time answering the complimentary letters until sportswriter Arthur Mann took over this responsibility. Mann responded to every letter, whether inspirational or insolent. Robinson "was flattered and captivated by most" of the letters "and insulted by some" of them. The Dodgers' star "reviewed, sometimes revised, and signed each response." Occasionally Robinson added a paragraph or a postscript.[118] Rachel noted that although she and Jackie were Methodists, numerous Catholics sent him religious medals. "We aren't the least superstitious," she added, "but we get all sorts of good luck charms."[119]

Some letters transgressed the boundaries of propriety. The twenty-year-old African American winner of the Miss Akron beauty contest, for example, professed her love for Robinson and invited him to meet with her clandestinely. She acknowledged that the baseball star was married, but told him, "You don't have to be an angel." "When I married Mrs. Robinson," Jackie responded, "I exchanged vows to love, honor and cherish her for the rest of my life." Any "sneaking, skulking escapade" would violate this promise. A woman as "attractive and intelligent as you sound," he admonished, "should have no difficulty in finding the right man and creating a sound, honest life together in marriage."[120]

Although Robinson's teammates supported him when opponents attacked him verbally or through dirty play, gaining their friendship and full acceptance was very challenging. Rickey argued in the foreword to Robinson's 1948 autobiography that the rookie's "greatest achievement" was "his tactful handling of his relationship with his fellow players, as well as his opponents."[121] After spending a day with the Dodgers in 1947, sportswriter Jimmy Cannon declared in mid-May, "In the clubhouse Robinson is a stranger. The Dodgers are polite and courteous with him, but it is obvious he is isolated by those with whom he plays." In covering the Dodgers, Cannon had not heard Robinson's teammates criticize him or treat him rudely. But "Robinson never is part of the jovial and aimless banter of the locker room. He is the loneliest man I have ever seen in sports."[122]

Developing amiable relationships with his teammates was challenging for Robinson because of the racist attitudes of several players and the initial unfriendliness of others, but the situation improved as the season progressed, thanks to Robinson's demeanor, personality, and performance on the field. The Dodgers most hostile toward Robinson were pitchers Kirby Higbe and Hugh Casey; outfielders Carl Furillo and Dixie Walker; catcher Bobby Bragan, a Texan; and third baseman Cookie Lavagetto from California.[123] Higbe told a radio interviewer that his pitching prowess sprang in part from his growing up in South Carolina "throwing rocks at Negroes."[124] Casey, Brooklyn's best relief pitcher, told Robinson that when he had bad luck at home in Georgia, "I used to go and find me the biggest, blackest nigger woman I could find and rub her teats to change my luck."[125] Furillo, a Pennsylvania native, repeatedly declared before the 1947 regular season began that "I won't play with that black sonuvabitch.'" However, after Rickey told him that he would lose his job if he did not accept Robinson, Furillo "was no longer a rebel."[126] Despite this ostracism, Robinson wrote this in a mid-May column: "Everyone I have come in contact with since I joined the Dodgers has been alright."[127]

Most southern-born Dodgers initially treated Robinson with cold indifference, refusing to sit next to him on the bench or speak to him, but they gradually mellowed as the season progressed.[128] Robinson's stoic response to taunts and spikings and his significant contributions to the Dodgers' pennant win evoked sympathy and admiration from most of his teammates. Both Walker and Bragan rescinded their request to be traded by midsummer. Walker gave Robinson advice about hitting, and they developed a civil relationship. Walker told the press that Robinson had done more than any other player, except perhaps catcher Bruce Edwards, to put the Dodgers in first place.[129] Although Walker's attitude toward Robinson improved, Rickey traded him to the Pittsburgh Pirates after the 1947 season.

The testimony of Robinson, his teammates, and sportswriters about when the rookie was fully accepted by his teammates is contradictory and confusing. In addition to the verbal assault in Philadelphia on May 9, the team meeting in Pittsburgh in mid-May, and the Slaughter spiking in mid-August described above, two other accounts shed light on Robinson's improving relationship with his teammates—the story of Pee Wee Reese putting his arm around Robinson on the ballfield and Ralph Branca's saving him from crashing into the dugout in St. Louis.

No one did more than Reese, the Dodgers' shortstop, to help Robinson feel welcome and accepted. When the rookie reported to spring training in 1947, Reese was the first Dodger to shake his hand. "It was the first time I'd ever shaken the hand of a black man," Reese later stated. "But I was the captain of the team. It was my job, I believed, to greet the new players."[130] Robinson insisted that Reese's support was "particularly significant" in helping him adjust to MLB.[131] "Of all my teammates," Robinson asserted, "there was nobody like Pee Wee Reese for me." "The courage and decency of a teammate who could easily have been my enemy rather than my friend," Robinson wrote, helped him get through various crises.[132] Robinson called Reese "a staunch friend"[133] and a "courageous guy who knew how to stand up and speak out on the race issue where and when it counted."[134] "Anyone who resented Robinson" because of "his color and aggressiveness," a sportswriter declared, "found himself contending not only with Jack, but with the captain."[135]

A life-size statue on Coney Island depicts Robinson and Reese arm in arm. Its inscription states that Reese "stood by Jackie Robinson against prejudiced fans and fellow players . . . silencing the taunts of the crowd" during a game in Cincinnati. This incident has often been portrayed as an important one in both baseball's and the nation's social history. Reese said it happened early in the 1947 season in Cincinnati; Robinson maintained it occurred in Boston in 1948; others claim the incident took place in Brooklyn.[136] No photographs exist; the first published account of the episode is in an August 1949 interview with Robinson in the *Washington Post*.[137] Ken Burns expressed regret in his 2016 PBS Jackie Robinson film that the incident is probably a myth, and many scholars have questioned its authenticity.[138]

The standard account of Reese's display of support and encouragement has it occurring in Cincinnati in May 1947. In response to the ridicule of Robinson by Reds' players in the dugout and fans in the stands, Reese walked from his shortstop position to first base and put his arm around the rookie's shoulder while talking to him. His action stopped the verbal abuse and defused the hostility. Robinson later insisted, "After Pee Wee came over like that, I never felt alone on a baseball field again."[139] In a 1949 *Washington Post* interview, he stated, "Pee Wee kind of sensed the sort of hopeless, dead feeling in me and came over and stood beside me for a while. He didn't say a word but he looked over at the chaps who were yelling at me through him and just stared. . . . Slowly the jibes died down like when you kill a snake an inch at a time, and then there was nothing but quiet from them."[140]

On September 11, in a game against the Cardinals in St. Louis, Robinson sprinted toward the Dodgers' dugout to catch a pop-up. After catching the ball, he tripped over a pitcher's warmup mound and was going to crash into the dugout. Branca, reacting quickly, jumped out of the dugout and caught him to keep him from falling. "He wound up in my arms. Someone said that Jackie and I looked like a married couple" embracing, Branca commented.[141] Robinson heard Cardinals' fans discussing the incident in the stands during the next couple of innings. "It seemed to break the ice between me and the Cardinal fans," he noted.[142] That occurrence "proved to me once and for all that I was among men who did not give a hoot about the color of my skin," Robinson later wrote. "What was important to them was that I was part of the team."[143]

Conclusion

Robinson was named MLB's 1947 rookie of the year (not until 1949 did the National and American Leagues begin giving separate awards). Several national publications, most notably *Time* and *Ebony*, had campaigned for Robinson's selection by detailing his life, highlighting his challenges and achievements, and portraying his photogenic family in feel-good September cover stories. *Ebony* pictured Robinson holding his infant son with Rachel and described him as an "ex-Sunday School teacher" and "a loyal family man warmly devoted to his pretty, trim, ex-nurse" wife.[144] A sidebar story emphasized that the Robinsons were a morally upright couple who did not drink or smoke, disliked nightclubs, and often went to the movies.[145] *Time* reported similarly that Robinson avoided tobacco and alcohol, instead consuming a quart of milk every day. It noted that Robinson spent a lot of time with his nine-month-old son and that "Jackie's idea of a fine way to spend a night off is to go to bed early."[146]

In addition to accentuating his exemplary moral character, *Time* highlighted Robinson's athletic ability and accomplishments. Along with Army halfback and Heisman Trophy–winner Glenn Davis and Babe Didrikson Zaharias, a star in numerous sports including track and golf, *Time* described Robinson as one of the great all-around athletes of his era. The rookie was "jackrabbit fast" and "one thought and two steps ahead of every base-runner" in the game. His crafty baserunning was "a combination of surprise, timing and speed." Daring, Robinson maintained, is "half my game." Bruce Edwards, Pee Wee Reese, Eddie Stanky, Hugh Casey, Ralph Branca, and Dixie Walker all made major contributions, *Time* argued, but no one was more responsible for the Dodgers' success than Robinson.[147]

The Sporting News, which before the season began had predicted that an African American could not succeed in MLB, also named Robinson its rookie of the year. Its editors insisted that the award was based solely on his performance on the field and value to his team. "The sociological experiment that Robinson represented, the trail-blazing that he did, [and] the barriers he broke down" played no role in his selection.[148]

Fueled by his faith, courage, intelligence, and determination, Robinson hit .297, led the National League in stolen bases, scored 125 runs (second highest in the league), ranked ninth in hits, and helped the Dodgers win the National League pennant for only the second time since 1920. He even finished fifth in the NL MVP balloting, won by Boston Braves' third baseman Bob Elliott. After the season, an Associated Press poll ranked Robinson the second-most-admired American, trailing only singer and actor Bing Crosby.

"The saga of Robinson's first season," Jules Tygiel asserts, is "part of American mythology—sacrosanct in its memory, magnificent in its retelling." His story "thrills and fascinates, combining the central themes of the illusive Great American Novel: the undertones of Horatio Alger, the inter-racial comradery of nineteenth-century fiction, the sage advisor and his youthful apprentice, and the rugged and righteous individual confronting the angry mob." "To black America," Robinson was "a savior, a Moses leading his people out of the wilderness" into the promised land.[149]

Once the MLB color barrier was broken, other African Americans with superior skills, beginning with Cleveland Indians' center fielder Larry Doby in July 1947, also entered MLB. However, Doby, described as "shy, quiet, and unassuming," would have had a much tougher time in the pioneering role than the "aggressive, outspoken and audacious" Robinson. Prior to 1947, black baseball players had typically been caricatured as "road-show clowns, far inferior to their white counterparts." Because Robinson, Doby, Dodgers' pitcher Don Newcombe, Giants' center fielder Willie Mays, and the sport's other racial trailblazers established such high standards, most above-average but not exceptional black players remained in the minors. Even though baseball executives no longer doubted the abilities of African Americans and did not fear a backlash at the box office, they still discriminated against them. They continued to argue disingenuously that talented African Americans were in short supply and to demand higher standards of conduct on and off the field for black players than white ones.

Racism remained prevalent in baseball in other ways, and the problems other black players faced received far less attention than Robinson's pioneering ordeal. For example, in 1949, one of every four black position players in AAA baseball (the highest level of the minor leagues) was hospitalized due to being hit in the head with a pitch. These players also made substantial contributions toward the cause of racial equality while receiving little acknowledgment.[150]

After the season ended, John Curran, a priest at St. Thomas Rectory, one of eight Catholic parishes in Harlem, wrote to Robinson, "Thank God you have what it took" to integrate MLB. Curran argued that the ballplayer had been "a tremendous boon" to "our underprivileged youth" and hoped that Robinson would "inspire our youth to bigger and greater things in all fields of endeavor." "We are all so extremely proud of you and your accomplishments in the face of almost insurmountable odds," Curran declared. "The responsibility resting on the shoulders of him who would dare to be a Daniel would be tremendous," he insisted.[151]

Robinson was thrilled to have helped the Dodgers win the pennant. He was equally delighted that from now on, to play in MLB, an African American would "simply have to be a good enough player. As Mr. Rickey says, a champion is a champion in America, black or white."[152] Reflecting on his first season, Robinson humbly stated, "Somebody else might have . . . done a better job, but God and Branch Rickey made it possible for me to be the one, and I just . . . did the best I knew how."[153]

The integration of baseball, fulfilling Wendell Smith's prediction, turned out to be good for the owners' pocketbooks. Thanks in part to Robinson, National League attendance in 1947 was 750,000 more than the all-time record set the previous year. The Dodgers attracted 1,807,526 home fans, up just 11,000 from 1946, but an even larger number—1,863,542—attended Dodgers' road games. While earning the league's minimum salary of $5,000, Robinson became baseball's biggest draw since Babe Ruth. Large numbers of blacks viewed games in Brooklyn and other National League cities; busloads of black fans from southern cities came to see him play in Chicago, St. Louis, and Cincinnati.[154] A headline on the front page of the April 19 *Courier* proclaimed, "Jackie Robinson Packing 'Em In." One Dodgers game at Wrigley Field in Chicago in late May set the Cubs' all-time attendance record.[155] Highlighting Robinson's box office appeal, Smith declared on May 31, "Jackie's nimble, Jackie's quick, Jackie's making the turnstiles click!"[156] Robinson observed that "Money is America's God, and business people can dig black power if it coincides with green power." The black fans flocking to ballparks helped to ensure "the success of Mr. Rickey's 'Noble experiment.'"[157]

While visiting the Robinsons in New York City in September 1947, Karl Downs experienced severe stomach pain. Downs refused to remain in Brooklyn for further treatment and returned to Austin. Jackie was devastated when his pastor, mentor, and friend suffered a relapse and died from complications to surgery in a segregated hospital ward in February 1948. Downs's ability and dedication, Robinson argued, were as great as that of Roy Wilkins, Whitney Young, and Martin Luther King Jr. Had he lived longer, Downs would have become a major national leader. "It was hard to believe," Jackie bemoaned, "that God had taken the life of a man with such a promising future." In his final autobiography, Robinson wrote, "We believe Karl would not have died if he had received proper care, and there are a number of whites who evidently shared this belief. After Karl's death, the doctor who performed the operation was put under such pressure that he was forced to leave town."[158]

After the season ended, Robinson, needing to supplement his income, traveled with three vaudeville acts, earning at least $2,500 per performance. He was also a popular guest on radio shows and signed contracts to coauthor an autobiography and to star in a Hollywood movie about his life. Despite his low salary from the Dodgers, only two baseball players—Bob Feller and Hank Greenberg—earned more money overall in 1947 than Robinson.[159] His rookie year was outstanding, but his faith would be further tried and tempered during his next nine MLB seasons.

5

"I Am a Religious Man": Major League Stardom

1948–1956

From 1948 to 1956, Jackie Robinson was one of MLB's biggest stars and attractions. He also began to discuss his faith more openly and to promote black civil rights more vigorously. Robinson's faith helped supply the moral courage and ideological foundation for battling social injustice in both baseball and American society. He served as chair of the Commission on Community Organizations for the National Conference of Christians and Jews. In 1956, he received the NAACP's Spingarn Medal, awarded "for the highest achievement of an American Negro."

In 1949, Robinson testified before the House Committee on Un-American Activities. He denounced communism as godless, declaring, "I am a religious man." In his testimony, he also expressed disagreement with black actor Paul Robeson's view that African Americans should not fight to defend the United States against the Soviet Union because of the racial discrimination to which they were subjected. Despite this patriotic stance, Robinson continued to receive death threats and to experience racism on and off the field, especially after he and Rachel built a house in North Stamford, Connecticut. Rachel played a critical role in both his success on the diamond and his civil rights activism.

The 1950s were arguably the most religious decade in American history as measured by church membership, attendance, and financial contributions; sales of Bibles and religious books; popularity of movies with religious themes; and influence of Christianity and Judaism in various aspects of society. In 1958, 49 percent of Americans attended church on a typical Sunday, more than 10 percent higher than in the 1940s and an all-time record.[1] Many congregations were thriving, and numerous churches and synagogues were constructing new buildings. In the context of the Cold War, belonging to a church or synagogue was widely viewed as essential to being a good American. Involvement in a religious congregation enhanced people's social respectability and often contributed to their success in business and the job market. Many schools opened their days with prayer, invocations preceded public events, the Ten Commandments were posted in many city courthouses and parks, the words "under God" were added to the Pledge of Allegiance in 1954, and in 1956 Congress made In God We Trust the national motto and added this declaration to US currency. Radio, television, and newspaper messages and national, state, and local leaders all encouraged Americans to pray and attend religious services. Billboards throughout the nation asserted that "true Americans had religious faith."[2] The nation's resurgence of popular piety was widely discussed in newspapers, magazines, and scholarly books. When asked in 1957, "What is your religion?" 96 percent of Americans declared they belonged to a specific group.[3]

Although many churches were overflowing, the religiosity of the 1950s tended to be shallow and superficial. Many churches and clergy promoted the self-help movement, patriotism, and an uncritical celebration of "the American way of life."[4] Ignoring the prophetic function of Christianity and Judaism, numerous pastors, priests, and rabbis endorsed cultural practices that clashed with the Bible. The nation's religious ethos emphasized "the dignity of the individual, the superiority of American democracy, and the pragmatic doctrine of 'deeds not creeds.'" Rather than being the highest value, religion became an "instrument for promoting other values that in practice" were more important to many people. Millions of Americans did not know or care "much about the particulars of their religious tradition."[5] Although Christianity was widely viewed as an essential foundation for American democracy and effective opposition to communism and was celebrated in the speeches of President Dwight Eisenhower and other politicians, biblical teachings were usually not considered in discussions of major political, economic, or military issues.[6]

During much of his playing career, Robinson participated in the racially mixed but predominantly black Nazarene Congregational Church (NCC) in Brooklyn. NCC was a "mink coat church" in the late 1940s and 1950s; most of its members, including prominent attorneys, judges, and businessmen, were educated, affluent African Americans.[7] The Robinsons became involved in the church, which had a long history of social activism, through their friendship with the Covington family; Lacy Covington was a part-time minister there.[8] Tony Carnes, publisher of *A Journey through NYC Religions*, contends that this church and Robinson's faith "were central to [his] success."[9] Two of the nation's most prominent black ministers pastored the church in the twentieth century: Henry Hugh Proctor and J. Archie Hargraves. The son of former slaves and a graduate of Yale, Proctor served the large First Congregational Church in Atlanta for twenty-five years and helped numerous black Congregational churches in the South become self-sufficient before coming to Brooklyn. Under his leadership from 1919 to 1933, NCC's membership increased from 167 to 800. Hargraves led the congregation from 1956 to the early 1960s. In 1959, the Congregationalist Board of Home Missions described the parish's neighborhood as possessing "almost every problem that plagued city churches throughout the country."[10] To minister to the needs of the sixty-two thousand people who lived within a one-mile radius of NCC, Hargraves established a four-point program: fighting gangs, conducting evangelism, promoting integration, and improving housing. He also erected the Nazarene Community Center building, which housed Brooklyn's first Head Start program.[11]

A prominent figure during Robinson's time at NCC was Robert Ross Johnson, head pastor from 1952 to 1954, before he founded St. Albans Congregational Church in Queens, where he would serve for thirty-six years. Johnson also served as a prison chaplain for twenty-three years and on both the local school board and New York City's Board of Higher Education. He and his parishioners actively participated in the protests, demonstrations, and marches of the civil rights movement.[12] While ministering in Brooklyn and Queens, Johnson worked with the NAACP and YMCA and belonged to the National Conference of Christians and Jews, three organizations Robinson highly valued. The baseball trailblazer undoubtedly found Johnson's Social Gospel preaching, efforts to register African Americans to vote, and civil engagement very attractive, as they mirrored his own perspective and priorities. In his own sermons during the 1960s, Robinson frequently echoed Johnson's argument that the church should be "a vital seven-day-week factor" in the lives of its congregants and community residents.[13]

In accepting the NAACP's Spingarn Medal in 1956, Robinson highlighted the faith of his mother, Mallie, and his own: "Her faith in God and her constant advice that I, too, place that same faith in Him, has proven itself time and time again. I am humbly thankful that God gave me such a mother."[14] Robinson insisted that the essence of Christianity was "people having faith in God, in themselves and in each other and putting that faith into action."[15] He lived out his own faith by helping others. Robinson raised funds for numerous charitable causes; participated in numerous religious events, including the Brotherhood Week of the National Conference of Christians and Jews; supported the B'nai Brith's United Jewish Appeal dinner; and volunteered with the Harlem YMCA.[16]

Convinced that playing sports enriched children's lives and prevented them from becoming delinquents, Robinson also spent many hours during the off-season as a coach and counselor at the YMCA. Announcing that he and Dodgers' catcher Roy Campanella would work with the Y after the 1948 season, Robinson declared that "we are crazy about children." To become future leaders, he argued, children must gain self-confidence, express their opinions, and make their own decisions.[17] On a radio show he hosted on New York City's WMCA between the 1948 and 1949 seasons, Robinson frequently discussed the problem of juvenile delinquency.[18] In addition, he played with boys who lived in neighborhoods near the Harlem YMCA, visited many sick children in area hospitals, and answered numerous letters from children.[19] Robinson drove three hours to spend time with one young white boy, an ardent Dodgers' fan, who was dying of polio.[20] No other major leaguer, *Sport* magazine argued in 1955, had spent more time helping kids than Robinson, and no one in the game was more approachable, friendly, and honest in answering "the most pointed questions."[21] Characteristically, Robinson insisted that his work with the Y had given him "great satisfaction"; he went on, "I've learned more from the kids than they've learned from me."[22]

During Robinson's decade in MLB, New York City was the epicenter of the baseball universe, as the world's three top teams—the Yankees, Giants, and Dodgers—all played there. New York was also the nation's media center.[23] Robinson was named the National League's Most Valuable Player in 1949 and was selected as an All-Star six times. His career batting average was .311 (ranking in the top 100 in MLB history). He scored more than 100 runs in six of his ten MLB seasons and led his league in stolen bases twice. Robinson was among the top three in the National League in on-base percentage each year from 1949 to 1953; his career on-base percentage of .409 currently ranks thirty-seventh in MLB history. From 1949 to 1954, Robinson batted .327, and he and Stan Musial were the National League's most dominant players. In his best season, 1949, Robinson led the league with a .342 batting average and 37 stolen bases, was second in RBIs (124) and hits (203), and was third in runs scored, doubles, and triples.

Robinson was also an electrifying base runner and a wizard with the glove. From 1947 to 1956, he was one of only two MLB players who stole at least 125 bases and had a slugging percentage over .425. Furthermore, he was one of the best-fielding second basemen in MLB history; his 1951 fielding percentage of .992 set an all-time record for the position.[24]

Robinson's versatility and bunting skill were also impressive. During his career, Robinson played all four infield positions and left and right field. In one game after the Dodgers clinched the pennant in 1952, as a publicity stunt, he played one inning at every position except pitcher and made no errors anywhere. "He had excellent range as an infielder, superb hands, and a good . . . arm," a sportswriter asserted. "During his five seasons as a second baseman, he was never knocked off his feet while turning a double play." Baseball had few better bunters than Robinson: "You could not roll the baseball with more accuracy than you got with a Robinson bunt."[25]

At crucial points in a game, declared Leo Durocher (who managed both the Dodgers and Giants during Jackie's career), "Robinson was the one man I feared the most." Birdie Tebbetts, an MLB player, manager, scout, and front office executive, asserted, "In one spot, in one ball game, where I needed the one big base hit, I'd rather have Jackie Robinson up there for me than any other man in baseball."[26] The editors of *Sport* described Robinson as "a daring and guileful baserunner," a "sharp and decisive hitter who was always at his best in the tightest moments," and "a bold and instinctive fielder" who never gave up on a ball or shied "away from flying spikes on a close tag play." No other player could "match Robinson's incredible knack for digging a little deeper and coming up with a little more in the clutch."

MLB had not had "a more exciting player" since Babe Ruth or a greater competitor since Ty Cobb.[27]

Robinson was inducted into the MLB Hall of Fame in 1962, and in 1999 he was selected by fans among the thirty players on MLB's All-Century Team. Many who watched Robinson play believe that in his prime he was a better overall player than Stan Musial or Ted Williams if hitting, fielding, and base running are all considered.[28] In his ten seasons, he led the Dodgers to six National League pennants, and they lost two more on the final day of the season in 1950 and 1951.

Through his brilliant performance, an early biographer contended, Robinson helped remove the shackles of "suspicion, hatred, bigotry and sectionalism."[29] He played with such "valor, tenacity and intelligence" that all black players will forever be indebted to him.[30] "Robinson did not merely play at center stage," Roger Kahn maintains. "He *was* center stage."[31] Those who booed him because of his race, *Sport* magazine claimed, were forced "into squirming acceptance of him by the sheer strength of his performance on the field."[32]

Robinson Dazzles on the Diamond

Robinson came to spring training in 1948 thirty pounds overweight, thanks to spending much of the off-season on the "fried chicken circuit" speaking at dozens of events. He got off to a slow start but rebounded to bat .296, smack thirty-eight doubles, score 108 runs, and drive in eighty-five. The Dodgers finished in third place, 7.5 games behind the Boston Braves. Robinson continued to honor his commitment to Rickey to be humble and soft-spoken, but he noted in August that when black players could dispute an umpire's decision "and no one makes anything of it . . . we have really arrived in the big leagues."[33] That summer, when Truman ordered that the US military be integrated, critics who claimed that housing black, Hispanic, and white soldiers in the same barracks would produce discord were confronted by the question, "What about Jackie Robinson and the Brooklyn Dodgers?"

In 1949, his MVP season, Robinson was the Dodgers' "bellwether," "spark-plug," and "take-charge player" who held the team together through "his consistency, dependability," and "penchant for doing something important or dramatic."[34] In August, as Robinson led the league in several batting categories, *Life* magazine proclaimed, "Negroes Are Americans: Jackie Robinson Proves It in Words and on the Ball Field."[35] Buddy Johnson wrote and recorded a song called "Did You See Jackie Robinson Hit That Ball?" which was also recorded later that summer by Count Basie and his band. The song, which peaked at number fourteen on the pop chart, proclaimed:

> And when he swung his bat,
> the crowd went wild,
> because he knocked that ball a solid mile. . . .
> But it's a natural fact,
> when Jackie comes to bat,
> the other team is through.
> Did you see Jackie Robinson hit that ball?
> Did he hit it boy, and that ain't all.
> He stole home.

As a baserunner, Robinson brought the "aggressive and flamboyant" style of the Negro leagues to MLB.[36] His exceptional combination of "prowess, panache, and passion" led the Dodgers' speedster to be labeled "Ty Cobb in Technicolor." Robinson had an uncanny ability to rattle pitchers with his brash and unpredictable moves on the basepaths as he executed jackrabbit-like stops and starts and was always a threat to steal bases, even home.[37] "He dances and prances off base keeping the enemy infield upset and off balance, and worrying pitchers," *Time* magazine observed. Who taught him this baserunning style? Branch Rickey replied, "Primarily God."[38] Robinson was the only baserunner of his era, sportswriter Red Smith argued, "who could bring a game to a stop just by getting on base." He preoccupied pitchers' attention, and his antics led television producers to introduce the split screen so that audiences could watch both the runner at first and the pitcher at the same time.[39] "The only way to beat the Dodgers," insisted Cincinnati Reds' president Warren Giles, "is to keep Robinson off the bases."[40] The rundown "was his greatest play. Robinson could start so fast and stop so short that he could elude anyone in baseball."[41] In his fifty-three years in baseball, declared Clyde King, a Dodgers' pitcher, MLB manager, and New York Yankees' pitching coach, scout, and general manager, Robinson was the best base runner he had ever seen, not in stealing bases or speed but in pure instinct.[42]

Robinson's signature exploit was stealing home. He did so nineteen times; that figure ties for ninth in MLB history, but everyone ahead of him retired by 1937. The three greatest base stealers after him—Rickey Henderson, Lou Brock, and Maury Wills—collectively stole home just six times.

Capitalizing on his performance and popularity, many stores sold Robinson hats, jackets, and dolls. In addition, the Dodger had his own weekly radio show and was a guest on many other radio and television programs. "Our clubhouse in Ebbets Field," outfielder Duke Snider reported, became "a hangout" for celebrities who wanted to meet Robinson; Douglas MacArthur, Dwight Eisenhower, Richard Nixon, actors Jonathan Winters and Danny Kaye, and many others came to meet him.[43] In 1949, the Robinsons bought a house in St. Albans, Long Island, and finally had a backyard for their son to play in. Count Basie and several other noted black musicians and their families lived on the same block.

The MVP award Robinson won in 1949 was ironically named for Kenesaw Mountain Landis, the commissioner who had helped keep African Americans out of baseball. During this "banner year," Robinson reported, Dodger players became much closer, as racial tensions "almost completely dissipated."[44] After finishing one game ahead of the Cardinals, the Dodgers again faced the Yankees in the 1949 World Series. Don Newcombe, Preacher Roe, and Ralph Branca held the Yankees to two runs over twenty-six consecutive innings, but the Dodgers also scored only two runs in this stretch, and the Yankees won the series in five games. The Dodgers hit a meager .210 as a team; Robinson was even worse at .188 (three for sixteen), although he drew four walks and drove in two runs.

During the 1949 season, Robinson started talking more openly about his faith, telling a *Washington Post* reporter that it sustained him during his trials. "I often get down on my knees. It's the best way to get close to God," he declared. Robinson prayed for himself and his team. "And when things go wrong, I pray harder. . . . If you pray for something like [winning] the pennant you must . . . work twice as hard as before," he argued. "You have to merit the things you pray for." Robinson regretted that playing on Sunday prevented him from attending church and wished that a chapel could be established at Ebbets Field where players of all faiths could worship.[45] During his ten seasons in the majors, Robinson gave numerous speeches about baseball and civil rights in which he often discussed his faith. For example, in February 1949, he spoke to eight hundred people at a Student Church event at Bucknell University in Pennsylvania. Robinson rejoiced that prejudice toward black players was declining even in the South. He told several stories to illustrate how his Dodgers' teammates had forgotten about his skin color and simply viewed him as "a star player on a pennant-winning team."[46]

After the season ended, he participated in filming *The Jackie Robinson Story*. Although the production quality of this low-budget movie, starring Robinson as himself and Ruby Dee as Rachel, was poor, audiences cried as they watched the ballplayer humbly endure the verbal and physical abuse heaped on him. Robinson believed that the film helped increase public awareness of racism, bigotry, and blatant discrimination in American society.[47] *Life* pointed out that Babe Ruth and Lou Gehrig did not have movies made about them until they had either retired or died, whereas this film was released while Robinson was at the top of his game. Moreover, he played his role with "the natural charm of a screen born personality."[48]

By 1950, Robinson was the Dodgers' highest-paid player, earning $35,000 (worth about $380,000 today, still far less than what current superstars earn). He also made $30,000 for his movie role, plus 15 percent of the film's profits. Robinson finished the season with stellar statistics: a .328 batting average, thirty-nine doubles, and ninety-nine runs scored. He also led second basemen in fielding percentage and set a National League record for most double plays by a second baseman. The Dodgers finished second, two games behind the Phillies.

In 1950, Robinson was featured in a national advertisement campaign called "Religion in American Life." Appearing in a photograph with Rachel and Jackie Jr., he declared, "Being without the help of God is something we cannot imagine."[49] Robinson suffered a major blow after the season when Branch Rickey sold his share of the Dodgers and became vice president and general manager of the Pittsburgh Pirates. They kept in touch through letters and phone calls, but Robinson sorely missed their in-person interactions. In a November 1950 letter, Robinson thanked Rickey for his "constant guidance" and insisted that it had been crucial to his success as a baseball player.[50] Branch B. Rickey claimed that his grandfather considered Robinson a second son and that God had brought the two men together at a critical time in history.[51] "I don't think any other man," Rickey declared, "could have done" what Robinson "did those first two or three years."[52] Rickey signed more black prospects as well as Roberto Clemente, the first of a new cohort of Latin Americans who entered MLB directly without playing in the Negro leagues and the first Latino to be elected to the Hall of Fame. Rickey continued to insist that people would embrace the brotherhood of humanity only when they recognized that all races were the children of God.[53]

Robinson felt the departure even more keenly because he had an unpleasant relationship with Rickey's successor, Walter O'Malley. The new general manager's "attitude toward me was viciously antagonistic," Robinson wrote. O'Malley considered him an "uppity nigger."[54]

Robinson's 1951 season was sizzling, but the Dodgers and their fans suffered a major heartbreak when the team lost a three-game playoff series to the Giants and did not go to the World Series. Robinson hit .338, the second-highest average of his career, with 185 hits, 106 runs, eighty-eight RBIs, and twenty-five stolen bases. He finished sixth in the MVP balloting, won by a teammate, catcher Roy Campanella.

The Dodgers had a thirteen-game lead over the Giants in mid-August, but the Dodgers went 26–22 in their final forty-eight games while the Giants finished with an astounding 37–7 stretch. On the last day of the season, playing in Philadelphia and needing a win to tie for first place, the Dodgers were tied, 8–8, in the bottom of the twelfth inning when, with the bases loaded and two outs, Eddie Waitkus smashed a low line drive to the right of second base. Robinson dove for the ball, amazingly caught it, and crashed to the ground, a play Red Smith called "the unconquerable doing the impossible." His teammates huddled around him as Robinson lay on the field for several minutes. He eventually got up and hit a game-winning home run in the fourteenth inning.[55]

In the deciding game of the three-game playoff series with the Giants, Robinson knocked in the Dodgers' first run and scored their last run as Brooklyn took a 4–1 lead into the ninth. An exhausted Don Newcombe, hurling for the fourth time in eight days, gave up a run and left two runners on base, as Ralph Branca entered the game. Bobby Thomson hit a three-run homer, "the shot heard around the world," and the Giants prevailed, 5-4. The despair Brooklyn fans experienced when "the league pennant was snatched at the last minute," wrote historian Jacques Barzun, was reminiscent of a Greek tragedy.[56] Robinson was the only Dodger who went to the Giants' locker room after the game to offer his congratulations.

In 1952, ten of MLB's sixteen teams still had no black player. The Dodgers won 96 games that year, taking the National League pennant by 4.5 games. Robinson batted .308, with 104 runs scored and seventy-five runs batted in. He also walked 106 times and had a league-leading on-base percentage of .440, both the highest of his career. Robinson finished seventh in the MVP balloting.

Robinson was also hit by fourteen pitches in 1952, the most for him in any season. Black and Latino players in the early 1950s complained that pitchers threw more brushback pitches and beanballs at them than at white players. Cuban Minnie Minoso was hit 63 times from 1951 to 1954, leading the American League in this category each season. From 1947 to 1954, Robinson was smacked by 66 pitches. To put this number in perspective, Hugh Jennings, who played from 1891 to 1903, is the MLB record holder with 287 hit-by-pitches (HBPs) and Craig Biggio, who played from 1988 to 2007, is second with 285. Jennings was struck once every 17 at bats, Biggio once every 38, Minoso once every 29, and Robinson once every 68. However, Biggio was happy to get hit as a free pass to first base, whereas Robinson often applied his incredible agility to avoid being struck because many pitches were thrown at his head.[57]

Led by center fielder Duke Snider and shortstop Pee Wee Reese, who both hit .345 and had twelve of the Dodgers' eighteen RBIs, and Joe Black, who pitched twenty-one innings with an earned run average of 2.53, the Dodgers took games one, three, and five of the 1952 World Series from the Yankees before losing the final two games, 3-2 and 4-2. Robinson had a poor series at the plate, hitting only .174, although he did walk seven times, steal two bases, and score one-fifth of his team's runs.

The Dodgers were spectacular in 1953, recording 105 victories and winning the pennant by thirteen games. They clinched the league championship two weeks before the season ended; they had won two pennants in a row for the first time. The Dodgers scored 955 runs, only 20 fewer than the 1927 "Murderers' Row" Yankees, who featured Babe Ruth and Lou Gehrig.[58] Robinson had another stellar season, hitting .329, scoring 106 runs, and driving in ninety-five. The Dodgers hit .300 as a team in the World Series but still lost again to the Yankees, this time four games to two. Robinson had the highest average of the six World Series in which he played, batting .320, with two doubles and three runs scored.

On one of Brooklyn's trips to Pittsburgh during the 1953 season, Robinson met with the youth group of a Northside Lutheran church pastored by Bob Herhold. The white minister had persistently invited Robinson to talk to his youth group members, most of whom were African Americans. Having the Dodgers' star visit, Herhold's son wrote, "was a coup for a young pastor trying to integrate his church."[59]

In 1953, in addition to chairing the Commission on Community Organizations of the National Conference of Christians and Jews (NCCJ), Robinson served as national chair of the NCCJ's nationwide Brotherhood Week events that February. He also served on a committee, chaired by Eleanor Roosevelt, to raise funds to rebuild Concord Baptist Church of Christ in Brooklyn, which had been demolished by fire.[60] Between the 1953 and 1954 seasons, Robinson, inspired both by his faith and by the expectations placed on him by the black community, lectured on behalf of the NCCJ in cities from Pittsburgh to Los Angeles on "his core beliefs"—the importance of religion, education, racial tolerance, and family life.[61]

Robinson had another good year at the plate in 1954, hitting .311 and making the All-Star team for the sixth consecutive year, as the Dodgers finished second, five games behind the Giants. On July 17, for the first time in MLB history, the Dodgers started a mostly nonwhite lineup, with Robinson at third base, Junior Gilliam at second, Campanella catching, Newcombe pitching, and Cuban Sandy Amoros in left field. In both the North and the South, Robinson complained, "crude jokes were cracked and snide caricatures printed" to mock this lineup.[62]

By the end of the season, Robinson was considering retirement. "I was tired of fighting the press [and] the front office," he explained, "and I knew I was reaching the end of my peak years as an athlete." He regretted that his outspokenness would probably prevent him from getting an administrative job in baseball.[63] If Robinson had retired in 1954, he would not have been eligible for the Hall of Fame, because inductees must play a minimum of ten seasons.

Robinson was correct about the decline in his ability. This, coupled with illnesses and injuries, reduced his playing time and hampered his performance during his last two seasons. In 1955, the Dodgers again played brilliantly, winning 98 games and taking the pennant by 13.5 games. Robinson appeared in only 105 games and hit .256, the lowest average of his career. Before the World Series against the Yankees, *Sports Illustrated* asserted that although Robinson was "aging, aching, tiring, [and] still crabby," he would likely play a significant role because of his experience and competitive nature.[64] After losing the first two games to the Yankees, the Dodgers took four of the last five to win their first world championship. Home runs by Campanella, again the National League MVP, helped propel the Dodgers to victory in games three and four. Brooklyn celebrated effusively as motorists honked their horns, factories blew their whistles, residents beat pots and pans on their front stoops, and the *New York Daily News* declared, "THIS IS NEXT YEAR."[65] Not fulfilling *Sports Illustrated*'s prediction, Robinson hit only .182 and did not even play in the decisive seventh game, which the Dodgers won, 2-0. His most memorable achievements came in game one, when he hit a triple and then stole home, sliding just under the tag of Yankee catcher Yogi Berra, who vehemently protested the call. Robinson was thrilled that the Dodgers had finally won the world championship by defeating "our jinx club, the Yankees."[66]

Two weeks before the 1956 season began, Robinson helped lead a national Methodist Church youth conference in Minneapolis.[67] Robinson predicted that the Dodgers would finish no higher than fourth in the National League that year, although he insisted that they were still passionate about winning.[68] Robinson was a poor prophet, as the Dodgers, led by Newcombe, who went 27-7 and received both the MVP and Cy Young awards, again won the pennant, edging Milwaukee by one game. Robinson rebounded slightly in 1956, hitting .275 in 117 games.

One incident during the 1956 season indicated that Robinson still had opponents. Bill Keefe, sports editor of the *New Orleans Times-Picayune*, blamed Robinson for Louisiana's passage of a law forbidding black and white athletes from playing together. The "persistently insolent and antegonistic [sic] trouble-making Negro," Keefe claimed, had "been the most harmful influence the Negro Race has suffered in the attempt to give the Negro nationwide recognition in the sports field."[69] When a white Louisiana priest pointed out that the Irish had also faced much discrimination in America, Keefe responded that God had made blacks inferior beings, as evidenced by the thickness of their skulls and their "ape-like arms and characteristic odor."[70] Robinson countered that he was not a rabble-rouser but a black American who was proud of his heritage. It was "unfair and un-American," he chastised Keefe in a personal letter, to allow "the accident of birth to make such a difference to you." He reminded the sports editor that as recently as fifty years earlier, want ads in newspapers in some states included the line "Irish and Italians need not apply." "Am I insolent, or am I insolent for a Negro (who has courage enough to speak against injustices)?" Robinson asked Keefe. Louisiana, he wrote, had taken a "step backward" and was depriving sports fans of the chance to watch "top attractions" play and robbing African Americans of the right to engage in "free and equal competition."[71]

The 1956 World Series was a showdown between MLB's most diverse team—the multicultural Dodgers—and the Yankees, who had only one nonwhite player, catcher Elston Howard. The Yankees won the series, 4–3, as Don Larsen pitched the only perfect game in World Series history in game five. Robinson hit .250 with a .379 on-base percentage for the series. His tenth-inning line drive off the left-field wall batted in game six's only run. That was the last great moment at Ebbets Field for both Robinson and the Dodgers. The Yankees won the seventh game, 9–0, and Robinson soon retired. Brooklyn finished third in the National League in 1957, and the Dodgers then relocated to Los Angeles.

Following the path Robinson paved, African Americans began dominating MLB. In 1949, four of MLB's five black players—Robinson, Larry Doby, Roy Campanella, and Don Newcombe—were named to their league's All-Star teams. By the time Robinson retired, thirteen of the sixteen major league teams fielded black players, and African Americans had won rookie of the year seven times and National League MVP awards six times. By 1959, one-fifth of National Leaguers were African Americans, and they often led the league in batting average, home runs, RBIs, and stolen bases. From 1953 to 1965, the batting average of black players was about twenty points higher than that of white ones.[72]

Meanwhile, MLB's signing of the most talented black players caused the demise of the Negro leagues. Attendance at Negro league games decreased dramatically beginning in 1947, as large numbers of African Americans began to attend MLB contests. Moreover, MLB owners rarely compensated their Negro league counterparts for grabbing their best prospects. The Negro National League disbanded in 1948, while the Negro American League limped along until folding in 1962.[73]

After the 1956 World Series, the Dodgers embarked on a goodwill tour of Japan, going 14–4–1 against Japanese teams. On November 13, Robinson drove in a run in his final at bat as a Dodger.[74] One month later, he was traded to the New York Giants, the Dodgers' archrival, for journeyman pitcher Dick Littlefield and $35,000 in cash, shocking him, Brooklyn fans, and the entire baseball world. Roger Kahn called the trade the most cynical move in baseball since the Yankees dumped Babe Ruth on the Boston Braves in 1935. Ruth was sent to the other league, Kahn noted, whereas "Robinson, the embodiment of the loud, brave, contentious Dodgers," was traded "to his team's greatest adversary."[75] "I was surprised and stunned" to be traded, Robinson declared.[76] The Giants offered him a $35,000 salary, but Robinson decided to retire.

Robinson's contentious relationship with Dodgers' owner Walter O'Malley contributed to his decision to void the trade and not to play for the Giants. So did Robinson's waning athletic ability, frustration with continued racism in MLB, a job offer from Chock Full o' Nuts, his desire to spend more time with Rachel and their three children, and his plan to work with the NAACP to promote civil rights. *Look* magazine paid Robinson $50,000 for the exclusive rights to his retirement story, titled "Why I'm Quitting Baseball." Robinson wrote that he had been thinking about retiring for almost four years and had finally found the kind of job he wanted a few weeks earlier.[77] Rachel "wondered why the Dodgers had no sense of history and didn't make" a "grand gesture and retire the number 42 instead of trading" her husband "for thirty pieces of silver."[78] "Robinson's exit from baseball," a sportswriter insisted, "has generated the same type of rhubarb as did his entrance."[79]

Although racial bigotry diminished in baseball during Robinson's career, it did not end. In 1949, the grand dragon of the Ku Klux Klan led efforts to prevent Robinson, Campanella, and other black Dodgers from playing in Atlanta during spring training. On May 20, 1951, Robinson received an anonymous note declaring, "We have already got rid of several like you. One was found in river just recently. Robinson, we are going to kill you if you attempt to enter a ballgame at Crosley Field" in Cincinnati. Undeterred, Robinson hit a three-run homer in game one of a double-header as the Dodgers clobbered the Reds, 10-3 and 14-4. When Robinson received another threatening letter that season, his teammates said they would "all put on black face and wear number '42' so the would-be killer wouldn't know who to shoot at," Robinson disclosed. "That made me feel real good."[80] On September 16, 1953, Dodgers' manager Burt Shotten, before a game in St. Louis, showed his players a note reading, "Robinson, you die, no use crying for the cops. You will be executed gangland-style in Busch Stadium." This was the tenth reported death threat against the Dodgers' star in seven years, perhaps another baseball record, although Henry Aaron may have received more as he neared breaking Babe Ruth's home run record in 1974. When the team took the field to warm up, Pee Wee Reese jokingly told Robinson not to stand too close to him.[81]

Despite Jackie's prominence in baseball and personal popularity, he and Rachel also confronted discrimination off the field. When they moved into an apartment in Brooklyn in July 1949, Rachel explained, "even in this pre-dominantly Jewish neighborhood, we heard rumors of a petition being cir-culated to prevent our black landlady from purchasing the house we were to live in."[82] Rachel later explained, however, that many of their Jewish neighbors were friendly to them.[83] In the mid-1950s, racism prevented the Robinsons from buying a home in Westchester, New York, and hampered their attempt to purchase property in North Stamford, Connecticut. Moved by their plight, a group of ministers in Stamford established a committee to combat racial bias in housing and circulated nondiscrimination petitions. Rachel met with the pastors, who promised to discuss the housing issue with their parishioners. Fifty North Stamford families signed a statement declaring that excluding people "solely for reasons of race, creed or na-tional origin could only lessen the spiritual, economic and social develop-ment of our area." Controversy erupted between those who insisted that they had a "Christian duty" to welcome the Robinsons to their neighbor-hood and those who feared that their coming would lower the value of their property.[84] The Robinsons were eventually able to buy a six-acre lot with a pond, where they built a house they occupied in 1955.[85]

Although Jackie was an American hero, when he and his family moved into this all-white neighborhood, numerous white people complained and many African Americans called him a sellout.[86] The man who sold the property to the Robinsons was ostracized, and several families on the block sold their houses. Many other North Stamford residents "righteously rationalized" that it was not them but their neighbors who "worried about their property values depreciating."[87] Building this house made Rachel feel "closer to being a real American," closer to removing "the nagging doubts and insecurities that are the heritage of the American Negro."[88] Later, when Jackie tried to join the nearby High Ridge Country Club to play golf, he was rejected because members feared that the Robinsons would participate in club social events. "In the North," Rachel observed, "racism was disguised, denied, and pernicious."[89]

Rachel's Indispensable Role

Jackie, his friends, biographers, and sportswriters all affirmed that Rachel's love, support, and partnership were critical to her husband's success as a baseball player and civil rights activist. And Rachel frequently said the same thing.

In his 1948 autobiography, Jackie explained that Rachel helped him cope with his temper. He said, without her assistance, he "might have turned out to be 'baseball's No. 1 flop.'"[90] In accepting the NAACP's Spingarn Medal in 1956, Jackie declared, "This great honor . . . is hers as much as it is mine," thanking Rachel for "her faith in me, her wise counsel—above all, the confidence which she instilled and endlessly renewed in me."[91] In a 1962 column in the *New York Amsterdam News*, Jackie profusely praised Rachel. "[I wonder] where I would be in life if I hadn't met Rac. . . . I can't imagine how I would have made it through the bad days" without her "understanding, love and devotion." He insisted, "She has been my critic, my companion, my comforter and inspiration. She was the force behind my drive to make good in the world of sports" and today "in the world of business. . . . She was there to say exactly the right word" and help "me realize that . . . the world hadn't come to an end. . . . Rae has been a full partner in anything I have done" since they became engaged.[92] In his 1972 autobiography, Jackie avowed, "[Rachel] has been strong, loving, gentle, and brave, never afraid to either criticize or comfort me."[93]

Dodgers' teammate Carl Erskine stated that Jackie greatly depended on Rachel during his first season. She "stood by Jackie, as the Good Book says, tempered his fire," and had a very positive influence. "She made Jackie a calmer person and in doing so made him a better player. I don't think he would have lasted without her by his side."[94]

"When the burden of his task became almost unbearable," Rachel "consistently provided sage counsel and wrapped a comforting arm around him."[95] Rachel was "Jackie's supporter, cheerleader, and helpmate, the person who comforted him when he faced abuse, and encouraged him when he was feeling discouraged."[96] "She was Jack's co-pioneer," a journalist maintains. "She had to live through the death threats, endure the vile screams of the fans and watch her husband get knocked down by pitch after pitch.... She was beautiful and wise and replenished his strength and courage."[97] "It's a sign of his character that he chose a woman who was his equal," declared Michelle Obama. "I don't think you would've had Jackie Robinson without Rachel."[98] Filmmaker Ken Burns succinctly stated, "I don't know how he [Jackie] could have done it alone."[99] "All her life," Jonathan Eig argued, "Rachel believed she could accomplish anything she set her mind to. She was a tender and loving woman who inspired great warmth." Rachel "set high standards for those around her, including her husband." Jackie relied on her tremendously.[100]

In a 1951 article in *McCall's* magazine, Rachel confessed that she liked a concert, a play, or a ballet performance more than she liked a baseball game; nevertheless, she was "vitally interested" in the sport because of Jackie and did not miss a home game during his first two seasons.[101] "I was the support person so often misidentified as the 'little woman behind the great man,'" Rachel declared, "but I was neither little nor behind him. I felt powerful by his side as his partner, essential, challenged, and greatly loved."[102] The incredible pressure they experienced, Rachel argued, "pushed [them] together." Their time at home provided "the healing and restoration that enabled Jackie to be the man he was and for the Robinsons to lead the rich, resolute life they lived." "We treated our home like a haven," she declared.[103]

Robinson and Robeson

A controversial incident in 1949 testified to Robinson's popularity and prominence and highlighted both his religious convictions and his concern about black civil rights. In April 1949, renowned African American actor Paul Robeson told a conference in Paris, "It is unthinkable that American Negroes would go to war on behalf of those who have oppressed us for generations against a country [the Soviet Union] which in one generation has raised our people to the full dignity of mankind."[104] Like Robinson, Robeson had been a remarkable college athlete. Both men earned varsity letters in football, basketball, baseball, and track. The Rutgers football star was named an all-American in 1917 and 1918, and Walter Camp, the "father of American football," called him the greatest defensive end of all time. Unlike Robinson, Robeson also excelled in the classroom; he was a Phi Beta Kappa debate champion and class valedictorian. After receiving a law degree at Columbia University, Robeson became a celebrated actor and singer, starring in plays by William Shakespeare, Eugene O'Neill, and Jerome Kern. Like Robinson, Robeson received death threats (for his part in an interracial marriage in O'Neill's *All God's Chillun Got Wings*). Serving as a goodwill ambassador for the United States, he visited the Soviet Union in 1934. His argument that Soviet racial policies and practices were much better than those of the United States elicited little negative response while Americans were more concerned about Nazi Germany and imperial Japan. After the Cold War began, however, Robeson's favorable perspective toward the USSR came under strong attack.

The religious dimensions of the Cold War help to provide a context for Robinson's response to Robeson. From its inception, the Soviet Union zealously sought to destroy Christian and Jewish belief, deploying schools, the media, and museums to discredit religion. Communists supplied "a substitute system of belief based on 'scientific atheism'" and encouraged citizens to join atheist brigades and clubs. While Soviet elites viewed traditional religious faith as a hindrance to the national interest and strove to abolish it, American elites saw religion as a bulwark for US values and interests and labored diligently to promote it. To them, religious faith was a powerful weapon in a holy crusade to stop the spread of communism. Religious revival and spiritual strength were considered vital in winning the United States' righteous war against the Soviets' propagation of an atheistic, immoral communist ideology. American leaders created committees, organizations, and advisory boards to help strengthen their citizens' faith in Christianity or Judaism and solidify religion's role as the bedrock of the nation's freedom.[105] In this context, Robeson's defense of Soviet ideology, values, and racial policies and practices needed to be refuted, preferably by a black American hero who professed faith in God.

The House Un-American Activities Committee (HUAC) was established in the late 1930s principally to investigate alleged communist and fascist undertakings; it strove to expose political deviants and subject them to public derision. To counter and discredit Robeson's position, the HUAC asked Robinson, the only African American other than Joe Louis with a comparable reputation, to testify against him at a July 1949 hearing. Robinson was conflicted about testifying. On one hand, he believed that Robeson was wrong about African Americans' unwillingness to defend their country against its enemies and feared that the actor's "statement might discredit blacks in the eyes of whites."[106] On the other, he disliked opposing another prominent black man, whom he admired in many ways. Millions of African Americans viewed Robeson as "both a glamorous entertainer and a black man of unusual courage," and many whites highly respected him.[107] Moreover, as noted, Robeson had campaigned in 1943 for big-league owners to integrate baseball and had rejoiced when the Dodgers signed Robinson in 1945.[108]

As he considered whether to testify, Robinson received a flood of letters, telegrams, and phone calls. Some sought to persuade him not to speak, others advised him what to say, and still others warned him that testifying would cause him to lose popularity in the black community or even be considered a traitor.[109] Encouraged by Rachel, Branch Rickey, and numerous African American leaders, Robinson agreed to speak. Rickey, a fervid anticommunist, insisted that Robinson's speech "must be a masterpiece of cheek-turning," and he again read passages from Papini's *Life of Christ* to Robinson to support his contention. Rickey argued further that Robinson's testimony must not alienate either black or white Americans, which would require a delicate balancing act.[110] Working with Lester Granger, head of the National Urban League, and some black social workers, Robinson carefully crafted a speech, which he memorized.[111]

In his testimony, Robinson called Robeson's claims that African Americans would not fight against the Soviet Union "silly" and "untrue."[112] Robinson referred to his role in baseball's great experiment, praised the United States' freedom of religion, and decried its racial discrimination. He noted that he had been called "the laboratory specimen in a great change in organized baseball," which, he rejoiced, had enabled other African Americans to play. He insisted, "I am a religious man. Therefore I cherish America where I am free to worship as I please, a privilege which some countries [including the Soviet Union] do not give. And I suspect that 999 out of 1,000 colored Americans will tell you the same." Robinson, however, affirmed Robeson's assertion about racism in the United States. "That it is a Communist who denounces injustices in the courts, police brutality, and lynching . . . doesn't change the truth of his charges." The baseball star argued that life was "mighty tough for people" who differed from the majority "in their skin, color, or the way they worship their God, or the way they spell their last names." White Americans should realize, he declared, "that the more a Negro hates communism because it opposes democracy, the more he is going to hate the other influences that kill off democracy in this country," including "racial discrimination in the Army, segregation on trains and buses, and job discrimination." African Americans would not stop fighting race discrimination until they had it licked. He added, "It means we are going to fight it all the harder because our stake in the future is so big." Black Americans "were stirred up long before there was a Communist party," Robinson argued, and they would be agitated "long after the party has disappeared" unless Jim Crow laws had "disappeared by then as well." He promised to continue combating discrimination in sports, but he insisted that African Americans did not want the help of communists to attain equal rights.[113]

Many of the nation's most prominent African Americans, including Granger, NAACP president Walter White, and educator Mary McLeod Bethune, also criticized Robeson's comments, but Robinson's testimony "was the most celebrated and castigated" protest against the actor. Numerous radio and television shows, magazine articles, and newspaper editorials quoted Robinson's words, focusing on his criticism of Robeson and largely ignoring his condemnation of American racism. A New York state representative arranged for 500,000 copies of Robinson's testimony to be distributed to public schools.[114] The New York Times printed Robinson's statement on page one and supported his position in an editorial. The Times did not even mention the press conference Robeson held to rebut the Dodgers' star.[115]

A *Life* magazine article defended Robinson against other blacks who disparaged his testimony. *Life* labeled Robeson's claim that black men would not fight to defend their country "a libel" and insisted that most African Americans were "deeply religious" and "respectable," as illustrated by Methodist Robinson, who said with "conviction, 'I am a religious man.'" *Life* heartily affirmed Robinson's contention that African Americans did not welcome the aid of communists.[116] Eleanor Roosevelt and other white luminaries also endorsed Robinson's testimony.

The responses in the black press, by contrast, were mixed.[117] On one hand, many black newspapers condemned Robeson's statement. The *Pittsburgh Courier* denounced the actor's claim that African Americans would never fight the Soviets as "pathetic," while the *Chicago Defender* declared, "Nuts to Mr. Robeson." The *Philadelphia Afro-American* proclaimed that Robeson did not speak for millions of African Americans. On the other hand, some black columnists, noting that Jim Crow laws still dominated in the South and Washington, DC, lynching continued in the South, and the Ku Klux Klan attacked black persons in many locales, supported Robeson and criticized Robinson.[118] Leading black intellectual W. E. B. Du Bois complained that many African Americans blindly followed white leaders.[119] Years later, Malcolm X accused Robinson of letting white politicians use him "to destroy Paul Robeson."[120]

Robeson paid a great price for praising the Soviet Union and denouncing American racism. The FBI continually harassed him; many of his musical performances were canceled, and he was unable to schedule new ones; the State Department revoked his passport for almost a decade, preventing him from performing abroad and causing his annual income to decline from $150,000 to $3,000. Robeson's reputation never recovered from the assault on his character, and he had little influence on the civil rights movement for the remainder of his life. He died a discouraged and defeated man in 1976 at age seventy-seven, and his arguments and accomplishments have been underappreciated.[121]

In his 1972 autobiography, Robinson explained that he did not want to be a pawn in "the white man's game" and allow himself "to be pitted against another black man." He recognized that Robeson was attacking "racial inequality in the way that seemed best to him," but he feared that Robeson's position, if not strongly refuted, would be seen as representing most African Americans and would harm the civil rights movement. Although Robinson had never regretted his statement, he wrote that if he had been asked to testify in 1972, he would have refused. Robinson declared that he had much more faith in the ultimate justice of the American white man in 1949 than he had in 1972. Over the years, he had grown more frustrated by America's unwillingness to treat African Americans equally. Moreover, he had "an increased respect for Paul Robeson," who had "sacrificed himself, his career, and the wealth and comfort he once enjoyed" to "help his people" over the previous twenty years.[122]

Most analysts of the Robinson-Robeson conflict view the actor more favorably than the athlete. In so doing, they often overlook "the inherent naivete of Robeson's flirtation with the Soviet Union" and Robinson's "powerful condemnation of segregation."[123] Robeson ignored the USSR's political, social, and religious oppression and Joseph Stalin's slaughter of millions of Russians. This episode is best seen "as the clash of two fiercely principled men who admired each other and became reluctant symbols of competing approaches to racial justice during the Cold War."[124]

Baseball and Civil Rights

From Reconstruction to the 1950s, black churches throughout the nation, whether Baptist, Methodist, Pentecostal, or independent, provided a place for African Americans to worship God, win souls to Christ, nurture believers in the faith, and enjoy warm fellowship. They stressed the inherent dignity of African Americans and the equality of black and white persons in the eyes of God. These churches enabled black Christians to exercise leadership roles and supplied many social and material benefits.

During World War II, many black Christians supported the "Double V for Victory" campaign, which called for eradicating racism and discrimination at home while defeating the Axis Powers abroad. Numerous African American Christian leaders criticized the Roosevelt administration's Jim Crow practices in both civilian and military agencies. Seeking to stop the plans of A. Philip Randolph, an influential African Methodist Episcopal (AME) labor leader, for a march of 100,000 African Americans on Washington in 1941 to demand "the Right to Work and Fight for Our Country," Franklin Roosevelt established a Fair Employment Practice Commission

(FEPC) to penalize defense plants that discriminated against minorities. Black Christians used other venues, including pulpits, newspaper articles, and public proclamations, to challenge segregation and systemic discrimination between 1940 and 1955.[125] In addition to Randolph, these activities were led by AME bishop Archibald Carey Sr.; his son, Archibald Jr., a Chicago politician; Charles H. Wesley, the president of Wilberforce University; Owen Whitfield, a Baptist pastor and labor organizer; Baptist minister Fred Shuttlesworth; AME laywoman and attorney Sadie Alexander, who worked through the NAACP, the National Council of Negro Women, and the National Bar Association; Ella Baker, who played a prominent role in the NAACP, the Southern Christian Leadership Conference, and Student Nonviolent Coordinating Committee; and AME minister Joseph De Laine, who sponsored a foundational case that eventually led to the Supreme Court's landmark public school desegregation decision in 1954.[126]

On the other hand, many black congregations and ministers did little from 1925 to 1955 to explicitly challenge the political, economic, and social status quo or to directly support civil rights organizations. Although African American clergy insisted that God would eventually bring justice on earth, they usually preached an otherworldly gospel and often "encouraged forbearance in the face of suffering and oppression."[127] Plagued by inadequately trained leaders, limited financial resources, and white antagonism and indifference, many black congregations struggled to survive, and their pastors rarely denounced systemic racism or overtly condemned Jim Crow laws.

Before the mid-1950s, Gayraud Wilmore argues, most black congregations "retreated into enclaves of moralistic, revivalistic Christianity" and were too otherworldly, apathetic, or preoccupied with their own institutional maintenance to mobilize their members to attack poverty and racism.[128] Civil rights leader and Baptist minister Ralph Abernathy complained that many older clergy preached about otherworldly themes and displayed little concern for social issues.[129] Meanwhile, many denominational leaders were preoccupied with "the powers and prerogatives" of their positions and the well-being and growth of their communions and gave "only perfunctory support to significant initiatives against white supremacy."[130] Large, social action–oriented, institutional churches like Adam Clayton Powell Sr.'s Abyssinian Baptist Church in Harlem were unusual, although they "sometimes set the pace for entire neighborhoods or sections of a city." "With a few outstanding exceptions," Wilmore contends, black churches focused on satisfying "the spiritual hunger of a dispossessed and exploited people who found emotional release from victimization" in the rituals and activities of black church life.[131] In the mid-1940s, about 8.3 million of the nation's 14 million blacks belonged to a Christian church. Nearly all were Protestants, with 7.5 million of them belonging to separate black denominations and only 500,000 being members of predominantly white communions.[132]

In July 1948, President Truman began to desegregate the armed forces. Nevertheless, many African Americans threatened to support Progressive Party candidate Henry Wallace in the fall election, arguing that Truman had done little to end racial discrimination. Most African Americans, however, voted for Truman, thereby playing a key role in his narrow victory over Republican Thomas Dewey. Most white Americans still did not support equal rights for black persons; 56 percent of white respondents to a 1948 Gallup poll opposed Truman's moderate civil rights program.[133] Racial discrimination remained rampant. Developers refused to sell new homes to African Americans in many locales. In 1950, every state had laws and local ordinances that mandated residential segregation as well as separate schools for African Americans, Latino Americans, Native Americans, and Asian Americans. Racially motivated violence still occurred frequently throughout the nation.[134] "White indifference to racial inequity was a compound of complacent distaste, ineffectual benevolence and mildly guilty inertia—comparable to the average city dweller's attitude today toward the homeless."[135]

After World War II, the perspective and approach of many black ministers and congregations began to change dramatically. Hundreds of African American pastors started emphasizing equality and justice and using biblical principles and language to combat racism. Inspired by Martin Luther King Jr. and other Christian civil rights activists, black churches became a major force in the battle to obtain African American rights. They functioned as the civil rights movement's institutional center, providing leaders who were generally independent of white society and capable of managing people and resources, an army of combatants, funding, and meeting places for planning tactics and strategies. Black churches also supplied the primary base for staging demonstrations and the moral and social support necessary to spur collective action. The Southern Christian Leadership Conference, founded by King and other African American ministers in 1957, served as "the decentralized political arm of the black church" in the struggle for civil rights.[136] The rise of the civil rights movement and a series of Supreme Court decisions in the 1950s reduced segregation on railway cars and in education.

Using his status as a sports celebrity, Robinson joined the campaign to challenge American racism. In numerous speeches, interviews, and newspaper columns, he denounced racial injustice.[137] Robinson gradually became more outspoken about organized baseball's racial policies and black civil rights in American society as he grew more disgusted with persistent racial hatred and discrimination. Even after he had proven himself on the playing field, Robinson remonstrated, African Americans were still denied equal rights in society; the reason he had willingly suffered humiliation, he professed, was to help "provide a better future for my children and for young black people everywhere, and because I naively believed that my sacrifices might help a little to make America the kind of country it was supposed to be."[138] Robinson argued that discrimination against black players in accommodations and travel must end. He protested that some MLB clubs resisted signing African Americans, that teams were reluctant to put too many black players on the field at the same time, and that some managers, players, umpires, and sportswriters censured black persons who expressed their views on racial matters. *The Sporting News*, for instance, complained that Robinson was a civil rights crusader rather than simply a baseball player.[139] Robinson should remember, a sportswriter argued in 1954, that he was "a ballplayer, not a symbol."[140] Throughout his baseball career, however, the Dodger was always both a ballplayer and a symbol, an athletic star and America's most visible, well-known African American. For most Americans, these two identities were indistinguishable.[141]

Robinson later explained that he had put his "freedom into mothballs" for a while and "accepted humiliation and physical hurt and derision and threats" to his family to "help make a lily white sport a truly American game." Many praised this approach as "the appropriate posture for a black man." He added, "But when I straightened up my back so oppressors could no longer ride upon it, some of the same people said I was arrogant, argumentative and temperamental."[142] Robinson agreed with *The Sporting News* editors that his notoriety and status imposed "definite obligations" on him, but he disagreed as to what those obligations were.

Many attacked Robinson for being so blunt about racism in baseball and society. Numerous commentators urged the Dodger to emulate Joe Louis's example and serve as a goodwill ambassador for his race; Robinson insisted instead that he must denounce social injustice. Irritated and even alienated by Robinson's increasing frankness about racial discrimination in baseball and society, many players (even some black ones), umpires, journalists, baseball executives, and fans urged him to be more like Roy Campanella or Willie Mays, who excelled on the diamond but did not make controversial, discomforting statements.[143] For example, Robinson reported in 1954 about a conversation with an umpire who said, "I liked you much better when you were less aggressive." Robinson responded that he did not care whether the umpire liked him or not. Rather, he wanted the umpire to respect him for standing up for what he believed. "I am not an Uncle Tom. I am in this fight to stay," Robinson declared.[144]

Robinson's smashing of baseball's color barrier and his increasing candor about racial discrimination in sports helped improve the status of African Americans and advance their civil rights in other areas of society. Baseball's boosters praised their game's positive influence on other sports. The NFL rapidly desegregated; only Washington fielded an all-white football team throughout the 1950s. During that decade, African Americans dominated the NBA. In 1955, the Supreme Court ordered that public golf courses be desegregated, and in 1957 Charlie Sifford became the first African American to win a tournament sponsored by the Professional Golfers Association. That year, tennis player Althea Gibson won both Wimbledon and the US Open. Because "baseball has always been loved and respected" in America, Robinson argued, when black athletes became stars, many Americans "began to look on them in a new light."[145] After *Brown v. Board of Education* and the rise of the civil rights movement, Rachel explained, she and Jackie "felt connected to something larger than the struggles in baseball, more intensely connected to the destiny" of their race.[146]

When they applauded Robinson, few white Americans thought they were supporting integration in other areas of society. Nevertheless, admitting that Robinson was a superb ballplayer helped diminish people's long-standing prejudice and racial hatred. Across the country, as people discussed Robinson and the Dodgers, they were forced to confront their own bigotry and the nation's institutional racism. That realization was arguably as important as *Brown* in advancing equality for African Americans.[147] By handling the racism of fellow players and fans and the discrimination he encountered in restaurants, hotels, trains, and other public venues with great dignity, Robinson "stirred the consciences of many white Americans, and gave black Americans a tremendous boost of pride and self-confidence."[148] Rachel argued similarly that "the single most important impact" of her husband's baseball career "was that it enabled white baseball fans to root for a black man, thus encouraging more whites to realize that all our destinies were inextricably linked." The Robinsons recognized that they symbolized black Americans' "hunger for opportunity" and "determination to make dreams long deferred possible."[149] Celebrating the tenth anniversary of integration in 1956, *The Sporting News* contrasted baseball's history of "gradual, voluntary, and peaceful advance" with the increasing militancy of civil rights leaders.[150] Although Jackie endured considerable abuse, MLB player, coach, and manager Harry Walker avowed, no violence occurred in ballparks as it did on the streets during the civil rights movement between 1956 and 1970. Ignoring baseball's continuing racial discrimination, he insisted that baseball had integrated sooner than the rest of American society "and did a better job of it. It's too bad it took so long for everything else to catch up."[151] Many others contended that baseball's "great experiment" furnished a model for promoting racial harmony for the United States and the world.[152]

In 1948, Branch Rickey leased a former naval station with its own airstrip at Vero Beach, Florida, for the Dodgers' spring training to provide a refuge from southern segregation. Black and white players could train, eat, and even room together there without interference from civil authorities.[153] As the Dodgers traveled in the late 1940s and early 1950s throughout Latin America and the South during spring training and to large cities in the East and Midwest during the regular season, they challenged segregation on buses and trains and in hotels and restaurants. "They forced parents to explain to their children and themselves why black Americans" had long been "excluded from the Great American Game."[154] MLB helped effect racial change in the South in the early 1950s, as communities in numerous states accepted interracial competition by hosting spring training games.[155]

Interracial baseball, however, faced renewed opposition after the *Brown* decision in May 1954. In the mid-1950s, racial violence and intimidation increased in the South as the Ku Klux Klan reemerged; beatings, shootings, and murders of blacks increased, most notoriously the brutal slaying of fourteen-year-old Emmett Till in 1955. By 1957, southern legislatures had passed more than one hundred new segregation statutes, including ones barring interracial competition.[156] By the mid-1950s, as the civil rights movement gained momentum, black athletes were often used to illustrate that integration was occurring, but life in spring training and on the road during the regular season reminded them of how limited their acceptance was. Despite some advancements, conditions remained very difficult for black baseball players, including Cardinals Bob Gibson and Curt Flood, who described their experience as an ordeal and the South as a "hellhole." African Americans faced severe hardships on road trips; they often were not allowed to eat in restaurants, stay in hotels, or even use public toilets. "Confronted by lingering prejudices on the playing field, in their private lives, and in Florida and Arizona training camps, black athletes, led once again by Jackie Robinson, changed from stoic pioneers, grateful to be accepted, to militant protestors, demanding equal treatment—foreshadowing the evolution of the civil rights movement."[157] Robinson exhorted MLB teams, which spent millions in the South every year, to exert more financial pressure to eradicate racism in baseball below the Mason-Dixon Line.[158] Meanwhile, until the mid-to-late 1960s, college athletics in the South remained segregated and many southern football teams refused to play against northern teams with black members.

By the mid-1950s, the media's "most blatant examples of racial stereotyping had disappeared"; overall, the media provided "highly sympathetic coverage" of baseball's integration.[159] The *New York Times*, for example, editorialized in 1954 that MLB had produced "some of the [nation's] most intelligent and effective work against racial discrimination." Black players had "done more than could have been accomplished by volumes of polemics to demonstrate the stupid folly of prejudice."[160] Meanwhile, the demolition of baseball's color line helped pave the way for the civil rights movement in the second half of the 1950s. Robinson argued that the integration that characterized baseball could "be achieved in every corner of the land." Despite the sport's continued mistreatment of minorities, he insisted that "integration in baseball has already proved that all Americans can live together in peaceful competition."[161]

During Robinson's MLB career, his faith helped guide his morality, determine his priorities, and direct his activities. It also inspired him to combat discrimination in baseball and society and to work with religious and civic organizations to eliminate racism and improve social conditions. After his retirement from baseball, Robinson's efforts to expand black civil rights and opportunities in society would intensify.

6

"Still Slaying Dragons": Civil Rights Activism

1956–1972

After retiring from baseball, Jackie Robinson arguably broke more barriers than he did as a player.[1] Through his civil rights, religious, and political activism and his business positions and enterprises, Robinson helped increase opportunities for people of color. In 1970 Random House declined to publish the Hall of Famer's final memoir because Robinson planned to discuss not only his career as a baseball player but also his work in other fields.[2]

In remembering her husband, Rachel Robinson emphasized his role "as an informal civil rights leader. That's the part" of his legacy "people forget."[3] Jackie "never wanted to run for office," she added, but used his athletic success "as a political forum" to promote causes about which he cared.[4] Robinson called himself a one-man "pressure group for civil rights."[5] Motivated by his faith, Robinson became a major civil rights spokesperson and activist during the last sixteen years of his life. Describing his promotion of civil rights, one sportswriter declared that Robinson "is still slaying dragons." Some people, he asserted, saw Robinson as "a fearless knight on a dashing white steed on his way to destroy evil," whereas others viewed him as "a swashbuckling, notorious villain."[6] Robinson was a pathbreaker in social and political activism; in his time, he was one of a handful of professional athletes who went beyond philanthropy and social service to challenge social institutions and practices through their words and deeds. "The scale, depth, and variety of Robinson's activism" were substantial enough to attract sharp criticism and cause the FBI to keep a file on him.[7]

Robinson's approach to civil rights is difficult to pigeonhole. Whereas many depict him as a civil rights champion, some black activists and scholars portray him much less favorably. To critics, his testimony against Paul Robeson, endorsement of Richard Nixon in 1960, enthusiastic campaigning for Nelson Rockefeller, and support for the Vietnam War greatly tarnish his reputation as a pioneer of integration and the "luminous mythos" often associated with his life story.[8] As inner cities burned and protesters were beaten and jailed, many younger black Americans saw Robinson as "on the wrong side of the barricades."[9]

Both black and white Americans blessed and damned him, Robinson observed in 1970. He had been labeled a "militant, radical, conservative and even [an] Uncle Tom."[10] Robinson's positions on racial issues became more progressive after his playing days ended, but many younger African Americans still viewed him as "an out-of-step old man" and shouted "Oreo" at him. Malcolm X and other black critics called him "a black man who was made by white people."[11] They argued that Robinson had "three fabulous, white godfathers—Mr. Rickey in baseball, Bill Black in business, and Nelson Rockefeller in politics."[12] Although many of his views were similar to those of Martin Luther King Jr., Robinson was "always defiantly independent in thought and action" and "forged his own distinctive and controversial path in politics and protest."[13]

The ex-Dodger served as the national chair of the NAACP's Freedom Fund Campaign, worked with the National Conference of Christians and Jews and the George Washington Carver Memorial Foundation, helped lead several civil rights marches, wrote columns on racial issues for the *New York Post* and the *New York Amsterdam News*, gave dozens of speeches and sermons, and labored energetically to provide better schools, housing, and jobs for African Americans. In countless media interviews and newspaper columns, and while hosting several radio and television shows himself, Robinson analyzed numerous global and domestic civil rights issues and challenged the views of black and white politicians and activists, including Adam Clayton Powell Jr., Roy Wilkins, Malcolm X, Dwight Eisenhower, John F. Kennedy, Richard Nixon, Ronald Reagan, and William Buckley. He sent dozens of letters to presidents, both criticizing and applauding their civil rights policies. He journeyed to many of the South's hot spots, speaking in Birmingham and marching in Selma, Alabama. Robinson participated in the August 1963 March on Washington and other protest events in the nation's capital and in New York City and convinced other prominent black athletes to join him at such events. As a businessman and civil rights advocate, he challenged both Republicans and Democrats to provide equal rights and help empower the nation's minorities.[14]

Independent, assertive, and persistent, Robinson charted his own course during the turbulent years from 1956 to 1972. Younger black militants castigated him for working through the nation's political and economic system to improve life for African Americans, while Robinson criticized the older generation of black leaders for moving too slowly. He was caught between a rock and a hard place, and he alienated some groups with his actions, including his denunciation of the anti-Semitism of Harlem blacks; his criticism of Powell for urging blacks to repudiate the NAACP; his resignation from the NAACP in 1967 because it refused to give more power to younger, more progressive blacks; and his censure of the New York City police for their brutal treatment of the Black Panthers in 1968.[15]

Robinson's faith, shaped by his mother, Mallie; Karl Downs; and Branch Rickey, inspired him in these battles just as it helped him endure the racist taunts, epithets, and beanballs during his baseball career. "There's nothing like faith in God," Robinson explained, "to help a fellow who gets booted around once in a while."[16] "Our faith had been important through[out] our lives," Rachel insisted. "We came from religious families," and had beliefs that "supported us in our activities," decisions, and plans.[17] Jackie argued that the Bible's mandate to proclaim liberty and abolish oppression required Christians to fight to obtain everyone's freedom.[18]

Robinson "leaned heavily on Scripture as the road map for improving race relations in America."[19] He described his work promoting civil rights as "hoeing with God"—using God's gifts to advance God's work.[20] Robinson often told a story about a man who worked from dawn to dusk to rejuvenate a sorely neglected farm. Noticing how rich his harvest looked, a neighbor declared, "The Lord has certainly been good to you." The farmer agreed but added, "You should have seen this [farm] before I started hoeing." "I have always believed," Robinson concluded, "that God will help us do anything we want to do that is decent and good" but wants believers to do "a little hoeing."[21]

Robinson insisted that the church had a vital role to play in procuring black equality. From 1964 to 1966, he served as president of United Church Men, a branch of the National Council of Churches. In promoting civil rights, he often partnered with black ministers, churches, and parachurch organizations. If "the church of the living God cannot save America in this hour of [racial] crisis," he declared, "what can save us?"[22] In 1963, the United Church of Christ gave Robinson its Churchman Award, describing him as "a Christian layman fulfilling your ministry to the world" and praising his "Christian commitment of time, energy and skill in the struggle for social justice."[23]

Using Every Means at Our Disposal

Robinson's constant criticism of club owners' greed and mistreatment of black players after his retirement in 1956 often made his relationship with MLB officials contentious. In 1960, Robinson noted that African Americans "are well integrated into the game," and "although problems exist, they are generally accepted as individuals whose personalities, interests and abilities vary just as much as" those of their white teammates.[24] Nevertheless, Robinson's 1964 book titled *Baseball Has Done It*, based on interviews with two dozen black stars, including Hank Aaron, Ernie Banks, and Frank Robinson, highlighted racial disparities. While lauding the sport's contributions to the civil rights movement, his book also contains numerous testimonies about the discrimination black players continued to face. Robinson also criticized baseball executives for refusing to address broader civil rights issues. "The main complaint" of black ballplayers, Robinson asserted, "is that integration in baseball will never be complete until there's integration everywhere."[25]

Baseball, Robinson insisted, is "a sociological experiment which has revealed certain truths about human relations, a research laboratory and proving ground for democracy in action." It had demonstrated that integration was possible. In baseball, blacks and whites sat side by side on dugout benches; used the same water fountains, toilets, showers, bats, balls, and gloves; traveled together on the same buses, trains, and planes; stayed in the same hotels; and ate in the same dining rooms. Robinson rejoiced that players of color, who constituted 15 percent of MLB players in 1963, were excelling and that no racial altercations had occurred. Many African American and Latino players complained, however, about conditions in Florida during spring training. Robinson urged MLB to protect black rookies against "insult, isolation and discouragement during spring training." He exhorted baseball executives to pressure "Southern towns to end all forms of discrimination" and to refuse to play in places that failed to "provide equal accommodations and services to all players at all times."[26]

God, Robinson stressed, gave African Americans certain unique qualities that they cherish as their heritage, just as other groups with a common heritage cherish theirs. In both baseball and society, black Americans were "no longer willing to wait until Judgment Day for equality"; he insisted, "We want it here on earth as well as in heaven." Robinson concluded, "We intend to use every means at our disposal to smash segregation and discrimination" in the United States. "We are staring into the face of our oppressors and demanding by what right of skin coloration do they consider themselves our superiors." The "falsehoods about our supposed inferiority" are being exposed and "must be destroyed."[27]

For the remainder of his life, Robinson prodded professional baseball to hire African Americans as coaches, managers, and executives. He refused to play in a 1969 old-timers' game because MLB had little "genuine interest in breaking the barriers" that denied African Americans "managerial and front office positions." He denounced the veiled argument that blacks lacked the brains to succeed in these roles. Nine days before his death, after throwing out the ceremonial first pitch before game two of the 1972 World Series and accepting a plaque commemorating the twenty-fifth anniversary of his MLB debut, he confessed, "I'm going to be tremendously more pleased and more proud when I . . . see a black face managing in baseball."[28] Although he worked in 1965 as the first black analyst for ABC's *Major League Baseball Game of the Week* program, Robinson would have welcomed the chance to manage a team and maintained that he could "have been a good manager."[29]

Moving beyond racial issues, Robinson also criticized baseball's overall employment structure, especially the reserve clause—which bound a player to a single team for his entire career unless he was unconditionally released—for creating a form of indentured servitude. After Cardinals' outfielder Curt Flood challenged the reserve clause in 1969, Robinson was one of the few former players to testify in court the next year on his behalf. Baseball claimed to be "a sacred institution dedicated to the public good," Robinson asserted, "but it is actually a big, selfish business," more ruthless than many businesses in other fields. He also accused MLB of exploiting young, gifted black and brown players and then discarding and forgetting about them after they had "given the best years and the best energies of their lives."[30] The reserve clause, he argued, "is one-sided in favor of the owners and should be modified to give the player some control over his destiny."[31] Free agency was introduced in MLB in 1976, enabling players with longer tenures to choose their teams and substantially increasing their salaries.

The Hall of Fame

Robinson deeply desired to be selected for the MLB Hall of Fame, but he recognized that his outspokenness and antagonistic relationship with numerous sportswriters (the group that determines who is elected) might prevent him from attaining the 75 percent vote required for admission. He did not deserve to be elected simply for being the first African American to play in MLB, Robinson argued, but he should not be rejected because his "fiery temper" flared against violations of his and other blacks' "personal dignity and civil rights." He should be judged by the same standard as all other candidates—performance on the field, sportsmanship, character, and contribution to one's team and baseball. He was not willing to violate his principles and integrity, Robinson insisted, to win "this high mark of baseball immortality."[32] Elated when he was chosen on the first ballot, Robinson proclaimed that if a former juvenile delinquent "whose parents were virtually slaves," who came from a broken home, and "whose mother worked as a domestic from sun-up to sun-down" could be elected, "then it can happen to you kids . . . who think that life is against you." His selection, Robinson argued, proved that many wonderful people of other races appreciated the abilities and achievements of black persons and the principles of democracy enough to stand up when it counted.[33]

Not since 1936 when Ty Cobb, Babe Ruth, Honus Wagner, and Walter Johnson became the Hall of Fame's initial honorees, declared sportswriter Sam Lacy, had an "induction ceremony attracted such wide attention" as in 1962.[34] In his induction speech on July 23, Robinson thanked the three people who had contributed the most to his success on the baseball field and in life—Mallie, Branch Rickey, and Rachel. He praised his mother for teaching him so many "important things early in life." Rickey was his advisor, "a wonderful friend," and "a man who I considered a father." Rachel had "been such a wonderful inspiration"; she had "guided and advised me throughout our entire marriage. I couldn't have been here today without her help."[35] Rickey insisted that the six pennants he had helped the Cardinals, Dodgers, and Pirates win had not given him as much satisfaction as Robinson's induction.[36] New York governor Nelson Rockefeller lauded Robinson for helping "make American democracy a genuine reality for every American."[37] In a message sent to a dinner at the Waldorf-Astoria Hotel in New York City honoring Robinson, President John F. Kennedy declared, "The vigor and fierce competitive spirit that characterized his performance as an athlete" were also evident in his efforts "to achieve equality of opportunity for all people."[38]

Taking a Stand

After retiring from baseball, Robinson participated in numerous picket lines and civil rights rallies. He served on the NAACP board of directors for eight years and was one of the organization's top fund-raisers for several years. He also solicited money for the Southern Christian Leadership Conference, the Congress of Racial Equality, and the Student Nonviolent Coordinating Committee. Surrounded by a hostile white crowd outside the building, Robinson spoke to the NAACP branch in Jackson, Mississippi, on February 16, 1958, urging the audience to press persistently but peacefully for their rights as American citizens.[39] On October 25, 1958, Robinson, along with singer Harry Belafonte, labor leader A. Philip Randolph, and Martin Luther King Jr.'s wife, Coretta Scott King, led ten thousand exuberant black and white youth in a march in Washington, DC, to protest segregated schools. Participants delivered a written statement to President Dwight Eisenhower explaining the march's purpose but were unable to meet with him or any members of his administration. On April 18, 1959, Robinson helped lead about twenty-five thousand activists in another Washington march, chanting, "Five, six, seven, eight, these United States must integrate."[40]

An incident on October 28, 1959, and events that followed, illustrates the impact of Robinson's determination to stand for civil rights. After speaking at an NAACP convention in Greenville, South Carolina, he went to the local airport to fly back to New York. While he and other African Americans were waiting for his plane to depart, airport officials asked them to move from the main lounge to the "colored lounge." Robinson and his NAACP associate Gloster Current refused to leave, arguing that as interstate passengers they had a right to sit in the main lounge. This federally subsidized facility had been built using black tax dollars, they contended, and was under the jurisdiction of the Interstate Commerce Commission (ICC); according to ICC regulations, black travelers could use it. Robinson and Current asked what Greenville law mandated that they move. In Robinson's version of the story, the police officers who had ordered them to move were befuddled and simply left, and Robinson and his entourage remained in the main lounge until his plane departed.[41] James Hall, a pastor with whom Robinson stayed in Greenville and who accompanied him to the airport, added another detail to the story. He claimed that just as the police officers were about to arrest the African American contingent for refusing to leave the main lounge, about one hundred black children arrived at the airport to see their hero and obtain his autograph. Seeing so many children in the terminal, the police decided not to lock up anybody. As "the Bible says, God sends us angels to have charge over us," Hall explained.[42]

For the next two months, the twenty-five-year-old Hall worked to organize a march on January 1, 1960, to protest this segregationist policy. One thousand Greenville residents marched peacefully that day from Hall's church to the airport and presented a resolution to officials, declaring the following: "We will not [be] satisfied with the crumbs of citizenship while other[s] enjoy the whole loaf only by right of a white-skinned birth." They pledged, "With faith in this nation and its God, we shall not relent, we shall not rest, we shall not compromise, we shall not be satisfied until every vestige of racial discrimination and segregation has been eliminated from all aspects of our public life."[43]

Black college students who learned of Robinson's experience of airport discrimination spread the story of the original incident and the march when they returned to their campuses throughout the Southeast after the Christmas break.[44] One month later, four African Americans who attended North Carolina Agricultural and Technical State University in Greensboro refused to leave a lunch counter at a Woolworth's in their city; their action inspired similar sit-ins throughout the nation. One of these sit-ins, at the whites-only Greenville Library, was co-led by Jesse Jackson, who was arrested for trespassing along with seven other Greenville residents. Jackson had graduated from the city's Sterling High School in the spring of 1959 and was playing football for the University of Illinois. He had heard Robinson speak in October at the NAACP event and participated in the New Year's Day march. Robinson's "sense of independence and character," Jackson insisted, made him "the most dominant figure in my formative years, way before I met Dr. Martin Luther King Jr. as an adult."[45] Later, Robinson would support Jackson's Operation Breadbasket in Chicago and Jackson would deliver the eulogy at Robinson's funeral.

James Hall baptized Jackson as a teenager and introduced him to Jesus, social action, and the methods of Mahatma Gandhi.[46] Inspired in part by Robinson, whom he called "an authentic hero," Hall became an unsung civil rights advocate, galvanizing his community to protest segregation and serving as vice president of the South Carolina State NAACP and president of the local chapter of the Congress of Racial Equality.[47] In 1963, Hall accepted a pastorate in Philadelphia, and six years later he founded Triumph Baptist Church there. He stayed for fifty years as the congregation grew to over five thousand members, combining evangelism, education, and economic development. It established a credit union, a scholarship fund for youth, a supermarket to serve nearby neighborhoods, and many other ministries.[48]

Another person who heard Robinson speak in Greenville in October and participated in the January 1, 1960, march, Leona Robinson-Simpson, observed that he spoke softly, "not with fire and brimstone," but "had a powerful presence."[49] Robinson-Simpson has represented the Greenville area in the South Carolina House of Representatives since 2012.

After speaking at an NAACP-sponsored luncheon in Cleveland on April 23, 1960, Robinson joined other activists in picketing the Woolworth store on Euclid Avenue, as part of a nationwide boycott of Woolworth stores and other five-and-dime chains that refused to allow blacks to eat at their lunch counters in their southern stores. Having learned that "it was a lot harder to turn the other cheek and refuse to fight back" than he had expected, Robinson praised civil rights demonstrators for acting nonviolently at sit-ins, marches, and freedom rides. This approach, he claimed, worked; sooner or later, those who attacked demonstrators felt ashamed.[50] Nevertheless, he admitted, "I am not and don't know how I ever could be nonviolent."[51] When the police used brutal tactics to suppress the Fruit Riot in Harlem in 1964, Robinson insisted he admired Dr. King deeply, but added, "I have not learned to return hatred with love."[52]

During the summer of 1962, Robinson became embroiled in a controversy between black nationalists and Jews in Harlem. The ex-Dodger defended the right of Frank Schiffman, the Jewish owner of the Apollo Theater in Harlem, to rent space to a white businessman to open an inexpensive steak house. Fearing that this prospective business would hurt a black-owned restaurant in Harlem, some local black residents, supported by Malcolm X and the Nation of Islam, picketed the Apollo Theater and shouted anti-Semitic epithets. Robinson, then vice president of Chock Full o' Nuts, debated Lewis Micheaux, the owner of the National Memorial African Book Store, on a local radio station about the Apollo dispute. Micheaux labeled the ex–baseball player "a flunky for whites," while Robinson called the bookstore owner "a bigot, a demagogue," and stupid. After an hour of "knock-down, drag-out quarreling," they began to listen to each other and search for common ground. They agreed that "anti-Semitism was despicable" and that blacks should never resort to it.[53] Undoubtedly influenced by the support Jews gave him while he played baseball, Robinson, in an *Amsterdam News* column, lambasted blacks, who were "as persecuted as anyone in the world," for standing by while a handful of their compatriots employed the same ethnic slurs the Nazis had used in Germany.[54] Robinson was ashamed of community leaders who were too afraid to denounce black anti-Semitism. How can blacks condemn anti-black prejudice, he asked, if they were "willing to practice or condone a similar intolerance"?[55]

Black militants responded angrily, even organizing a "hate Jackie Robinson campaign," and some of them picketed the Chock Full o' Nuts coffee shop in Harlem.[56] Civil rights leaders, including Roy Wilkins, the executive director of the NAACP, backed Robinson, as did pastors George Lawrence of the Antioch Baptist Church in Brooklyn and Thomas Kilgore of Friendship Baptist Church in Harlem. Lawrence, a community activist and close associate of Martin Luther King Jr., promised to urge his church's four thousand members to eat at Chock Full o' Nuts shops and buy its coffee to support Robinson's "magnificent stand against anti-Semitism."[57] Antioch's "courageous and witty pastor," Robinson wrote, was right in proclaiming—as the company's advertisements heralded—that Chock Full o' Nuts was "a heavenly coffee" that Christians should drink.[58]

In January 1963, Robinson returned to Jackson, Mississippi, to strengthen the morale of blacks suffering from "economic and political oppression." In May, he and heavyweight champion Floyd Patterson went to Birmingham, Alabama, to support racial protesters who had stood "fast against fire-hoses, police-dogs, riot clubs, guns and bombs." Speaking to large crowds in two churches, they denounced racial violence. Robinson complained that he and Patterson were watched like criminals who had come to Birmingham to rob a bank, or "like potential despoilers of Southern womanhood." He was deeply moved at the August 23, 1963, March on Washington for Jobs and Freedom, where he marched with 250,000 passionate demonstrators and heard King's "I Have a Dream" speech. Robinson urged civil rights advocates to continue to march, sing, work, pray, and go to jail together until, as King said, one day all black Americans would be free at last.[59]

Robinson was outraged by the massacre of four innocent little black girls by "murderous bombers" while they were learning about "God's love in a Sunday-school class" in Sixteenth Street Baptist Church in Birmingham on September 15, 1963. This act, Robinson lamented, displayed the "depths to which the godless will go."[60] The twenty-first bombing in the city in eight years (none of which had been solved) also bloodied and dazed several dozen people and destroyed the church's basement. If one of his children had died in this explosion, Robinson confessed, he would have responded violently. "God bless Dr. Martin Luther King," he declared. "But, I'm afraid he would have lost me as a potential disciple of his credo of nonviolence."[61] In August 1964, after the KKK killed three civil rights activists in Meridian, Mississippi, Robinson cochaired a campaign to build a memorial center there to honor them.

Unlike most Christians, Robinson praised black athletes who censured racism in American and international sports.[62] He strongly supported American track stars Tommie Smith and John Carlos, who, when receiving their medals at the Mexico City Olympics in 1968, raised their fists while the national anthem was played to protest US racism. He called their action "the greatest demonstration of personal conviction and pride" he'd ever seen.[63] In his 1972 autobiography, long before quarterback Colin Kaepernick knelt during the playing of "The Star-Spangled Banner" in 2016 to protest police brutality and racial inequality, Robinson, disillusioned by the nation's persistent denial of black rights, declared, "I cannot stand and sing the anthem. I cannot salute the flag."[64] His memorable statement has been quoted hundreds of times, since many other NFL players have followed Kaepernick's example.

The Power of Words

Robinson's position with Chock Full o' Nuts afforded him ample time to write columns, grant interviews, and traverse the country delivering speeches. He "wielded his pen with remarkable talent and energy."[65]

In 1959 and 1960, Robinson wrote three columns a week for the *New York Post*. From 1962 to 1968, he penned a weekly column for the *New York Amsterdam News*, the nation's oldest black newspaper, titled "Home Plate." His op-eds in both papers were nationally syndicated; his *Post* column was the first one written by an African American for a white-owned and white-operated newspaper. Robinson had assistance in writing both columns; he teamed with playwright William Branch in the *Post* and sportswriter Alfred Duckett in the *Amsterdam News*. However, he "made absolutely sure that his voice was front and center" in his op-eds.[66] "I never hid the fact that Al Duckett ghosted my column," Robinson asserted, but it was a joint effort and "never expressed anything that wasn't sincerely my conviction."[67] Robinson sought "to prod and provoke, inflame and infuriate, and sway and persuade" people on racial violence, busing, social welfare policies, voting rights, and other major civil rights issues. The often frustrated and impatient prophet repeatedly condemned African Americans' second-class citizenship.[68]

While Robinson was playing, various Jewish journalists had exhorted baseball executives to sign more black players. Shirley Povich, for example, wrote a fifteen-part series in the *Washington Post* in 1953 on African American contributions to baseball. Thankful for the support he had received from Jews as a Dodger and appreciative of the strenuous efforts of Jewish people to provide civil rights for all Americans, Robinson strongly supported various Jewish causes after his retirement from baseball. He encouraged black and Jewish civil rights groups to work together and helped the Anti-Defamation League develop a congenial relationship with some black organizations.[69] Rachel explained that her husband "believed that positive relations between blacks and Jews were critical to both."[70] In a 1959 column, Robinson praised a decision by New York Supreme Court justice Henry Epstein prohibiting the Arabian-American Oil Company from discriminating against Jews.[71] In a January 1960 op-ed, he condemned the painting of swastikas on the walls of synagogues, Jewish businesses, and homes as "another symptom of rabid sickness in our society." Because every person "is a member of some vulnerable minority—whether it be by race, religion, national origin, political party, education, occupation, or other differences—none of us is safe once group-hate is unleashed against any other."[72] In the 1960s, Robinson often staunchly defended the Jews against charges of racism after it became unpopular among African Americans to do so.[73]

Although he applauded Robinson's civil rights activism, *Post* editor James Wechsler did not renew his contract after the 1960 election because he was disappointed with the quality of the columns (in part because he thought that Branch's prose clashed with the ex-Dodger's personality) and with Robinson's support of Nixon.[74] Describing his columns in the *Post*, *Time* declared that sometimes "Jackie has been chock full o' zeal" while other times he had been "chock full o' nonsense." On civil rights, his favorite topic, Robinson was willing to cross swords with anyone, including Eisenhower (for allegedly remaining on the sidelines of the battle) and Bing Crosby (for refusing to condemn segregated golf tournaments).[75]

Robinson used his columns in both the *Post* and the *Amsterdam News* to decry racism and discuss how individuals could combat it. Racism, he argued, is a vicious, contagious disease that afflicted the entire nation.[76] He called on black labor leader A. Philip Randolph in 1964 to craft a statement recommitting blacks to an "unyielding, aggressive, intelligent and courageous fight for liberty and justice" for all Americans based on "the Judeo-

Family ca. 1925: Mallie Robinson with her children (left to right) Mack, Jackie, Edgar, Willa Mae, and Frank | HULTON ARCHIVE / GETTY IMAGES

Jackie at football practice, 1939–1940 | AP PHOTO

Jackie doing track at UCLA
ARCHIVE PL / ALAMY STOCK PHOTO

Jackie and Rachel, February 26, 1946
AP PHOTO / ED WIDDIS

Karl Downs (right) and Jackie
KARL E. DOWNS COLLECTION, HTU.2021.005.1 /
COURTESY OF HUSTON-TILLOTSON UNIVERSITY,
AUSTIN, TX, USA

Branch Rickey and Jackie sign a one-year contract for the Brooklyn Dodgers, 1945.

Rachel and children help Jackie blow out a candle on a cupcake as they celebrate Jackie's thirty-fifth birthday January 31, 1954, at home at St. Aldans, NY. Sharon is four, David is twenty months, and Jackie Jr. is seven.

AP PHOTO

Jackie, as the Montreal Royals' shortstop, crosses the plate in Roosevelt Stadium, Jersey City, NJ, after hitting a home run in the third inning against the Jersey City Giants. He's congratulated by Montreal outfielder George Shuba. The umpire is Art Gore. The game was Jackie's pro debut, April 18, 1946.

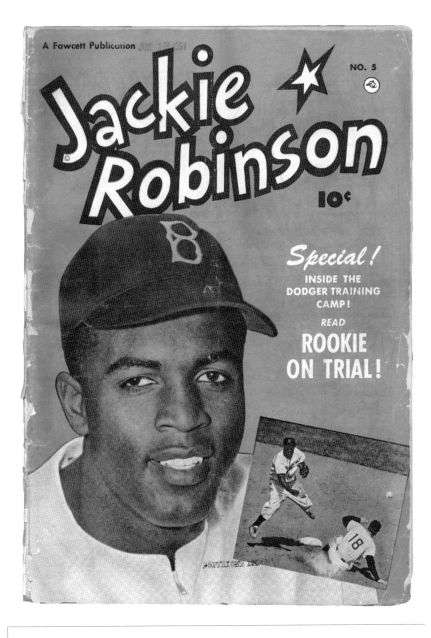

Comic book, ca. 1951 | LIBRARY OF CONGRESS

Left to right: John Jorgensen, Pee Wee Reese, Ed Stanky, and Jackie Robinson, before a game against the Boston Braves at Ebbets Field in Brooklyn, April 15, 1947

Jackie with bat in Dodgers uniform, 1954

Jackie sliding into home | SCIENCE HISTORY IMAGES / ALAMY STOCK PHOTO

Jackie signing autographs for kids | SCIENCE HISTORY IMAGES / ALAMY STOCK PHOTO

The family in front of their Stamford, CT, home, February 8, 1962.
Jackie Jr. is fifteen, David is nine, and Sharon is twelve.

Jackie, Rachel, and David at the March on Washington, August 28, 1963

Jackie confers with Gov. Nelson Rockefeller on his new post as a special assistant to the governor on community affairs in Albany, NY, February 8, 1966.

Jackie speaks to crowd, with Branch Rickey at left, in Wesley Center AME Zion Church for the NAACP fundraiser "1957 Fight for Freedom Fund" in Pittsburgh, January 1957.

Jackie Sr.'s body is carried from the church after his funeral in New York, October 27, 1972. Carrying the casket are Bill Russell and Ralph Branca at left and Don Newcombe and Pee Wee Reese at right. Roy Campanella is at left in wheelchair.

BETTMANN / GETTY IMAGES

Christian principles of our heritage."[77] "Northern-style" discrimination, Robinson contended in 1964, was "as insidious as any open and frank Southern brutalities." The region's "bleeding heart liberals suddenly realized they didn't want job competition" from African Americans; they did not want black children "infiltrating their schools" or black families as neighbors. Robinson denounced "the counterrevolution of white people in America against the aims and aspirations" of blacks as "ugly."[78] He exhorted readers to avoid prejudice, give everyone the same respect and esteem they desired for themselves, and support the NAACP, National Urban League, National Conference of Christians and Jews, and Anti-Defamation League.[79] He also urged African Americans to boycott aluminum, car, and tire companies that sponsored golf tournaments from which black persons were excluded.[80]

Robinson, who loved boxing, defended Muhammad Ali's conversion to Islam in 1964; the heavyweight champion had "as much right to ally himself with the Muslim religion" as other people had to be Christians. Robinson downplayed the widespread fear that large numbers of African Americans would embrace the Nation of Islam; most black people, he insisted, wanted to participate equitably in mainstream American life, not live in a small part of the nation "in splendid isolation," as that movement advocated.[81] Although initially critical, Robinson later defended Ali's refusal to serve in the army. He praised Ali for "standing up for his principle" and his willingness to accept the penalty for his draft evasion. The boxer's actions, however, would likely reduce the influence "his splendid career and prospects" would have made possible.[82]

Robinson frequently deplored racial injustice in South Africa. In 1967 he warned Avery Brundage, president of the International Olympic Committee (IOC), that if the IOC allowed South Africa to participate in the 1968 Summer Olympics in Mexico City, civil rights organizations would urge African Americans to withdraw from competition.[83] "I would rather cut off my right arm," Robinson declared, than give American approval to South African apartheid by having the US team participate in the Olympics.[84]

Meanwhile, Robinson continued to protest racial inequality at home. For example, in July 1967, he wrote to the *New York Times* objecting to its assertion that black Americans "are economically the most prosperous large group of non-whites in the world, enjoying a higher average income than the inhabitants of any nation in Africa, Asia or Latin America." Robinson berated the *Times* for comparing the status of African Americans to that of nonwhites in other nations instead of to white Americans, thereby implying that "we never had it so good."[85]

Rejecting "Go Slow" Gradualism

In numerous letters to Presidents Eisenhower, Kennedy, and Nixon, Robinson prodded them to promote equal rights for all Americans more actively. Black people had "proven beyond a doubt" that they had been more than patient in seeking their rights as American citizens, Robinson declared on *Meet the Press* in 1957. He was tired of hearing "be patient; let's take our time; things will come." African Americans had been waiting for equal rights since the Civil War ended ninety-three years earlier; "if that isn't patience," he said, "I don't know what is."[86] "Barred from the basic rights of a citizen—the vote—and hemmed in by restrictions on opportunities for education, jobs, housing, culture and every other activity," Robinson wrote in a 1959 *New York Post* column, it is "amazing that Negroes have 'behaved themselves' as well as they have."[87]

Robinson's perspective clashed with that of Eisenhower (who had been influenced by evangelist Billy Graham) and other prominent white leaders who advocated a slower, more indirect approach to attaining black civil rights and urged African Americans to stoically endure racial injustice.[88] On September 13, 1957, Robinson chastised Eisenhower for not using his power as president to denounce racial injustice. People around the world would laud him if he put his "office behind the efforts for civil rights."[89] Two weeks later, however, after Eisenhower sent army troops to Little Rock, Arkansas, to ensure that nine black students could attend Central High School, Robinson praised him for doing "the right thing at the crucial time." He added, "May God continue giving you wisdom to lead us in this struggle."[90] Soon disappointed again with Eisenhower's "go slow" approach, Robinson wrote to Vice President Nixon in February 1958 that the nation's progress should be measured not by what advances blacks had made recently but by how far they had to go before they achieved full first-class citizenship.[91]

In May 1958, Robinson attended a summit meeting of black leaders at which Eisenhower spoke. The president asserted that the nation's racial crisis had "no revolutionary cures" and that laws could not "solve problems that have their roots" in human hearts and emotions; he also urged black activists to exercise "patience and forbearance."[92] The next day, a frustrated Robinson told Eisenhower that African Americans "have been the most patient of all people." Seventeen million black Americans could not "wait for the hearts of men to change." The only way they could enjoy the rights they were entitled to was to "pursue aggressively goals which all other Americans achieved over 150 years ago." The nation's chief executive, Robinson complained, was unwittingly crushing "the spirit of freedom in Negroes by constantly urging forbearance" and giving encouragement to pro-segregation leaders such as Arkansas governor Orval Faubus who wanted to strip African Americans of the few freedoms they currently enjoyed.[93] Eisenhower responded to Robinson that individuals, organizations, and government should work to enable all Americans to enjoy "all the privileges of citizenship spelled out in our Constitution." He praised the former baseball star for helping "lead the way towards the goals we seek."[94]

On April 24, 1959, a white mob removed twenty-three-year-old African American Mack Charles Parker from his jail cell in a Mississippi courthouse. Its members shot Parker, who had been charged with raping a white woman, several times and threw his body into the Pearl River. An enraged Robinson blamed Parker's death, which his biographer called the "last classic lynching in America," on "the weak-kneed 'gradualism' of those entrusted with enforcing and protecting civil rights."[95] The next month, after an all-white jury acquitted a white man charged with raping a black woman in front of numerous witnesses in Monroe, North Carolina, an incensed Robinson asked how black Americans could be asked to simply "wait, hope and pray" that people's hearts would change while such horrific acts occurred. If you do not keep someone from choking you, Robinson asserted, you will not "live to save his soul."[96] Robinson accused Eisenhower of refusing to acknowledge that racism still plagued the South and that its bigoted white residents would do all they could to maintain segregation. He exhorted the Eisenhower administration "to be proactive, rather than passive and employ every political and economic weapon at its disposal" to require recalcitrant southern states to comply with federal laws.[97]

In a May 1959 *Post* column, Robinson argued that African Americans had been patiently waiting for ninety-six years "for people's hearts to change." Nevertheless, it would be tragic for blacks or whites to try to solve civil rights problems "by hate, violence and spite, no matter how provoked" they felt.[98] In a June speech, Eisenhower insisted that civil rights would improve as individuals were motivated by moral laws, not compelled by statutory laws, because statutory laws could not change the human heart or eliminate prejudice. Robinson agreed with the president that "laws alone will not change people's personal feelings," but he insisted that blacks were much more concerned about stopping overt, vicious acts than eliminating prejudice. "When a man has his foot on your throat, you can worry later about changing his heart." Eisenhower's approach, Robinson averred, had encouraged bigots to conduct campaigns of terror and intimidation against black Americans. The vast majority of white southerners, he claimed, would obey laws and court decisions if the government protected them from their region's "actively vicious element."[99] Moreover, in speeches at many black churches, Robinson beseeched Eisenhower and other elected officials to combat racial violence and injustice immediately and directly.

Martin Luther King Jr. and the Vietnam War

Of all of America's civil rights leaders, Robinson most respected and had the closest friendship with Martin Luther King Jr. Moved by King's calm response to the bombing of his house in Montgomery, Alabama, on January 30, 1956, Robinson arranged to meet him shortly afterward through their mutual friend Alfred Duckett. The ballplayer was impressed by King's many "remarkable qualities that made him a great leader," including his "Godliness, strength, courage, and patience in the face of overwhelming odds."[100] "If ever a man was placed on this earth by divine force to help solve the doubts and ease the hurts and dispel the fears of mortal man, I believe that man is Dr. King," Robinson asserted.[101] Similarly, King admired Robinson's courageous actions in smashing baseball's color barrier and his willingness not to fight back early in his career.[102] For several years Robinson hosted a summer jazz festival at his home in North Stamford to help fund King's Southern Christian Leadership Conference. In 1962, King asked Robinson to lead a campaign to finance the rebuilding of southern churches destroyed by arsonists. Robinson and King advocated similar tactics to procure black civil rights, and their common Christian faith further strengthened their bond. Their public disagreement about the Vietnam War strained their relationship, but they continued to work together on numerous matters.

King told Robinson in 1960 that he and all Americans were "deeply indebted" to Robinson for his "unswerving devotion to the cause of freedom and justice" and his "willingness at all times to champion the cause of the underdog."[103] Robinson responded, "I respect sincerely your great efforts and hope God gives you strength to continue. You have been a true inspiration."[104] In May 1962, King stated that Robinson's "baseball prowess" and "inflexible demand for equal opportunity for all" had made all African Americans proud.[105] At the 1962 dinner at the Waldorf-Astoria celebrating Robinson's induction into the Hall of Fame, King's assistant read a statement praising the former ballplayer's honesty, courage, and conviction and his denunciation of religious and racial hatred. "Thank God for" Robinson, King declared, who stood his ground and proclaimed, "I have spoken what I believe to be the truth." Robinson had suffered trauma, humiliation, and loneliness as a pilgrim walking on "the high road of Freedom," King argued. "He was a sit-inner before the sit-ins, a freedom rider before the freedom rides," and his accomplishments had created "a rich legacy of confidence and hope" for African Americans.[106] Two years later, King told Robinson, "I don't know what we would have done through these past years without your ardent support." He concluded, "May God continue to enable you to maintain the high level of leadership and integrity which has been yours throughout your career."[107]

Although Robinson's perspective changed in the early 1970s, he strongly supported the Vietnam War during the second half of the 1960s. Influenced by the rabid anticommunism of Branch Rickey and repulsed by the atheism of the Soviet Union, Robinson saw stopping the spread of communism in Southeast Asia as a crucial component of the Cold War. He faulted King for blaming the United States exclusively for the conflict and ignoring the Vietcong's responsibility. In a 1967 television interview, Robinson claimed that the United States had "a moral commitment" to Vietnam and that the Vietcong had slaughtered many women and children without any provocation.[108] In an open letter to King in May 1967, he agreed with the Baptist minister that the United States had been "terribly wrong" in its treatment of blacks and that the Vietnam War is one "we could do without." It was unfair, however, to put all the "blame upon the United States and none upon the Communist forces we are fighting." He objected to King calling the United States "the greatest purveyor of violence on earth." Robinson asked King why he didn't "suggest that the Viet Cong cease, stop, and withdraw also." "I respect you deeply," he concluded. "But I also love this imperfect country."[109] "No matter how much we disagreed," Robinson later wrote, he had faith in King's "sincerity, his capacity to make the hard, unpopular decision, and his willingness to accept the consequences."[110]

Robinson also feared that King's criticism of the war would detract from his civil rights activism and diminish Lyndon Johnson's support for the civil rights movement. Robinson respected King's right as an individual and a Christian to oppose the war, but it was more important for his "voice to cry out in the American wilderness" against racial injustice.[111] Robinson's own son was fighting in Vietnam, and like Jackie Jr., he believed that blacks had a duty "to support the president and our Congress in its decisions on foreign policy."[112] In April 1967, Robinson wrote Johnson that thousands of blacks were fighting in Vietnam because they believed the American position was just and that many African Americans applauded his efforts to achieve an "honorable solution to the war." He concluded, "I hope God gives you the wisdom and strength to come through this crisis at home, and that an end to the war in Viet Nam is achieved very soon."[113] Robinson also praised Johnson's attempts to end the war. "It strikes me that our President has made every effort," Robinson asserted in a May 13 open letter to King in the *Amsterdam News*, "to convert the confrontation from the arena of the battlefield to the atmosphere of the conference table."[114]

Sharon Robinson explained that her father strongly believed that "the United States should honor its commitment" to South Vietnam "and not back down in the face of an aggressive enemy."[115] Jackie also defended the frequently used argument that US military might was needed to deter communist aggression. "I am convinced we must deal from a position of strength," Robinson wrote in an October 1967 *Amsterdam News* column. It is "a good policy in athletics" and "probably the best policy in war." He pointed out that the Vietcong had used a respite from US bombing to refortify their positions instead of to pursue peace, which justified the resumption of bombing. Johnson, Robinson declared, "deserves the support and confidence of the American people" in combating communism.[116] The baseball star also castigated opponents of the war for denigrating black soldiers as "willing dupes of imperialism."[117]

Robinson was devastated by King's incredibly "disturbing and distressing" assassination on April 4, 1968.[118] He hoped that "King's last full measure of devotion to the cause of brotherhood would not prove to have been in vain."[119] Robinson attended King's funeral and, in dealing with King's death, turned again to his faith. "I do not pretend that I have begun to reach the mountaintop which God showed the man who, in my view, was the greatest leader of the Twentieth Century," he declared. "But I have been able to regard his death as perhaps one of those great mysteries with which the Almighty moves—his wonders to perform."[120] A month after King's assassination, Robinson told the Texas Association of Christian Churches that "a sane and saintly man of God" who had provided "calm and benevolent leadership" had been struck down by a "sick man" who was the "product of a sick society." Creating scholarships and awards, endowing foundations, building monuments, and passing civil rights bills were insufficient responses to King's "suffering and his crucifixion." King could be properly honored only if people committed themselves "thoroughly and absolutely" to providing racial justice.[121]

In an *Amsterdam News* column, Robinson reflected upon a deeply moving sermon King preached in 1957 after the bombing of black homes and churches. Where, King asked, was "God in the midst of falling bombs"? His answer was that "God is all-powerful and all good." He "never plans or creates evil, sickness or war or death or other sin. But sometimes God allows evil to exist to change the hearts and minds of men so that he can then exercise his creative, redemptive will."[122] In his column, Robinson suggested that God had permitted whites to destroy black churches and houses to effect racial reconciliation in Montgomery and had allowed King to be murdered to promote racial understanding in the nation. Perhaps positive change would happen after African Americans' anger subsided and they were no longer bent on revenge.[123] Mourning the assassination of Robert Kennedy two months later, Robinson protested that some were trying to stop "dissent and opposition and the call to freedom and justice with bullets." He warned readers that, as Jesus said, "He who lives by the sword will die by the sword." "Let us hope," he added, "that a merciful God will delay the retribution which we deserve."[124]

Roberto Clemente and his Pittsburgh Pirates' teammates voted to not play their first two games in 1968 after MLB commissioner William Eckert permitted teams to decide whether to play games scheduled on April 8 or 9, with King's funeral set for April 9. The Pirates, who had eleven black players (the most of any MLB team), stated, "We are doing this because we white and black players respect what Dr. King has done for mankind." Players on other teams voted to follow the Pirates' example, and all MLB season openers were played the day after King's funeral. Baseball had not postponed any games during World War II and would not do so again until after the September 11, 2001, attacks.[125]

By 1971, Robinson's view about the Vietnam War had shifted. He had rejected the domino theory that the fall of Vietnam would lead to communist domination of all Southeast Asia and had become "bitterly disillusioned" about the United States.[126] In addition, he concluded that the forces the United States was supporting in Vietnam were corrupt. His son's traumatic postwar experiences underscored the problems many American soldiers were suffering.

Robinson and the NAACP

Robinson strongly supported the NAACP from the early 1950s until 1967. As chair of the organization's million-dollar Freedom Fund Drive, a position he assumed in 1956, Robinson spoke in black churches around the nation to recruit volunteers, raise funds, and solicit members. In this role, he worked with Franklin Williams, a "brilliant young lawyer" who later served as US ambassador to Ghana. Together they traversed the country, with Robinson explaining why people should support the NAACP's work and Williams making "the professional money pitch."[127] When he received the NAACP's Spingarn Medal in 1956, Robinson declared that the organization "represents everything a man should stand for"—human dignity, brotherhood, and fair play.[128] The next year, Robinson extolled the NAACP as "the tireless champion of the rights and well-being of the Negroes" and "of all Americans who cherish the principles on which this country was founded."[129] In 1963, Robinson called the NAACP America's greatest organization working to provide "freedom and human dignity for the black man in America."[130] Foreshadowing his break with the organization, however, Robinson complained to its president in 1966 that some of its leaders were more interested in personal gain than "the good of the masses."[131]

Further disillusioned with its growing conservatism, exclusion of younger, more progressive black leaders, and distance from the black masses, Robinson resigned in early 1967 from the NAACP board of directors after serving for five years. He explained in his *Amsterdam News* column that he was "a longtime admirer of the organization" who "has traveled thousands of miles and raised hundreds of thousands of dollars for the organization." He added, "I am terribly disappointed in the NAACP and deeply concerned about its future" because of "the strangling political grip which [its executive director] Roy Wilkins and a clique of the Old Guard" had on it. Wilkins, Robinson charged, was a dictator, insensitive to contemporary trends, and "unresponsive to the needs and aims" of the black community, especially its younger members, who saw the NAACP as archaic.[132]

Rankled by this criticism, Wilkins told Robinson that someday "before you are seventy some down-to-earth wisdom will find a way into your life" and "stop you from believing that 'because I see it this way I have to say it.'" Wilkins added, "If you had played ball with a hot head instead of a cool brain, you would have remained in the minors. You need that cool brain in the weighing of issues in the critical area of civil rights."[133] "I don't intend to remain silent," Robinson responded, "when I see things I believe to be wrong."[134] Robinson continued to agree with the NAACP's stated goals and hoped his censure would help the organization recapture its original mission. "I still have my doubts about the NAACP," Robinson declared in 1972, but "I made a grave error in resigning rather than remaining in the inside to try to fight for reform."[135]

Robinson and Kennedy

As with Eisenhower, Robinson wrote several letters to John F. Kennedy, to condemn and commend him regarding various civil rights matters. Robinson also met with Kennedy to discuss this subject. Influenced by Robinson, King, and the growing protest movement, Kennedy delivered a historic speech in June 1963 that censured inequality on moral grounds and contributed to the passage of the Civil Rights Bill of 1964. Robinson, who had frequently disparaged Kennedy's lack of action on civil rights, applauded the Democrat's changed approach toward African Americans.

Robinson was disappointed by Kennedy's victory in 1960, but he told the president, "I will continue to hope and pray for your aggressive leadership . . . in our struggle for human dignity." He warned Kennedy, as he had Eisenhower, that black patience with slow progress was wearing thin and promised he would criticize the president if he did not make civil rights a priority. "May God give you the strength and the energy," he concluded, "to accomplish your most difficult task"—providing equal rights for all citizens.[136]

Robinson's most blunt critique of Kennedy was his May 5, 1962, open letter in the *Amsterdam News*. He pointed out that Kennedy had displayed great anger, taken a strong stand, and negotiated a rollback of the price of steel after major companies had raised their rates. Robinson urged Kennedy to "think about the high cost of race prejudice," just as he had contemplated the high cost of steel, and "get angry again." If he did that, he could "go down in history" as the chief executive "who won the battle against the bigots in this country who are working harder to destroy it from within than any foreign power is working to destroy it from without." He warned Kennedy that black Americans would not "continue to turn the other cheek" as their children were denied good schools, sufficient food, the right to vote, and the opportunity to live where they wanted.[137] Numerous black leaders praised Robinson's challenge to Kennedy. King told him that his "inflexible demand for equal opportunity for all" made all American blacks proud, while Ralph Abernathy, another prominent activist, declared that Robinson had spoken "like a prophet, a scholar and a great American," with "authority and power."[138]

Robinson criticized Kennedy for refusing to meet with one hundred black ministers in the summer of 1962. The president failed to recognize that no group was "closer to the pulse" of African Americans than pastors. "From the cradle to the grave, the minister remains in intimate contact with his people," Robinson wrote. "He christens or baptizes our babies, counsels, praises and chastises our youth, conducts our marriages, seeks to help prevent divorces and administers the funerals of our loved ones. In crisis, sickness and in triumph, the minister is a power, an influence and a leader."[139] Robinson also castigated Kennedy for not intervening in a civil rights crisis in Albany, Georgia, in August 1962 that led to King's arrest. The nation had sunk to a new low, he protested, "when men are beaten, jailed and intimidated because they turn to God for an answer, because they fall upon their knees to pray."[140]

For the next year, Kennedy's approach to civil rights was faltering and ineffectual, and Robinson continued to denounce vociferously his lack of progress. As protesters were being brutally attacked in Birmingham in May 1963, Robinson criticized the president for keeping few of the civil rights promises he had made in 1960. "The pace at which our country is moving toward total equality for all peoples is miserably slow," Robinson complained. The "atrocities" inflicted on African Americans in the South were "disgusting." Police dogs, high-power hoses, and beatings, he insisted, could not squelch the black revolt against racism. Moreover, the United States was providing a poor example for the newly established African nations. Robinson warned Kennedy that many would seriously doubt the sincerity of his administration unless he faced the nation's racial discrimination as forcefully as he had handled the steel industry and the Cuban missile crisis. Robinson concluded, "The eyes of the world are on America and Americans of both races are looking to you."[141]

Growing social unrest, violent responses to civil rights demonstrators, and criticism from Robinson, King, and other activists prompted Kennedy, in a nationally televised address on June 11, 1963, to pledge to propose a civil rights bill. He declared, "We are confronted primarily with a moral issue. It is as old as the scriptures and is as clear as the American Constitution": whether all Americans would be "afforded equal rights and equal opportunities, whether we are going to treat our fellow Americans as we want to be treated." Congress, Kennedy asserted, must pass legislation to ensure that all citizens were treated equally.[142] An ecstatic Robinson thanked Kennedy in his June 12 *Amsterdam News* column for providing "the inspired leadership that we so desperately needed." Robinson reminded readers that he had often criticized Kennedy's lack of action on civil rights, but he declared that the president's address demonstrated his courage, wisdom, and sincerity. It was "one of the finest declarations ever issued in the cause of human rights."[143] After Kennedy's assassination, Robinson insisted that he had "done more for civil rights than any other president."[144]

Robinson and Nixon

Robinson would have supported Hubert Humphrey had he received the 1960 Democratic nomination for president, and he campaigned for him in 1968. In a speech in May 1968, Robinson declared, "I once believed in Mr. Nixon as ardently and sincerely committed to racial justice."[145] In August, Robinson blasted the Nixon-Agnew ticket as "racist in nature" and claimed that Nixon had "prostituted himself to get the Southern vote."[146] Nevertheless, after Nixon's victory, Robinson frequently wrote to urge him to promote racial justice and black progress. "We are a divided nation searching our souls for answers," he told Nixon on January 22, 1969. These answers could "only come from sincere, dedicated leadership. I pray to God you have the capacity" to help the nation avoid a racial "holocaust."[147] As a member of the Black Economic Council, an organization dedicated to improving economic opportunities for African Americans, Robinson joined White House picketers who were urging the Nixon administration to provide more loans for businesses in the nation's inner cities.[148] Despite Nixon's expression of condolences after Jackie Jr.'s death in June 1971 and his laudatory comments about Robinson's athletic achievements, Robinson continued protesting the president's policies. He acknowledged that some blacks, believing they should not "put all of their eggs in one political basket," thought it might be best to back Nixon in the 1972 election. Agnew's regressive stance on race relations, however, prevented Robinson from supporting the Republican ticket.[149] In March 1972, Robinson criticized Nixon's call for a moratorium on busing, without which, the baseball star argued, African Americans could not obtain equal educational opportunities. Robinson wanted desperately to "love this nation" as he once had, but he had become disillusioned by its continued racist practices.[150]

Robinson and Malcolm X

Robinson's most antagonistic relationship with a black civil rights activist was with Malcolm X. When Robinson shattered baseball's color barrier in

1947, Malcolm Little (his original name) was serving an eight-to-ten-year prison sentence for burglary. The twenty-one-year-old, who called himself Robinson's most "fanatic fan," hoped that the Dodgers' rookie's performance on the diamond would help destroy the degrading stereotypes of black inferiority. Calculating Robinson's batting average after every game helped Little pass the time. He admired the ballplayer's courage, which he believed could inspire other African Americans to combat injustice.[151] By 1963, nine years after his discharge from prison, Malcolm X saw Robinson as a major adversary, not a hero. Until Malcolm X's assassination on February 21, 1965, they would be each other's most vocal critics.

Robinson and Malcolm X both strove to enhance black freedom and equality, but they had very different approaches. Robinson advocated integration and, like King, was willing to work with whites to end racism. Malcolm X, by contrast, argued that African Americans should live separately from whites and rejected white assistance. Living segregated within white society made black Americans second-class citizens, he thought, but living separately in their own section of the United States would enable them to become politically and economically independent. Robinson also criticized Malcolm's opposition to King's nonviolent approach. Robinson did concur with Malcolm X, however, that blacks could justifiably use physical force to defend themselves.[152]

Malcolm X called Robinson a pawn of the white liberal establishment; Robinson shot back that Malcolm's separatist strategy and calls to support the Nation of Islam would lead blacks down the road to destruction. After Muhammad Ali (then Cassius Clay) defeated Sonny Liston in February 1964, Malcolm X stated provocatively that Robinson was "the white man's hero" and Clay "the black man's hero."[153] After Robinson wrote a column criticizing Elijah Muhammad, members of the Nation of Islam allegedly plotted to physically assault the former ballplayer but confused him with boxer Sugar Ray Robinson. After not finding Sugar Ray at home, they abandoned their plan.[154]

Malcolm X lambasted Robinson for campaigning for Nixon in 1960 and for being "very faithful to [his] White Benefactors"—Branch Rickey, William Black, and Nelson Rockefeller. After "Rickey picked you up from obscurity and made you a Big Leaguer," Malcolm X asserted, "you never let Mr. Rickey down; and since Mr. Black has given you a well-paying position with Chock-Full-O-Nuts, you have never let Mr. Black down . . . and now with Mr. Rockefeller promising to make you the Boxing Commissioner of New York State, we know that you can't afford to let Ole Rocky down." Malcolm X also claimed that Robinson did not appreciate the support the black community had given him and warned that if he ever militantly advocated for "our oppressed people," his white friends would put a bullet or dagger into his back. Robinson was so gullible that he would "die thinking they are still" his white friends, and "that the dagger" in his back "is only an accident!" If, however, "whites were to murder me for the religious philosophy that I represent and stand for," Malcolm X insisted, "I would die KNOWING that it was at the hands of OPEN ENEMIES OF TRUTH AND JUSTICE!"[155]

If he was so unappreciative of the black community, Robinson asked, then why did NAACP branches around the nation invite him to speak, why had the NAACP given him its highest award, and why did King constantly invite him to participate in the southern fight for freedom? Robinson further protested that Malcolm's "militancy is mainly expressed in Harlem where it is safe." He rejected Malcolm's "racist views," hatred of white people, and call for creating a separate black state where Elijah Muhammad, head of the Nation of Islam, could be the ruler and Malcolm X his successor. The ex-Dodger insisted that he was willing to work with "decent Americans of either race who believe in justice for all." He thanked God for civil rights activists such as King, Ralph Bunche, Roy Wilkins, and A. Philip Randolph.[156]

Robinson accused Malcolm X and Harlem congressman Adam Clayton Powell Jr. of talking "one hell of a civil rights fight" but doing "very little to back up their statements." Robinson had earlier considered Powell a hero because of his hard-hitting, courageous championing of the black cause, and he deeply respected Malcolm X's intelligence and eloquence. Both men, however, were misleading blacks and taking positions to obtain "sensational headlines." Robinson was astounded by their attack on "one of the world's most distinguished and honorable citizens," United Nations under secretary-general Ralph Bunche, who had served "with great skill and integrity."[157] Malcolm X accused Bunche of failing to condemn racism to keep his job.[158] Robinson countered that Bunche had generally followed a long-standing diplomatic practice of not commenting on the United States' racial policies and practices, but he had occasionally deplored US racial discrimination. Powell, by contrast, typically made grandstanding, publicity-seeking, outlandish promises that he failed to keep, while Malcolm X ignored the fact that whites had helped make the Nation of Islam popular among black people by putting its leaders on television. Malcolm X talked "the language of the segregationists—a language which the Negro people scorn." Robinson wished that Powell and Malcolm X had one-twentieth of the "integrity and leadership" of Bunche, whose record made a mockery of their "unjust and unfounded criticism."[159]

Shortly after Malcolm's pilgrimage to Mecca that led him to leave the Nation of Islam, Robinson wrote in the *Chicago Defender* on July 18, 1964, "If Malcolm were sincere and honest in his new visions, he would reflect on how harshly and unjustly he has belittled and sought to discredit our national responsible leaders who have been working in the struggle for so long."[160] After Malcolm X was assassinated, Robinson lamented not only that his murderers had "stilled his articulate voice," but also that by making him a martyr they had increased his influence and fueled a senseless, brutal war in which blacks fought each other.[161] In his 1972 autobiography, however, Robinson called Malcolm's assassination a "tragedy of the first order" and praised him for admitting in his posthumously published *Autobiography of Malcolm X* that his separatist approach had been "mistaken and misguided."[162]

The black press avidly followed this debate between two prominent African Americans, whereas white media largely ignored it. Their dispute further isolated Robinson as he became "more uncertain about where he was going, what he was doing, and how and where he fit in" to the civil rights movement.[163]

Robinson was also frequently attacked by other African Americans who despised whites, did not want their help to achieve civil rights, and preferred to live separately from them. In the early 1960s, Robinson began to receive hate mail from fellow blacks. For example, a July 18, 1962, letter signed by "The 'Hate White' Movement" declared, "Uncle Toms do not belong in our ranks. . . . You are a traitor to . . . the cause that compels the Black Man to destroy the white races to make this world a better place to live. . . . To us a good white man is a dead white man."[164] Robinson rejected pleas from black activists to refuse to participate in civil rights organizations they did not control, such as the NAACP, which had many Jewish leaders. Robinson also repudiated the idea that blacks should refrain from criticizing each other to maintain their unity. He refused to "blindly endorse a man simply because he is black."[165] "I have enough moral stamina," Robinson insisted, "to always speak for myself, regardless of who likes or doesn't like what I say."[166] Despite threats to his life, he promised in 1967 to continue to write and say what he believed. "I don't seek to be anyone's martyr or hero, but telling it like I think it is—that's the only way I know how to be me."[167]

Robinson and Black Power

Robinson castigated the Black Power Movement and the Black Panthers for many of the same reasons he criticized Malcolm X. The slogan "black power" became popular in connection with a June 1966 march organized by James Meredith to mobilize African Americans to vote in Mississippi. Its proponents stressed black unity and self-determination. Created by Bobby Seale and Huey Newton in October 1966 in Oakland, California, the Black Panthers censured capitalism and blended black nationalism with Marxist doctrines. Like King, Robinson applauded black power and the Black Panthers for emphasizing racial pride and agreed with much of their critique of American society, but he objected to their inflammatory rhetoric, endorsement of violence, hatred of whites, and calls for racial separation.[168] He saw the rising popularity of black power as an ominous development.

"It is both frustrating and frightening to see the hordes of Negro people, so many of them the restless young, exploding into the most sickening kind of violence," Robinson declared.[169] He denounced Black Panther leader H. Rap Brown as "a sensationalist, dangerous, irresponsible agitator" who ignited fires and then abandoned those "he agitated to face the flames" alone.[170] In contrast, although he often criticized Powell and would actively support the congressman's opponent in the 1970 Democratic primary, in a 1966 column Robinson praised Powell's understanding of black power as "*first and foremost*, Godly power," as "our sincere faith and trust in God." "If black power means the intelligent and concerted use of economic and political strength as leverage" to advance black rights, Robinson avowed, "I am for it," but if it meant "black supremacy" and loathing whites, even ones who displayed "understanding and good will and love for justice," he would staunchly oppose it. Black power, rightly defined as using "our ballot and our dollars wisely," coupled with personal responsibility and black initiative and productivity, would enable African Americans to advance.[171] Rejecting the separatist approach of Malcolm X and black power proponents, Robinson insisted, "Total integration is the only cure for the disease of the hatred" afflicting America.[172]

Conclusion

Although Robinson repudiated the more radical solutions for ending American racism offered by Malcolm X, the Black Panthers, and others, his criticism of conditions in the United States became increasingly caustic during the final five years of his life. Dismayed by the numerous inner-city disturbances during the summer of 1967, he argued, "Riots begin with the hopelessness which lives in the hearts of people who, from childhood, expect to live in a rundown house, to be raised by one parent, to be denied proper recreation, to attend an inferior school, to experience police brutality, [and] to be turned down when seeking a decent job."[173] That fall, in a sermon in New Rochelle, New York, Robinson declared, "The good Lord has showered blessings upon me and this country and its people, black and white, have been good to me." But no matter how much wealth and privileges or how many powerful friends he had, he would not be satisfied until the poorest African American had everything he needed to have an "equal opportunity with his white brother. He should not seek more. He cannot settle for less."[174] In his 1972 autobiography, Robinson expressed similar sentiments: "I cannot possibly believe that I have it made while so many of my Black brothers and sisters are hungry, inadequately housed, insufficiently clothed, denied their dignity, live in slums or barely exist on welfare." Robinson could not "rejoice in the good things" he had achieved "while the humblest of my brothers is down in a deep hole hollering for help and not being heard. That is why I have devoted and dedicated my life to service." He concluded, "until hunger is not only immoral but illegal; until hatred is recognized as a disease, a scourge, and epidemic, and is treated as such; until racism and sexism and narcotics are conquered and until every man can vote and any man can be elected if he qualifies—until that day," neither he nor any "one else can say he has made it."[175]

After King's death, the civil rights advocate Robinson most admired was Jesse Jackson. The ex-ballplayer was very impressed with Jackson personally and with his Operation Breadbasket in Chicago, which worked to expand economic opportunities for blacks. Jackson, Robinson argued, supplied "the most viable leadership for blacks and oppressed minorities in America."[176] This "young, brave Black Moses" could "take us some giant steps along the way to the Promised Land of which Dr. King spoke."[177] Robinson served on Operation Breadbasket's board of directors and praised the organization for enhancing the "dignity and self-respect" of African Americans.[178] In 1971, Jackson left Operation Breadbasket to establish PUSH (People United to Save Humanity) to pursue similar goals, and Robinson agreed to serve as its first vice president. The ex-Dodger made numerous trips to Chicago to support PUSH's efforts to increase job security for African Americans, organize black residents earning low wages, and aid black-owned businesses. In response to its lobbying, Coca-Cola, 7 Up, Burger King, and several other corporations agreed to hire more African Americans, do more business with minority companies, and donate more money to black colleges and civic organizations.[179]

From 1956 to 1960, Jackie Robinson arguably was the nation's most prominent civil rights advocate, but his support for Nixon damaged his reputation. That, coupled with the social tumult and increasing radicalism of other black leaders during the 1960s, David Falkner contends, made Robinson seem increasingly like "an old timer" and "a cautious conservative," even "an Uncle Tom," who was "out of step with the times."[180] Robinson's influence in the civil rights movement, however, remained substantial until his death in 1972. Robinson had many critics and broke with the NAACP in 1967. But through working with that organization for a decade; partnering with King, Jackson, and other prominent black leaders; helping lead marches; participating in demonstrations; writing hundreds of opinion pieces; giving scores of speeches; corresponding with US presidents; and encouraging and advising other activists, he played a significant role in the civil rights movement for sixteen years after retiring from baseball.

Many more people cheered for Jackie Robinson the athlete and Hall of Famer than for Jackie Robinson the social activist. Many blacks and whites alike, though often from different vantage points, urged Robinson to stop discussing the problems of racial minorities, the poor, and homeless "and just smile and accept his trophies."[181] His disposition, faith, and life experiences, however, did not allow him to do that. Robinson's tireless, courageous advocacy and substantial impact justify remembering him not only as the man who integrated MLB but as one of the nation's greatest civil rights activists.

7

Religion, Politics, and Business:
The Pulpit, the Ballot, and the Buck

1956–1972

After retiring from baseball, Jackie Robinson engaged in many religious, business, and political activities, most of them related to his civil rights activism. During the last sixteen years of his life, he was involved with numerous religious organizations and participated in various endeavors designed primarily to promote social justice. From 1956 to 1964, he served as vice president and director of personnel at Chock Full o' Nuts, a national chain of coffee shops; he was the first black vice president of a major American company and one of the nation's foremost black corporate executives. In 1964, Robinson helped establish Freedom National Bank in Harlem; in 1970, he founded the Jackie Robinson Construction Company to build affordable housing.

Robinson frequently lobbied politicians to pass antidiscrimination legislation and change governmental, business, and social policies and practices that contributed to racism and poverty. At the same time, his understanding of Scripture and life experiences led him to emphasize personal responsibility, and he feared the unintended negative consequences of extensive government welfare programs. These convictions contributed to his support of Republicans Richard Nixon in the 1960 presidential election and Nelson Rockefeller throughout the 1960s.

Robinson often stressed that God suffered with the oppressed, victims of racial prejudice, the vulnerable, and captives. He spent much of his post-baseball years fighting to improve the welfare of these groups. Robinson's last years were plagued by tragedy and illness. His son Jackie Jr. struggled with drugs, fought in Vietnam, and died in a car accident at age twenty-four. Robinson suffered from diabetes and other health problems for many years before dying of a heart attack in 1972 at age fifty-three. He was posthumously awarded the Presidential Medal of Freedom in 1984 and the Congressional Gold Medal in 2005 in recognition of his achievements in sports, business, civil rights, and public service.

Religious Activism

For most of his life, Robinson was affiliated with Christian congregations— Scott Methodist Church in Pasadena, Nazarene Congregational Church in Brooklyn, and North Stamford Congregational Church (NSCC)—but he rarely attended church services regularly. His travel schedule as a baseball player and civil rights advocate made church attendance difficult for much of his adult life. Sharon Robinson asserts that although her "father was raised in a Christian home and believed in the power of prayer," his church attendance was "an occasional activity rather than a regular source of comfort."[1] Why Robinson did not go to church consistently after his retirement is a mystery, especially given the popularity of church attendance in America during that time.

After they moved to North Stamford in 1955, the Robinsons joined the Congregational church at the end of the block on which they lived, and it became the center of both their religious and their community activities. They were the only black family in the congregation, which affiliated with the United Church of Christ (UCC) in 1961. Rachel explained that she and Jackie sought to model their faith for their children because "observation and practice, not didactic discussion," was "the best teacher." She added that they became active in the church to help their children and "hoped the lessons they learned" there would reinforce their parents' "spiritual and ethical teachings."[2] Like the Nazarene Congregational Church in Brooklyn, NSCC promoted a variety of social causes, and its mostly affluent members included a stockbroker, a department store owner, a vice president at Pitney-Bowes, and the president of a bottling company. Considering that its minister, E. King Hempel, who served from 1962 to 1967, had previously pastored Unitarian and Universalist congregations, NSCC's members were probably liberal in their theology. Jackie presumably felt comfortable in the church because of its commitment to social reform and because many of its members were businessmen like him.

Robinson's religious activism focused primarily on the social-transformation implications of Christianity, with little reference to the personal spiritual transformation emphasized by evangelical Protestants, many black Protestants, and some mainline Protestants. Robinson contended that the church had a pivotal role to play in the battle to procure black rights, and he frequently praised the work of African American ministers. If Christians acted as if they all belonged to God's family, Robinson argued, the church could be the nation's "most powerful force" for racial uplift.[3] In a 1963 *Saturday Evening Post* article, Robinson rejoiced that the nation's leading denominations were issuing statements, raising funds, and executing policies "to expose the hypocrisy of acknowledging the fatherhood of God on Sunday" and denying the brotherhood of humanity throughout the week.[4] In accepting the UCC's Churchmanship Award that year, Robinson asserted similarly that Christians must practice their faith every day.

Robinson often spoke in churches, sometimes preaching the Sunday morning or evening sermon, and to Christian organizations.[5] He frequently exhorted Christians to work more vigorously to remedy social ills, especially racial discrimination. For example, in a May 3, 1968, speech to the Texas Association of Christian Churches, Robinson insisted that only Christian congregations could clean up the nation's "terrible mess" of drug use, crime, and riots and assist war veterans who had returned from Vietnam physically, mentally, or psychologically impaired. "Sunday-go-to-meeting Christians," "Monday morning halfback Christians," "just-let-John-do-it Christians," or "I-don't-want-to-get-involved Christians" could not achieve these objectives. Only "dedicated Christians," he avowed, could solve these problems. He urged Christians to create a nation where presidents would not hesitate to tell the truth out of fear that doing so would cause "the stock market of public opinion" to crash.[6]

In the 1960s, Robinson enjoyed friendships with many "fine clergymen." He especially admired Dr. Gardner Taylor, pastor of the Concord Baptist Church in Brooklyn. Called the "dean of the nation's black preachers," Taylor served Concord from 1948 to 1990. When he arrived, the church had eight thousand members, making it the nation's second-largest

Baptist congregation. In 1961 Taylor and Martin Luther King founded the Progressive National Baptist Convention, which strongly supported King's civil rights activism.[7] Robinson greatly respected King and other ministers, black and white, who had "lived out the meaning of Christianity in the South" while "facing criticism, insults, and personal danger."[8]

Enraged by racist attacks on churches, Robinson led a fund-raising drive to rebuild two black churches in Albany, Georgia, that were razed in 1962 because their members had helped register black voters. Robinson worked for almost two years to obtain the money to rebuild these two churches and a third in Lee County, Georgia. He solicited sizable donations from New York governor Nelson Rockefeller and William Black, his boss at Chock Full o' Nuts. Rockefeller told Robinson, "As a Baptist layman" who wanted to ensure that all American had "the right to worship . . . I count it a high privilege" to contribute to the fund.[9]

In giving Robinson the Churchmanship Award in 1963, the UCC praised his work to promote social justice and his "courage in the face of racial discrimination."[10] In July 1963, the UCC adopted the strongest civil rights resolution of any US denomination, imploring Christians to reject "patience, moderation, and gradualism" and fight vigorously to provide equal justice in employment, housing, education, voting, and the judicial system.[11] In an *Amsterdam News* column that month, Robinson extolled the UCC for staunchly supporting racial justice and endorsing interracial marriage. He lauded ministers, priests, and rabbis who had heroically promoted civil rights, but he added that many activists were disappointed that "denominations and conferences acted either timidly or not at all on the question of civil rights." Robinson urged other communions and parachurch organizations to recognize that the United States "has too long stopped payment on the blank check" of "justice and equality which is the rightful legacy of every American."[12]

While commending churches that opposed racial discrimination, Robinson reminded Christians that much work remained. Speaking at a UCC general synod meeting in 1963, Robinson told of an African American boy whose family moved into a white community that was hostile toward black persons. When the boy tried to go to Sunday school at a church across the street from his house, an usher prohibited him, declaring "this church is for white people" only. Frustrated, the boy sat on the church step and began to weep. "Do you know what God did?" Robinson asked. "He sat right down at the little boy's side and started to cry, too," because God had been trying to get into that church for many years. For decades, he added, echoing a point that King frequently made, "it has been a national shame that 11 a.m. was the most segregated hour in America." Thankfully, however, the consciences of many denominational leaders and clergy had "been stirred." Robinson hoped that other denominations would join the UCC in denouncing racial prejudice in all sectors of society.[13] Many Christians, however, substituted "the doctrine of 'patience' and 'education'" for "forthright action to implement all" God's laws "regarding the brotherhood of humans and the fatherhood of the Maker."[14]

From 1964 to 1966, Robinson served as president of United Church Men (UCM), a nationwide organization of about ten million Protestant and Orthodox laymen. The National Council of Churches established UCM in 1950 to combine the resources of the men's agencies of twenty constituent denominations. UCM had supported sit-ins, the 1963 March on Washington, and other civil rights demonstrations, and as president, Robinson pushed it to combat racial discrimination even more vigorously. UCM denounced segregation as a violation of the Bible's teaching on love and supported legislation to end it.[15] In 1965 Robinson told Branch Rickey that his work as UCM president was quite time consuming. Robinson received many invitations to speak, some of which he accepted, but we have no record of what else his work as president entailed.[16]

Political Activism

During the last sixteen years of his life, Robinson participated actively in politics. He wrote numerous opinion pieces on political issues; sent dozens of letters to presidents, senators, governors, and other elected and appointed officials; campaigned for various candidates; and lobbied for specific policies and bills. His support for Republicans, especially Richard Nixon in 1960, and his close relationship with New York governor Nelson Rockefeller damaged his reputation and diminished his social capital among some African Americans.

Although Robinson considered other factors important, especially character and commitment to capitalism, a politician's position on civil rights and track record in promoting black advancement served as his primary litmus test for determining whom to back. In elections, he usually favored the candidate who pledged to provide the most assistance to African Americans in their battle for equality.[17] In a 1963 open letter to Nixon, Robinson asserted, "I am neither a Republican nor a Democrat. I vote for people who I believe in, regardless of their party affiliations."[18]

Despite such statements, Robinson generally supported the Republican Party, and he did so at an inopportune time. In nominating Nixon in 1960 and 1968 and Arizona senator Barry Goldwater in 1964, the party adopted reactionary and sometimes racist policies. The Democratic Party, because of the statements of John F. Kennedy, Hubert Humphrey, and Lyndon B. Johnson, the passage of civil rights acts in 1964 and 1965, and the implementation of Johnson's Great Society program, came to be widely seen as the party of progressivism and racial progress. Furthermore, by campaigning for liberal Democrats in the 1964 and 1968 presidential elections, Robinson impaired his standing in the GOP, becoming perceived as "a loose cannon, a force the party could not count on, and perhaps even a showboat." Although his staunch independence often made him seem "noble in his loyalty to principle," it led some to consider him "self-righteous and even undependable."[19]

Several factors caused Robinson to favor the Republican Party. He was influenced by Branch Rickey's staunch commitment to the party, the Republican emphasis on individual initiative and free enterprise, the party's long association with Abraham Lincoln and emancipation, and his belief that blacks should not put all their political resources in one bin. Robinson liked the GOP's "toughness on communism" and support of business. Its moral image, he believed, had not been sullied, as the Democrats had, by southern bigotry or the sordid corruption of some urban political machines.[20] Moreover, the New York politicians who most strongly supported black civil rights in the late 1950s and 1960s were Republicans Nelson Rockefeller, Jacob Javits, and John Lindsay.

Robinson repeatedly claimed that the Democratic Party was taking blacks for granted while some Republicans, especially Rockefeller, were "genuinely interested in helping them."[21] He encouraged blacks to vote for Republicans because doing so gave them political leverage and avoided allying themselves with southern redneck racists.[22] "It would make everything I worked for meaningless if baseball is integrated but political parties were segregated," Robinson asserted.[23] The sooner the United States developed "a strong two party system," Robinson maintained, "the sooner we get our Rights."[24] He had "no maudlin love for the Republican Party," Robinson declared in a 1965 newspaper column, but maintaining a two-party system was critical to ensure that minorities had "the bargaining power necessary" to obtain "the best of everything in our society."[25]

Like Robinson, many of New York City's prominent black ministers were moderate or liberal Republicans during the first half of the 1960s. While promoting social Christianity, the NAACP, and the Urban League, and supporting government efforts to aid the disadvantaged, many clergy, most notably Sandy F. Ray, the pastor of Brooklyn's large Cornerstone Baptist Church, campaigned for Nelson Rockefeller and other Republicans.[26] Wyatt Tee Walker, a Southern Christian Leadership Council board member before becoming pastor of Canaan Baptist Church in Harlem, served as the governor's urban affairs liaison.

Robinson and Nelson Rockefeller

Of all the nation's Republican politicians, Robinson was most attracted to Nelson Rockefeller, who served as New York's governor from 1959 to 1973. Robinson admired him personally and liked many of his policies. Of all the politicians he had met, Robinson told the governor in 1961, Rockefeller had "the greatest potential" to make "America the country we all want it to be."[27] Robinson actively supported three of Rockefeller's gubernatorial campaigns as well as his bids to gain the Republican nomination for president in 1964 and 1968. Robinson argued that Rockefeller inspired minorities more than any other Republican.[28]

Despite his great respect for Rockefeller, Robinson did not hesitate to criticize him at times. He urged the governor in February 1965 to appoint an African American to "an important position who will tell you what you should hear, not what you want to hear."[29] Robinson warned Rockefeller in January 1966 that unless he appointed more African Americans, black journalists could justifiably criticize Robinson for being too favorable toward the governor in his *Amsterdam News* columns.[30] Shortly thereafter, Rockefeller named Robinson as a special assistant for community affairs, and the ex–baseball player later praised the governor's "unprecedented appointments of blacks to high positions."[31] Robinson was also impressed that Rockefeller listened to the reproaches and recommendations of African Americans and implemented many of their suggestions.

Robinson enthusiastically supported Rockefeller's reelection campaign in 1966. In an August 1966 *Amsterdam News* column, for example, the baseball star urged African Americans to vote for the governor because he had personally helped fund the civil rights movement and had promoted legislation to provide education, medical insurance, and better housing for the poor. Robinson also energetically campaigned for Rockefeller in predominantly black communities and helped arrange a public meeting for the governor with residents of St. Albans, a neighborhood in Queens, where he had lived while playing for the Dodgers. Robinson claimed in mid-August that he had "made great gains" in convincing African Americans to vote for Rockefeller.[32]

After Rockefeller's reelection, Robinson urged him to "make America the place we dream of," so that New Yorkers would "*remember* Gov. Rockefeller as the greatest Gov. the state has ever had." Robinson insisted that Rockefeller would prove that he was "a great man."[33] When racial tensions flared in Buffalo during the long, hot summer of 1967, Rockefeller sent the baseball trailblazer, as the governor's special assistant for urban affairs, to help quell the city's riots. Robinson greatly enjoyed his work in this position. In January 1968, he told Rockefeller, "1967 has been one of the most rewarding years of my life because of your understanding, commitment and direction."[34] That same month, Robinson insisted in the *Amsterdam News* that he had worked for Rockefeller because he deeply believed in him and "his dedication to justice for all people."[35]

Although Robinson sometimes called himself a Rockefeller Republican and extolled the governor as "a man of great integrity and ability," he became disillusioned with the governor toward the end of his life.[36] In 1971, Robinson, while still professing great admiration for Rockefeller, publicly criticized his plan to make welfare benefits more difficult to receive.[37] Troubled by this issue, Rockefeller's support of Nixon's proposed one-year moratorium on busing students to integrate schools, and some of his other policies, Robinson complained in May 1972 that "the one man in public life" in whom he "had complete faith" was no longer measuring "up to his previous highly laudable" stances. He protested that "getting ahead politically" seemed to be more important to the governor "than what is right." A "good friend," Robinson lamented, "has let me down."[38]

Presidential Elections: 1960, 1964, 1968

Had Hubert Humphrey won the Democratic nomination in 1960, Robinson would have supported his candidacy. Robinson was impressed by Humphrey's stance on civil rights as mayor of Minneapolis and as US senator.[39] During the 1960 Democratic primaries, Robinson stumped in Wisconsin for Humphrey, whom he considered one of the Senate's "ablest" members, and strongly opposed Kennedy, the "Fair-haired boy of the Southern segregationists."[40]

After Kennedy captured the nomination, Robinson was forced to choose between him and Nixon. Viewing Robinson's support as essential to winning black voters, both candidates courted him. Robinson's political philosophy; his affinity for Republican policies on business, foreign relations, and social issues; his previous relationship with Nixon; an unpleasant meeting with Kennedy in June 1960; the Democrats' acceptance of the racist Dixiecrats; and the candidates' apparent positions on civil rights led him to support the vice president rather than the senator, a decision he later regretted. Robinson was upset that during their meeting, Kennedy did not look him in the eyes, which to him was a clear indication of insincerity and dishonesty. He was also alarmed by Kennedy's frank admission that he knew few African Americans and lacked an understanding of black people and their problems.[41]

Robinson believed that Nixon would work to advance black civil rights. The vice president had supported a 1957 civil rights bill and had visited Africa. After Nixon stated in 1957, "We shall never be satisfied" until "equal opportunity becomes a reality for all Americans," Robinson promised his "steadfast cooperation" to help achieve this objective.[42] As vice president, Nixon, Robinson averred, "had a fairly good track record in civil rights" and had pledged to move faster to advance racial equality than had Eisenhower.[43] He had also selected racially progressive Massachusetts senator Henry Cabot Lodge Jr. as his running mate. In addition, Robinson and Nixon had a friendly relationship, based in part on their shared love of sports. After meeting with Nixon in May 1960, Robinson declared that the

Republican seemed committed to using "the influence and prestige of the presidency to advance equal rights and human dignity."[44]

In his *New York Post* columns, Robinson attacked Kennedy's position on civil rights and his willingness to meet in June 1959 with Alabama's racist governor, John Patterson. This prompted Kennedy to meet with Robinson in late June 1960 to discuss his candidacy. Their conversation went poorly. Robinson was upset that the Democrat knew few black Americans personally. Robinson later explained that Kennedy "knew little or nothing about black problems and sensibilities" and had "a bleak record on civil rights."[45] Two days after their meeting, Kennedy lauded Robinson's civil rights efforts, professed his desire to end discrimination, and asserted he did not agree with Patterson's segregationist position.[46] Robinson replied that he wanted more evidence to verify Kennedy's "sincerity in these matters," but he was willing to wait and see what developed at the convention and what Kennedy did if nominated.[47] After Kennedy's nomination, Robinson complained in a July 15 column that the senator had voted to send the 1957 civil rights bill back to committee to try to kill it, had met with Patterson, and had not actively promoted black civil rights. Although Democrats had adopted the "strongest civil rights plank in history," Robinson declared, they had added Lyndon Johnson to the ticket to appease southern bigots. Kennedy, Robinson protested, "is willing to ruthlessly gamble with the rights—and the very lives—of millions of Southern Negro Americans to satisfy his own personal ambition to be President."[48]

Robinson took leave from writing for the *New York Post* in September to campaign for Nixon. He began to lose confidence in the vice president, however, when Nixon refused to help Martin Luther King Jr. gain release from a Georgia prison in October or to answer questions about whether his cabinet would include African Americans.[49] Nixon declined to even call King, arguing that doing so would be "grandstanding," whereas Kennedy phoned King's wife and Robert Kennedy enlisted a local judge to help obtain his release.

Kennedy's role in this incident convinced many African Americans to vote for the Democratic candidate, but Robinson clung to the hope that Nixon would honor his promises to help black citizens. Robinson gave many speeches on Nixon's behalf, often in black churches and sometimes alongside Nelson Rockefeller. Rockefeller's frequent argument that the United States was founded on the principle of "the brotherhood of man under the fatherhood of God," one of Robinson's favorite themes, undoubtedly contributed to his growing admiration for and friendship with the New York governor.[50] As the campaign went on, Kennedy began to look more attractive, but Robinson continued to argue that "blacks must be represented in both parties."[51] During the campaign, most black leaders also endorsed Nixon, while King remained neutral.[52]

The 1964 presidential election presented Robinson with another unwelcome choice. He had campaigned vigorously to help Rockefeller obtain the Republican nomination and was deeply disappointed when it went instead to Goldwater. "A Barry Goldwater victory would insure that the G.O.P. would become completely the white man's party," Robinson warned in the *Saturday Evening Post* in early 1964. Robinson was appalled when right-wing delegates derided Rockefeller at the Republican National Convention in San Francisco. Their criticism conveyed "a revulsion for all he stood for," Robinson complained, "including his enlightened attitude toward Black people." After the convention, he wrote, "I had a better understanding of how it must have felt to be a Jew in Hitler's Germany."[53] Robinson supported the National Negro Republican Assembly, created in 1964 to protest Goldwater's nomination and to promote black rights and concerns within the Republican Party.

Robinson had earlier decried Lyndon Johnson as a segregationist, but in mid-1964 he praised the Texan's stance on civil rights. The baseball star joined Republicans for Johnson and spoke frequently to white, black, and mixed audiences about why Goldwater must be defeated.[54] He argued that Johnson was "saying and doing bold and forthright things in civil rights," while the Arizona senator sought to win the presidency "by capitalizing on white resentment to Negro demands for justice."[55] Robinson denounced Goldwater as "a bigot, an advocate of white supremacy and more dangerous" than George Wallace, Alabama's segregationist governor.[56]

Robinson was disheartened that the Republican Party chose Nixon over Rockefeller as its presidential nominee in 1968. In a September 1967 *Amsterdam News* column, Robinson had warned that if the GOP nominated Nixon or Ronald Reagan, "it would be telling the black man it cares nothing about him or his concerns."[57] During the primaries, he told Rockefeller, "Each man is placed upon this earth with a destiny to fulfill." He contended that Rockefeller was one of the few Americans who by his integrity, vigor, temperament, political philosophy, and persuasive power could help the Republican Party, the nation, and the world meet "the awesome challenges of our time."[58] When Republicans nominated Nixon instead of Rockefeller, Robinson called it a sign "of the sick and troubled times." The GOP had stupidly not taken advantage of "Rockefeller's quality and courage to carry their standard. They deserved the man they got—a double-talker, a two-time loser, an adjustable man with a convertible conscience."[59]

Robinson backed Humphrey in 1968 primarily because of his position on civil rights and worked enthusiastically for his election. He was "terribly disappointed" by Nixon's victory in November 1968 but prayed that his administration would be successful.[60] Shortly after the election, Humphrey thanked Robinson for his support, confidence, and trust, declaring, "You were a tower of strength for me and the causes that we worked for."[61]

Some pundits criticized Robinson's political electioneering. Black journalist A. S. "Doc" Young, for example, insisted that politicians courted and welcomed Robinson's political support because they believed that African Americans "who idolized him as a player would become properly starry-eyed at the polls." The athlete, who had benefited personally from "racial militant action," sold out his own people and beggared "his hard-earned popularity" by shilling for politicians "whom he merely knows casually, whose real beliefs, opinions and practices he knows not."[62] *National Review* founder William Buckley accused Robinson of being a "pompous moralizer" and advocating reverse racism.[63] Robinson's support of Nixon, Rockefeller, Lindsay, and other Republicans has prompted many scholars to label him naïve, credulous, and misguided.[64] Others counter that Robinson was "as tough-minded and combative in the political arena as he was running base paths in National League ballparks" and "was far more open-minded" and shrewder than the ideologues who criticized him "from both ends of the political spectrum." Before 1964, numerous African American leaders agreed with Robinson that as long as it included so many white segregationists, the Democratic Party would not promote civil rights.[65]

For many years, the Republican Party sought to capitalize on Robinson's support of some of its candidates. Its website long stated, "Not only was he a great athlete, [but] Jackie Robinson was a great Republican." After many complaints, Robinson's photograph and this statement were finally removed from the website in 2012.[66]

Economics and Business

Robinson's business life is less well remembered than his athletic exploits and his civil rights activism, but from 1956 until his death, he participated in numerous business endeavors to give his life meaning, pay his bills, and improve the lives of black Americans. Robinson concluded that during his postbaseball years the best way to aid African Americans was to concentrate on political empowerment and economic development—"the ballot and the buck."[67] Robinson's favorable view of free enterprise and his belief in the power of economic development to uplift African Americans was similar to that of many white Christians, especially evangelicals, who from 1940 on touted the benefits of capitalism and used funds supplied by business tycoons and business methods to advance their ministries.[68] Robinson insisted that blacks must create their own businesses and manage their own financial institutions; they must be producers, not merely consumers. Robinson used his name, prestige, and time to promote several business enterprises and helped pave the way for other athletes and entertainers of color to engage in similar activities. Black business success, he argued, could bolster civil rights activism.[69] He insisted in *I Never Had It Made* that African American demands for equality would be much more effective "if we were negotiating from the strength of our own self-reliance" rather than asking for charity. Robinson wanted black Americans to participate in the nation's mainstream economy.[70] Rachel argued that her husband "was in the forefront of thinking about black economic development."[71]

From 1957 to 1964, Robinson was a vice president of Chock Full o' Nuts—a job he was offered, he asserted, because of "the mysterious and miraculous way in which God works in the lives of people."[72] In addition, he helped found Freedom National Bank; created a company called Seahost to market frozen fish to the black community; started Jackie Robinson Associates, a group of business leaders who supplied loans to help build affordable housing and establish minority-owned businesses; and established the Jackie Robinson Construction Corporation to build apartments for low- and middle-income residents of metropolitan New York. His skepticism about the value of government welfare programs and his belief in the importance of individual initiative and hard work inspired him to engage in these activities. Robinson claimed that economic development was as important as civil rights legislation in enhancing the well-being of black Americans.[73] While challenging politicians to pass laws and adopt economic policies that helped eliminate racism and alleviate poverty, Robinson repeatedly argued that African Americans must take responsibility for their own lives. He believed, as did many black ministers, including Leon Sullivan and Jesse Jackson, that African Americans could make significant economic progress "by working within the confines of electoral politics and the capitalist economy."[74] Robinson urged black Americans "to become producers, manufacturers, developers, and creators of businesses."[75]

Robinson continually exhorted African Americans to take the initiative to improve their lives. In a June 1959 speech at Tuskegee, Alabama, the home of Booker T. Washington's Tuskegee Institute, he lauded black residents for building a shopping center, establishing a savings and loan association, and starting a car dealership and other businesses despite white efforts to politically disenfranchise them. He praised them for developing "new pride, industry and sense of importance in life."[76] In his 1967 sermon "Cast the First Stone," Robinson argued that the constant talk about helping black Americans was making them weary. Poverty programs, he insisted, had largely "fallen flat on their faces" and were mere handouts; better schools, housing, and jobs would better enable the indigent to improve their situation. "God helps mankind," Robinson declared, "but he helps those who help themselves." To underscore this argument, Robinson described a farmer who spent many hours planting his new crop. After a neighbor inspected his bountiful harvest and declared that God is good, the farmer agreed, but added, "You should have seen the mess this land was in before I got out here with these tools and gave God a little help."[77]

Three-quarters of the one thousand workers at Chock Full o' Nuts were black, leading racists to call the company "Chock Full o' Niggers." As the coffee company's vice president and director of personnel, Robinson strove to provide black employees with more training, pay, and management positions.[78] He sought to give employees the resources they needed to work more effectively and enhanced their benefits, including medical insurance and sick pay. He also helped many employees who had previously relied on loan sharks to procure loans from banks.[79] The company's president, Bill Black, called Robinson an "advisor, friend, and father confessor" who had greatly boosted African American employees' morale.[80] Whereas the baseball pioneer saw his position as providential, Black had a pragmatic motive for hiring Robinson, believing that his black employees "would worship" him and would thus be more diligent and productive.[81] Robinson was grateful that Black permitted him to spend a substantial amount of time volunteering with the NAACP, but their partnership ended in 1964 largely because Black did not give Robinson the authority he desired to make personnel-related decisions.

In 1964, Robinson helped establish Freedom National Bank in Harlem to help rectify the community's "serious deficiency of banking facilities." Its founders sought to create "the first national bank organized by, directed by, and attuned to the needs of the Harlem community." New York's white-owned banks, Robinson complained, were doing little to serve Harlem residents. African Americans were generally considered bad credit risks because of their lower median income and the belief that they could not be trusted; as a result, they had difficulty getting mortgages and business loans. Redlining—discrimination against racial minorities in lending—kept many black Americans from owning homes. Samuel Pierce Jr., who later served as US secretary of Housing and Urban Development in the Reagan administration, helped establish Freedom Bank to enable "blacks to move into the financial world." In 1972, Robinson contended, Freedom Bank, with two branches in Brooklyn and one in Harlem, was enabling these communities' black residents to "negotiate from strength and self-respect" and had become a major source of pride for black people as well as one of the nation's largest African American banks.[82] For several years, Robinson chaired the bank's board. Joe Black, Robinson's roommate on the 1952 Dodgers and later a senior vice president with Greyhound, reported that Robinson "used his fame to lure black people into the bank. He'd walk the streets in Harlem, he'd be at the Apollo, he'd go to the Y." Robinson used "his charisma to help make the bank" attractive to African Americans. Robinson believed that "if black people were going to move ahead," they had to start their own businesses, which the bank would help them to do.[83]

During Robinson's years with the Dodgers, discriminatory federal policies, redlining, and prejudiced white homeowners had combined to force most African Americans in Brooklyn to live in certain neighborhoods where they paid high rents for dilapidated apartments, garbage was collected only sporadically, and few recreation centers, parks, or pools existed.[84] After Robinson retired, conditions in the city's black enclaves continued to worsen. Concerned about these developments, Robinson and three partners started a construction company in 1970 to remodel Brooklyn's decaying nineteenth-century brownstones. By using black workers to repair and clean these buildings, the Jackie Robinson Construction Company could supply good jobs and affordable housing for Brooklyn's black community.[85] After her husband's death, Rachel took over the company and continued to provide homes for people unable to afford other accommodations in New York's expensive housing market. By 1987, the company had built more than 1,300 low- and moderate-income units in East Harlem, Brooklyn, and Yonkers.[86]

Not all of Robinson's business ventures were successful. Seahost, the frozen fish company, did not last long. He invested in a line of women's beauty products with Harlem physician Arthur Logan and his wife, Marian, but this enterprise also foundered. In 1965 Robinson, Logan, and other businessmen founded the Gibraltar Insurance Company, which failed as well. Robinson convinced Nelson Rockefeller to help fund the creation of New Communities, Inc., on a 4,800-acre tract of land in southwest Georgia, where eight hundred low-income, rural southern families could live, engage in intensive farming, and learn industrial skills.[87] New Communities hoped to develop a prototype that could be duplicated throughout the nation, but the enterprise was only moderately successful.[88]

Robinson promoted black economic development in other ways. In October 1964, he traveled to Philadelphia to speak to seven hundred students attending the Opportunities Industrialization Center (OIC), established that year by the city's black clergy to train African Americans for skilled and semiskilled positions.[89] The OIC's principal leader was Leon Sullivan, pastor of the six-thousand-member Zion Baptist Church, whom Robinson called "a mover and shaker who gets things going not for personal greed, gain, or glory—but to fulfill his mission as a man of God."[90] Robinson commended Sullivan, a prominent civil rights activist, for designing economic programs to enable black Americans to help themselves.[91]

Appearing before a Senate subcommittee in January 1970, Robinson criticized Nixon for failing to keep his pledge to promote black capitalism, and he wrote op-eds and sent letters to the president exhorting him to fulfill this commitment.[92] Despite his concerns about the potential negative effects of welfare, Robinson protested New York's reduced welfare payments in March 1971. The vast majority of recipients, he argued, were children, the aged, the disabled, or parents who had to stay home to care for their children. Most able-bodied recipients preferred work over welfare but could not find jobs; only 2 to 3 percent were loafers taking advantage of the system. Robinson called for creating more child-care centers to enable parents to work. The United States was neglecting the poor, he complained, while spending "billions searching for rocks on the moon."[93]

"One of the Greatest Men of Our Time"

Branch Rickey, over his physicians' objections, left a hospital to speak at his induction into the Missouri Sports Hall of Fame on November 13, 1965. While telling the biblical story of Zacchaeus, the eighty-three-year-old collapsed; he died less than a month later. Robinson grieved deeply, as the two had enjoyed a very close and meaningful relationship for twenty years.

In 1962, Robinson wrote to Rickey, "your life has been such an inspiration to me. I am a better man for having had the rich years of association with you. May God give you the strength to carry on. America needs more Mr. Rickeys—and personally—I need the assurance of a man I respect, admire and love."[94] Rickey, Robinson declared, was "the greatest human being" he had ever known and the person who "inspired" him the most.[95] "God has called [home] one of the greatest men of our time," Robinson wrote in the *Amsterdam News*. Robinson revealed that when he was at risk of dying in 1963 after surgery, Rickey, who himself had been ill, traveled to New York to see him. "He talked with me and treated me like a son."[96] Robinson's relationship with Rickey had deepened after he retired from baseball, and he felt almost as if he had lost his own father. Robinson was disappointed that only a couple of African American baseball players attended Rickey's funeral and that black superstars did not send telegrams.[97]

"Her Strength Gave Me Strength"

After Jackie retired from baseball, Rachel's life and activities changed significantly, but while pursuing her own career, she remained an equal partner and a major contributor to his work. When her children were young, Rachel derived great satisfaction from her role as a mother and homemaker. "Being home," she declared, "allowed me to enjoy my children and support their development. I was one of those suburban mothers so often caricatured as den mother [and] scout leader." Rachel participated "in neighborhood drives and causes"; raced "with a car full of children to events, lessons, [and] games"; and was "home for talks, snacks, and homework."[98]

After her youngest child started school, Rachel earned a master's degree in psychiatric nursing at New York University in 1959 and then worked as a nurse-therapist and researcher at the Albert Einstein College of Medicine in New York. While there, she helped establish the nation's first day hospital for acutely ill psychiatric patients. In 1965, Rachel became a professor at Yale's School of Nursing and the nursing director at the Connecticut Mental Health Center, positions she held until Jackie died in 1972. After his death, Rachel became president of the Jackie Robinson Construction Company and established the Jackie Robinson Foundation to provide educational scholarships.

Rachel's encouragement, wise counsel, and collaboration were as important to Jackie in his business, political, and religious work as they had been to his baseball career. Her mother, Sharon Robinson avows, was "a symbol of perfection—beautiful, gracious, available, and attentive as wife and mother."[99] "Jackie and Rachel were united as civil rights activists," Chris Lamb argues; "they knew, as Rachel put it, 'that the issue wasn't simply baseball but life and death, freedom and bondage, for a lot of people.'"[100] In accepting an award in 1971 as "The Man of 25 Years in Sports," Jackie, as he had done many times, thanked Rachel. "Her strength gave me strength," he declared, "and I question how far I would have come without her. Everything I have done, has been because of her."[101] "Publicly and privately," Sharon adds, "Dad never failed to appreciate how essential my mother was to all of us."[102]

God Is Good

During the last ten years of his life, Robinson had many health problems: diabetes, hypertension, two mild heart attacks, excruciating pain in his legs, aching knees that required surgery, and failing eyesight. While facing these trials, he testified frequently to God's goodness to him. Reflecting on his struggle with diabetes and his knee surgery in early 1963, Robinson wrote in the *Amsterdam News*, his experience made him realize "how wonderful" God had been to him. After visiting a five-year-old who had been badly burned, he "pledged to be grateful to God for all of his blessings." He went on, "I have suffered but witnessing the suffering of an uncomplaining, pain-stricken five-year-old makes you feel the power of God's blessings."[103] Pondering his precarious health, Robinson declared, "God has a lot of work left for me to do and wants to give me time to do it the best I possibly can."[104] After a minor heart attack in June 1968, Robinson wrote to a friend: "I guess the good Lord has a job for me or else I could or would have had some serious heart damage."[105] One of her father's favorite sayings, Sharon Robinson reports, "was that God was testing him and would not give him more than he could bear."[106]

Tragedy Strikes

Jackie Robinson Jr. was born on November 18, 1946, shortly after his father's first season in white professional baseball ended. Robinson had high aspirations for his son and desired to give him a better childhood than his own in Pasadena. Robinson hoped that his son would go to college and follow him into MLB. But most of all, he wanted Jackie Jr. "to grow up to be a fine man" who could "take care of himself in this rough, tough outside world."[107]

An article in *Parents Magazine* in 1955 insisted that "their wise, warmhearted parents" were rearing the Robinson children "in an atmosphere of love, lofty ideals and mutual respect."[108] Beneath the surface, however, trouble was brewing. Jackie Jr. had been under a microscope from his birth. When their son was very young, Rachel reported, everyone wanted "something from him." Cameramen wanted him to pose for pictures; kids wanted to play with him; women wanted to cuddle him.[109] The *Parents* article noted, "Because of his famous name, Jackie Jr. presents a special problem. When he was younger, grownups tried to spoil him by invariably giving him things, hugging and even mobbing him."[110] Being in "his father's spotlight and shadow," Rachel later reflected, had a much greater impact on Jackie Jr. than she and Jackie recognized at the time. He was born before most people "understood the stress that celebrity status could have on families," the impact of learning disabilities, the importance of educating children about the dangers of drugs, or the debilitating effects of the Vietnam War on soldiers.[111] Sharon Robinson explains, "we were an enviable family living the American Dream. Our perfection was immortalized on the front covers of magazines, through television medium, and in newsprint. Everywhere we went people stared, whispered, pointed, smiled, and admired us from afar." "Dad's bigger-than-life stature and my mother's perfection played havoc with our developing adolescence and self-esteem," she asserts. "Jackie, David, and I were just average kids—we brought home report cards with more C's than D's; we were good athletes, but not outstanding." They did not expect to excel as their father had.[112] All the teasing Jackie Jr. received about being renowned someday like his father, the baseball star insisted, chipped away at his son's self-esteem.[113] "At times," Sharon maintains, "the pressure associated with Dad's fame was obviously beyond Jackie's ability to cope." He increasingly disliked being around strangers; he quit Little League baseball because other fathers constantly compared him to his father; although he was strong, muscular, and very well coordinated, he refused to play high school sports.[114]

Adding to these pressures, Jackie Jr. received insufficient attention from his father. After his retirement from baseball, Robinson visited a YMCA, school, or hospital at least twice a week to talk with youngsters who needed guidance about good sportsmanship and citizenship and their problems.[115] Incongruously, however, this man who cared so deeply about young people's development struggled to raise and connect with his older son. Robinson admitted that he had not nurtured Jackie Jr. enough, in large part because of the travel that baseball entailed. He told reporters when he posted bail for his son in March 1968, "I guess I had more of an effect on other people's kids than I had on my own," and "My problem was my inability to spend more time at home."[116]

"Dad was too absorbed in baseball to establish a strong relationship with his firstborn," Sharon argued. "Later, when Dad had tried to be the disciplinarian, Jackie wouldn't listen." Jackie Jr.'s quest to escape from his father's image intensified their estrangement.[117] Robinson regretted that he and his son did not communicate effectively and "rubbed each other the wrong way." Jackie Jr. was undoubtedly upset that his father had "tremendous rapport" with his younger brother, David, and that they enjoyed doing many things together.[118] In addition, Jackie Jr. was less self-disciplined and "more dependent, pampered and needy" than Sharon or David. "To compensate for his perceived vulnerability," the women in the Robinson household—his mother, grandmother Wilmette Bailey (who lived with the Robinsons for fifteen years), and Sharon—"ran around anticipating Jackie's needs before he had time to express them."[119]

Jackie Jr. struggled in school and in life. His poor grades and disciplinary infractions became a "real disaster" in junior and senior high, prompting his parents to send him to a private school in the Berkshires, but this did not work out.[120] Jackie Jr. "wanted to be great at *something*," his father declared, so he decided at a young age "to be a great crook" and began to smoke pot.[121] Ironically, Robinson had long labored to prevent juvenile delinquency. In addition to working with the Harlem YMCA, he helped create an organization of professional athletes to "guide wayward young boys," served on the Connecticut State Prison's three-person parole board, testified before a Senate subcommittee on juvenile delinquency, and wrote numerous newspaper columns about the problem. Robinson argued that the best way to reduce teenage crime was to provide homes where youth felt they were loved and their concerns were understood.[122]

Jackie Jr. did not feel he had such a home. In spring 1964, he ran away to California; shortly thereafter, he joined the army. But the army did not end his discontentment. "Bored, lost, and troubled," he spent his off-duty time at Fort Riley, Kansas, smoking marijuana and popping pills. In July 1964, the army sent him to Cam Ranh Bay in Vietnam, where he saw no military action for the first two months. "He had joined the Army looking for discipline and a sense of purpose," Sharon asserted, but instead experienced "boredom, underutilization, and terror." "We prayed endlessly for his safety," Rachel declared.

In November 1965, Jackie Jr. was wounded by shrapnel from an explosion that killed two soldiers standing next to him. He was awarded the Purple Heart and honorably discharged in June 1967. He returned to Connecticut, in Rachel's words, "spiritless, wounded in body and soul, cynical, afraid, and worst of all, though we didn't know it at the time, a drug addict."[123]

For the next nine months, Jackie Jr. seemed lost, unable to keep a job or live permanently in one place.[124] "Caught between the allure of two worlds, the street life which offered him anonymity and the one connected to our father, which promised only disappointment," Sharon argued, Jackie Jr. chose to live in hotels in the Stamford area instead of at home.[125] His son could use drugs and commit crimes without his parents knowing, Robinson explained, because he was "a great liar."[126] On March 5, 1968, "the roof fell in on" the Robinsons, as Jackie Jr. was arrested for possessing marijuana, heroin, and a .22 revolver.[127]

In late March, Robinson shared with Barry Goldwater his hope that "with God's help things will right themselves for Jackie Jr. in the days to come."[128] Instead, the next three months were a horrible stretch. On April 4, Jackie's good friend Martin Luther King Jr. was assassinated in Memphis, Mallie Robinson died in May, Robert Kennedy was killed in June, and Sharon, who had married an abusive boyfriend, soon divorced. Meanwhile, Jackie Jr. "became a harbinger of the devastation that would decimate" many African American males in the 1980s.[129]

Jackie Jr. soon entered Daytop, an eighteen-to-twenty-four-month "self-help program staffed and run entirely by ex-addicts" and based in Seymour, Connecticut, that helped individuals grow in self-understanding and find fulfillment without drugs.[130] On August 23, Jackie Jr. was arrested for "using females for immoral purposes." Although he had pointed a revolver at the police, he was placed on probation and allowed to return to Daytop. Thereafter, Jackie Jr. began to change. He recognized, as the Daytop philosophy asserted, that "drugs are not the problem" but "the manifestation and the symptom of the problem." He explained, "I was haunted by the image of being the son" of "a great man. So, when I found I couldn't deal with him as a man and found that my father couldn't identify with me as his son . . . I tried to eliminate the desire that I thought would never be fulfilled." This led him to lie, cheat, steal, and patronize prostitutes. However, he continued, "at Daytop I found not only myself but love." Although he did not always recognize it and "didn't always call on him," he realized that his father "was always there" for him.[131] Robinson rejoiced that his son was growing in self-esteem and confidence and learning about "the massive power of love."[132]

After his son's arrest, Robinson declared, "God is testing me."[133] Robinson prayed that God would help Jackie Jr. with his recovery. "We can only hope and pray," he told Caroline Wallerstein, because "Jackie has lots of problems and only he [Jackie Jr.] can solve them."[134] Robinson also responded to this trial by enlisting in the battle against drugs. The September 10, 1970, issue of *Jet* magazine declared on its cover, "Jackie Robinson Joins War against Dope in the Ghettoes." Calling drugs a new "form of slavery," the ex-ballplayer lamented that many youth, especially black ones, were graduating from high school or returning from Vietnam "with no real future" and "seemingly no one" to help them. "I'm only sorry," he confessed, that it required a personal tragedy for him to "recognize the seriousness of this problem." He hoped that other black parents would not wait until drugs struck them personally to become involved. He also revealed that he and Rachel had received numerous letters gloating about their son's troubles.[135]

In a speech he delivered during this period, Robinson declared, "I know what it is to wake up one morning and find my whole world" and that of "those nearest and dearest to me, changed, threatened, transformed, because my son had become addicted." Jackie Jr. "got into trouble" because of societal pressures and "constantly being compared" to his father. Robinson urged parents to keep supporting their youngsters, regardless of the severity of their drug problems. As they grew up, youth had to deal with communication problems, the Vietnam War, and many other maladies. Adults were drinking martinis, chain-smoking, and taking tranquilizers, he argued, and then were surprised when their children became "defeatist and cynical."[136]

On June 14, 1971, Jackie Jr. spoke at Nazarene Congregational Church in Brooklyn, which his family had attended in the 1950s, about the drug menace. The pastor, Sam Varner, advised him to use the experience of "the prodigal son who landed in the gutter, broke and destitute" as the basis for his talk. Varner pointed out that "the prodigal son's father had instilled in him the belief that wherever he went, whatever he did," he would always take him back. Jackie Jr. said, "Yes, that's like my father. I knew I could always go back to him. But I kept . . . trying to escape because I was still haunted by . . . being the son of . . . a great man." Daytop, however, helped him find the father he "had lost."[137]

Four days later, Jackie Jr. lost control of his car about 2:00 a.m. while driving to New York City. Crashing into a fence and an abutment, he broke his neck and died almost instantly. Rachel and Jackie were both devastated by their son's death. Few people know, Jackie declared, what it is like "to lose a son, find him, and lose him again."[138] Jackie, however, derived more comfort from his faith than Rachel did. Some religious philosophers, he noted, assure you that "he's in the arms of God" or that "he's better off," but that provided little solace. He believed, however, that "there had to be a deep meaning to Jackie's being taken away" from them "at this particular time. Not so with Rachel," who "grieved as a mother." "She didn't want to hear about God knowing best, or any other clichés that people use to make you feel better," Jackie explained. Jackie Jr. had been clean for three years and had begun working at Daytop. "God had taken her son" just as "he had begun to help a lot of other youngsters less fortunate than" him.[139]

Jackie was especially thankful for Jesse Jackson's pastoral comfort and David's ability to console his mother. A few days after Jackie Jr.'s death, Jackson met with the family at their house. When he asked them to hold hands and pray with him, Rachel and Sharon angrily demanded to know "why had God taken Jackie just as he was beginning to live." Jackson "skillfully calmed our hysteria and assured us," Sharon explained, that someday his death "would make sense." Her father, she surmised, was probably the one most grateful for Jackson's words, but they were all consoled by his prayer.[140] "I shall never get over the loss" of Jackie Jr., the baseball pioneer declared, "but he thanked God for the comfort David furnished to Rachel at her lowest moment. While grieving for their son, he concluded, they learned about the positive influence Jackie Jr. had on many peers and older people. Richard Nixon acknowledged that nothing "could relieve the pain that this loss has brought you," but promised the Robinsons that he and his wife "will be praying that God may give you the strength and courage to persevere."[141] Capturing Robinson's grief, Red Barber wrote, after reading the ex-ballplayer's account of Jackie Jr.'s life and death in *I Never Had It Made*, that he thought of "King David, alone in his chamber, weeping and saying, 'O my son Absalom, my son . . . would God I had died for thee, O Absalom, my son, my soul!'"[142]

Jackie Jr.'s funeral was held at the Antioch Baptist Church in Brooklyn, the church where Rachel's mother worshiped. Pastors George Lawrence and Lacy Covington, both family friends, conducted the service, attended by 1,500 people. Jackie Jr.'s service in Vietnam and his fight against drugs at home, Lawrence insisted, made him a hero. David read a poem he had written. Gospel singer Joyce Bryant performed a solo, and the Daytop choir sang "Bridge over Troubled Waters" and "Still the Water Runs Deep." An organist played a joyous rendition of "We Shall Overcome."[143]

Ten days after Jackie Jr.'s death, the Robinsons held an "Afternoon of Jazz" at their home in North Stamford, which their son had organized to raise money for Daytop; more than three thousand people heard Roberta Flack, Herbie Mann, Dave Brubeck, and other prominent artists perform. Jesse Jackson then discussed the many obstacles Jackie Jr. had overcome and encouraged the audience to focus on his accomplishments. Jackson stressed that the length of a person's journey on earth mattered less than the deeds he performed along the way. Jackson then led the attendees in praying for the Robinson family. Reflecting on the many "young people, parents, clergy, and counselors he had reached with his antidrug message," Sharon concluded that maybe her brother "hadn't died in vain."[144]

While battling numerous health problems and dealing with Jackie Jr.'s troubles, Robinson, aided greatly by Rachel's love, support, and wise counsel and motivated and comforted by his Christian faith, worked diligently to advance religious causes, influence political outcomes, challenge politicians to promote civil rights, and create and operate businesses to improve the lives of African Americans. As he battled racial discrimination in the church, political arena, business world, and society and dealt with personal heartbreak, Jackie Robinson's relationship with God provided inspiration, direction, and consolation. His faith empowered him to cope with frustration and failure and resolutely pursue the causes that mattered most to him—social justice and economic advancement for African Americans.

Conclusion

The Faith and Impact of Jackie Robinson

Jackie Robinson's Christian faith played a major role in his professional and personal life. It shaped his understanding of who he was, the nature of the world, and his calling. Many of his personal traits were consistent with the biblical fruit of the Spirit (Gal. 5:22), especially love, kindness, goodness, faithfulness, and self-control. Robinson is one of many Christians in MLB history who strove to display his faith through his performance on the diamond; relationships with teammates, opponents, and fans; verbal testimony; and off-the-field activities. Beyond his remarkable legacy as MLB's first black player, Robinson arguably did more to improve American society after retiring from baseball than any other athlete.

Robinson's Faith

Assessing Robinson's faith is challenging because he did not speak frequently about what it meant to him or describe his personal beliefs. He rarely explained specifically how his relationship with God or his specific Christian convictions directed his thinking or inspired his actions.[1] As a baseball player, he often asked God to help him cope with the trials and troubles he faced. His faith clearly helped sustain him as he faced the taunts, the insults, and the immense pressure that came with trying to integrate MLB. His faith, nurtured and nourished by his mother, Branch Rickey, Karl Downs, and other minister friends, helped shape his character and motivated many of his actions. It influenced his perspective of life, his goals, and his battle to improve the lives of African Americans.

Throughout his life, Robinson participated in mainline Methodist, Congregationalist, and United Church of Christ congregations and was comfortable in both black and white Christian communities. His faith is best understood in the context of the mainline Protestantism of the 1950s and 1960s. His perspective on the Bible, his spirituality, and his commitment to serving others were similar to those of many other mainline Protestants.

From 1950 to the early 1960s, mainline Protestant churches—most significantly, the United Methodist Church, Congregationalists (the United Church of Christ beginning in 1957), the Presbyterian Church (USA), the Episcopal Church, the American Baptist Convention, the Disciples of Christ, and the Lutheran Church in America—were in their heyday in terms of number of members and cultural influence.[2] Sixty percent of Protestants were affiliated with mainline Protestant communions in 1950, and the majority of Protestants still belonged to mainline congregations in 1970.[3] Members of these denominations held major leadership roles in politics, business, education, science, and the arts. They (especially Episcopalians and Presbyterians) tended to be wealthier than other Americans and highly educated. Culturally dominant, and generally socially progressive, mainline Protestants saw themselves as the shepherd of the nation's soul and the custodians of its values.[4] They felt responsible for shaping and leading society, not protecting Christians from it. During the 1950s, their moral values were widely embraced in the larger culture. They were the backbone of the National Council of Churches, founded in 1950 to promote Christian unity and engage collectively in Christian mission and social amelioration. Until at least 1964, most mainline Protestants were Republicans.[5] They tended to be theological moderates (sometimes also called evangelical liberals) who viewed the Bible as divinely inspired but not inerrant. They believed that the Bible furnished norms and guidance for everyday life, but that it should be interpreted in the context of its original cultural settings by using the tools of higher criticism and God-given reason. Most mainliners accepted the divinity of Christ, the general accuracy of the New Testament accounts, and Jesus's bodily resurrection and biblical miracles. Whereas evangelical Protestants emphasized a born-again experience, during the 1950s and 1960s members of mainline denominations were more likely to maintain that children became Christians gradually through being nurtured in faith by believing parents and in Sunday school and confirmation classes. Mainliners also tended to stress the concept of a spiritual journey over the need for a conversion experience. Many mainline Protestant congregants were concerned about social issues and saw serving others as their principal mission in life.[6]

Mainline Protestant spokespersons carried great moral authority and influence in the 1950s, but during the next decade, the high status and hegemony of mainline churches were challenged by increasing religious and ideology pluralism (including growing interest in yoga, transcendental meditation, Buddhism, and Hinduism), the election of the nation's first Catholic president, and the social upheaval brought by civil rights protests, the Vietnam War, the feminist movement, and changing sexual mores. All these developments challenged traditional Protestant teachings and some of the positions and actions of mainline leaders and members.

Civil rights became a major concern of mainline churches in the 1960s, and their members played a more active role in combating racism during the decade than did evangelical Protestants. The *Christian Century*, mainline Christianity's flagship magazine, endorsed the movement in numerous articles as the decade began.[7] In October 1963, fifty-three Episcopal clergy and laypeople went to Washington, DC, to lobby for passage of civil rights legislation. At a national convention in 1963, the United Church of Christ called for immediate action to eliminate discrimination in voting, employment, housing, education, and the judicial system. The next year, the Lutheran Church in America expressed enthusiastic support for black civil rights and denounced racism at its biennial convention, claiming that those who used the Bible to justify discrimination had a faulty understanding of God and Scripture.[8]

Robinson shared many of the theological convictions and social concerns of other mainline Protestants. "Connected to Protestant institutions throughout his life," Robinson, like many of them, "saw faith as a source of inspiration, hope," and identity. He subscribed to a traditional moral code on such issues as smoking, drinking, and premarital and extramarital sex. Like many mainline Protestants, Robinson had a strong commitment to the social-justice implications of Christianity. He insisted that believers must combat racism in American society and that true Christianity promoted racial equality and complained that many white Christians were not practicing what they preached.[9] Robinson spoke in scores of black churches to promote civil rights, raised money for religious causes and the NAACP, and enjoyed friendships with numerous black ministers. He had much less contact with white evangelicals. Strikingly, Billy Graham apparently never invited Robinson to speak at any of his crusades, including the 1957 crusade in New York City, at a time when the evangelist was reaching out to other Christian celebrities to give testimonies.[10]

"I cannot claim to be a deeply religious man," Robinson confessed in a 1968 *Amsterdam News* column.[11] "I don't [wear] religion on my sleeve," he declared. "There are many better Christians than I." Robinson insisted, however, "I believe in God, in the Bible and in trying to do the right thing as I understand it."[12] He protested that some people laughed and sneered at individuals like Branch Rickey "who are not ashamed of having faith."[13] "I would have to be pretty stupid, and certainly, ungrateful not to have some of the deep religious conviction of my mother" and Rickey "rub off on me."[14] Robinson emphasized his devout Methodist upbringing and, while acknowledging that he was not "the greatest churchgoer in the world," argued that "a person can be quite religious and at the same time militant in the defense of his ideals." He added, "I have practiced [the Golden Rule] all my life. Some of my friends tell me that I go overboard . . . that I do too much to others and get left out on a limb."[15]

Robinson resonated with some biblical characters and stories. He had "a special affinity for Job," partly because he believed black Americans had suffered a similar experience. Like Job, African Americans had lost their wealth, civilization, language, land, and health as they were "brutalized by slavery"; often, they even lost their families. African Americans had been "kept in bondage, enduring the scornful eye of the community and the revulsion of our masters." "But like Job we answer, 'I am a man, and therefore worthy. Though you slay me, I will maintain my own ways before you." Robinson concluded that he did not have "the status of Job" or his innocence, goodness, or courage. But, he pointed out, "as a black man I understand him."[16]

Family, friends, and scholars all testified that Robinson's faith helped direct his life and inspire his actions. Rachel asserted that her husband's humility stemmed from his religious faith and his conviction that God had given him talents to serve others.[17] Presbyterian pastor Richard Stoll Armstrong, who participated with Robinson in May 1964 on an NBC television program hosted by the National Council of Churches on the topic "Morality in Sports," maintained that the ex-Dodger was a man of "deep faith."[18] Robinson's fierce resolve to smash baseball's color barrier and end racial discrimination in all areas of American life was fueled by his belief that God made him a black man and gave him extraordinary athletic talent to help him achieve his objectives. His faith helped empower him to surmount great obstacles and "plow ahead mercilessly."[19] Father Jerome Ledoux contended that Robinson's "remarkable restraint under racial fire and baiting" would not have been "possible without the faith inherited from his mother, without the faith-driven, stern guidance of Rev. Karl Downs and the powerful ensuing spiritual motivation that drove and sustained him." Moreover, his faith "powered Jackie relentlessly in pursuit of civil rights."[20]

Robinson's sense of worth as a black man was grounded primarily in his faith in God, not a general "admiration for the African past."[21] Robinson counseled a boy living in an orphanage in Fort Wayne, Indiana, who was struggling with being black, "Be proud of what God gave you. I, too, felt the pains you must feel, but I never have been ashamed of what God has given me." He added, "God put us here on earth and gave us a color that is distinctive, and then put problems before us to see what would happen." These challenges, Robinson insisted, benefited African Americans.[22]

Robinson believed that God providentially directed all earthly events. God expected people to exert their maximum effort, but he would determine the outcome of their endeavors—and whatever God did was right, even when individuals did not understand all God's plans.[23] Robinson insisted that "Providence was at work in his life, and that Providence deserved all the thanks." God was guiding his life, Robinson averred, to achieve important purposes.[24] "God has been good to me," the baseball star told a Jewish boy with whom he frequently corresponded, "and I intend to work as hard as I can to repay all the things people have done for me."[25] Rachel reported that "Jackie believed that he was God's creature, and he saw his opportunities as a way of carrying out God's plan."[26] The obstacles he encountered, Jackie insisted, made him "fight all the harder." But he would not have been able "to fight at all" if he had not been "sustained by the personal and deep-rooted belief" that his "fight had a chance." "My faith in God," he argued, "sustained me in my fight," and he believed that he must do for others what God had done for him.[27]

Because the God who controlled the universe loved and suffered with victims of racial oppression, Robinson was confident that his hard work would pay dividends and that black rights would eventually be achieved.[28] "I am an eternal optimist," he wrote in a 1968 column.[29] Like most mainline and black Christians, he maintained an abiding hope that God's will would be accomplished on earth.[30]

Robinson believed in people's integrity, the warmth of human hearts, and the goodness of society. However, a good society could be created and maintained only if people "are willing to fight" to achieve it and able to overcome "obstacles and prejudices."[31] "Life is not a spectator sport," he proclaimed. Spending one's "whole life in the grandstand just watching what goes on" was not truly living.[32]

Robinson's Personal Characteristics

Many of Robinson's personal traits testify to his Christian faith. Sportswriters, friends, teammates, and scholars praise his sense of dignity, intelligence, candor, righteous indignation, competitiveness, charisma, courage, integrity, persistence, and loyalty. "Robinson's obvious intelligence, self-deprecating wit, and public willingness to forgive and understand his tormentors," a scholar asserts, "made him an American hero."[33] "Bright, articulate, and willing to engage in verbal combat with the press, Robinson soon became the focus of the Dodger locker-room interviews," a biographer explained.[34] "Proud, courageous, and defiant," Robinson repeatedly asserted "his rights as an American and as a black man, even in the face of personal risk."[35] Rachel praised her husband's "integrity and strength."[36] "Outspoken, controversial, combative, he created critics as well as loyalists."[37]

Throughout his life, Robinson complained, he had to deal with "friendly counselors" who thought they knew what he "should do, feel, and think." These advisors, Robinson explained, included "power-seeking politicians who wanted to buy my loyalty," envious individuals "who wanted me to get on my knees in gratitude for what baseball had done for me," and "the mentally disturbed who longed for my downfall."[38]

Given his personality, Robinson's lack of retaliation during his first two MLB seasons was "a miracle of self-restraint."[39] As Rachel explained, Jackie was inclined to fight back immediately against mistreatment, but he had promised Rickey that he would turn the other cheek for two years. So he bided his time, knowing that after two years, he could soon be himself.[40] In 1949, Robinson changed his approach and became "a fiery, no-holds-barred competitor, ready to do battle with opponents, teammates, management or press," a style that continued for the rest of his baseball career.[41]

Robinson was extremely competitive. "I just can't stand to lose at anything," he declared.[42] Numerous observers extolled this trait. Dodgers' teammate Duke Snider called Robinson a great competitor who taught him mental toughness. He added, "I've seen him beat a team with his bat, his ball, his glove, his feet and, in a game in Chicago one time, with his mouth."[43] Branch Rickey called Robinson "the most competitive man" he had known since Ty Cobb. Robinson, Dodgers' manager Leo Durocher proclaimed, "didn't just come to play. He came to beat ya."[44] The best word to describe Jackie Robinson, sportswriter Red Smith declared, "is 'unconquerable.'" He refused to allow another team or the hardships of life to defeat him.[45]

Robinson's competitiveness and outspokenness frequently evoked criticism and condemnation. The media publicized his outbursts of anger on the field. From 1949 to 1954, *The Sporting News* frequently disparaged Robinson's outspokenness in editorials such as "A Problem Grows in Brooklyn" and "Robinson Should Be a Player, Not a Crusader."[46] During his fifth season, National League president Warren Giles exhorted "all Dodgers and especially Jackie Robinson to strive for courtesy in their address to umpires."[47] Robinson was so painfully honest, Red Barber insisted, that "he was often severely abrasive."[48] Rachel said her husband was "impatient for signs of progress, and unwilling to accept affronts to his dignity." Some sportswriters labeled his forcefulness "black rage."[49]

"I made up my mind a long time ago," Robinson declared in a 1968 speech, "that I would rather be true to myself and to my beliefs and principles than to buy popularity at the cost of truth."[50] Robinson realized that he would have been more admired if he avoided "hot subjects," but he had refused to do so.[51] "If I think [a sportswriter] is wrong," Robinson avowed, "I blast him."[52] From his third season in the majors until his retirement,

Robinson engaged in numerous verbal battles with umpires, all of whom were white, when he believed they abused their power and strove to "put him in his place."[53] As soon as he began to argue and protest, Robinson claimed, he was denounced as "a swellhead, a wise guy, an 'uppity' nigger," "a pop-off, a troublemaker, and a rabblerouser."[54] Robinson and some sportswriters argued that he was being judged by a different standard from white players. "If I'm a troublemaker," he stated, "it's only because I can't stand losing." "Many people think," he protested, that blacks "must always be humble—even in the heat of sports competition."[55] When Eddie Stanky, Billy Martin, or Enos Slaughter acted aggressively, they were praised as "all-out-to-win" competitors, declared the editors of *Sport* magazine in 1955. "But when Robinson does it, he is condemned as a 'showboat.' That doesn't make sense to Jackie and it doesn't make sense to us."[56] Speaking for many, Lawrence Spivak asked Robinson on *Meet the Press* in 1957, "Is it the game itself that stirred up the competitive spirit or was it partly the way you were treated as the first Negro in baseball that resulted in your so-called tart tongue and terrible temper?"[57]

Robinson's belligerence also flared in his business and political activities.[58] Robinson was "too intense sometimes" about both baseball and social justice, declared Dodgers' teammate Carl Erskine.[59] His fiercely competitive spirit sometimes threatened to undermine his accomplishments.[60] But Robinson's fury, sportswriter Roger Kahn countered, "enabled him to do the great and immensely difficult thing that he did."[61] Robinson claimed that he recognized that he was not always right "in my squawks." When he made mistakes, he insisted, he quickly apologized.[62]

Some of Robinson's personal characteristics and actions clashed with biblical principles and virtues. According to Kahn, Robinson frequently employed vulgar language.[63] Umpire Jocko Conlan called him "the most difficult ballplayer" he had to deal with and complained that Robinson frequently fired obscenities at him.[64] Rachel stated that her husband never swore at home, but, she added, "I understand from his teammates that he could manage the language very well in the locker room."[65] Scott Simon asserted that Robinson "harangued opposing players, and sometimes his own teammates, with graphic epithets of the kind that would have once been considered legal provocation for a duel (although the epithets were never racial and rarely sexual)."[66] Kahn claimed that Robinson admitted to having sexual liaisons before and during his marriage, and that when he was at UCLA, he "didn't have to make much of a move" to get white coeds to go to bed with him. Kahn contended that "Jackie always had a keen eye for the ladies" and that he spent a night with a white woman inw1956.[67] Another sportswriter insisted that Robinson was stubborn, sometimes overzealous, and unreasonably suspicious.[68] Dodgers' owner Walter O'Malley, who treated Robinson very poorly at the end of his career, called him "the most shameless publicity seeker" he had ever met.[69]

Christians in Major League Baseball

Throughout professional baseball history, many players have shared Robinson's strong Christian faith. Briefly examining other notable Christian baseball players helps provide a context for understanding Robinson's faith. Like him, these players have used their success on the diamond as a platform for presenting God's goodness, love, and call to serve others.

The first baseball player to achieve notoriety because of his faith was Billy Sunday, a heavy-drinking outfielder who converted to Christianity in 1886. After eight seasons of professional baseball, Sunday left the game to work as an evangelist. For the next thirty years, he crisscrossed the United States, preaching the gospel, using countless athletic allusions, sharing his faith journey, and recording millions of conversions.[70]

The archetypical Christian ballplayer was New York Giants' pitcher Christy Mathewson, who won 373 games from 1900 to 1916 (tying him for third in all-time wins) and was a member of the inaugural class inducted into MLB's Hall of Fame. Mathewson "was the first truly national baseball figure who captured the country's admiration and hero worship by combining all the ideal elements of baseball, religion, and American culture."[71] Labeled "the Christian gentleman," Mathewson long refused to pitch on Sundays, taught Sunday school, served as a church elder, and promoted "muscular Christianity." In the 1910s, Protestant pastors and magazine editors often referred to Mathewson's character and exploits to make their messages more attractive. They also highlighted the college-educated, clean-living, churchgoing pitcher to make baseball more acceptable to America's "respectable classes."[72] "His family values, virtues, and larger-than-life persona epitomized the myth of what 'baseball' was supposed to be and contributed to its unchallenged status as the 'national pastime' and America's 'civil religion.'"[73] During Robinson's fifth season, Mathewson was one of four athletes portrayed in the magnificent Sports Bay at the Cathedral Church of Saint John the Divine in New York City, which opened in 1951.

The leading Christian major leaguer in the next generation was probably Cardinals' outfielder Pepper Martin, who played from 1928 to 1944. The devoted Baptist penned an article about his faith for *Guideposts*. When anyone asked what his goal in life was, his daughter reported, "he would say, 'To get to heaven.'" After he died, a newspaper cartoon depicted him sliding into heaven.[74]

As a player, Robinson benefited from having three devoted Christians on his team—Carl Erskine, Gil Hodges, and Ralph Branca. Another committed Christian during Robinson's playing days was Cleveland Indians' pitcher Bob Feller.[75] Feller, who won 266 games and entered the Hall of Fame in 1962 with Robinson, spoke at some Methodist events to promote church attendance and Christian faith.[76]

As Robinson was retiring in 1956, New York Yankees' second baseman Bobby Richardson, who became the most outspoken Christian player during the next decade, was beginning his career. The seven-time All-Star helped create the Fellowship of Christian Athletes and Baseball Chapel, worked as an evangelist after his playing days, and wrote several books about his faith, most notably *Grand Slam: Principles of Baseball and the Christian Life* (1978). Other outspoken Christians between 1956 and 1975 included Dominican-born outfielder and manager Felipe Alou, catcher Manny Sanguillén, and pitchers Al Worthington and Lindy McDaniel. McDaniel became a minister in the Church of Christ and often preached on Sundays during the off-seasons of his playing career.[77]

Hank Aaron, one of four MLB players to have more than six hundred home runs and three thousand hits and the game's all-time leader in RBIs and total bases, faithfully attended a Baptist church in Mobile, Alabama, as a youth. Aaron was very impressed that the "emotional, explosive" Robinson, during his rookie year, "didn't lose his temper in spite of a steady barrage of insults from fans and other players." Aaron "learned later that he prayed a lot for help." Robinson's great "sense of destiny about what he was doing" led him, Aaron argued, to see "God's presence with him" and "put aside his pride and quick temper" to accomplish his goal of integrating baseball. Aaron declared in 1973, "God is my strength. He gave me a good body and some talent and the freedom to develop it. He helps me when things go wrong. He forgives me when I fall on my face. He lights the way." On the verge of breaking Babe Ruth's record, Aaron stated, "The Lord willing, I'll set a new home-run record. If I don't, that's okay too," because God had already blessed him greatly.[78]

Baseball Chapel was founded in 1973 to provide chaplains and chapel services for major and minor league players, umpires, and ballpark personnel. However, some prominent players during the 1970s, including Phillies' third baseman Mike Schmidt and Mets' catcher Gary Carter, both Hall of Famers, complained that many of their teammates viewed Christians as undependable weaklings and ostracized them.[79]

In the late 1980s and 1990s, the number and influence of Christians in MLB increased significantly as numerous high-profile players testified to their faith. Leading the way were pitcher Orel Hershiser, designated hitter Paul Molitor, and first baseman Sid Bream. Speaking for all of them, Bream declared, "God has orchestrated my life to give glory to Him" and "has provided opportunities to share my faith."[80] The most dramatic faith story from these two decades is that of Dave Dravecky, who amazingly made his way back to the majors in 1989 after having a cancerous tumor removed from his pitching arm. He won his first game, but during his second game his humerus bone snapped, ending his career. After working through his frustration, anger, despair, and depression, Dravecky shared his testimony about God's sustaining love with hundreds of audiences across America and wrote several books about his experience, including *When You Can't Come Back: A Story of Courage & Grace* (1994).[81]

During the 1990s, half the players on some teams regularly attended chapel services and numerous players penned testimony cards that were distributed under the auspices of Baseball Chapel.[82] Hall of Fame pitchers John Smoltz, Pedro Martinez, and Mariano Rivera; catcher Mike Piazza; and two other pitchers, Andy Pettitte (256 wins) and Curt Schilling (216 wins), who all played into the middle of the new century's first decade, frequently discussed their relationship with God. Smoltz described his decision to accept Christ as his savior while playing for the Braves in 1995 and his efforts to follow Christ in *Starting and Closing: Perseverance,*

Faith, and One More Year (2013). *The Closer* (2014) explains how Rivera's Christian commitment "kept him grounded amid the glitz and glamour of professional sports."[83]

Some of today's top players openly share their faith in Christ. Los Angeles Dodgers' pitcher Clayton Kershaw, who has won three Cy Young Awards, insists that "Being a Christian means . . . you're supposed to be different, you're supposed to act boldly in your faith." He and his wife, Ellen, have funded several mission projects in the United States and abroad and coauthored *Arise: Live Out Your Faith and Dreams on Whatever Field You Find Yourself* (2012).[84] Since becoming a Christian in 1998, first baseman Albert Pujols, a three-time National League MVP, has sought to serve others and share God's good news.[85] Kershaw, Pujols, Andrew McCutchen, Aaron Judge, Adam Wainwright, Ben Zobrist, and many other current players discussed their faith in film documentaries such as *Champions of Faith* (2008); books, including Kevin and Elizabeth Morrisey's *God's Lineup! Testimonies of Major League Baseball Players* (2012), Rob Maaddi's *Baseball Faith: 52 MLB Stars Reflect on Their Faith* (2017), and Del Duduit's *Dugout Devotions* (2019); scores of magazine and newspaper articles; and hundreds of interviews. Many players identify themselves as followers of Jesus on their homepages and Twitter accounts. For example, the introductory blurb for Judge's account reads, "Christian. Faith, Family, then Baseball."[86] The faith of the 2007 Colorado Rockies' manager and players was featured after they won twenty-one of their last twenty-two games to make it into the World Series.[87] Paul Kent's *Playing with Purpose: Baseball Devotions; 180 Spiritual Truths Drawn from the Great Game of Baseball* (2015) highlights the faith of many MLB players. Since early in the twenty-first century, many MLB teams have hosted "Faith Nights" that feature Christian bands, worship, and testimonies by players, coaches, and managers.

Aided by Baseball Chapel and several parachurch organizations, many MLB players during the last fifty years have been more outspoken about their Christian faith than Robinson and most other earlier Christian ballplayers. Richardson, Hershiser, Dravecky, Bream, Kershaw, McCutchen, and numerous other recent and current players have frequently discussed their personal relationship with Jesus and urged others to accept Christ as their savior, which Robinson did not do. Although Robinson repeatedly referred to praying and thanked God for his help in dealing with adversity, he focused primarily on biblical themes of social justice rather than on personal spirituality during both his playing career and his postbaseball activities.

Heading Home

On October 24, 1972, Jackie Robinson died of a heart attack at his home in North Stamford, Connecticut, at age fifty-three. Three days later, 2,500 people gathered at Riverside Church in Manhattan, an imposing Gothic cathedral funded by John D. Rockefeller, to say farewell to the legendary ballplayer. The funeral service's music and message testified to Robinson's Christian faith. Attendees included Governor Nelson Rockefeller, New York mayor John Lindsay, vice presidential candidate Sargent Shriver, MLB commissioner Bowie Kuhn, NAACP executive director Roy Wilkins, comedian Dick Gregory, television show host Ed Sullivan, singers Ella Fitzgerald and Cab Calloway, and sports stars Joe Louis, Bill Russell, Willie Mays, Hank Aaron, Ernie Banks, Larry Doby, Roy Campanella, Willie Stargell, and Hank Greenberg. President Nixon sent a forty-person delegation led by cabinet secretary Robert Finch. Five of Robinson's former Dodgers' teammates—Jim Gilliam, Don Newcombe, Ralph Branca, Pee Wee Reese, and Joe Black—served as pallbearers.

George Lawrence, pastor of the Antioch Baptist Church in Brooklyn, conducted the service; Lacy Covington, a minister at Nazarene Congregational Church in Brooklyn, read Scripture; Harlem pastor and civil rights activist Wyatt Tee Walker preached a sermon; and Jesse Jackson gave the eulogy. The sixty-member Canaan Baptist Choir sang "Precious Lord," which proclaims, "Take my hand, precious Lord, and lead me home," and "If I Can Help Somebody," which conveyed Robinson's philosophy of life: "If I can help somebody, as I travel along . . . my living shall not be in vain." Pop artist Roberta Flack performed the Negro spiritual "I Told Jesus It Will Be All Right If I Change My Name."[88] After the funeral, tens of thousands of mourners lined the streets, cried, and chanted, "Goodbye, Jackie," as his body was transported from the church through Harlem to Cypress Hills Cemetery in Brooklyn, a few miles from the site of Ebbets Field, and buried next to Jackie Jr.[89]

In his eulogy, Jackson highlighted Robinson's faith and legacy. The Lord protected Jackie as he went "through dangers seen and unseen," Jackson declared, and God enabled him "to wear glory with grace. Jackie's body was a temple of God." He was an "instrument of peace" who rejected "the idle gods of fame and materialism." Robinson, Jackson proclaimed, was "a co-partner of God." God mercifully ended his physical afflictions "and permitted him to steal away home" to heaven, where there are no umpires and "only the supreme judge of the universe speaks." Jackson continued, "All of us are better off because [Robinson] passed this way." "His powerful arms" smashed barriers. Jackson argued that Robinson bore the burden of all black people. "When he hit the ball, it was for all the poor; he caught for all the dispossessed. He played the game for all the downtrodden; he went to bat for all the neglected," and "his victories were for all humanity." His triumph helped African Americans "ascend from misery, to hope." Jackie "realized that to live is to suffer," but he found meaning in his suffering. Robinson challenged the assumptions of racial superiority, American laws, and nearly three hundred years of slavery that African Americans are less intelligent, hardworking, and patriotic than whites, and more violent. He proved that black athletes could "succeed when the playing field is level." Jackson concluded, "Jackie won, the Dodgers won, America won because God sent this very special person our way to make us better." Robinson now "belongs to the ages, and we will be eternally grateful to him and forever remember" him.[90]

"Jackie Robinson Marked the Trail Well"

The list of those Robinson influenced, personally in many cases, is long and impressive. Among those who directly expressed having been inspired by Robinson are author James Baldwin; comedian Dick Gregory; singer-songwriters Nina Simone, Chuck Berry, and Harry Belafonte; activists Rosa Parks, Martin Luther King Jr., and Harry Edwards; politicians John Lewis, Shirley Chisholm, and Barack Obama; and athletes Jim Brown, Bob Gibson, Muhammad Ali, and Reggie Jackson.[91]

The day before the Dodgers-Phillies series in May 1947, in which Robinson was so ruthlessly taunted, Gil Jonas, a white Brooklyn high school student, interviewed him for his school newspaper. Observing how Robinson responded to a barrage of obscenities the next day, Jonas declared, "I watched people who were hardhearted or antagonistic . . . change. It was palpable." His own racial views were transformed by his experience that day. Jonas served as the principal fund-raiser for the NAACP from 1965 to

1995 and wrote *Freedom's Sword: The NAACP and the Struggle against Racism in America, 1909-1969* (2005).[92]

Numerous blacks credited Robinson with giving them the opportunity to play major league baseball. Hank Aaron said that Jackie Robinson "meant everything" to him.[93] Hearing Robinson speak at a grocery store in Mobile, Alabama, as a fourteen-year-old transformed his life.[94] "I would have never thought about being a professional baseball player," Aaron asserted, if Robinson had not opened "the door for blacks to play in the big leagues."[95] "He was a pillar of strength, and he gave me strength."[96] When Robinson died in 1972, Aaron sent Rachel a telegram stating, "My own success in baseball has been in large measure because Jackie Robinson marked the trail well."[97] Playing in the South as a member of the Atlanta Braves, Aaron experienced racial discrimination and received numerous death threats, especially as he neared breaking Babe Ruth's home run record in April 1974. Aaron admired Robinson for turning the other cheek and accepting "blows for the love and future of his people."[98]

Boston Celtics' great Bill Russell declared, "if it hadn't been for Jackie," he might not have become a professional basketball player. Robinson "was someone that young black athletes could look up to."[99] Los Angeles Laker Kareem Abdul-Jabbar, the NBA's all-time scoring leader, declared in 1989, "The courage and competitiveness of Jackie Robinson affects [*sic*] me to this day. If I patterned my life after anyone, it was him."[100]

Another outstanding athlete who followed in Robinson's footsteps was decathlete Rafer Johnson, who won the silver medal at the 1956 Olympics and gold in 1960. Influenced by Robinson, Johnson attended UCLA, where he starred in track and field and also in basketball for legendary coach John Wooden. Like Robinson, he had an impressive record of public service after his sports career ended, working with the Peace Corps, Red Cross, March of Dimes, Muscular Dystrophy Association, numerous boards at UCLA, and most notably the Special Olympics. Like Robinson, Johnson was a committed Christian, although he was more vocal about his faith. Johnson was long involved with the Fellowship of Christian Athletes and shared his testimony in numerous speeches and publications; he loved, he said, "Jesus Christ with all my heart" and competed in sports "for the glory of my Lord."[101]

Without Robinson leading the way, Martin Luther King Jr. insisted, the journey to justice would have been even more arduous: "Jackie made my work less difficult."[102] Calvin Morris, the associate director of Operation Breadbasket, told Robinson that for those who had few black male role models, "you were as a shining beacon" by "the way you talked, walked, and carried yourself" on and off the field. Robinson, he declared, had inspired many black youth "to hold fast to their dreams."[103] Film producer and director Spike Lee testifies that the baseball star has long "been an inspiration" to him, and that black children growing up in Brooklyn in the 1960s revered no one more than Jackie Robinson. He "was spoken of with the same respect and awe as Dr. King, as Joe Louis, as Jesus Christ." Robinson's ability to perform at a high level "with the entire weight" of his race on his shoulders, "while being ridiculed, lambasted, and having racial epithets hurled" at him and being unable to respond, Lee argues, "is one of the great American stories."[104]

Pastor Vince Antonucci grew up being verbally abused and feeling unloved by his father. Captivated and empowered by Jackie Robinson's life, Antonucci concluded that he too could "defy the odds" and do something with his life despite "the pain and mess" of his childhood. Learning that Robinson was inspired by Karl Downs and ultimately by Jesus, Antonucci eventually became a pastor, ministered to many troubled individuals on the Las Vegas strip, and wrote *Renegade: Your Faith Isn't Meant to Be Safe* (2014) to describe Robinson's impact on his life.[105]

African American Claire Smith was a sports columnist for the *New York Times* and then a news editor for ESPN. She was the first woman to win the J. G. Taylor Spink Award for outstanding writing about baseball. Smith stated, "What Robinson did, what he stood for, what he conveyed not only to black America, but to all of America, has resonated with me for as long as I can remember, and nothing else played as big a role in fueling my desire to be a writer, a recorder of history, a storyteller." As a third grader, she watched the 1950 *Jackie Robinson Story* with her classmates at school and first learned about a man who, she said, "showed us all how to be strong enough not to fight back but rather to fight on and on."[106]

Other Impressive Postbaseball Contributors

Jackie Robinson arguably contributed more to American society after he retired from baseball than any other player. His three principal competitors for that title seem to be pitcher Jim Bunning and outfielders Henry Aaron and Dave Winfield. Bunning was a Hall of Fame pitcher who, during his seventeen-year career, won over two hundred games, struck out nearly three thousand batters, and pitched a no-hitter in both the American and National Leagues. After his playing days ended, he served in public office for thirty-four years, including six terms in the US House of Representatives (1987–1999) and two in the US Senate (1999–2011).

After his retirement, Aaron worked diligently to persuade MLB to hire more black executives, umpires, and physicians and a black commissioner. Aaron worked as a player development manager for the Atlanta Braves' minor-league farm system. In 1990, he was named senior vice president and assistant to the president of the Braves. Aaron complained that most baseball players of his time, unlike Robinson, had "no discernible social conscience" or "sense of self-sacrifice." He claimed that Robinson would be "bitterly disappointed if he saw the way today's black players have abandoned the struggle" to improve society. Aaron exhorted ballplayers to dedicate themselves and their money to furnishing camps, counseling centers, and baseball programs for inner-city youth.[107] Aaron was a board member for Turner Broadcasting System (TBS) and vice president of business development for the CNN Airport Network. During the last thirty years of his life, he and his second wife, Billye, participated actively in community affairs and philanthropy. They established the Hank Aaron Chasing the Dream Foundation in the late 1990s to help needy children fulfill their aspirations. It has dispensed several million dollars in scholarships, primarily to students attending historically black colleges and universities. Aaron, like Robinson, also became a successful businessman and owned several car dealerships and eighteen Krispy Kreme franchises in Atlanta.[108]

A third Hall of Famer, Dave Winfield, created a foundation for underprivileged youth in 1977, while in his fifth year as a player, becoming the first active player to establish a charitable foundation. For forty-five years, it has focused on providing college scholarships, sponsoring health clinics, and preventing and treating substance abuse.[109] After playing for twenty-two years, Winfield was the San Diego Padres' executive vice president and senior advisor from 2001 to 2013; he has also worked as a baseball analyst for ESPN. Although the contributions to society of Bunning, Aaron, and Winfield are impressive, they are arguably less notable than those of Robinson detailed in this book.

Never Forget: The Legacy of Jackie Robinson

Historian Steve Riess argues that the saga of Jackie Robinson "is to Americans what the Passover story is to Jews: it must be told to every generation so that we never forget."[110] Jackie Robinson was "a complicated man who left multiple legacies, on and off the field, that defy easy characterization."[111] The integration of MLB remains a pivotal event in American history, and Robinson's teammates testified to how difficult the challenge was. "He knew that the future of blacks in baseball depended" on how well he did, fellow Dodger Duke Snider declared. "The pressure was enormous, overwhelming, and unbearable at times. I don't know how he held up. I know I never could have."[112] "I don't know any other ball player who could have done what he did," Pee Wee Reese stated. What he did, Reese said, was "the most tremendous thing I've ever seen in sports."[113]

Robinson's success on the diamond helped pave the way for black athletes to participate in baseball and other professional sports. Three African Americans joined MLB teams in July 1947, most notably Larry Doby, the first black to play in the American League. The Dodgers added pitcher Dan Bankhead in August 1947, catcher Roy Campanella in 1948, and pitcher Don Newcombe in 1949. By 1951, twenty African Americans had played in MLB, including Satchel Paige and Willie Mays. The National Basketball Association, formed in 1946, added its first three black players in 1950. A black woman, Althea Gibson, played tennis in the US Nationals in 1950, and black men first competed in 1959. An African American man played golf in the US Open in 1948; Gibson switched sports and in 1963 became the first black woman to play on the LPGA Tour. A handful of black Americans played in the National Football League from 1920 to 1933, but then none until 1946. The popularity of professional football in the 1940s, however, paled compared with that of MLB.

"If Jackie hadn't conducted himself as he did," declared Frank Robinson, the first black baseball manager, African Americans probably would not have made so much progress. "His play on the field, the classy way he was off the field," and his effective responses to critics, removed "all the excuses for not having blacks in every part of the game."[114] Robinson's exploits also helped darker-skinned Latinos break into MLB in the early 1950s, and the success of early black players "created a new era for all Latinos," most notably Luis Aparicio, Juan Marichal, and Orlando Cepeda.[115]

Hank Aaron called Robinson "the Dr. King of baseball."[116] He symbolized "the new American black," who was "proud, defiant, articulate, no longer patiently waiting to receive his civil rights."[117] "No black man had ever shone so brightly for so long as the epitome not only of stoic endurance but also of intelligence, bravery, physical power, and grit. Because baseball was lodged so deeply in the average white man's psyche," Robinson's success had a huge impact.[118] Even more than the feats of Jesse Owens and Joe Louis, those of Jackie Robinson helped change the way millions of African Americans viewed themselves, giving them a sense of pride and hope that they would someday be treated equally. Thousands of black parents named their children after him.

Like African Americans, many Jews carefully watched and applauded Robinson's performance on the diamond. To most Jews, the Dodger was "a surrogate whose successes were as much Jewish as African American triumphs." Jews were powerfully drawn to Robinson, as they had been to Joe Louis. They deeply admired his undaunted courage and unshakable dignity as he confronted racist taunts, physical attacks, and death threats and combated the forces of prejudice that harmed all minority groups. They also empathized with Robinson because the few Jews who played in the major leagues before 1947, most notably Hank Greenberg, had frequently endured anti-Semitic heckling from opposing players and fans.[119]

Although Robinson was not forgotten after his death by either African American baseball players or the general public, his status was greatly elevated in 1997 as the fiftieth anniversary of the smashing of the color barrier was widely celebrated and his number was retired throughout MLB. Baseball's rich, "quasi-intellectual tradition"; sportswriters determined to tell his story; and his remarkable career and personality all contributed to the greater emphasis on his exploits.[120] Highlighting Robinson's legacy also enabled MLB to appeal to African Americans to play baseball and to help increase the percentage of minorities working in front offices and as managers, while directing attention away from baseball's problems, including the lack of competitive balance and many players' use of steroids and other performance-enhancing drugs.[121] Also in 1997, the Jackie Robinson Foundation coproduced *Jackie Robinson: Breaking Barriers*, a film that included interviews with family members, his Dodger teammates, and contemporaries. Jewish organizations celebrated Robinson's jubilee year with conferences and exhibits and extolled him "as a symbol of the fight against bigotry." The Simon Wiesenthal Center's Museum of Tolerance produced a traveling exhibition, *Stealing Home: How Jackie Robinson Changed America*, portraying Robinson as a model of racial and religious tolerance.[122]

Jackie Robinson's story "has become a kind of American parable" similar to that of Abraham Lincoln the railsplitter emerging from the prairies to end slavery, Charles Lindbergh flying alone across the Atlantic, and Franklin Roosevelt "rising from the despair of polio to put steel in the spine of a nation."[123] Jessie Jackson argues that Robinson was a therapist for the black masses; by succeeding with great style, flair, and drama, he made baseball a game for people of all races, "with excellence the only test for success."[124] Robinson's successful integration of baseball, a black journalist insists, was indisputably "America's proudest story of democracy in action," its greatest "proof that people of all races and colors and creeds can work or play together in harmony for the greater good of all."[125] Civil rights activist Roger Wilkins maintains that Robinson helped instill pride in blacks; he "lifted us up" as "he marched through both the muck of white racism and the pain of culturally shriveled black spirits." Robinson's exploits inspired many to join the NAACP and to participate in demonstrations in numerous locales.[126] *Ebony* magazine declared, "Jackie became a symbol. . . . He was doctor, engineer, mathematician, professor, airline pilot, business executive and everything else a young black man might aspire to be."[127] When somebody asked Roger Kahn "what Jackie Robinson had done for his race," he replied, "His race was humanity, and he did a great deal for us."[128]

The many awards and honors bestowed on Robinson testify to his contributions to American society. In 1956 he received the NAACP's Spingarn Medal. The next year the Interfaith Committee of Washington, DC, honored him for his diligent efforts to improve race relations. He received his denomination's Churchmanship Award in 1963 for his outstanding work as a Christian layman. In 1971, *Sport* magazine named him the greatest athlete of the previous twenty-five years. In 1972, the Dodgers retired

Robinson's number, 42, along with the numbers of Sandy Koufax and Roy Campanella, the first three numbers the franchise retired. President Ronald Reagan awarded Robinson the Presidential Medal of Freedom in 1984, declaring that "he struck a mighty blow for equality, freedom and the American way of life." In 1997 MLB retired number 42, the first time that MLB, the NFL, the NBA, or the NHL had ever retired a number.[129] In 1999, *Time* magazine included Robinson among the 100 most influential people of the twentieth century, while *The Sporting News* put him on its list of baseball's 100 greatest players. In 2005 President George W. Bush awarded Robinson the Congressional Gold Medal, the nation's highest civilian honor. A highway from Queens to Brooklyn is named for Robinson, as are the rotunda at the New York Mets' Citi Field and dozens of schools. Even with all these posthumous accolades, Robinson would undoubtedly still say, as he did in 1963, that his most prized possession was not any of his trophies and plaques but the loving cup their three children presented to Rachel and him that year, inscribed "To the best parents."[130] The Jackie Robinson Foundation is currently creating a museum in lower Manhattan as a tribute to his pioneering legacy and to publicize his "unswerving commitment to social justice and equal opportunity."[131]

Myths, Jackie Robinson, and Baseball

Jackie Robinson has become fixed in America's cultural ethos. "The mythic Robinson exists" as a series of impressions "of solitude, strife and flashing spikes, of base-running bravado and beanballs, of pennants and provocations and perseverance." Robinson's "legend has reverberated in the national imagination" as an "epitome not only of stoic endurance," Arnold Rampersad argues, "but also of intelligence, bravery, physical power and grit."[132] The story of his baseball career, especially his captivating first season, has become part of American folklore. It features many of the central themes of American legends, life, and literature, most notably that through hard work individuals can conquer all obstacles and rise to great heights. Robinson shines brightly in America's cultural firmament, pointing the way toward what talented, energetic, courageous, persevering people can achieve regardless of their race, class, or religious convictions. To many, Robinson's saga "is redemptive and transporting. . . . Robinson is a secular saint, revered for his skill and his bravery" in carrying out "the noble experiment of desegregating baseball."[133]

Robinson has often been portrayed more as a legendary figure than as a human being. His story frequently attains mythical proportions and contains numerous highly suspect episodes. The contention that he singlehandedly integrated baseball in April 1947 ignores the history of Native American, Latino, and other African American players and the contributions of thousands of black sportswriters, politicians, religious and union leaders, and civil rights activists. It is doubtful that Robinson and Pee Wee ever embraced on the baseball diamond or that in May 1947 the St. Louis Cardinals threatened to strike if Robinson played against them. Although Robinson himself, as well as the media during his playing days, often portrayed him as impervious to the racist taunting and discrimination he experienced in accommodations and restaurants, beneath the surface he was infuriated. Moreover, Branch Rickey is often given too much credit for integrating baseball. As we have seen, many others contributed to this breakthrough.

Because of his intense struggles, impressive accomplishments, and inspiring character, Robinson's entire life, or at least his baseball career, has often been depicted as larger than life. He has been presented as a civil rights champion, an athletic hero, and even as the embodiment of all the good traits baseball commonly represents in American history. Robinson may have "personified blacks in baseball" during his playing career and for the remainder of his life, but his achievements have often been overemphasized, leading to an underappreciation of numerous other African Americans—most notably Larry Doby, Ray Campanella, Willie Mays, Hank Aaron, and Frank Robinson—who, by their demeanor and performance on the field, also helped advance the status of black Americans.[134]

Robinson would have been the first to admit that he was a flawed human being, not a saint. He had incredible strengths, but he also had weaknesses that made his life more difficult. His story includes much pathos: his inner turmoil as he dealt with abusive physical and verbal treatment on the baseball diamond; his struggle to relate to his eldest son and cope with Jackie Jr.'s tragic death; his battles with other black civil rights leaders; and the challenges Jackie and Rachel faced in their marriage as she strove to be her own person and have her own career, not simply to be the wife of a famous ballplayer. Ken Burns's 2016 documentary, made in collaboration with Rachel, helps strips away "the heroic veneer and liberates" Jackie from some of the legends surrounding him, "which makes him feel more raw and human" and, as a result, even more admirable.[135]

That Robinson's life and accomplishments have been shrouded in myths is not surprising; baseball itself has long been cloaked in mythology. As John Thorn, the official historian for MLB, argues, "in no field of American endeavor is invention more rampant than in baseball, whose whole history is a lie from beginning to end, from its creation myth to its rosy models of commerce, community, and fair play. The game's epic feats and revered figures, its pieties about racial harmony and bleacher democracy, its artful blurring of sport and business—all of it is bunk. . . . Yet we love both the game and the flimflam because they are both so . . . American."[136]

This uniquely American game has embodied quintessential American values ever since its invention, allegedly by Abner Doubleday in Cooperstown, New York, in 1839. Historians insist that Doubleday had no role in founding the sport, which evolved incrementally from earlier English games using bats and balls. Baseball has long been a symbol of a simpler, rural past and the nation's highest aspirations. Perhaps nothing better epitomizes this symbolism than the 1989 nostalgic movie *Field of Dreams*. In the movie, Terrence Mann, a Boston author, tells an Iowa corn farmer that America "has been erased like a blackboard, rebuilt, and erased again, but baseball has marked the time. This field [which the farmer constructs on his property], this game, it's a part of our past. . . . It reminds us of all that once was good and could be again."[137]

Randy Roberts argues that myths about baseball have been persistent and deep and that many players, owners, sportswriters, and fans have viewed the sport in terms of myths rather than realities. He repudiates common contentions that baseball has been democratic, that it has built character, and that it has served as "an assimilating and acculturating agent for immigrants." Benevolent and civil-minded owners of professional baseball teams allegedly brought bucolic serenity into New York, Chicago, Boston, and other bustling cities, enabling all Americans, regardless of class, creed, or citizenship, to be instructed in "traditional American values like hard work, sacrifice, self-reliance, and independence." In reality, Roberts claims, the game was invented and played principally in urban centers, and owners sought primarily to make money or advance political aims. A game that allegedly symbolized many virtues of rural America was ironically controlled by men who epitomized much of urban America's corruption. From its inception, professional baseball was a business and team owners were "as tight-fisted and dictatorial as the most ruthless nineteenth-century robber barons." They treated players "as semiskilled labor, to be used for several seasons, paid as little as possible, and then discarded."[138]

Myths serve a variety of purposes. At their most basic level, they help make sense of life by providing answers to timeless concerns about the origin of humanity and the world, human nature, the meaning of existence, good and evil, and the afterlife. Some myths challenge human expectations, beliefs, and actions, while others furnish role models, reassurance, and hope. Myths supply instruction and social norms; they celebrate or lament aspects of the human experience. They help justify particular social systems and cultural practices. Myths guide and comfort people and provide a sense of belonging. They furnish personal meaning and teach individuals who they are and their place in the universe.[139]

The myths about Jackie Robinson and baseball have served many of these purposes. They have helped reassure Americans that their nation is unique, special, and virtuous and that individual character, teamwork, arduous labor, risk taking, and persistence pay off. These myths affirm that Americans value fair play, camaraderie, self-sacrifice, and loyalty. For black Americans, Robinson's story has been particularly uplifting and inspiring. It demonstrates that talented individuals who work diligently can prosper despite the barriers of race and class. Robinson's experience suggests that racial prejudice and discrimination can be defeated or at least diminished by the acts of tenacious, courageous individuals.

Robinson's heroic performance and his story's appeal to cherished American values prompted many white people to acknowledge the nation's institutional racism and change their attitudes toward black people.[140] Robinson's saga forced many white Americans to confront their own prejudices, to think about the injustices African Americans faced, and in some cases, to resolve to help end them. For the first time in their lives, some white Americans identified with a black person and strove to understand the plight of his compatriots. Some of them saw the world anew through his eyes and experiences, his pleasures and pains.[141] Numerous white Americans thanked him for stimulating them to reject racial prejudice, and some white entrepreneurs, influenced by his accomplishments, integrated their businesses and factories.[142] Undoubtedly speaking for many, Dodgers' announcer Red Barber confessed that Robinson forced him to reexamine his beliefs and led him to become more understanding and tolerant.[143] Robinson proved by his deeds that "black Americans had been held back not by their inferiority but by systemic discrimination." That, Jonathan Eig contends, is his "true legacy."[144]

Rachel's Legacy

Rachel Robinson's accomplishments are also impressive. After her husband's death, she kept his legacy alive, promoting his favorite causes and new ones as well. She served as president of the Jackie Robinson Development Corporation from 1972 to 1986. Rachel founded the Jackie Robinson Foundation in 1973 to provide scholarships for college students and promote leadership development. Its stated purpose is to help "promising minority youths in realizing their full potential as well-educated and active participants in the process of social change."[145] The foundation has provided $85 million in program assistance, including $26 million in direct financial aid, to more than 1,500 students. Scholarship recipients also receive summer jobs and internships and academic, emotional, social, and career counseling. A remarkable 98 percent of Jackie Robinson scholars have graduated from college, including from Harvard, Yale, Georgetown, and UCLA.[146]

In addition, Rachel has continued, as Jackie did, to prod MLB to hire more minorities as managers and executives. In 2014, the Baseball Reliquary named her to its Shrine of Eternals, an alternative Hall of Fame celebrating the sport's "rebels and renegades." In 2017, Rachel received the MLB Hall of Fame's John Jordan "Buck" O'Neil Lifetime Achievement Award for her tireless efforts to increase racial equality in baseball and throughout American society. Jackie and Rachel are the only husband and wife team enshrined in Cooperstown. Fittingly, Rachel has been acknowledged and honored as "one of the most important women in baseball history."[147] She is "an outright national treasure," asserts Claire Smith, who "is as integral to the legend of No. 42 as Jackie himself."[148]

Conclusion

Throughout American history, sports have been not just a form of entertainment and competition. Rather, they have embodied and reflected numerous cultural trends and debates and are one of the nation's primary venues for hotly contested battles over religion, gender, sexual identity, patriotism, and race. Since the 1940s, sports, along with universities, movies and television, and popular music, have served as a major platform for society's clashes over social norms. In recent years, racial and anti-Semitic slurs and domestic violence incidents involving college and professional players and coaches have been widely condemned and have had major consequences. On the other hand, many athletes have censured racism, police brutality, and unfairness in voting rights.[149] Not surprisingly, when athletes protest conditions in American society, as NBA players did in 2020 after the death of George Floyd and other African Americans and the shooting of Jacob Blake, the name of Jackie Robinson is often invoked.[150]

Baseball and some other sports moved more quickly toward racial equality than most other areas of American society, thereby contributing to the desegregation of other institutions and social practices. Beginning in the 1950s, African Americans and Latinos enjoyed greater opportunities in sports than in almost any other area of society. By practicing and playing together in the 1960s, black and white athletes helped demolish some "racial barriers in the South that would have been conventionally impenetrable," but they rarely socialized after leaving the field.[151] During this decade, black football pioneers in the South, such as Southern Methodist University running back and wide receiver Jerry LeVias, endured "racist verbal and physical assaults from opponents, hate mail, and death threats," just as Robinson had earlier. Like Robinson, these "martyr-like historical figures" suffered emotional scars that remained throughout their lives.[152] Integration gave black athletes "more opportunities and resources, but at the stiff price of fractured communities and a loss of culture."[153]

Moreover, racism continued in sports, negative racial stereotypes were often associated with blackness, and, off the field, African Americans were still treated as second-class citizens. By the mid-1960s, led by former football star and sociologist Harry Edwards, increasing numbers of African Americans began to challenge the treatment of their race. Edwards exhorted black athletes to stop complacently accepting relegation to an inferior status. Those who joined his black athletic revolt, especially those who participated in boycotts and protests, were constantly criticized for not appreciating their opportunities and for undermining sporting ideals, whereas black athletes who sought only to excel in their sports were praised. Both the written and unwritten rules of conduct in sports inhibited black athletes from fully engaging in the battle against discrimination. Edwards and his allies were typically portrayed as extremists with unrealistic and destructive demands.[154]

From the late 1960s to the present, racial and gender prejudice have continued. When black athletes such as basketball star Michael Jordan, Olympic sprinter Michael Johnson, or golfer Tiger Woods triumph, the media presents their success as an inspiring example for all minorities, but the off-the-field problems of black athletes such as boxer Mike Tyson or football receiver Terrell Owens have been more highlighted than those of their white counterparts. Previously marginalized groups have received unprecedented inclusion as players, but few members of minority groups are team owners, general managers, or coaches in any major sport.[155]

Jackie Robinson broke down the racial wall that had kept baseball completely white and had long prevented African Americans from playing, but the sport has been slow to recognize or change some of its practices.[156] In 2020, MLB finally decided to count the statistics of 3,400 African Americans who played in seven different Negro leagues operating between 1920 and 1948 as part of official MLB records. These leagues, MLB commissioner Rob Manfred declared, "produced many of our game's best players, innovations and triumphs against a backdrop of injustice." In 2021, however, only two MLB teams had African American managers and only one had a black head of operations. After peaking at more than 18 percent in the mid-1970s and again in the mid-1980s, the percentage of African American players in 2020 was 7.8, only slightly higher than the 6.7 percent total in 1956, Robinson's last season, and well below the black proportion of the overall US population, currently 13.4 percent.[157] Several factors have produced this decline: many African Americans do not play baseball as children, the best black athletes tend to gravitate to other sports, and the percentage of Latino and foreign-born players has increased substantially (30 and 28.5 percent, respectively, in 2021, although there is considerable overlap between the two groups). Mexican American businessman Arturo Moreno, who has owned the Los Angeles Angels since 2003, is the only person of color who is the majority owner of an MLB team. Three African Americans—Derek Jeter, Earvin "Magic" Johnson, and LeBron James—are part owners of the Miami Marlins, Los Angeles Dodgers, and Boston Red Sox, respectively.[158]

"Racism was in the amniotic fluid out of which our nation was born." It was present in the environment in which the American people, culture, and nation developed. The virus of racism infected churches, the Constitution and laws, and American attitudes and ideologies.[159] Attorney Bryan Stevenson, who created the Equal Justice Initiative to abolish excessive and unfair sentencing and exonerate innocent death-row prisoners, asserts that the greatest evil of American slavery "was the fiction that black people . . . aren't the equals of white people," that they are less evolved, human, capable, worthy, or deserving than whites.[160] Jackie Robinson spent his life trying to demolish this fiction by his performance on the baseball field, civil rights activism, publications, and speeches. "The resiliency, creativity, industry, and indomitable faith" of Jackie Robinson and many other African Americans despite "all they have suffered is nothing short of miraculous." Their innovations, entrepreneurship, art, music, films, poetry, books, sermons, hymns, and athletic achievements have greatly benefited the world.[161]

Robert Ellis argues that watching or participating in sports can provide moments of transcendence that elevate us above the routines of everyday life; during these moments, people can "witness the work of the divine amid the seemingly ordinary."[162] Although Robinson never explicitly stated this idea, I believe it summarizes how he viewed his athletic career. Through his integration of MLB and varied activities after his playing career, Robinson demolished racial barriers, opened opportunities for other people of color, denounced racism, and helped build a better America. Discrimination continues, however, as evident in education, employment, housing, the criminal justice system, life expectancy, and other areas. The median household income of whites is almost $30,000 greater than that of blacks, while the median white household's wealth is almost eight times as high as that of the median black household. Black Americans fear being accosted by the police and are disproportionately likely to be arrested and shot by the police. We have a long way to go to eliminate discrimination, but inspired by his Christian faith, Jackie Robinson moved our society forward, and his life continues to inspire progress toward racial equity. He deserves to have the last word: "If I had a room jammed with trophies, awards and citations, and a child of mine came into that room and asked what I had done in defense of black people and decent whites fighting for freedom, and I had to tell that child that I had kept quiet, that I had been timid, I would have to mark myself a total failure at the whole business of living."[163]

Abbreviations

BR	Branch Rickey
JFK	John F. Kennedy
JR	Jackie Robinson
JRP	Jackie Robinson Papers
LBJ	Lyndon Baines Johnson
LOC	Library of Congress
MLB	Major League Baseball
MLK	Martin Luther King Jr.
NR	Nelson Rockefeller

Notes

Preface

1. Cornel West, introduction to *I Never Had It Made: Jackie Robinson, an Autobiography* (New York: HarperCollins, 1995), ix. Originally published by Putnam in 1972.

2. Jon Meacham, "Jackie Robinson's Inner Struggle," *New York Times*, July 20, 2020, https://www.nytimes.com/2020/07/20/books/review/jackie-robinson-inner-struggle.html (first quotation); Robinson, *I Never*, 279 (second quotation).

3. Jason Sokol, "Jackie Robinson's Life Was No Home Run for Racial Progress," *Time*, July 4, 2015, https://time.com/3942084/jackie-robinson-racial-progress/.

4. "Jackie Robinson: This I Believe," NPR, March 25, 2008, https://www.npr.org/templates/story/story.php?storyId=89030535.

5. Michael G. Long and Chris Lamb, *Jackie Robinson: A Spiritual Biography; The Faith of a Boundary-Breaking Hero* (Louisville: Westminster John Knox, 2017), 10.

6. Chris Lamb, "Hall of Famer Continues to Inspire," Michigan Conference, The United Methodist Church, October 24, 2017, https://michiganumc.org/hall-famer-continues-inspire/.

7. Ed Henry, *42 Faith: The Rest of the Jackie Robinson Story* (Nashville: W Publishing, 2017), 19.

Introduction

1. Edna Rust and Art Rust Jr., *Art Rust's Illustrated History of the Black Athlete* (Garden City, NY: Doubleday, 1985), 60.

2. Red Barber, "It Was Never a Game for Jackie," review of *I Never Had It Made*, by Jackie Robinson, *New York Times*, November 12, 1972, https://timesmachine.nytimes.com/timesmachine/1972/11/12/91354522.pdf?pdf_redirect=true&ip=0.

3. Christopher Evans and William Herzog II, "Introduction: More Than a Game," in *The Faith of 50 Million: Baseball, Religion, and American Culture*, ed. Christopher Evans and William Herzog II (Louisville: Westminster John Knox, 2002), 6.

4. "A Little Rusted Up," *New York Times*, February 11, 1971, 61.

5. John Kelly, "Integrating America: Jackie Robinson, Critical Events and Baseball Black and White," *International Journal of the History of Sport* 22, no. 6 (2005), doi:10.1080/09523360500286742.

6. Jules Tygiel, *Baseball's Great Experiment: Jackie Robinson and His Legacy* (New York: Oxford University Press, 2008), 9.

7. Patrick Henry, "Kareem's Omission? Jackie Robinson, Black Profiles in Courage," in *Jackie Robinson: Race, Sports, and the American Dream*, ed. Joseph Dorinson and Joram Warmund (Armonk, NY: M. E. Sharp, 1999), 209.

8. John Held, "Great Grandaddy vs. Jackie Robinson," *Southern Exposure* 7 (Fall 1979): 14.

9. Langston Hughes, *Montage of a Dream Deferred* (New York: Holt, 1951).

10. Jackie Robinson, *Breakthrough to the Big League: The Story of Jackie Robinson* (New York: Harper & Row, 1965), xii.

11. Jules Tygiel, introduction to *The Jackie Robinson Reader: Perspectives on an American Hero*, ed. Jules Tygiel (New York: Penguin, 1997), 9.

12. Simon Henderson, *How American Sports Challenged the Black Freedom Struggle* (Lexington: University Press of Kentucky, 2013); C. K. Pace, ed., *Race and Sport: The Struggle for Equality on and off the Field* (Jackson: University Press of Mississippi, 2004).

13. Howard Bryant, *The Heritage: Black Athletes, a Divided America, and the Politics of Patriotism* (Boston: Beacon, 2018), ix.

14. Scott Simon, *Jackie Robinson and the Integration of Baseball* (Hoboken, NJ: Wiley & Sons, 2007), 9 (quotation), 5.

15. Adrian Burgos, *Playing America's Game: Baseball, Latinos, and the Color Line* (Berkeley: University of California Press, 2007), 201 (second quotation); Joseph Arbena, review of *Playing America's Game*, by Adrian Burgos, *Americas* 64 (January 2008): 446 (first quotation). See also Peter Bjarkmann, *Baseball with a Latin Beat* (Jefferson, NC: McFarland, 1994).

16. On blacks in baseball, see Robert Peterson, *Only the Ball Was White: A History of Legendary Black Players and All-Black Professional Teams* (New York: Oxford University Press, 1992); Bill Kirwin, *Out of the Shadows: African American Baseball from the Cuban Giants to Jackie Robinson* (Lincoln: University of Nebraska Press, 2005); and Donn Rogosin, *Invisible Men: Life in Baseball's Negro Leagues* (New York: Kodansha, 1995).

17. See Jeffrey Powers-Beck, "'Chief': The American Indian Integration of Baseball, 1897–1945," *American Indian Quarterly* 25 (Fall 2001): 508–38. Powers-Beck lists forty-nine Native Americans who either played in MLB between 1887 and 1945 or were in the minors by 1947 and played in MLB after 1947. See also Powers-Beck, *The American Indian Integration of Baseball* (Lincoln: University of Nebraska Press, 2009), and Tom Swift, *Chief Bender's Burden: The Silent Struggle of a Baseball Star* (Lincoln: University of Nebraska Press, 2008).

18. Burgos, *Playing America's Game*, xiv, 4 (first quotation), 179–80 (second quotation), 185.

19. John Bloom, review of *Playing America's Game*, by Adrian Burgos, *American Quarterly* 60 (March 2008): 194. For context on baseball's history of segregation, see George Lipsitz, *The Possessive Investment in Whiteness* (Philadelphia: Temple University Press, 1998); and Michael Omi and Howard Winant, *Racial Formations in the United States: From the 1960s to the 1980s* (New York: Routledge, 1994).

20. Burgos, *Playing America's Game*, xiv, 2–4, 12. See also Burgos, "Robinson's Legacy Includes Assist for Latinos," La Vida Baseball, April 16, 2019, https://www.lavida baseball.com/jackie-robinson-latino-followers/.

21. Carl Rowan, *Wait Till Next Year: The Life Story of Jackie Robinson* (New York: Random House, 1960), 339.

22. "Baseball Honors Jackie Robinson," CNN, April 15, 1997, http://www.cnn.com /US/9704/15/robinson/.

23. "L.A. Dodgers, Major League Baseball Celebrate Jackie Robinson Day," *Los Angeles Daily News*, April 15, 2012, https://www.dailynews.com/2012/04/15/la -dodgers-major-league-baseball-celebrate-jackie-robinson-day/.

24. "Jackie Robinson: A Hero for 60 Years," *Los Angeles Daily News*, April 16, 2007, https://www.dailynews.com/2007/04/16/jackie-robinson-a-hero-for-60-years/.

25. Tygiel, *Baseball's Great Experiment*, 319, 320 (quotation).

26. Tygiel, *Baseball's Great Experiment*, 327.

27. Richard Stoll Armstrong, "My Reactions to '42,'" *Minding What Matters*, September 28, 2013, http://rsarm.blogspot.com/2013/09/my-reactions-to-42.html.

28. On Methodism, see Frederick Norwood, *The Story of American Methodism: A History of the United Methodists and Their Relations* (Nashville: Abingdon, 1974).

29. Russell E. Richey, Kenneth E. Rowe, and Jean Miller Schmidt, *The Methodist Experience in America*, vol. 2, *Sourcebook* (Nashville: Abingdon, 2000), 563 (first quotation), 564 (second and third quotations).

30. Gary Dorrien, *The New Abolition: W. E. B. Du Bois and the Black Social Gospel* (New Haven: Yale University Press, 2016); Evelyn Brooks Higginbotham, *Righteous Discontent: The Women's Movement in the Black Baptist Church, 1880–1920* (Cambridge, MA: Harvard University Press, 1993); Gary Scott Smith, *The Search for Social Salvation: Social Christianity and America, 1880–1925* (Lanham, MD: Lexington Books, 2000), 213–32.

31. Randal Maurice Jelks, "A Methodist Life," in *42 Today: Jackie Robinson and His Legacy*, ed. Michael G. Long (New York: New York University Press, 2021), 21 and passim.

32. Jacques Barzun, *God's Country and Mine* (Boston: Little, Brown, 1954), 159.

33. John Thorn, "Why Baseball?" in Geoffrey Ward and Ken Burns, *Baseball: An Illustrated History* (New York: Knopf, 1994), 61.

34. Christopher Evans, "Baseball as Civil Religion: The Genesis of an American Creation Story," in Evans and Herzog, *Faith of 50 Million*, 15. At the same time, MLB owners marketed the game to help promote baseball's inherent uniqueness. See G. Edward White, *Creating the National Pastime: Baseball Transforms Itself, 1903–1953* (Princeton: Princeton University Press, 2014).

35. Bart Giamatti, *Take Time for Paradise: Americans and Their Games* (New York: Summit Books 1989), 93.

36. Evans and Herzog, "Introduction," 7.

37. Burgos, *Playing America's Game*, 73. See also Susan Birrell and Mary McDonald, eds., *Reading Sport: Critical Essays on Power and Representation* (Boston: Northeastern University Press, 2000); and John Bloom and Michael Nevin Willard, eds., *Sports Matters: Race, Recreation, and Culture* (New York: New York University Press, 2002).

38. See also Kenneth Robson, ed., *A Great and Glorious Game: Baseball Writings of A. Bartlett Giamatti* (Chapel Hill, NC: Algonquin Books, 1998).

39. Evans and Herzog, "Introduction," 1.

40. Quoted in John Rossi, *The National Game: Baseball and American Culture* (Chicago: Ivan R. Dee, 2000), 9.

41. Evans, "Baseball as Civil Religion," 20, 21 (quotation), 22.

42. Harold Seymour, *Baseball: The Early Years* (New York: Oxford University Press, 1960), v–vii.

43. See Steven Riess, *Touching Base: Professional Baseball and American Culture in the Progressive Era* (Westport, CT: Greenwood, 1980).

44. Evans and Herzog, "Introduction," 2.

45. See Peter Levine, *A. G. Spalding and the Rise of Baseball: The Promise of American Sport* (New York: Oxford University Press, 1985).

46. David Heim, "The Kingdom of Baseball," *Christian Century* 119 (June 5, 2002): 36. On the history of baseball, see also David Voigt, *American Baseball*, 3 vols. (University Park: Pennsylvania State University Press, 1983), and Harold Seymour, *Baseball: The People's Game* (New York: Oxford University Press, 1990).

47. See Scott Boras, "We Have to Bring Baseball Back," *New York Times*, May 5, 2020, https://www.nytimes.com/2020/05/05/opinion/scott-boras-mlb-baseball-coronavirus.html.

48. Artemis Moshtaghian, "MLB and All 30 Teams Sue Insurance Providers, Citing Billions in Losses Due to Covid-19," CNN, December 5, 2020, https://www.cnn.com/2020/12/05/us/mlb-sue-insurance-losses-coronavius-trnd/index.html.

49. Becky Little, "Why the Star-Spangled Banner Is Played at Sporting Events," History.com, September 25, 2017, https://www.history.com/news/why-the-star-spangled-banner-is-played-at-sporting-events.

50. Rachel Robinson with Lee Daniels, *Jackie Robinson: An Intimate Portrait* (New York: Abrams, 1996), 10.

51. Roosevelt to Landis, January 15, 1942, in *Public Papers and Addresses of Franklin D. Roosevelt*, ed. Samuel Rosenman, 13 vols. (New York: Harper, 1938–50), 11:62.

52. Doug Glanville, "Baseball Is Playing for Its Life, and Ours," *New York Times*, August 2, 2020, https://www.nytimes.com/2020/08/02/opinion/baseball-coronavirus-Marlins.html.

53. NBC Sports Washington, July 20, 2020, https://www.nbcsports.com/washington/nationals/dr-anthony-fauci-will-throw-out-first-pitch-nationals-home-opener. See also George Will, "Our National Sports Withdrawal Is Agony," *Washington Post*, June 24, 2020, https://www.washingtonpost.com/opinions/our-national-sports-withdrawal-is-agony/2020/06/23/2755d4bc-b573-11ea-a8da-693df3d7674a_story.html; and Daniel Krauthammer, "Baseball's Return: Why We Care," *Washington Post*, July 22, 2020, https://www.washingtonpost.com/opinions

/why-we-are-inspired-by-the-return-of-baseball/2020/07/22/5c4c2fc4-c9f8-11ea
-bc6a-6841b28d9093_story.html.

54. David Adler, "MLB Sees Fan Growth across the Board in 2019," MLB.com, September 30, 2019, https://www.mlb.com/news/mlb-increased-viewership -attendance-in-2019.

55. Quoted in John Sexton, *Baseball as a Road to God* (New York: Gotham, 2014), 215.

56. See, for example, Franklin H. Zimmerman, "The Healing Power of Baseball," *New York Times*, May 1, 2020, https://www.nytimes.com/2020/05/01/well/baseball -coronavirus-masks-quarantine-war-influenza.html.

57. Renford Reese, "The Socio-Political Context of the Integration of Sport in America," *Journal of African American Men* 3 (Spring 1998): 7–8, quotation from 8.

58. Evans and Herzog, "Introduction," 6.

59. Christopher Evans, "The Kingdom of Baseball in America," in Evans and Herzog, *Faith of 50 Million*, 45.

60. Jackie Robinson, *Baseball Has Done It* (Brooklyn, NY: Ig, 2005), 23, 28; quotations in that order.

Chapter 1

1. Jackie Robinson, *Baseball Has Done It* (Brooklyn, NY: Ig, 2005), 39.

2. Jackie Robinson, *Breakthrough to the Big League: The Story of Jackie Robinson* (New York: Harper & Row, 1965), 169.

3. Arthur Morse, "Jackie Wouldn't Have Gotten to First Base," *Better Homes and Gardens*, May 1950, 279.

4. Arnold Rampersad, *Jackie Robinson: A Biography* (New York: Knopf, 1997), 22.

5. Jackie Robinson, "My Greatest Day," unpublished manuscript, n.d., but probably written in 1961, JRP, box 11, folder 12, Manuscript Division, LOC, Washington, DC, 2–3.

6. "Mrs. Robinson's Notes," miscellaneous manuscript, n.d., JRP, Manuscript Division, LOC, Washington, DC, 2.

7. Michael G. Long and Chris Lamb, *Jackie Robinson: A Spiritual Biography; The Faith of a Boundary-Breaking Hero* (Louisville: Westminster John Knox, 2017), 17.

8. "Mrs. Robinson's Notes," 4.

9. Quoted in Rampersad, *Jackie Robinson*, 24.

10. Meyer Liebowitz, "On Jackie Robinson Day, 100 Photos of the Icon on the Field and with Family," *New York Times*, January 31, 2019, https://www.nytimes .com/2019/01/31/sports/jackie-robinson-photos-100th-birthday.html.

11. Jackie Robinson, "My Greatest Day," 3.

12. Jackie Robinson, *Baseball Has Done It*, 40 (first phrase); Jackie Robinson, *Breakthrough*, 16 (second phrase).

13. Jackie Robinson, *Breakthrough*, 7.

14. Jackie Robinson, "My Greatest Day," 3.

15. Jackie Robinson, *I Never Had It Made: Jackie Robinson, an Autobiography* (New York: HarperCollins, 1995), 5, 269; quotations in that order.

16. "Ex-Dodger Happy: Robinson Recalls Humble Beginning," *Wilmington (OH) News Journal*, January 24, 1962, 13.

17. Jackie Robinson, "Home Plate," *New York Amsterdam News*, May 28, 1966, 17.

18. Interview with Willa Mae, n.d., in David Falkner, *Great Time Coming: The Life of Jackie Robinson from Baseball to Birmingham* (New York: Simon & Schuster, 1995), 20.

19. Rachel Robinson with Lee Daniels, *Jackie Robinson: An Intimate Portrait* (New York: Abrams, 1996), 14.

20. "Interview with Rachel Robinson," *Scholastic*, February 11, 1998, https://www .scholastic.com/teachers/articles/teaching-content/interview-rachel-robinson/.

21. "Rookie of the Year," *Time*, September 22, 1947.

22. Jules Tygiel, introduction to *The Jackie Robinson Reader: Perspectives on an American Hero*, ed. Jules Tygiel (New York: Penguin, 1997), 2.

23. Rampersad, *Jackie Robinson*, 32; all quotations but the last phrase, which is from Michael Anderson, "Baseball in Black and White: Whoever Wants to Know the Heart and Mind of America Had Better Learn the Jackie Robinson Story," *New York Times*, October 19, 1997, https://archive.nytimes.com/www.nytimes.com/books/97/10/19 /reviews/971019.19anderst.html.

24. Arthur Mann, *The Jackie Robinson Story* (New York: Grosset & Dunlop, 1951), 37.

25. Long and Lamb, *Jackie Robinson*, 25.

26. "Mrs. Robinson's Notes," 5; Long and Lamb, *Jackie Robinson*, 22.

27. Morse, "Jackie Wouldn't," 315.

28. "Mrs. Robinson's Notes," 5.

29. Jackie Robinson (as told to Ed Reid), "Robinson Never Forgets Mother's Advice," *Washington Post*, August 23, 1949, 12–13.

30. Fred Glennon, "Baseball's Surprising Moral Example: Branch Rickey, Jackie Robinson, and the Racial Integration of America," in *The Faith of 50 Million: Baseball, Religion, and American Culture*, ed. Christopher Evans and William Herzog II (Louisville: Westminster John Knox, 2002), 154.

31. Jackie Robinson, "Robinson Never Forgets," 12.

32. "Rookie of the Year."

33. Morse, "Jackie Wouldn't," 279.

34. See Marne Campbell, *Making Black Los Angeles: Class, Gender, and Community, 1850–1917* (Chapel Hill: University of North Carolina Press, 2016).

35. Jackie Robinson, *Baseball Has Done It*, 41.

36. Morse, "Jackie Wouldn't," 278.

37. Long and Lamb, *Jackie Robinson*, 21.

38. Rampersad, *Jackie Robinson*, 24.

39. Interview with Willa Mae, n.d., in Rampersad, *Jackie Robinson*, 33.

40. *Jackie Robinson: My Own Story* (New York: Greenburg, 1948), 7.

41. Mann, *The Jackie Robinson Story*, 39.

42. Jackie Robinson, *I Never*, 5–6.

43. Mann, *The Jackie Robinson Story*, 38.

44. Mann, *The Jackie Robinson Story*, 35, 36; Rachel Robinson, *Jackie Robinson*, 222.

45. Ray Bartlett interview, March 6, 1992, in John Vernon, "Beyond the Box Score: Jackie Robinson, Civil Rights Crusader," *Negro History Bulletin* 58 (October–December 1995): 16.

46. Sharon Robinson, *Stealing Home: An Intimate Family Portrait by the Daughter of Jackie Robinson* (New York: HarperPerennial, 1997), 36.

47. Jackie Robinson, *Breakthrough*, 5.

48. *Jackie Robinson: My Own Story*, 8; Jackie Robinson, *Breakthrough*, 17.

49. Roger Kahn, "The Jackie Robinson I Remember," *Journal of Blacks in Higher Education* 14 (Winter 1996/1997): 90; Jackie Robinson, *I Never*, 6.

50. Long and Lamb, *Jackie Robinson*, 24.

51. Jerome Ledoux, "Untold Part of Jackie Robinson Story Centers on Faith," *Daily World*, May 28, 2017, https://www.dailyworld.com/story/opinion/2017/05/28/untold -part-jackie-robinson-story-centers-faith/102097256/.

52. Jackie Robinson, *I Never*, 7.

53. Long and Lamb, *Jackie Robinson*, 24.

54. Jackie Robinson, *Breakthrough*, 19.

55. Vernon, "Beyond the Box Score," 15. On Robinson's athletic prowess in high school, see "Classic Faces in the Crowd," *Sports Illustrated*, July 19, 1993, 73; Woodie Strode and Sam Young, *Goal Dust* (New York: Madison Books, 1990), 30; and Harvey Frommer, *Jackie Robinson* (New York: Watts, 1984), 10–14.

56. Long and Lamb, *Jackie Robinson*, 28.

57. Randal Maurice Jelks, "A Methodist Life," in *42 Today: Jackie Robinson and His Legacy*, ed. Michael G. Long (New York: New York University Press, 2021), 20–21. Jelks explains how the Methodist emphasis on a personal relationship with God, the pursuit of holiness, and efforts to improve society provided a foundation for Robinson's life and social activism (18–20).

58. Rampersad, *Jackie Robinson*, 56.

59. Rampersad, *Jackie Robinson*, 57; Ray Bartlett, interview with Rampersad, n.d.

60. Rachel Robinson, *Jackie Robinson*, 18.

61. Quoted in John Maher, "Huston College President Guided Jackie Robinson Down Historic Path," *Austin American-Statesman*, August 24, 2013, https://www .statesman.com/article/20130824/SPORTS/308249735.

62. Jackie Robinson, *I Never*, 7 (first quotation), 8 (second quotation); Jackie Robinson, "My Greatest Day," 8 (third quotation).

63. Rampersad, *Jackie Robinson*, 58.

64. Jackie Robinson, "My Greatest Day," 6.

65. Jackie Robinson, *I Never*, 9 (first and third quotations); Jackie Robinson, "My Greatest Day," 8 (second quotation).

66. Rachel Robinson, *Jackie Robinson*, 18.

67. Jackie Robinson, *I Never*, 8.

68. Jackie Robinson, "My Greatest Day," 7.

69. Ada C. Anderson, "Downs, Karl Everette (1912–1948)," Texas State Historical Association, Handbook of Texas, accessed October 7, 2021, https://www.tshaonline .org/handbook/entries/downs-karl-everette; Falkner, *Great Time Coming*, 34.

70. Quoted in Maher, "Huston College President Guided Jackie Robinson Down Historic Path."

71. Jackie Robinson, *I Never*, 8.

72. Jackie Robinson, *Baseball*, 42.

73. Jackie Robinson, "My Greatest Day," 9–10.

74. Karl Downs, *Meet the Negro* (Pasadena, CA: Login, 1943), 21.

75. Chris Lamb, "Jackie Robinson Day Is April 15—Here's a Story about Robinson

You May Not Know," *Huffington Post*, April 12, 2017, https://www.huffpost.com/entry/jackie-robinson-day-is-april-15-heres-a-story-about_b_58ea0e5e4b0145a227cb6cb.

76. Mann, *Jackie Robinson*, 139 (quotation), 98.

77. Karl Downs, "Did My Church Forsake Me? A Negro Methodist Asks a Question," *Zion's Herald*, March 9, 1938, 308. This article is the source for discussing this episode.

78. "Made Good," *Time* 31 (March 21, 1938): 53.

79. William N. Jones, "Day by Day," *Baltimore Afro-American*, April 9, 1938, 4.

80. "NAACP to Hear Carl Downs," *Baltimore Afro-American*, November 12, 1938.

81. Long and Lamb, *Jackie Robinson*, 31.

82. Karl Downs, "Timid Negro Students," *Crisis*, June 1936, 171, 187; quotations in that order.

83. Maher, "Huston College President Guided Jackie Robinson Down Historic Path"; Anderson, "Downs, Karl Everette (1912–1948)."

84. Quoted in Maher, "Huston College President Guided Jackie Robinson Down Historic Path."

85. Paul Putz, "Who Was Karl Downs? Exploring the Life and Legacy of Jackie Robinson's Mentor," *Faith & Sports*, March 12, 2021, https://blogs.baylor.edu/faithsports/2021/03/12/who-was-karl-downs-exploring-the-life-and-legacy-of-jackie-robinsons-mentor/#_edn1.

86. Jackie Robinson, *Baseball Has Done It*, 45.

87. Mann, *Jackie Robinson*, 90.

88. Jackie Robinson, *Breakthrough*, 22.

89. Jackie Robinson, *Breakthrough*, 23.

90. Jackie Robinson, *Baseball Has Done It*, 44.

91. Jackie Robinson (as told to Ed Reid), "Jackie Finds Louis Real Champ," *Washington Post*, August 25, 1949, 17.

92. *Jackie Robinson: My Own Story*, 10.

93. Peter Dreier, "Honoring Rachel Robinson, Baseball Pioneer and Civil Rights Activist," *Huffington Post*, July 20, 2014, https://www.huffpost.com/entry/honoring-rachel-robinson-_b_5602717.

94. Gary Libman, "Rachel Robinson's Homecoming: She Recalls a Legend and Her Days in L.A.," *Los Angeles Times*, September 2, 1987.

95. J. K. Pollack, "A Family Named Robinson," *Parents Magazine*, 1955, in Tygiel, *The Jackie Robinson Reader*, 207.

96. Libman, "Rachel Robinson's Homecoming."

97. "Interview with Rachel Robinson" (quotation); Libman, "Rachel Robinson's Homecoming."

98. Jackie Robinson, *I Never*, 22–23.

99. Rampersad, *Jackie Robinson*, 81; Sharon Robinson, *Stealing Home*, 39.

100. Rampersad, *Jackie Robinson*, 82.

101. Mann, *Jackie Robinson*, 72.

102. Tygiel, introduction to *The Jackie Robinson Reader*, 3.

103. Jelks, "A Methodist Life," 23.

104. Jackie Robinson, *Breakthrough*, 25, 28, 34.

105. Jackie Robinson, "Jackie Finds Louis Real Champ," 17.

106. Jackie Robinson, *Breakthrough*, 35.

107. Jackie Robinson, *I Never*, 12.

108. Mann, *Jackie Robinson*, 83.

109. Quoted in Patrick Washburn, *The African-American Newspaper: Voice of Freedom* (Evanston, IL: Northwestern University Press, 2006), 144–47.

110. Jackie Robinson, *Breakthrough*, 36.

111. Paul Putz and Art Remillard, "Ten Christian Athletes Who Were Tebowing before Tebow," *Christianity Today*, September 28, 2016, https://www.christianityto day.com/history/2016/september/ten-christian-athletes-who-were-tebowing-before -tebow.html. On Louis's faith, see also Chris Mead, *Champion—Joe Louis, Black Hero in White America* (New York: Scribner, 1985), and Richard Bak, *Joe Louis: The Great Black Hope* (New York: Perseus, 1998).

112. Vernon, "Beyond the Box Score," 16. See also Jackie Robinson, "Jackie Finds Louis Real Champ," 17.

113. Rampersad, *Jackie Robinson*, 99.

114. Quoted in Jules Tygiel, "The Court-Martial of Jackie Robinson," in Tygiel, *The Jackie Robinson Reader*, 45.

115. Long and Lamb, *Jackie Robinson*, 43.

116. Ronald E. Franklin, "Jackie Robinson Court Martialed for Fighting Discrimination," Owlcation, December 9, 2017, https://owlcation.com/humanities/The -Jackie-Robinson-Court-Martial.

117. Paul E. Pfeifer, "The Court-Martial of Jackie Robinson," The Supreme Court of Ohio & the Ohio Justicial System, November 17, 1999, http://test.supremecourt .ohio.gov/SCO/justices/pfeifer/column/1999/jp111799.asp.

118. Rampersad, *Jackie Robinson*, 106.

119. Vernon, "Beyond the Box Score," 17. See also Michael Lee Lanning, *The Court-Martial of Jackie Robinson: The Baseball Legend's Battle for Civil Rights during World War II* (Lanham, MD: Stackpole Books, 2020).

120. Tygiel, "Court Martial," 50.

121. Tygiel, "Court-Martial," 51.

122. Jackie Robinson, *Baseball Has Done It*, 49.

123. Rachel Robinson interview, in Rampersad, *Jackie Robinson*, 106.

124. Rampersad, *Jackie Robinson*, 112.

125. "Rookie of the Year."

126. Falkner, *Great Time Coming*, 93 (quotation); Jackie Robinson, "What's Wrong with Negro Baseball?," *Ebony* 3 (June 1948): 16–18.

127. Chris Lamb, "Hall of Famer Continues to Inspire," Michigan Conference, The United Methodist Church, October 24, 2017, https://michiganumc.org/hall-famer -continues-inspire/.

128. Rampersad, *Jackie Robinson*, 118.

129. "Jackie Robinson Negro League Stats," Baseball Almanac, accessed October 7, 2021, https://www.baseball-almanac.com/players/p_robij3.shtml.

130. Scott Simon, *Jackie Robinson and the Integration of Baseball* (Hoboken, NJ: Wiley & Sons, 2007), 7.

131. Jules Tygiel, *Baseball's Great Experiment: Jackie Robinson and His Legacy* (New York: Oxford University Press, 2008), 41.

132. *Jackie Robinson: My Own Story*, 17–18.

Chapter 2

1. "Wesley's Sermon Reprints: The Use of Money," Christian History Institute, accessed October 8, 2021, https://christianhistoryinstitute.org/magazine/article/wesleys-sermon-use-of-money.

2. On Rickey's family and childhood, see Lee Lowenfish, *Branch Rickey: Baseball's Ferocious Gentleman* (Lincoln: University of Nebraska Press, 2007); Murray Polner, *Branch Rickey: A Biography* (New York: Athenaeum, 1982); and Roger Kahn, *Rickey & Robinson: The True, Untold Story of the Integration of Baseball* (New York: Rodale, 2014).

3. Lowenfish, *Branch Rickey*, 13–15; Polner, *Branch Rickey*, 30–31.

4. Arthur Mann, *The Jackie Robinson Story* (New York: Grosset & Dunlop, 1951), 11.

5. Lowenfish, *Branch Rickey*, 105.

6. Lowenfish, *Branch Rickey*, 280.

7. Arnold Rampersad, *Jackie Robinson: A Biography* (New York: Knopf, 1997), 120.

8. Lee Lowenfish, email correspondence with Long, July 10, 2016, in Michael G. Long and Chris Lamb, *Jackie Robinson: A Spiritual Biography; The Faith of a Boundary-Breaking Hero* (Louisville: Westminster John Knox, 2017), 52.

9. Lowenfish, *Branch Rickey*, 26–27. Because Rickey refused to play on Sundays, the Reds traded him to the Chicago White Sox, who traded him to the St. Louis Browns.

10. May 1906 interview with *Cleveland Press*, as cited by Polner, *Branch Rickey*, 42.

11. Branch Rickey, "'One Hundred Percent Wrong Club' Speech," Atlanta, January 20, 1956, LOC, Washington, DC, https://www.loc.gov/collections/jackie-robinson-baseball/articles-and-essays/baseball-the-color-line-and-jackie-robinson/one-hundred-percent-wrong-club-speech/.

12. E.g., Kahn, *Rickey & Robinson*, 2; Lowenfish, *Branch Rickey*, 390.

13. *Bridgeport Post*, Newspaper Archives, March 18, 1967, 4.

14. Peale to Mary Iams Rickey, November 2, 1971, as quoted in Lowenfish, *Branch Rickey*, 598.

15. Lowenfish, *Branch Rickey*, 216.

16. Lowenfish, *Branch Rickey*, 289; see *Time*, May 30, 1938, 58; John Evans, "Methodism to Shift Gears to Face New Age," *Chicago Tribune*, February 5, 1938, 13.

17. Lowenfish, *Branch Rickey*, 340.

18. "History," The Church-in-the-Gardens, accessed October 8, 2021, http://thecitg.org/info/history.

19. Quoted in Fred Glennon, "Baseball's Surprising Moral Example: Branch Rickey, Jackie Robinson, and the Racial Integration of America," in *The Faith of 50 Million: Baseball, Religion, and American Culture*, ed. Christopher Evans and William Herzog II (Louisville: Westminster John Knox, 2002), 150.

20. Lowenfish, *Branch Rickey*, 306, 340–41, 510.

21. Ed Henry, *42 Faith: The Rest of the Jackie Robinson Story* (Nashville: W Publishing, 2017), 185–86.

22. On Rickey's faith, see also John Chalberg, *Rickey and Robinson: The Preacher, the Player, and America's Game* (Wheeling, IL: Harlan Davidson, 2000).

23. Dan Dodson, "The Integration of Negroes in Baseball," in *The Jackie Robinson Reader: Perspectives on an American Hero*, ed. Jules Tygiel (New York: Penguin, 1997), 158.

24. Roger Kahn, *The Boys of Summer* (Evanston, IL: Holtzman, 1972), 94.

25. Larry Powell, "Jackie Robinson and Dixie Walker: Myths of the Southern Baseball Player," *Southern Cultures* 8 (Summer 2002): 60.

26. "Rookie of the Year," *Time*, September 22, 1947; Jack Orr, "Jackie Robinson: Symbol of the Revolution," *Sport* 29 (March 1960): 55.

27. Bill Horlacher, "When Leadership Smashed the Color Barrier," *Success Factors* 1, no. 1 (Fall 1998): 5, https://static1.squarespace.com/static/517aa696e4b0ab 81ac8d9aef/t/51c480bde4b0895fa6de3948/1371832509726/Jackie_Robinson.pdf.

28. Editorial page, *St. Louis Post-Dispatch*, October 31, 1955.

29. David Prince, "The 'Ferocious Christian Gentleman' behind Jackie Robinson's Famous Moment," Prince on Preaching, April 15, 2015, https://www.da vidprince.com/2015/04/15/the-ferocious-christian-gentleman-behind-jackie -robinsons-famous-moment-2/.

30. Jules Tygiel, *Baseball's Great Experiment: Jackie Robinson and His Legacy* (New York: Oxford University Press, 2008), 48.

31. "Rookie of the Year."

32. Polner, *Branch Rickey*, 122.

33. Scott Simon, *Jackie Robinson and the Integration of Baseball* (Hoboken, NJ: Wiley & Sons, 2007), 83.

34. Tommy Holmes, *Dodger Daze and Knights* (New York: David McKay, 1953), 180–81.

35. Rampersad, *Jackie Robinson*, 121.

36. Lowenfish, *Branch Rickey*, 280.

37. Slaughter quoted in "Sports Buzz," *Birmingham News*, June 2, 1999; Stanky quoted in Carl Prince, *Brooklyn's Dodgers: The Bums, the Borough, and the Best of Baseball* (New York: Oxford University Press, 1996), 65; Kahn, *The Boys of Summer*, 94.

38. Simon, *Jackie Robinson*, 70.

39. Ed Fitzgerald, "Branch Rickey, Dodger Deacon," *Sport*, November 1947, 58.

40. Roger Launius, *Seasons in the Sun: The Story of Big League Baseball in Missouri* (Columbia: University of Missouri Press, 2002), 20.

41. Tygiel, *Baseball's Great Experiment*, 49.

42. Benjamin Verser, "Branch Rickey: Baseball's Lincoln," *Drover Review* 2 (2019), https://droverreview.files.wordpress.com/2019/06/drvol2201914verser.pdf.

43. Interview with Rachel Robinson, in Tygiel, *Baseball's Great Experiment*, 49.

44. Quoted in Robert Peterson, *Only the Ball Was White: A History of Legendary Black Players and All-Black Professional Teams* (New York: Oxford University Press, 1970), 176.

45. Peter Dreier, "The Real Story of Baseball's Integration That You Won't See in 42," *Atlantic*, April 11, 2013, https://www.theatlantic.com/entertainment/archive

/2013/04/the-real-story-of-baseballs-integration-that-you-wont-see-in-i-42-i/274
886/.

46. Peter Dreier, "Jackie Robinson: A Legacy of Activism," *American Prospect*,
January 31, 2019, https://prospect.org/civil-rights/jackie-robinson-legacy-activism.

47. *New York Amsterdam News*, December 26, 1942, quoted in Chris Lamb, *Conspiracy of Silence: Sportswriters and the Long Campaign to Desegregate Baseball* (Lincoln:
University of Nebraska Press, 2012), 223.

48. Larry Lester, "Can You Read, Judge Landis?," *Black Ball* 1 (Fall 2008): 74.

49. "Equality Laws Mock Negroes," *Northwest Enterprise*, November 8, 1944, 1.

50. The material in this paragraph is from Steven Norword and Harold Brackman,
"Going to Bat for Jackie Robinson: The Jewish Role in Breaking Baseball's Color Line,"
Journal of Sport History 26 (Spring 1999): 115–41; quotation from 118. See also Murray
Friedman, *What Went Wrong? The Creation and Collapse of the Black-Jewish Alliance*
(New York: Free Press, 1995); Stuart Svonkin, *Jews against Prejudice: American Jews
and the Fight for Civil Liberties* (New York: Columbia University Press, 1997); Neal
Gabler, *Winchell: Gossip, Power, and the Culture of Celebrity* (New York: Knopf, 1994);
Rebecca Alpert, *Out of Left Field: Jews and Black Baseball* (New York: Oxford University
Press, 2011).

51. Jules Tygiel's study relies heavily on the work of Wendell Smith and Sam Lacy
(*Baseball's Great Experiment*, ix).

52. *Jackie Robinson: My Own Story* (New York: Greenburg, 1948), 56.

53. See Patrick Washburn, "The Pittsburgh Courier's Double V Campaign in
1942," *American Journalism* 3 (Spring 1986): 73–86.

54. Jesse Washington, "Joe Louis and Jackie Robinson's Pittsburgh Story," *Undefeated*, February 28, 2018, https://theundefeated.com/features/book-smoketown-joe
-louis-and-jackie-robinson-pittsburgh-story/. See also Mark Whitaker, *Smoketown: The
Untold Story of the Other Great Black Renaissance* (New York: Simon & Schuster, 2019).

55. Wendell Smith papers, file MS-1, National Baseball Hall of Fame, Cooperstown, NY.

56. Washington, "Joe Louis and Jackie Robinson's Pittsburgh Story"; Brian Carroll,
"This Is IT! The PR Campaign by Wendell Smith and Jackie Robinson," *Journalism
History* 37, no. 3 (2011): 154; Rickey to Smith, January 8, 1946, Wendell Smith papers,
file MS-1. See also David Wiggins, "Wendell Smith, the Pittsburgh Courier-Journal
and the Campaign to Include Blacks in Organized Baseball, 1933-1945," *Journal of
Sport History* 10 (Summer 1983): 5–29.

57. Adrian Burgos, *Playing America's Game: Baseball, Latinos, and the Color Line*
(Berkeley: University of California Press, 2007), 181, 183.

58. Chris Lamb, "Breaking the Color Line: The Politics of Signing Jackie Robinson," *New Republic*, April 13, 2016, https://newrepublic.com/article/132646/breaking
-color-line-politics-signing-jackie-robinson.

59. John Kelly, "Integrating America: Jackie Robinson, Critical Events and Baseball Black and White," *International Journal of the History of Sport* 22, no. 6 (2005):
1011–35, doi:10.1080/09523360500286742. See also Kelly Rusinack, "Baseball on
the Radical Agenda: The Daily Worker and Sunday Worker Journalistic Campaign
to Desegregate Major League Baseball, 1933-1947," in *Jackie Robinson: Race, Sports,*

and the American Dream, ed. Joseph Dorinson and Joram Warmund (Armonk, NY: M. E. Sharp, 1999), 75–85.

60. Quoted in Brad Snyder, *Beyond the Shadow of the Senators: The Untold Story of the Homestead Grays and the Integration of Baseball* (Chicago: Contemporary Books, 2003), 193.

61. Tygiel, *Baseball's Great Experiment*, 37.

62. Lamb, "Breaking the Color Line."

63. Dreier, "The Real Story of Baseball's Integration That You Won't See in *42*."

64. Tygiel, *Baseball's Great Experiment*, 35.

65. "Jackie Robinson Says," *Pittsburgh Courier*, July 3, 1948, 10.

66. Lamb, *Conspiracy of Silence*, 133–35.

67. Tygiel, *Baseball's Great Experiment*, 33.

68. Tygiel, *Baseball's Great Experiment*, 39.

69. "Another Revolution in Race Relations Brewing," *Christian Century* 59 (September 2, 1942): 1045–46; all quotations except the last one from 1045. The Pirates also promised to give tryouts to two black players in August 1943, but they did not follow through in either case.

70. Ronald Smith, "The Paul Robeson–Jackie Robinson Saga and a Political Collision," in Tygiel, *The Jackie Robinson Reader*, 176–78.

71. Neil Lanctot, *Negro League Baseball: The Rise and Ruin of a Black Institution* (Philadelphia: University of Pennsylvania Press, 2004), 236, 444. Some scholars dispute Veeck's story, but Lanctot offers strong evidence that Veeck's version of events is correct.

72. Tygiel, *Baseball's Great Experiment*, 30, 32 (quotation), 33.

73. *The Sporting News*, October 4, 1945.

74. Larry Schwartz, "Jackie Changed Face of Sports," ESPN.com, accessed October 8, 2021, https://www.espn.com/sportscentury/features/00016431.html#:~:text=Chandler%2C%20a%20former%20governor%20and,selected%20Robinson%20to%20integrate%20baseball.

75. Long and Lamb, *Jackie Robinson*, 63; Lowenfish, *Branch Rickey*, 359; quoted phrases in that order.

76. Steven Lawson, *Running for Freedom: Civil Rights and Black Politics in America Since 1941* (Philadelphia: Temple University Press, 1991), 6–26.

77. Rickey to Alfred Knopf, May 9, 1956, box 14, Frank Tannenbaum Papers, Rare Book and Manuscript Library, Columbia University, New York. See also Norword and Brackman, "Going to Bat," 126.

78. Tygiel, *Baseball's Great Experiment*, 55.

79. Lowenfish, *Branch Rickey*, 378.

80. Dodson, "Integration," 164.

81. Dodson, "Integration," 164.

82. "St. Martin's Church: A Parish History," Mount Morris Park Community Improvement Association, accessed October 8, 2021, https://mmpcia.org/st-martins-episcopal-church-a-parish-history/; Wolfgang Saxon, "The Rev. John Howard Johnson, Religious and Civic Leader, 98," *New York Times*, May 25, 1995, B16; "A Renaissance Man in Harlem," At the Corner of Genealogy and History, December 6, 2019,

https://cornerofgenealogy.com/a-renaissance-man-in-harlem/; Lawrence Hogan, "The Real First Citizen of Harlem," *First Things*, December 18, 2007, https://www.firstthings.com/web-exclusives/2007/12/the-real-first-citizen-of-harl; Brett Hoover and Stephen Eschenbach, "Ivy Blackball," Ivy@50, accessed October 8, 2021, http://ivy50.com/blackhistory/story.aspx?sid=2/14/2007; Lawrence Hogan, *Shades of Glory: The Negro Leagues and the Story of African-American Baseball* (Washington, DC: National Geographic and National Baseball Hall of Fame, 2007).

83. Rebecca Alpert, "Jackie Robinson: Jewish Icon," *Shofar: An Interdisciplinary Journal of Jewish Studies* 26 (Winter 2008): 51; Prince, *Brooklyn's Dodgers*.

84. Corey Weiss, "Sermon: Jackie and Branch," Congregation Beth Shalom Rodfe Zedek, Connecticut, October 22, 1999.

85. Melody Wilensky, "For Jewish Fans, Baseball's Still the Name of the Game," *Jewish Advocate*, October 28, 1999, 189.

86. Irwin Cohen, "Jackie Robinson and the Jews: Celebrated Baseball Player Was a Vocal Opponent to Antisemitism," *Detroit Jewish News*, July 24, 2020, https://thejewishnews.com/2020/07/24/jackie-robinson-and-the-jews-celebrated-baseball-player-was-a-vocal-opponent-to-antisemitism/.

87. Adrian Burgos, *Playing America's Game: Baseball, Latinos, and the Color Line* (Berkeley: University of California Press, 2007), 186.

88. Kelly, "Integrating America"; Dreier, "Jackie Robinson."

89. Roger Kahn, "The Jackie Robinson I Remember," *Journal of Blacks in Higher Education* 14 (Winter 1996/1997): 91.

90. Simon, *Jackie Robinson*, 63.

91. John Holway, *Voices from the Great Black Baseball Leagues* (New York: Da Capo, 1975), 10.

92. Tygiel, *Baseball's Great Experiment*, 27.

93. Renford Reese, "The Socio-Political Context of the Integration of Sport in America," *Journal of African American Men* 3 (Spring 1998): 12.

94. Simon, *Jackie Robinson*, 63.

95. Lowenfish, *Branch Rickey*, 369.

96. Rachel Robinson interview with Henry, April 2011, in Henry, *42 Faith*, 237.

97. Rickey, "One Hundred Percent."

98. Arthur Mann, *Branch Rickey: American in Action* (Boston: Houghton Mifflin, 1957), 217.

99. "Rookie of the Year."

100. Tygiel, *Baseball's Great Experiment*, 58 (quotation), 63.

101. Kelly, "Integrating America."

102. Jackie Robinson, *I Never Had It Made: Jackie Robinson, an Autobiography* (New York: HarperCollins, 1995), 28.

103. Quoted in Thomas Gilbert, *Baseball at War: World War II and the Fall of the Color Line* (New York: Grolier, 1997), 112.

104. Quoted in Orr, "Jackie Robinson," 56.

105. A. S. Young, "Jackie Robinson Remembered," *Ebony*, February 1997, 108.

106. Jackie Robinson, *I Never*, 31, 33.

107. See Charles Phillips, "A Prophet in Italy," *Catholic World* 104 (1921): 210–19.

In the 1930s, Papini became a fascist and supported some of Benito Mussolini's policies, including his 1938 racial discrimination laws.

108. Giovanni Papini, *Life of Christ* (New York: Harcourt, Brace, 1923), 106–8.

109. Rampersad, *Jackie Robinson*, 126.

110. Jackie Robinson, *I Never*, 34.

111. Kelly, "Integrating America."

112. Jackie Robinson, *I Never*, 34.

113. Paul Roth, *The Game: How Baseball Overcame Segregation* (n.p.: n.p., 2013), 47, https://issuu.com/paulyroth/docs/the_game.

114. Horlacher, "When Leadership Smashed the Color Barrier."

115. Jackie Robinson, *I Never*, 33, 34; quotations in that order.

116. Horlacher, "When Leadership Smashed the Color Barrier."

117. Henry, *42 Faith*, 48.

118. Branch Rickey, *The American Diamond: A Documentary of the Game of Baseball* (New York: Simon & Schuster, 1965), 46.

119. Jackie Robinson, "Home Plate," *New York Amsterdam News*, April 25, 1960, 68.

120. Chris Lamb, "Hall of Famer Continues to Inspire," Michigan Conference, The United Methodist Church, October 24, 2017, https://michiganumc.org/hall-famer-continues-inspire/.

121. Jackie Robinson, "Trouble Ahead Needn't Bother You," *Guideposts*, August 1948, available under the headline "Guideposts Classics: Jackie Robinson on Facing Challenges," https://www.guideposts.org/better-living/entertainment/sports/guideposts-classics-jackie-robinson-on-facing-challenges.

122. Branch Rickey III statement to Henry, March 2011, in Henry, *42 Faith*, 104.

123. Al Parsley, "'Guess I'm Just a Guinea Pig,' Says Jack Robinson," *The Sporting News*, November 1, 1945, 2.

124. Chris Lamb, *Blackout: The Untold Story of Jack Robinson's First Spring Training* (Lincoln: University of Nebraska Press, 2004), 48.

125. Wendell Smith, "The Sports Beat," *Pittsburgh Courier*, December 29, 1945, 16.

126. Quoted in "'Good' and 'Bad': Varied Comment of O.B., Writers on Negro's Case," *The Sporting News*, November 1, 1945, 5, 6.

127. Arthur Mann, "The Negro and Baseball: The National Game Faces a Racial Challenge Long Ignored," in Tygiel, *The Jackie Robinson Reader*, 79; these are Mann's words, not Rickey's.

128. Jackie Robinson, "Robinson's Own Story," *Pittsburgh Courier*, November 3, 1945. See also "Jackie Robinson Says," *Pittsburgh Courier*, June 26, 1948, 10.

129. Sam Maltin, *Pittsburgh Courier*, November 10, 1945; Dan Parker, *The Sporting News*, March 28, 1946; Tygiel, *Baseball's Great Experiment*, 74.

130. Chris Lamb, "The White Media Missed It," in *42 Today: Jackie Robinson and His Legacy*, ed. Michael G. Long (New York: New York University Press, 2021), 64–65.

131. Tygiel, *Baseball's Great Experiment*, 74; e.g., *Montreal Gazette*, October 25, 1945.

132. Tygiel, *Baseball's Great Experiment*, 78–79; quotation from 79.

133. Both are quoted in "'Good' and 'Bad,'" 6.

134. *Chicago Defender*, November 3, 1945.

135. Orr, "Jackie Robinson," 56.

136. Mann, *Jackie Robinson*, 130.

137. Carl Rowan, *Wait Till Next Year: The Life Story of Jackie Robinson* (New York: Random House, 1960), 122.

138. Quoted in Mann, *Jackie Robinson*, 137.

139. Quoted in Rampersad, *Jackie Robinson*, 128.

140. Dan Daniels, "Negro Player Issue Heads for Showdown," *The Sporting News*, November 1, 1945, 1.

141. Tygiel, *Baseball's Great Experiment*, 78.

142. Quoted in Simon, *Jackie Robinson*, 86. See Leroy "Satchel" Paige and David Lipman, *Maybe I'll Pitch Forever* (New York: Doubleday, 1962), 172–73.

143. Quoted in "'Good' and 'Bad,'" 6.

144. Jackie Robinson, *I Never*, 32.

145. Jackie Robinson, *Breakthrough to the Big League: The Story of Jackie Robinson* (New York: Harper & Row, 1965), 53, 83.

146. *Pittsburgh Courier*, November 3, 1945.

147. Polner, *Branch Rickey*, 130.

148. Tygiel, *Baseball's Great Experiment*, 52–53.

149. Tim Cohane, "A Branch Grows in Brooklyn," *Look* 10 (March 19, 1946): 70.

150. Dodson, "Integration," 156.

151. Quoted in Bill Weaver, "The Black Press and the Assault on Professional Baseball's Color Line, October 1945–April 1947," *Phylon* 11 (Winter 1979): 306.

152. *Miami Herald*, October 24, 1945, quoted in Long and Lamb, *Jackie Robinson*, 54.

153. Tygiel, *Baseball's Great Experiment*, 52.

154. Kahn, *Rickey & Robinson*, 48.

155. Lowenfish, *Branch Rickey*, 24.

156. A. S. Young, "The Black Athlete in the Golden Age of Sports: Branch Rickey Launched Negroes to Stardom with Signing of Jackie Robinson," *Ebony*, November 1968, 154.

157. Chris Lamb, "Did Branch Rickey Sign Jackie Robinson to Right a 40-Year Wrong?," *Black Ball* 6 (Spring 2013): 5–18.

158. *Miami Herald*, October 24, 1945, quoted in Long and Lamb, *Jackie Robinson*, 54. Scott Simon insists that no reporters ever heard Rickey tell the part of the Charles Thomas story about "damned black skin" before spring training in 1946 (*Jackie Robinson*, 74), but this claim is impossible to verify.

159. Mark Harris, "Branch Rickey Keeps His 40-Year Promise to a Negro Dentist," *Negro Digest*, September 1947, 4–7.

160. Michael Anderson, "Baseball in Black and White: Whoever Wants to Know the Heart and Mind of America Had Better Learn the Jackie Robinson Story," *New York Times*, October 19, 1997, https://archive.nytimes.com/www.nytimes.com/books/97/10/19/reviews/971019.19anderst.html.

161. Rampersad, *Jackie Robinson*, 121.

162. John Chamberlain, "Brains, Baseball, and Branch Rickey," *Harper's*, April 1948.

163. Quoted in David Falkner, *Great Time Coming: The Life of Jackie Robinson from Baseball to Birmingham* (New York: Simon & Schuster, 1995), 134.

164. Jackie Robinson, *Baseball Has Done It* (Brooklyn, NY: Ig, 2005), 52.

165. Rickey, "One Hundred Percent."

166. Quoted in Jimmy Breslin, *Branch Rickey* (New York: Viking, 2011), 6.

167. Jackie Robinson, *Breakthrough*, 169.

168. Roscoe McGowen, "Ringing Up a Run for the Dodgers to Help Extend Their Winning Streak," *New York Times*, May 14, 1945, 12.

169. June Fifield, "Branch Rickey's 'Day of Decision,'" in Kahn, *Rickey & Robinson*, 40.

170. Fifield, "'Day of Decision,'" 40–41; first quotation from 41; second and third from 41.

171. Jackie Robinson, *Breakthrough*, 169.

172. Quoted by Phil Pepe, *New York Daily News*, December 10, 1965.

173. Jackie Robinson, *Breakthrough*, 167.

174. "Jackie Robinson," *New York Post*, June 8, 1959, 64; all his *Post* columns had this title and did not use headlines.

175. "Jackie Robinson," *New York Post*, May 13, 1960, 96.

176. Lamb, "Hall of Famer" (first quotation); Clemente Lisi, "Jackie Robinson's Forgotten Christianity: How Being a Devout Methodist Impacted His Life," *Religion Unplugged*, February 20, 2019, https://religionunplugged.com/news/2019/2/19/jackie-robinson-and-christianity-how-being-a-devout-methodist-impacted-his-life. "Muscular Christianity" emerged in the mid-nineteenth century as a movement promoting Christian values in athletics, masculinity, self-discipline, and self-sacrifice. See Clifford Putney, *Muscular Christianity: Manhood and Sports in Protestant America, 1880–1920* (Cambridge, MA: Harvard University Press, 2003).

177. Simon, *Jackie Robinson*, 78.

178. Interview with Jackie Robinson, n.d., in Tygiel, *Baseball's Great Experiment*, 67.

179. Rachel Robinson with Lee Daniels, *Jackie Robinson: An Intimate Portrait* (New York: Abrams, 1996), 38.

180. Dodson, "Integration," 75.

181. Lowenfish, *Branch Rickey*, 367–68; Lamb, *Blackout*, 37–38, 67–68.

182. Lamb, *Blackout*, 51–52.

183. Powell, "Jackie Robinson and Dixie Walker," 60.

184. "Jackie Robinson," *New York Post*, June 8, 1959.

185. Jackie Robinson, *Baseball Has Done It*, 51.

186. George Richardson to Rickey, April 17, 1947, JRP, box 3, folder 7, LOC, Manuscript Division, Washington, DC.

187. Jackie Robinson, *I Never*, xxiii.

188. Quoted in *The Sporting News*, February 25, 1948.

189. Verser, "Branch Rickey," 95; Dodson, "Integration," 75–76; Lamb, *Conspiracy of Silence*, 307–8.

190. "Rookie of the Year."

191. Lamb, "Breaking the Color Line."

192. Bill Mardo, "Robinson-Robeson," in Dorinson and Warmund, *Jackie Robinson*, 102–3.

193. Albert (Happy) Chandler with Vance H. Trimble, *Heroes, Plain Folks, and Skunks: The Life and Times of Happy Chandler* (Chicago: Bonus Books, 1989), 229.

194. "Baseball's Color Bar Broken," *Christian Century* 64 (April 23, 1947): 517.

195. See Harold Fey, "Racial and Religious Freedom Proclaimed by Federal Council on Fortieth Anniversary," *Christian Century* 65 (December 15, 1948): 1371.

196. Wendell Smith, "The Sports Beat," 16.

Chapter 3

1. Arnold Rampersad, *Jackie Robinson: A Biography* (New York: Knopf, 1997), 134.

2. Steven Norword and Harold Brackman, "Going to Bat for Jackie Robinson: The Jewish Role in Breaking Baseball's Color Line," *Journal of Sport History* 26 (Spring 1999): 115.

3. Peter Dreier, "The Real Story of Baseball's Integration That You Won't See in 42," *Atlantic*, April 11, 2013, https://www.theatlantic.com/entertainment/archive/2013/04/the-real-story-of-baseballs-integration-that-you-wont-see-in-i-42-i/274886/.

4. Chris Lamb, *Blackout: The Untold Story of Jack Robinson's First Spring Training* (Lincoln: University of Nebraska Press, 2004), 63–65.

5. Peter Dreier, "Honoring Rachel Robinson, Baseball Pioneer and Civil Rights Activist," *Huffington Post*, July 20, 2014, https://www.huffpost.com/entry/honoring-rachel-robinson-_b_5602717.

6. Carl Rowan, *Wait Till Next Year: The Life Story of Jackie Robinson* (New York: Random House, 1960), 132; Chris Lamb, "'I Never Want to Take Another Trip like This One': Jackie Robinson's Journey to Integrate Baseball," *Journal of Sport History* 24, no. 2 (Summer 1997): 177–91.

7. Jackie Robinson, *Breakthrough to the Big League: The Story of Jackie Robinson* (New York: Harper & Row, 1965), 89.

8. *Jackie Robinson: My Own Story* (New York: Greenburg, 1948), 74.

9. Jules Tygiel, *Baseball's Great Experiment: Jackie Robinson and His Legacy* (New York: Oxford University Press, 2008), 4.

10. Patrick Sauer, "The Year of Jackie Robinson's Mutual Love Affair with Montreal," *Smithsonian*, April 6, 2015, https://www.smithsonianmag.com/history/year-jackie-robinsons-mutual-love-affair-montreal-180954878/.

11. Quoted in Art Rust Jr., *Get That Nigger Off the Field* (New York: Delacorte, 1976), 79.

12. Rachel Robinson with Lee Daniels, *Jackie Robinson: An Intimate Portrait* (New York: Abrams, 1996), 52.

13. Lamb, *Blackout*, 103–5.

14. Michael G. Long and Chris Lamb, *Jackie Robinson: A Spiritual Biography; The Faith of a Boundary-Breaking Hero* (Louisville: Westminster John Knox, 2017), 75.

15. Rachel Robinson, *Jackie Robinson*, 52.

16. Tygiel, *Baseball's Great Experiment*, 112.

17. National Negro Publishers Association, "Churchmen Protest Jacksonville's Stand on Robinson, Wright," *New Journal and Guide*, April 6, 1946, A19, ProQuest Historical Newspapers.

18. Lee Lowenfish, *Branch Rickey: Baseball's Ferocious Gentleman* (Lincoln: University of Nebraska Press, 2007), 392.

19. Paul Parizeau, *Le Canada*, a Montreal newspaper, in "'Good' and 'Bad': Varied

Comment of O.B., Writers on Negro's Case," *The Sporting News*, November 1, 1945, 5, 6.

20. Quoted in "'Good' and 'Bad,'" 5.

21. Quoted in Long and Lamb, *Jackie Robinson*, 9.

22. Jackie Robinson, *Baseball Has Done It* (Brooklyn, NY: Ig, 2005), 54.

23. Quoted in Jackie Robinson, *I Never Had It Made: Jackie Robinson, an Autobiography* (New York: HarperCollins, 1995), 47.

24. Tygiel, *Baseball's Great Experiment*, 124.

25. Quoted in Sauer, "The Year of Jackie Robinson's Mutual Love Affair with Montreal." Sadly, many other black persons were discriminated against in employment, in housing, and in Montreal's social life. See Dorothy Williams, "The Jackie Robinson Myth: Social Mobility and Race in Montreal, 1920–1960" (MA thesis, Concordia University, 1999, https://www.collectionscanada.gc.ca/obj/s4/f2/dsk2/ftp01/MQ39047.pdf); Dorothy Williams, *The Road to Now: A History of Blacks in Montreal* (Montreal: Véhicule, 1997).

26. Baz O'Meara, *Montreal Daily Star*, April 19, 1946.

27. Rowan, *Wait Till Next Year*, 150.

28. Sauer, "The Year of Jackie Robinson's Mutual Love Affair with Montreal."

29. Wendell Smith, "It Was a Great Day in Jersey," *Pittsburgh Courier*, April 27, 1946, 26. Jackie told Rachel: "God must have smiled on me today" (*Jackie Robinson: My Own Story*, 103).

30. William Nunn, "American Way Triumphs in Robinson 'Experiment,'" *Pittsburgh Courier*, April 27, 1946, 1.

31. Rampersad, *Jackie Robinson*, 149.

32. Tygiel, *Baseball's Great Experiment*, 132 (quotation), 135.

33. *Montreal Star News*, July 27, 1946.

34. Mel Jones, *The Sporting News*, August 20, 1946.

35. Jackie Robinson, *Baseball Has Done It*, 54.

36. Rowan, *Wait Till Next Year*, 162–63.

37. Sauer, "The Year of Jackie Robinson's Mutual Love Affair with Montreal."

38. *The Sporting News*, October 16, 1946.

39. Jackie Robinson, *I Never*, 49, (first quotation) 54 (second and third quotations).

40. Jackie Robinson, "Batting It Out," *Pittsburgh Courier*, March 22, 1947, 15.

41. Barton Bernstein, ed., *The Politics and Policies of the Truman Administration* (Chicago: Quadrangle Books, 1970), 269–76.

42. Patrick Henry, "Jackie Robinson: Athlete and American Par Excellence," *Virginia Quarterly Review* 73 (Spring 1997): 193–94.

43. Tygiel, *Baseball's Great Experiment*, 125; "Top 100 Teams," MILB.com, accessed October 10, 2021, http://www.milb.com/milb/history/top100.jsp?idx=84.

44. Interview with John Welaj, in Tygiel, *Baseball's Great Experiment*, 141.

45. Sam Maltin, "Jackie's Dazzling Play Wins 'Little World Series' for Montreal," *Pittsburgh Courier*, October 12, 1946.

46. Jackie Robinson, *I Never*, 52.

47. Quoted in Patrick Henry, "Jackie Robinson," 191; "Jackie Robinson Says," *Pittsburgh Courier*, July 19, 1947, 15.

48. Rampersad, *Jackie Robinson*, 154.

Chapter 4

1. *Jackie Robinson: My Own Story* (New York: Greenburg, 1948), 111.

2. Larry Powell, "Jackie Robinson and Dixie Walker: Myths of the Southern Baseball Player," *Southern Cultures* 8 (Summer 2002): 56.

3. See Joram Warmund, "In the Eye of the Storm: 1947 in World Perspective," in *Jackie Robinson: Race, Sports, and the American Dream*, ed. Joseph Dorinson and Joram Warmund (Armonk, NY: M. E. Sharp, 1999), 3–12.

4. See Anthony Leviero, "Guardian for Civil Rights Proposed by Truman Board; Report Asks End of Biases," *New York Times*, October 30, 1947, 14–15.

5. Steven Lawson, *Running for Freedom: Civil Rights and Black Politics in America Since 1941* (Philadelphia: Temple University Press, 1991), 26.

6. Jules Tygiel, introduction to *The Jackie Robinson Reader: Perspectives on an American Hero*, ed. Jules Tygiel (New York: Penguin, 1997), 9.

7. Steven Norword and Harold Brackman, "Going to Bat for Jackie Robinson: The Jewish Role in Breaking Baseball's Color Line," *Journal of Sport History* 26 (Spring 1999): 130.

8. "Jackie Robinson Says," *Pittsburgh Courier*, May 10, 1947, 14.

9. Scott Simon, *Jackie Robinson and the Integration of Baseball* (Hoboken, NJ: Wiley & Sons, 2007), 34, 38 (first quotation), 40 (second quotation).

10. Arthur Daley, "Sports of the *Times*: The Dodger Deacon Discourses," *New York Times*, February 12, 1943, 32.

11. Rudy Marzano, *The Brooklyn Dodgers in the 1940s: How Robinson, MacPhail, Reiser, and Rickey Changed Baseball* (Jefferson, NC: McFarland, 2005), 135.

12. Roger Kahn, "The Jackie Robinson I Remember," *Journal of Blacks in Higher Education* 14 (Winter 1996/1997): 92 (quotations); Leo Durocher with Ed Linn, *Nice Guys Finish Last* (New York: Pocket Books, 1976), 177–79.

13. Arthur Mann, *The Jackie Robinson Story* (New York: Grosset & Dunlop, 1951), 169; Murray Polner, *Branch Rickey: A Biography* (New York: Athenaeum, 1982), 193.

14. Red Barber with Robert Creamer, *Rhubarb in the Catbird Seat* (Garden City, NY: Doubleday, 1968), 272, 274; Red Barber, *1947: When All Hell Broke Loose in Baseball* (New York: Da Capo, 1984), 63–64.

15. Jackie Robinson, *I Never Had It Made: An Autobiography* (New York: Harper-Collins, 1995), 56.

16. Mike Klingaman, "Robinson Was Covered in Mainstream Papers Mostly by Invisible Ink: AN AMERICAN HERO," *Baltimore Sun*, April 15, 1997, https://www.baltimoresun.com/news/bs-xpm-1997-04-15-1997105101-story.html.

17. Wendell Smith, "Fans Swamp Jackie," *Pittsburgh Courier*, April 26, 1947, 5.

18. Branch Rickey, "'One Hundred Percent Wrong Club' Speech," Atlanta, January 20, 1956, LOC, Washington, DC, https://www.loc.gov/collections/jackie-robinson-baseball/articles-and-essays/baseball-the-color-line-and-jackie-robinson/one-hundred-percent-wrong-club-speech/.

19. Joe Marren, "1947 Dodgers: Branch Rickey and the Mainstream Press," Society for American Baseball Research, accessed October 11, 2021, https://sabr.org/journal/article/1947-dodgers-branch-rickey-and-the-mainstream-press/ (second quotation); Mann, *The Jackie Robinson Story*, 160–65 (first quotation from 163).

20. Milton Gross, "The Emancipation of Jackie Robinson," *Sport*, October 1951, 13ff.

21. "Rookie of the Year," *Time*, September 22, 1947.

22. Bill Roeder, *Jackie Robinson* (New York: A. S. Barnes, 1950), 78–79; "33 Brooklyn Leaders Here Aided Jackie," *New York Amsterdam News*, October 25, 1947; Jonathan Eig, *Opening Day: The Story of Jackie Robinson's First Season* (New York: Simon & Schuster, 2007), 53.

23. "Rickey and Robinson," *Crisis*, May 1947, 137.

24. Sam Lacy, "Looking 'Em Over," *Baltimore Afro-American*, May 3, 1947, 13.

25. Jackie Robinson, "My Greatest Day," unpublished manuscript, n.d., but probably written in 1961, JRP, box 11, folder 12, Manuscript Division, LOC, Washington, DC, 10–11, quotation from 10.

26. Robinson, *I Never*, xxii.

27. Jackie Robinson, "Guest Speaker at Freedom Dinner of Southern Christian Leadership Conference—Tuesday Evening, September 25 [1962] at Birmingham, Alabama," JRP, box 12, folder 8, Manuscript Division, LOC, Washington, DC.

28. Robinson, "My Greatest Day," 11.

29. "Jackie Robinson Says," *Pittsburgh Courier*, April 19, 1947, 18.

30. Wendell Smith, "The Sports Beat," *Pittsburgh Courier*, April 12, 1947, 14. Smith argued that Robinson's greatest challenge was to gain the acceptance of other Dodgers' players based on his performance on the field and his personality.

31. *Boston Chronicle*, April 19, 1947.

32. Quoted in Steve Goode, "Legends of the Games," *Hartford Courant*, April 22, 2007, https://www.courant.com/news/connecticut/hc-xpm-2007-04-22-070 4200247-story.html.

33. "Jackie Robinson Says," *Pittsburgh Courier*, April 5, 1947, 14.

34. Rickey quoted in Smith, "Fans Swamp Jackie," 1; Tygiel, *Baseball's Great Experiment*, 192.

35. "Rookie of the Year."

36. Editors of *Sport* magazine, "Hurray for Jackie Robinson," *Negro History Bulletin* 18 (January 1955): 93.

37. Jack Orr, "Jackie Robinson: Symbol of the Revolution," *Sport*, March 1960, 57.

38. Simon, *Jackie Robinson*, 4.

39. Patrick Henry, "Jackie Robinson: Athlete and American Par Excellence," *Virginia Quarterly Review* 73 (Spring 1997): 194.

40. William Nack, "The Breakthrough: Why May 1947 Was Crucial for Jackie Robinson," *Sports Illustrated*, April 15, 2015, https://www.si.com/mlb/2015/04/15/jackie -robinson-day-william-nack-si-vault.

41. Dan Burley, "Yankee Razzing Angers Jackie. Jockeying Worse Than Phillies; Fails to Affect His Playing," *New York Amsterdam News*, October 4, 1947, 27. The Yankees, Robinson complained, were "dirty cowards" who hid in the dugout and made nasty, racist remarks and had "descended to new lows in invective."

42. Roeder, *Jackie Robinson*, 127–28. These are Roeder's words, not Robinson's.

43. Patrick Henry, "Jackie Robinson," 195.

44. Simon, *Jackie Robinson*, 111.

45. "Debut 'Just Another Game' to Jackie," *The Sporting News*, April 23, 1947; Eig, *Opening Day*, 61.

46. Klingaman, "Robinson Was Covered."

47. Nack, "The Breakthrough"; Tygiel, *Baseball's Great Experiment*, 190.

48. Simon, *Jackie Robinson*, 117.

49. Eig, *Opening Day*, 85.

50. Nack, "The Breakthrough."

51. Nack, "The Breakthrough."

52. Roger Kahn, *The Boys of Summer* (Evanston, IL: Holtzman, 1972), xv; William Marshall, *Baseball's Pivotal Era: 1945–1951* (Lexington: University Press of Kentucky, 1999), 140–41.

53. Jackie Robinson, *I Never*, 58.

54. Mann, *The Jackie Robinson Story*, 180.

55. Roger Kahn, "We Don't Need No Niggers Here," in *The Phillies Reader*, ed. Richard Orodenker (Philadelphia: Temple University Press, 1996), 58.

56. Jackie Robinson, *I Never*, 59, 72 (quotations).

57. Quoted in Jackie Robinson, *I Never*, 60.

58. Tygiel argues that Stanky, an Alabama native, was Robinson's principal defender against all the "taunts, brushbacks, and spikes of opposing players" during his first season (*Baseball's Great Experiment*, 195).

59. Jackie Robinson, *I Never*, 61.

60. Carl Rowan, *Wait Till Next Year: The Life Story of Jackie Robinson* (New York: Random House, 1960), 184.

61. *The Sporting News*, May 7, 1947.

62. *Jackie Robinson: My Own Story*, 145.

63. *Sporting News*, May 14, 1947; Tygiel, *Baseball's Great Experiment*, 183. For an earlier example of ethnic discrimination, see Lawrence Baldassaro, *Yankee Tony Lazzeri: Yankees Legend and Baseball Pioneer* (Lincoln: University of Nebraska Press, 2021).

64. Jon Meacham, "Jackie Robinson's Inner Struggle," *New York Times*, July 20, 2020, https://www.nytimes.com/2020/07/20/books/review/jackie-robinson-inner -struggle.html. What Robinson told fans contradicted his true feelings. Chapman, he wrote, "impressed me as a nice fellow. I don't think that he really meant the things he was shooting at me." "Jackie Robinson Says," *Pittsburgh Courier*, May 17, 1947, 14.

65. Stanley Woodward, "Views of Sport," *New York Herald Tribune*, May 9, 1947.

66. Jackie Robinson, *I Never*, 62.

67. Kahn, *The Boys of Summer*, 45.

68. *Jackie Robinson: My Own Story*, 154, 156; quotations in that order.

69. Warren Corbett, "The 'Strike' against Jackie Robinson: Truth or Myth?," *Baseball Research Journal*, Spring 2017, https://sabr.org/journal/article/the-strike-against -jackie-robinson-truth-or-myth/. Robinson describes this episode in detail in *Jackie Robinson: My Own Story*, 151–56.

70. "Jackie Robinson Says," May 17, 1947, 14.

71. Maury Allen, "Pepper Street, Pasadena," in Tygiel, *The Jackie Robinson Reader*, 24.

72. Vince Johnson, "Pirate Homers Rout Bums, 7–3," *Pittsburgh Post-Gazette*, May 16, 1947, 20.

73. *Jackie Robinson: My Own Story*, 146–47. See also Rebecca Alpert, "Jackie Robinson: Jewish Icon," *Shofar: An Interdisciplinary Journal of Jewish Studies* 26 (Winter 2008): 43–44.

74. Wendell Smith, "The Sports Beat," *Pittsburgh Courier*, May 24, 1947, 14. See also Sam Lacy, "From A to Z," *Baltimore Afro-American*, May 17, 1947, 12; Dan Burley, "Major League Dozens' Playing," *New York Amsterdam News*, June 25, 1947.

75. *Hank Greenberg: The Story of My Life*, ed. Ira Berkow (New York: Times Books, 1989), 189–91; quotation from 190–91.

76. Smith, "Sports Beat," May 24, 1947, 14.

77. Nack, "The Breakthrough."

78. "Greenville Jurors Allow Twenty-Eight Confessed Lynch Murderers to Go Free," *New York Age*, May 31, 1947, 1.

79. Nack, "The Breakthrough." In the third game of the series, Robinson went three for four with a home run.

80. Wendell Smith, "Chapman Says Jackie Keeping Brooklyn in Race by Brilliant Playing!" *Pittsburgh Courier*, June 28, 1947, 14.

81. *Jackie Robinson: My Own Story*, 149.

82. Tygiel, *Baseball's Great Experiment*, 202; "Jackie Robinson Says," *Pittsburgh Courier*, July 5, 1947, 14.

83. Langston Hughes, "Here to Yonder," *Chicago Defender*, August 9, 1947, 14.

84. Quoted in Ed Henry, *42 Faith: The Rest of the Jackie Robinson Story* (Nashville: W Publishing, 2017), 169.

85. John Grindrod, "Remembering Jackie Robinson and Revenge, 7 Decades Later," *Lima (OH) News*, April 11, 2017, https://www.limaohio.com/news/238730/john-grindrod-remembering-jackie-robinson-and-revenge-7-decades-later.

86. Michael G. Long and Chris Lamb, *Jackie Robinson: A Spiritual Biography; The Faith of a Boundary-Breaking Hero* (Louisville: Westminster John Knox, 2017), 95.

87. Jackie Robinson, "Trouble Ahead Needn't Bother You," *Guideposts*, August 1948, available under the headline "Guideposts Classics: Jackie Robinson on Facing Challenges," https://www.guideposts.org/better-living/entertainment/sports/guideposts-classics-jackie-robinson-on-facing-challenges.

88. "Rookie of the Year."

89. Vince Johnson, "Dugout Diary," *Pittsburgh Post-Gazette*, August 25, 1947, 15.

90. *Jackie Robinson: My Own Story*, 163.

91. "Rookie of the Year."

92. Tygiel, *Baseball's Great Experiment*, 204.

93. Simon, *Jackie Robinson*, 148–49; Eig, *Opening Day*, 232–33.

94. Simon, *Jackie Robinson*, 146–47.

95. *Jackie Robinson: My Own Story*, 134–35 (quotation from 135); Tygiel, *Baseball's Great Experiment*, 202. "Bojangles" starred in fourteen movies. In 1936, he cofounded the New York Black Yankees, based in Harlem, which played in the Negro National League until 1948.

96. "Robinson Reveals Written Threats: Dodgers' Negro Star Told in Anonymous Letters to 'Get Out of Baseball,'" *New York Times*, May 10, 1947; Eig, *Opening Day*, 104.

97. "Rookie of the Year."

98. Rachel Robinson with Lee Daniels, *Jackie Robinson: An Intimate Portrait* (New York: Abrams, 1996), 70; Eig, *Opening Day*, 154–55, 234. Jonathan Eig reports that Rachel claimed that she and Jackie never attended church in 1947, although "religion stirred passionate feelings" in both her husband and Branch Rickey (*Opening Day*,

152). Although baseball games often prevented Jackie from attending, this strikes me as unlikely, given their relationship with the Covingtons.

99. Eig, *Opening Day*, 85; Michael Anderson, "Baseball in Black and White: Whoever Wants to Know the Heart and Mind of America Had Better Learn the Jackie Robinson Story," *New York Times*, October 19, 1997, https://archive.nytimes.com/www.ny times.com/books/97/10/19/reviews/971019.19anderst.html (quotation).

100. Jackie Robinson, "Now I Know Why They Boo Me!," in Tygiel, *The Jackie Robinson Reader*, 198. Rachel reported that, later, she "became particularly close to Joan Hodges, the wife of Gil Hodges, Betty Erskine, the wife of Carl Erskine, and Pee Wee Reese's wife, Dotty, as well as the wives of the black players—Roy Campanella and Don Newcombe" ("Interview with Rachel Robinson," *Scholastic*, February 11, 1998, https://www.scholastic.com/teachers/articles/teaching-content/interview -rachel-robinson/).

101. Jackie Robinson, *I Never*, 278.

102. Bill Horlacher, "When Leadership Smashed the Color Barrier," *Success Factors* 1 (Fall 1998): 6, https://static1.squarespace.com/static/517aa696e4b0ab81ac8d9aef /t/51c480bde4b0895fa6de3948/1371832509726/Jackie_Robinson.pdf.

103. Many of these letters and telegrams also quoted biblical verses to inspire and encourage Robinson. In addition, the Jackie Robinson Papers at the Library of Congress (box 1, folder 290) contain hundreds of telegrams to Branch Rickey expressing optimism about Robinson's prospects for success.

104. Jackie Robinson, "Trouble Ahead Needn't Bother You."

105. "Ralph Branca on the Quiet Strength of Jackie Robinson," *Guideposts*, September 4, 2013, https://www.guideposts.org/better-living/entertainment/sports /ralph-branca-on-the-quiet-strength-of-jackie-robinson.

106. Quoted in Ed Henry, *42 Faith*, 6.

107. Neither Robinson nor Smith explained how they produced these columns, but there are clear signs of Smith's close and regular involvement (Brian Carroll, "This Is IT! The PR Campaign by Wendell Smith and Jackie Robinson," *Journalism History* 37, no. 3 [2011]: 155.

108. For his praise of black athletes, see "Jackie Robinson Says," *Pittsburgh Courier*, July 12, 1947, 15; July 26, 1947, 15; August 9, 1947, 14; September 6, 1947, 14. On Doby, see Joe Moore, *Pride against Prejudice: The Biography of Larry Doby* (New York: Praeger, 1988).

109. "Jackie Robinson Says," *Pittsburgh Courier*, May 3, 1947, 15. He added that players on other teams had shouted similar things at him.

110. "Jackie Robinson Says," *Pittsburgh Courier*, May 24, 1947, 14; "Jackie Robinson Says," *Pittsburgh Courier*, June 7, 1947, 14.

111. "Jackie Robinson Says," *Pittsburgh Courier*, May 27, 1947, 15.

112. Nack, "The Breakthrough."

113. *Pittsburgh Courier*, April 19, 1947; Bill Weaver, "The Black Press and the Assault on Professional Baseball's 'Color Line,' October 1945–April 1947," *Phylon* 40 (Winter 1979): 315.

114. Carroll, "This Is IT!," 160.

115. Rachel Robinson, "I Live with a Hero," *McCall's*, March 1951, 108.

116. Rachel Robinson, *Jackie Robinson*, 72.

117. Kahn, *The Boys of Summer*, 405.

118. Mann, *The Jackie Robinson Story*, 186 (first quotation), 189, 190; Tygiel, *Baseball's Great Experiment*, 198 (second quotation).

119. Rachel Robinson, "I Live with a Hero," 106.

120. Tygiel, *Baseball's Great Experiment*, 199 (first quotation); Mann, *The Jackie Robinson Story*, 194–95 (remaining quotations).

121. Branch Rickey, foreword to *Jackie Robinson: My Own Story*.

122. Nack, "The Breakthrough."

123. Polner, *Branch Rickey*, 192; Art Rust Jr., *Get That Nigger off the Field* (New York: Delacorte, 1976), 68.

124. Eig, *Opening Day*, 42.

125. Jackie Robinson, *I Never*, 78.

126. Interview with Bobby Bragan, in David Falkner, *Great Time Coming: The Life of Jackie Robinson from Baseball to Birmingham* (New York: Simon & Schuster, 1995), 152–53; quotation from 152.

127. "Jackie Robinson Says," *Pittsburgh Courier*, May 17, 1947, 14.

128. Powell, "Dixie Walker," 63.

129. Marshall, *Baseball's Pivotal Era*, 142.

130. Ira Berkow, "Reese Helped Change Baseball," *New York Times*, March 31, 1997, C1.

131. Jackie Robinson, *Breakthrough*, 117.

132. Jackie Robinson, *I Never*, 63.

133. Jackie Robinson, *I Never*, xxii.

134. Jackie Robinson, "Home Plate," *New York Amsterdam News*, July 7, 1962, 11.

135. Kahn, *The Boys of Summer*, 312.

136. Bill Plaschke, "Pee Wee Was a Giant," *Los Angeles Times*, August 15, 1999, https://www.latimes.com/archives/la-xpm-1999-aug-15-sp-512-story.html; Joe Posnanski, "The Embrace," NBC Sports, accessed October 11, 2021, https://sportsworld.nbcsports.com/the-embrace/; Jackie Robinson, *Breakthrough*, 122–23. Carl Erskine said that the incident happened in Cincinnati and was intended to show fans that "Jack was completely acceptable" to Reese and the other Dodgers (Jackie Robinson, *Baseball Has Done It*, 80).

137. Jackie Robinson does not mention the incident in his 1948 autobiography.

138. Tygiel, *Baseball's Great Experiment*, 351.

139. Jack Doyle, "Reese & Robbie, 1945–2005," Pop History Dig, June 29, 2011, https://www.pophistorydig.com/topics/pee-wee-and-jackie/.

140. *Washington Post*, August 28, 1949, as quoted in Posnanski, "The Embrace."

141. Ralph Branca with David Ritz, *A Moment in Time: An American Story of Baseball, Heartbreak, and Grace* (New York: Scribner's, 2011), 82.

142. Jackie Robinson, "A Kentucky Colonel Kept Me in Baseball," *Look*, February 8, 1955, 84.

143. Jackie Robinson, "I Was Part of the Team," *Reader's Digest*, April 1953, back cover.

144. Jackie Robinson, "Family Man Jackie Robinson: First Negro in Big Leagues Also Tops as a Father," *Ebony*, September 1947, 15–16.

145. "Robinsons Plan for Day When They Have Own Home," *Ebony*, September 1947, 16.

146. "Rookie of the Year."

147. "Rookie of the Year."

148. *The Sporting News* as quoted in Jackie Robinson, *I Never*, 68.

149. Tygiel, *Baseball's Great Experiment*, 206 (first and second quotations), 196 (third quotation).

150. Tygiel, *Baseball's Great Experiment*, 207, 214 (first quotation), 252 (second quotation), 286–87, 256, 258 (third quotation).

151. John Curran to JR, October 7, 1947, JRP, box 12, folder 11, Manuscript Division, LOC, Washington, DC.

152. Jackie Robinson, "Trouble Ahead Needn't Bother You."

153. Quoted in Ed Henry, *42 Faith*, 7.

154. Roeder, *Jackie Robinson*, 143; Tygiel, *Baseball's Great Experiment*, 205.

155. Wendell Smith, "Jackie Robinson Packing 'Em In," *Pittsburgh Courier*, April 19, 1947, 1; Wendell Smith, "46,572 Pack Wrigley Field," *Pittsburgh Courier*, May 24, 1947, 15.

156. Wendell Smith, "Jackie Helps Dodgers Near Record Gate," *Pittsburgh Courier*, May 31, 1947, 15.

157. Jackie Robinson, *I Never*, xxii.

158. Jackie Robinson, *I Never*, 69–70; quotations in that order.

159. *The Sporting News*, October 22, 1947.

Chapter 5

1. Michael Hirsley, "It's Not Just Old-Time Religions," *Chicago Tribune*, May 5, 1991, https://www.chicagotribune.com/news/ct-xpm-1991-05-05-9102090796 -story.html.

2. Jonathan Herzog, *The Spiritual-Industrial Complex* (New York: Oxford University Press, 2011), 5. See also Patrick Allitt, *Religion in America Since 1945* (New York: Columbia University Press, 2003), 1–80.

3. William Petersen, "Religious Statistics in the United States," *Journal for the Scientific Study of Religion* 1 (Spring 1962): 169.

4. See, for example, Will Herberg, *Protestant, Catholic, Jew: An Essay in American Religious Sociology* (Garden City, NY: Doubleday, 1955); and William Lee Miller, *Piety along the Potomac: Notes on Politics and Morals in the Fifties* (Boston: Houghton Mifflin, 1964).

5. George Marsden, *The Twilight of the American Enlightenment: The 1950s and the Crisis of Liberal Belief* (New York: Basic Books, 2014), 99.

6. Alan Bean, "The Twilight of the American Enlightenment: The 1950s and the Crisis of Liberal Belief," *Baptist News Global*, February 4, 2015, https://baptistnews .com/article/the-twilight-of-the-american-enlightenment-the-1950s-and-the-crisis -of-liberal-belief/.

7. Pastor Conrad Tillard, as quoted in Beth J. Harpaz, "A Guide to Exploring Jackie Robinson's Brooklyn," *Brooklyn Daily Eagle*, April 15, 2013, https://brooklyneagle.com /articles/2013/04/15/a-guide-to-exploring-jackie-robinsons-brooklyn/.

8. Rachel Robinson with Lee Daniels, *Jackie Robinson: An Intimate Portrait* (New York: Abrams, 1996), 70.

9. Harpaz, "A Guide to Exploring Jackie Robinson's Brooklyn."

10. "The Church Will Go to the People," *Plain Standard*, April 22, 1959, 19.

11. "The History of Nazarene," Nazarene Congregational United Church of Christ, accessed October 12, 2021, http://www.nazareneucc.org/our-history; "Congregationalists Mark 85th Anniversary," *New York Age*, November 7, 1959, 8. Hargraves helped establish the East Harlem Protestant Parish, considered by some "the most significant experiment in American Protestantism" in the twentieth century. Hargraves also cofounded the West Side Organization, a prototype for American community-based organization. Hargraves was named one of the "Ten Churchmen of the Decade" during the 1970s. See Mark Wild, "Liberal Protestants and Urban Renewal," *Religion and American Culture: A Journal of Interpretation* 25 (Winter 2015): 122; Lowell Livezey, "Church as Parish: The East Harlem Protestant Parish," *Christian Century*, December 9, 1998, 1176.

12. "History of SACC," St. Albans Congregational Church, accessed October 12, 2021, http://www.saccucc.org/history; Wolfgang Saxon, "Rev. Robert Ross Johnson, 79, First Pastor of Queens Church," *New York Times*, April 6, 2000, C25.

13. "Urges 7-Day Week for All Churches," *New York Daily News*, December 18, 1955, 553. See also "'Register to Vote' Parade Held by Non-Partisan Group," *Brooklyn Daily Eagle*, September 28, 1953, 8.

14. Samuel Haynes, "'High Point of My Career'—Jackie of Spingarn Award," *Baltimore Afro-American*, December 8, 1956, 3.

15. Jackie Robinson, "My Greatest Day," unpublished manuscript, n.d., but probably written in 1961, JRP, box 11, folder 12, Manuscript Division, LOC, Washington, DC.

16. John Vernon, "Beyond the Box Score: Jackie Robinson, Civil Rights Crusader," *Negro History Bulletin* 58 (October–December 1995): 19.

17. "Jackie Robinson Says," *Pittsburgh Courier*, September 4, 1948, 10.

18. "Jackie Robinson Says," *Pittsburgh Courier*, October 9, 1948, 11.

19. Arthur Mann, *The Jackie Robinson Story* (New York: Grosset & Dunlop, 1951), 221–22; Rachel Robinson, "I Live with a Hero," *McCall's*, March 1951, 114; J. K. Pollack, "A Family Named Robinson," *Parents*, 1955, in *The Jackie Robinson Reader*, ed. Jules Tygiel (New York: Penguin, 1997), 210; Arnold Rampersad, *Jackie Robinson: A Biography* (New York: Knopf, 1997), 203.

20. Rachel Robinson, "Hero," 106.

21. Editors of *Sport* magazine, "Hurray for Jackie Robinson," *Negro History Bulletin* 18 (January 1955): 93.

22. Rachel L. Swarns, "Solving a Jackie Robinson Mystery," *New York Times*, accessed October 12, 2021, https://www.nytimes.com/interactive/projects/cp/national/unpublished-black-history/jackie-robinson-lectures-city-college-baseball.

23. See Roger Kahn, *The Era, 1947–1957: When the Yankees, the Giants, and the Dodgers Ruled the World* (New York: Diversion Books, 2012); Carl Prince, *Brooklyn's Dodgers: The Bums, the Borough, and the Best of Baseball* (New York: Oxford University Press, 1996).

24. Bill James, *The New Bill James Historical Baseball Abstract* (New York: Free Press, 2001), 502–3.

25. Roger Kahn, "The Jackie Robinson I Remember," *Journal of Blacks in Higher Education* 14 (Winter 1996/1997): 90.

26. Both quoted in Jack Orr, "Jackie Robinson: Symbol of the Revolution," *Sport* 29 (March 1960): 59.

27. Editors of *Sport* magazine, "Hurray for Jackie Robinson," 93.

28. Roger Kahn, *The Boys of Summer* (Evanston, IL: Holtzman, 1972), 393.

29. Mann, *The Jackie Robinson Story*, 221.

30. Orr, "Jackie Robinson," 53.

31. Kahn, *The Boys of Summer*, 393.

32. Editors of *Sport* magazine, "Hurray for Jackie Robinson," 93.

33. "Jackie Robinson Says," *Pittsburgh Courier*, August 14, 1948, 12.

34. Mann, *The Jackie Robinson Story*, 217.

35. "Negroes Are Americans: Jackie Robinson Proves It in Words and on the Ball Field," *Life*, August 1, 1949, 22.

36. Jules Tygiel, introduction to Tygiel, *The Jackie Robinson Reader*, 9.

37. Vernon, "Beyond the Box Score," 18.

38. "Rookie of the Year," *Time*, September 22, 1947.

39. Red Smith, "Death of an Unconquerable Man," *New York Times*, October 25, 1972, 53.

40. Dave Anderson, "Jackie Robinson, First Black in Major Leagues, Dies," *New York Times*, October 25, 1972, 56.

41. Kahn, *The Boys of Summer*, 394.

42. William Nack, "The Breakthrough: Why May 1947 Was Crucial for Jackie Robinson," *Sports Illustrated*, April 15, 2015, https://www.si.com/mlb/2015/04/15/jackie-robinson-day-william-nack-si-vault.

43. Maury Allen, *Jackie Robinson: A Life Remembered* (New York: Franklin Watts, 1987), 117–18.

44. Jackie Robinson, *I Never Had It Made: Jackie Robinson, an Autobiography* (New York: HarperCollins, 1995), 86.

45. "Robinson Never Forgets Mother's Advice," *Washington Post*, August 23, 1949, 12.

46. Eric Scicchitano, "A Lasting Legacy: Robinson Led Way in Baseball, Civil Rights," *Sunbury (PA) Daily Item*, April 14, 2017, https://www.dailyitem.com/news/a-lasting-legacy-robinson-led-way-in-baseball-civil-rights/article_ff443bac-2106-11e7-9c91-07e76e967aee.html; quotation from the *Bucknellian*, February 10, 1949.

47. Rachel Robinson, *Jackie Robinson*, 115.

48. "Jackie Robinson's Double Play," *Life*, May 8, 1950, 129.

49. "Jackie Robinson Featured in Go-to-Church Advertising," *Los Angeles Sentinel*, November 2, 1950.

50. JR to BR, ca. November 1950, JRP box 3, folder 7, LOC, Washington, DC.

51. BR to Arnold Rampersad, February 24, 1997, in Rampersad, *Jackie Robinson*, 220.

52. Bill Horlacher, "When Leadership Smashed the Color Barrier," *Success Factors* 1 (Fall 1998): 6, https://static1.squarespace.com/static/517aa696e4b0ab81ac8d9aef/t/51c480bde4b0895fa6de3948/1371832509726/Jackie_Robinson.pdf.

53. "Branch Rickey Calls for an End to Racial Bias," *Pittsburgh Courier*, August 30, 1952, 27. Rickey called for "aggressive and unrelenting insistence" on racial justice.

54. Jackie Robinson, *I Never*, 92, 95; quotations in that order.

55. Patrick Henry, "Jackie Robinson: Athlete and American Par Excellence," *Virginia Quarterly Review* 73 (Spring 1997): 190.

56. Jacques Barzun, *God's Country and Mine* (Boston: Little, Brown, 1954), 159.

57. Jules Tygiel, *Baseball's Great Experiment: Jackie Robinson and His Legacy* (New York: Oxford University Press, 2008), 308, 133.

58. Kahn, *The Boys of Summer*, 180.

59. Scott Herhold, "A Story about Jackie Robinson and a Persistent Pastor," *San Jose Mercury News*, April 15, 2013, https://www.mercurynews.com/2013/04/15/herhold-a-story-about-jackie-robinson-and-a-persistent-pastor/.

60. "Brooklyn Pastors United to Aid Concord Efforts," *New York Amsterdam News*, February 14, 1953.

61. Rampersad, *Jackie Robinson*, 247. Robinson also chaired Brotherhood Week in February 1968.

62. "Jackie Robinson," *New York Post*, August 17, 1959, 48.

63. Jackie Robinson, *I Never*, 118.

64. Robert Creamer and Roy Terrell, "Preview: The World Series, This Year the Dodgers?," *Sports Illustrated*, September 26, 1955, 19.

65. Damon Rice, *Seasons Past* (New York: Praeger, 1976), 414–15.

66. Jackie Robinson, *I Never*, 120; Jackie Robinson, "How We Won," *Dell Baseball Annual*, 1956 (quotation).

67. "Jackie Robinson to Lead Parade at Methodist Meeting," *Chicago Defender*, March 31, 1956, 17.

68. Jackie Robinson, "How We Won."

69. Bill Keefe, "Enemy of His Race," *New Orleans Times-Picayune*, July 18, 1956.

70. "Bill Keefe Says We're Ape-Like," *Pittsburgh Courier*, August 25, 1956, https://www.newspapers.com/clip/31413512/8-25-56keefejackie-feud/.

71. JR to Bill Keefe, July 23, 1956, in Michael G. Long, ed., *First Class Citizenship: The Civil Rights Letters of Jackie Robinson* (New York: Holt, 2007), 16.

72. Aaron Rosenblatt, "Negroes in Baseball: The Failure of Success," *Transactions* 4 (September 1967): 51–53; Larry Moffi and James Kronstadt, *Crossing the Line: Black Major Leaguers, 1947–1959* (Jefferson, NC: McFarland, 1994).

73. Robert Peterson, *Only the Ball Was White: A History of Legendary Black Players and All-Black Professional Teams* (New York: Oxford University Press, 1992), 183–206.

74. "Brooks Criticized at End of Tour," *New York Times*, November 14, 1956.

75. Kahn, *The Boys of Summer*, 387.

76. Jackie Robinson, *I Never*, 121.

77. Jackie Robinson, "Why I'm Quitting Baseball," *Look*, January 22, 1957, 91.

78. Rachel Robinson, *Jackie Robinson*, 139.

79. Carl Rowan, *Wait Till Next Year: The Life Story of Jackie Robinson* (New York: Random House, 1960), 284.

80. Jackie Robinson, "Five Years in White Man's Baseball: An Exclusive Focus Interview," *Focus*, July 1952, 7.

81. Scott Simon, *Jackie Robinson and the Integration of Baseball* (Hoboken, NJ: Wiley & Sons, 2007), 154; Tygiel, *Baseball's Great Experiment*, 325.

82. Rachel Robinson, *Jackie Robinson*, 88.

83. Rachel Robinson, "Hero," 111.

84. "Jackie Robinson Buying Home in Connecticut, Stirs Dispute," *St. Louis Post-Dispatch*, December 14, 1953, 38.

85. Jason Sokol, "Jackie Robinson's Life Was No Home Run for Racial Progress," *Time*, July 4, 2015, https://time.com/3942084/jackie-robinson-racial-progress/; Robinson, *I Never*, 107.

86. Jackie Robinson, "Now I Know Why They Boo Me!," *Look*, January 25, 1955, 26.

87. Jamal Powell, "North Stamford Congregational Church Remembers Jackie Robinson," *Stamford (CT) Patch*, February 13, 2012, https://patch.com/connecticut/stamford/north-stamford-congregational-church-remembers-jackie-robinson; Rachel Robinson, *Jackie Robinson*, 132; Pollack, "A Family Named Robinson," 205 (quotation).

88. Quoted in Sokol, "Jackie Robinson's Life Was No Home Run for Racial Progress."

89. *Jackie Robinson: My Own Story*, 133.

90. *Jackie Robinson: My Own Story*, 112, 116.

91. Long, *First Class Citizenship*, 343.

92. Jackie Robinson, "Home Plate," *New York Amsterdam News*, February 10, 1962, 9. Cf. "Home Plate," *New York Amsterdam News*, May 28, 1966, 17.

93. Jackie Robinson, *I Never*, xxiv.

94. Carl Erskine and Burton Rocks, *What I Learned from Jackie Robinson: A Teammate's Reflections on and off the Field* (New York: McGraw-Hill, 2005), 29.

95. David McMahon and Sarah Burns, "Why Jackie Robinson's Legacy Matters Today," *Time*, April 11, 2016, https://time.com/4282838/jackie-robinson-legacy/.

96. Peter Dreier, "Jackie Robinson: A Legacy of Activism," *American Prospect*, January 31, 2019, https://prospect.org/civil-rights/jackie-robinson-legacy-activism.

97. Roger Wilkins, "Jack and Rachel Robinson," *Nation*, April 21, 1997, 4–5.

98. Quoted in Peter Dreier, "In Ken Burns' New Documentary, Rachel Robinson Finally Gets Her Due," *Huffington Post*, April 8, 2016, https://www.huffpost.com/entry/in-ken-burns-new-document_b_9645502.

99. Peter J. Kaplan, "Rachel Robinson," Peter J. Kaplan, July 15, 2020, https://petejkaplan.medium.com/rachel-robinson-edca2f4038ef.

100. Jonathan Eig, *Opening Day: The Story of Jackie Robinson's First Season* (New York: Simon & Schuster, 2007), 84.

101. Rachel Robinson, "Hero," 39–40.

102. Rachel Robinson, *Jackie Robinson*, 144.

103. Kostya Kennedy, "Rachel Robinson Reflects on Her Life with Jackie and the Movie 42," *Sports Illustrated*, April 11, 2013, https://www.si.com/mlb/2013/04/11/rachel-robinson-jackie-robinson-chadwick-boseman-42, including both Rachel Robinson quotations.

104. Associated Press, "Robeson Assaults Stettinius," April 20, 1949.

105. Herzog, *The Spiritual-Industrial Complex*, 4–7; quotation from 4. See also Diane Kerby, ed., *Religion and the Cold War* (New York: Palgrave Macmillan, 2003); David Foglesong, *The American Mission and the "Evil" Empire* (New York: Cambridge University Press, 2007); Paul Froese, *The Plot to Kill God: Findings from the Soviet Experiment in Secularization* (Berkeley: University of California Press, 2008); T. Jeremy

Gunn, *Spiritual Weapons: The Cold War and the Forging of an American National Religion* (Westport, CT: Praeger, 2009).

106. Jackie Robinson, *I Never*, 83.

107. Rampersad, *Jackie Robinson*, 203.

108. Sam Maltin, "Paul Robeson, Canadian Press, Hail the Signing," *Pittsburgh Courier*, October 27, 1945, 1.

109. Jackie Robinson, *I Never*, 84.

110. Bill Roeder, *Jackie Robinson* (New York: A. S. Barnes, 1950), 154.

111. Rachel Robinson, "Hero," 111.

112. "He Fights and Steals," *Quick*, August 1, 1949, 57.

113. "Sworn Testimony of Jack Roosevelt Robinson," in *Hearings before the Committee on Un-American Activities, House of Representatives Eighty-First Congress First Session* (Washington, DC: GPO, 1949), 479–83, as quoted in "Negroes Are Americans," 22.

114. Vernon, "Beyond the Box Score."

115. Joseph Dorinson, "Paul Robeson and Jackie Robinson: Athletes and Activists at Armageddon," *Pennsylvania History* 66 (Winter 1999): 20.

116. "Negroes Are Americans," 22.

117. Martin Duberman, *Paul Robeson: A Biography* (New York: Knopf, 1988), 360–61. Illustrative of the support Robinson received from black leaders is a July 19, 1949, letter from Lester Granger, praising his testimony (JRP box 3, folder 7, LOC, Washington, DC).

118. Ronald Smith, "The Paul Robeson–Jackie Robinson Saga and a Political Collision," in Tygiel, *The Jackie Robinson Reader*, 181. The *Chicago Defender* argued that every "responsible" black leader and all major black organizations were anticommunist (April 30, 1949, 6).

119. W. E. B. DuBois, *Daily Worker*, May 2, 1949.

120. Malcolm X, open letter to Jackie Robinson, *New York Amsterdam News*, November 30, 1963, in Long, *First Class Citizenship*, 183.

121. Peter Dreier, "Half a Century before Colin Kaepernick, Jackie Robinson Said, 'I Cannot Stand and Sing the Anthem,'" *Nation*, July 18, 2019, https://www.thenation.com/article/archive/huac-jackie-robinson-paul-robeson/. See also Peter Dreier and Robert Elias, *Baseball Rebels: The Reformers and Radicals Who Shook Up the Game and Changed America* (Lincoln: University of Nebraska Press, 2022).

122. Jackie Robinson, *I Never*, 83 (first three quotations), 85–86 (fourth quotation).

123. Tygiel, introduction to Smith, "The Paul Robeson–Jackie Robinson Saga and a Political Collision," in Tygiel, *The Jackie Robinson Reader*, 170.

124. Dreier, "Half a Century before Colin Kaepernick, Jackie Robinson Said, 'I Cannot Stand and Sing the Anthem.'"

125. The AME, for example, adopted an African Methodist Social Creed at its 1952 General Conference to protest racial segregation and discrimination in education, housing, criminal justice, and other areas of American society.

126. See Dennis Dickerson, *African American Preachers and Politics: The Careys of Chicago* (Jackson: University Press of Mississippi, 2010); Dennis Dickerson, *The African Methodist Church: A History* (New York: Cambridge University Press, 2020); Erik Gellman and Jarod Roll, *The Gospel of the Working Class: Labor's Southern Prophets in New Deal America* (Urbana: University of Illinois Press, 2016); Jarod Roll, *Labor and*

Religion in the New Cotton South (Urbana: University of Illinois Press, 2016); Andrew Manis, *A Fire You Can't Put Out: The Civil Rights Life of Birmingham's Fred Shuttlesworth* (Boston: South End, 1980); and Barbara Ransby, *Ella Baker and the Black Freedom Movement: A Radical Democratic Vision* (Chapel Hill: University of North Carolina Press, 2003).

127. Michael Emerson, *Divided by Faith: Evangelical Religion and the Problem of Race in America* (New York: Oxford University Press, 2001), 45.

128. Gayraud Wilmore, *Black Religion and Black Radicalism* (Maryknoll, NY: Orbis, 1983), 161.

129. Ralph Abernathy, *And the Walls Came Tumbling Down* (New York: Harper-Perennial, 1989), 114.

130. Dickerson, *African Methodist Episcopal Church*, 352 (first quotation), 366 (second quotation), 370.

131. Wilmore, *Black Religion and Black Radicalism*, 161 (first quotation), 165 (second quotation). Both Charles Eric Lincoln and Lawrence Mamiya, *The Black Church in African American Experience* (Durham, NC: Duke University Press, 2005), 121, and Sylvester Johnson, *African American Religion, 1500–2000* (New York: Cambridge University Press, 2015), 334, affirm Wilmore's analysis of the black church from 1930 to 1955. See also Harry Richardson, *Dark Glory: A Picture of the Church among Negroes in the Rural South* (New York: Friendship, 1947), especially 34–49; and David Cohn, *Where I Was Born and Raised* (Boston: Houghton-Mifflin, 1948), 173–84.

132. Frank Loescher, *The Protestant Church and the Negro* (Westport, CT: Negro Universities Press, 1971), 76, 52.

133. Steven Lawson, *Running for Freedom: Civil Rights and Black Politics in America Since 1941* (Philadelphia: Temple University Press, 1991), 35, 38, 39.

134. Jack Doyle, "Reese & Robbie, 1945–2005," Pop History Dig, June 29, 2011, https://www.pophistorydig.com/topics/pee-wee-and-jackie/.

135. Michael Anderson, "Baseball in Black and White: Whoever Wants to Know the Heart and Mind of America Had Better Learn the Jackie Robinson Story," *New York Times*, October 19, 1997, https://archive.nytimes.com/www.nytimes.com/books/97/10/19/reviews/971019.19anderst.html.

136. Lawson, *Running for Freedom*, 66–67; Aldon Morris, *The Origins of the Civil Rights Movement: Black Communities Organizing for Change* (New York: Free Press, 1984), 4, 91 (quotation); David Chappell, "Religious Revivalism in the Civil Rights Movement," *African American Review* 36 (Winter 2002): 581–95.

137. Dreier, "Jackie Robinson."

138. Jackie Robinson, *I Never*, 75.

139. Henry, "Jackie Robinson," 198.

140. Joe Williams, *The Sporting News*, May 23, 1954.

141. Tygiel, *Baseball's Great Experiment*, 325.

142. JR to Michael Hamilburg, October 10, 1970, in Long, *First Class Citizenship*, 303.

143. Vernon, "Beyond the Box Score," 19.

144. Jackie Robinson, *Baseball Has Done It* (Brooklyn, NY: Ig, 2005), 21–22.

145. Jackie Robinson, "A Kentucky Colonel Kept Me in Baseball," *Look*, February 8, 1955, 89–90.

146. Rachel Robinson, *Jackie Robinson*, 120.

147. Kahn, *The Boys of Summer*, xvii.
148. Dreier, "Jackie Robinson."
149. Rachel Robinson, *Jackie Robinson*, 66.
150. *Sporting News*, September 16, 1956.
151. Quoted in Larry Powell, *Bottom of the Ninth: An Oral History on the Life of Harry "The Hat" Walker* (New York: Writers' Digest, 2000), 140–41.
152. Tygiel, *Baseball's Great Experiment*, 333.
153. Tygiel, *Baseball's Great Experiment*, 316.
154. Juan Williams, "After the Cheering Stopped, Jackie Robinson Played Harder Than Ever," *Washington Post*, April 12, 1987, https://www.washingtonpost.com/archive/lifestyle/magazine/1987/04/12/after-the-cheering-stopped-jackie-robinson-played-harder-than-ever-in-1947-he-broke-baseballs-color-line-then-unlike-so-many-of-todays-star-athletes-he-used-fame-as-a-way-tohelp-his-people/a06b8ec8-8c04-420a-b0d4-dcd10f7bb715/.
155. Tygiel, *Baseball's Great Experiment*, 268, 276.
156. C. Vann Woodward, *The Strange Career of Jim Crow* (New York: Oxford University Press, 1974), 162.
157. Tygiel, *Baseball's Great Experiment*, 311, 279, 304.
158. *The Sporting News*, June 6, 1956.
159. Tygiel, *Baseball's Great Experiment*, 306.
160. "Baseball Discrimination," *New York Times*, March 20, 1954, 14.
161. Jackie Robinson, *Baseball Has Done It*, 28, 23; quotations in that order.

Chapter 6

1. Juan Williams, "After the Cheering Stopped, Jackie Robinson Played Harder Than Ever," *Washington Post*, April 12, 1987, https://www.washingtonpost.com/archive/lifestyle/magazine/1987/04/12/after-the-cheering-stopped-jackie-robinson-played-harder-than-ever-in-1947-he-broke-baseballs-color-line-then-unlike-so-many-of-todays-star-athletes-he-used-fame-as-a-way-tohelp-his-people/a06b8ec8-8c04-420a-b0d4-dcd10f7bb715/.
2. Jeff Crosby, review of *Jackie Robinson: A Spiritual Biography; The Faith of a Boundary-Breaking Hero*, by Michael G. Long and Chris Lamb, *Englewood Review of Books*, April 3, 2017, https://englewoodreview.org/jackie-robinson-a-spiritual-biography-review/.
3. Quoted in "Jackie Robinson, Civil Rights Advocate," National Archives, last revised September 25, 2019, https://www.archives.gov/education/lessons/jackie-robinson.
4. Peter Golembock, *Bums: An Oral History of the Brooklyn Dodgers* (New York: Putnam, 1984), 227.
5. Quoted in Roger Kahn, *The Boys of Summer* (Evanston, IL: Holtzman, 1972), 398.
6. Jack Orr, "Jackie Robinson: Symbol of the Revolution," *Sport* 29 (March 1960): 53, 58; quotations in that order.
7. Peter Dreier, "The First Famous Jock for Justice," in *42 Today: Jackie Robinson and His Legacy*, ed. Michael G. Long (New York: New York University Press, 2021), 134, 136 (quotation), 137.
8. Abraham Khan, "Jackie Robinson, Civic Republicanism, and Black Political

Culture," in *Sports and Identity: New Agendas in Communication*, ed. Barry Brummett (New York: Routledge, 2014), 84–85, available at https://www.academia.edu/15605045/Jackie_Robinson_Civic_Republicanism_and_Black_Political_Culture.

9. Dave Zirin, *What's My Name, Fool? Sports and Resistance in the United States* (Sydney: Accessible Publishing System, 2010), 20.

10. JR to Michael Hamilburg, October 10, 1970, in *First Class Citizenship: The Civil Rights Letters of Jackie Robinson*, ed. Michael G. Long (New York: Holt, 2007), 302.

11. Howard Bryant, *The Heritage: Black Athletes, a Divided America, and the Politics of Patriotism* (Boston: Beacon, 2018), 43–44 (quotation); Kahn, *The Boys of Summer*, 401.

12. Jackie Robinson, *I Never Had It Made: Jackie Robinson, an Autobiography* (New York: HarperCollins, 1995), 259.

13. Jules Tygiel, introduction to *The Jackie Robinson Reader: Perspectives on an American Hero*, ed. Jules Tygiel (New York: Penguin, 1997), 11.

14. John Vernon, "Beyond the Box Score: Jackie Robinson, Civil Rights Crusader," *Negro History Bulletin* 58 (October–December 1995): 20; Jackie Robinson, *Baseball Has Done It* (Brooklyn, NY: Ig, 2005), 25–27.

15. Patrick Henry, "Jackie Robinson: Athlete and American Par Excellence," *Virginia Quarterly Review* 73 (Spring 1997): 200.

16. Jackie Robinson (as told to Ed Reid), "Robinson Never Forgets Mother's Advice," *Washington Post*, August 23, 1949, 12–13.

17. Interview with Ed Henry, in *42 Faith: The Rest of the Jackie Robinson Story*, by Ed Henry (Nashville: W Publishing, 2017), 285–86.

18. Long and Lamb, *Jackie Robinson*, 115. They report that he cited Leviticus 25:10–14 to support his argument.

19. Ed Henry, *42 Faith*, 16.

20. Long and Lamb, *Jackie Robinson*, 108.

21. Jackie Robinson, "My Greatest Day," unpublished manuscript, n.d., but probably written in 1961, JRP, box 11, folder 12, Manuscript Division, LOC, Washington, DC, 11.

22. Jackie Robinson, "Cast the First Stone," October 15, 1967, JRP, box 8, folder 3, Manuscript Division, LOC, Washington, DC, 7.

23. "Jackie Robinson, President," *Living Church* 147 (November 24, 1963): 13.

24. "Jackie Robinson," *New York Post*, March 23, 1960, 88.

25. Jackie Robinson, *Baseball Has Done It*, 212, 219 (quotation).

26. Jackie Robinson, *Baseball Has Done It*, 109, 211 (quotation). See also Larry Moffi and Jonathan Kronstadt, *Crossing the Line: Black Major Leaguers, 1947-1959* (Jefferson, NC: McFarland, 1994); Rick Swayne, *Black Stars Who Made Baseball Whole: The Jackie Robinson Generation in the Major Leagues* (Jefferson, NC: McFarland, 2005); Steve Jacobson, *Carrying Jackie's Torch: The Players Who Integrated Baseball—and America* (New York: Lawrence Hill Books, 2007).

27. Jackie Robinson, *Baseball Has Done It*, 22 (first three quotations), 23, 21 (remaining quotations).

28. Quoted in Peter Dreier, "Jackie Robinson: A Legacy of Activism," *American Prospect*, January 31, 2019, https://prospect.org/civil-rights/jackie-robinson-legacy-activism.

29. Robinson, *I Never*, 265.

30. Robinson, *I Never*, 261–62, 261; quotations in that order.

31. Quoted in Long, *First Class Citizenship*, 300. See Lee Lowenfish and Tony Lupien, *The Imperfect Diamond: The Story of Baseball's Reserve System and the Men Who Fought to Change It* (New York: Stein & Day, 1980).

32. Jackie Robinson, "Home Plate," *New York Amsterdam News*, January 12, 1962, 1, 11. See also Robinson, *I Never*, 142–43.

33. Jackie Robinson, "Home Plate," *New York Amsterdam News*, February 3, 1962, 9.

34. Sam Lacy, "Hall of Famer Still on Cloud 9," in Tygiel, *The Jackie Robinson Reader*, 220. Lacy omitted Christy Mathewson, who was also in this initial class.

35. Jackie Robinson, Hall of Fame speech, July 23, 1962, American Rhetoric, Online Speech Bank, accessed October 13, 2021, https://www.americanrhetoric.com/speeches/jackierobinsonbaseballhofinduction.htm.

36. Quoted in Lacy, "Hall of Famer," 221.

37. "900 Attend Tribute to Jackie Robinson," *New York Times*, July 21, 1962, 10.

38. JFK to Chairman, Jackie Robinson Testimonial Dinner, July 18, 1962, JRP, Manuscript Division, LOC, Washington, DC.

39. Jackie Robinson, "Patience, Pride and Progress," address for rally sponsored by the Mississippi State Conference of NAACP Branches, February 16, 1958, JRP, Manuscript Division, LOC, Washington, DC.

40. "Eisenhower Cites Integration as the Goal," *New York Times*, April 19, 1959, 64.

41. Orr, "Jackie Robinson," 53; Current to Robert Carter, October 28, 1959, in Long, *First Class Citizenship*, 75; "Jackie Robinson," *New York Post*, October 28, 1959; Patrick Obley, "How Jackie Robinson Ignited Greenville's Civil Rights Movement," *Columbia (SC) State*, April 6, 2013, https://www.thestate.com/news/local/civil-rights/article14425475.html.

42. Valerie Russ, "Triumph Baptist Church Honors Pastor James S. Hall Jr. for 65 Years of Preaching and Activism," *Philadelphia Inquirer*, November 19, 2016, https://www.inquirer.com/philly/news/20161120_Triumph_Baptist_Church_honors_Pastor_James_S_Hall_Jr_for_65_years_of_preaching_and_activism.html.

43. Obley, "How Jackie Robinson Ignited Greenville's Civil Rights Movement."

44. Obley, "How Jackie Robinson Ignited Greenville's Civil Rights Movement."

45. Quoted in Obley, "How Jackie Robinson Ignited Greenville's Civil Rights Movement."

46. Roger Bruns, *Jesse Jackson: A Biography* (Westport, CT: Greenwood, 2005), 11.

47. Obley, "How Jackie Robinson Ignited Greenville's Civil Rights Movement" (quotation); Samaria Bailey, "Honored and Humbled: South Carolina Honors Triumph Baptist Pastor Rev. James Hall," *Philadelphia Tribune*, October 26, 2019, https://www.phillytrib.com/honored-and-humbled-south-carolina-honors-triumph-baptist-pastor-rev-james-hall/article_5f15b0f5-4e19-578d-b14f-72e03c9d175d.html.

48. J. Whyatt Mondesire, "A Conversation with Rev. James S. Hall Pastor of Triumph Baptist Church and a Celebration of 60 Years of Ministry and Service," *Philadelphia Sun*, November 20, 2011, https://www.philasun.com/freedom-quest/a-conversation-with-rev-james-s-hall-pastor-of-triumph-baptist-church-and-a-celebration-of-60-years-of-ministry-and-service/.

49. Obley, "How Jackie Robinson Ignited Greenville's Civil Rights Movement."

50. "Jackie Robinson," *New York Post*, April 25, 1960, 68.

51. Jackie Robinson, "Home Plate," *New York Amsterdam News*, July 13, 1963, 11.

52. Jackie Robinson, "Home Plate," *New York Amsterdam News*, June 13, 1964.

53. Jackie Robinson, *I Never*, 148, 150 (quotations).

54. Jackie Robinson, "Home Plate," *New York Amsterdam News*, July 14, 1962.

55. Jackie Robinson, *I Never*, 147.

56. Arnold Rampersad, *Jackie Robinson: A Biography* (New York: Knopf, 1997), 340.

57. Lawrence to William Black, July 15, 1962, JRP, Manuscript Division, LOC, Washington, DC. On Lawrence, see "Our History," Antioch Baptist Church, accessed October 13, 2021, https://www.antiochbaptistbrooklyn.com/our-history.

58. Jackie Robinson, *I Never*, 148.

59. Jackie Robinson, "Home Plate," *New York Amsterdam News*, September 7, 1963, 11.

60. Jackie Robinson, *Baseball Has Done It*, 25, 26, 28; quotations in that order.

61. Jackie Robinson, "Home Plate," *New York Amsterdam News*, September 28, 1963. On Robinson's complicated views about violence, see Mark Kurlansky, "A Champion of Nonviolence?," in Long, *42 Today*, 42–56.

62. Paul Putz, "Black Christians Play a Crucial Role in Athlete Activism," *Christianity Today*, August 31, 2020, https://www.christianitytoday.com/ct/2020/august-web-only/nba-protests-christian-athletes-jacob-blake-fca-sports-mini.html.

63. Lou House Black Journal, episode 20, National Educational Television, New York, January 1970.

64. Jackie Robinson, *I Never*, xxiv.

65. Michael G. Long, "Introduction," in *First Class Citizenship*, 2.

66. Michael G. Long, ed., *Beyond Home Plate: Jackie Robinson on Life after Baseball* (Syracuse, NY: Syracuse University Press, 2013), xxv.

67. Robinson, *I Never*, 150.

68. Long, *Beyond Home Plate*, xxv (quotation), xxvi.

69. Rampersad, *Jackie Robinson*, 210.

70. Rachel Robinson with Lee Daniels, *Jackie Robinson: An Intimate Portrait* (New York: Abrams, 1996), 162.

71. "Jackie Robinson," *New York Post*, July 27, 1959.

72. "Jackie Robinson," *New York Post*, January 6, 1960.

73. Rebecca Alpert, "1947 Dodgers: Jackie Robinson and the Jews," Society for American Baseball Research, accessed October 13, 2021, https://sabr.org/journal/article/1947-dodgers-jackie-robinson-and-the-jews/.

74. Long, *Beyond Home Plate*, xxviii; James Wechsler to JR, November 8, 1960, in Long, *First Class Citizenship*, 115–16.

75. "Keeping Posted with Jackie," *Time*, April 11, 1960, 93.

76. Jackie Robinson, "Home Plate," *New York Amsterdam News*, January 28, 1967, 15.

77. JR to Randolph, March 28, 1964, in Long, *First Class Citizenship*, 196.

78. Jackie Robinson, "Home Plate," *New York Amsterdam News*, April 25, 1964, 11.

79. "Jackie Robinson," *New York Post*, June 10, 1959, 88.

80. Jackie Robinson, "Home Plate," *New York Amsterdam News*, February 23, 1963, 11.

81. Jackie Robinson, "Home Plate," *New York Amsterdam News*, March 14, 1964, 13.

82. Jackie Robinson, "Home Plate," *New York Amsterdam News*, October 14, 1967, 17.

83. JR to Brundage, March 21, 1967, in Long, *First Class Citizenship*, 251. In May 1968 the IOC voted to exclude South Africa, as it had in 1964.

84. Jackie Robinson, "The Church and the World," 27, May 3, 1968, JRP, box 8, folder 3, Manuscript Division, LOC, Washington, DC.

85. JR, letter to the editor of the *New York Times*, July 30, 1967, 26, responding to "Black Racism," *New York Times*, July 24, 1967, 25.

86. "Meet the Press," April 14, 1957, Library of Congress, https://www.loc.gov /collections/jackie-robinson-baseball/articles-and-essays/baseball-the-color-line -and-jackie-robinson/meet-the-press/.

87. "Jackie Robinson," *New York Post*, June 10, 1959, 88.

88. Long and Lamb, *Jackie Robinson*, 108–9.

89. JR to Eisenhower, September 13, 1957, in Long, *First Class Citizenship*, 40.

90. JR to Eisenhower, September 25, 1957, in Long, *First Class Citizenship*, 40.

91. JR to Nixon, February 5, 1958, in Long, *First Class Citizenship*, 49.

92. Dwight D. Eisenhower, "Remarks at Meeting of Negro Leaders Sponsored by the National Newspaper Publishing Association," American Presidency Project, May 12, 1958, https://www.presidency.ucsb.edu/documents/remarks-meeting-negro -leaders-sponsored-the-national-newspaper-publishers-association; Felix Belair Jr., "Eisenhower Bids Negroes Be Patient about Rights," *New York Times*, May 13, 1958, 1.

93. JR to Eisenhower, May 13, 1958, in Long, *First Class Citizenship*, 56.

94. Eisenhower to JR, June 4, 1958, in Long, *First Class Citizenship*, 57.

95. Colton Jeffries, "The Lynching of Mack Charles Parker," Clio: Your Guide to History, April 30, 2015, https://www.theclio.com/entry/13793. See also Howard Smead, *Blood Justice: The Lynching of Mack Charles Parker* (New York: Oxford University Press, 1986). Robinson, as quoted in David Falkner, *Great Time Coming: The Life of Jackie Robinson from Baseball to Birmingham* (New York: Simon & Schuster, 1995), 271.

96. "Jackie Robinson," *New York Post*, June 12, 1959.

97. John Vernon, "A Citizen's View of Presidential Responsibility: Jackie Robinson and Dwight Eisenhower," *Negro History Bulletin* 62 (December 1999): 16.

98. "Jackie Robinson," *New York Post*, May 29, 1959, 72.

99. "Jackie Robinson," *New York Post*, June 12, 1959, 92.

100. Jackie Robinson, *I Never*, 211.

101. Jackie Robinson, "Home Plate," *New York Amsterdam News*, July 1, 1967, 17.

102. Long and Lamb, *Jackie Robinson*, 110.

103. MLK to JR, June 19, 1960, in Long, *First Class Citizenship*, 105.

104. JR to MLK, June 29, 1960, in Long, *First Class Citizenship*, 106.

105. MLK to JR, May 14, 1962, in Long, *First Class Citizenship*, 147.

106. Martin Luther King Jr., "Hall of Famer," *New York Amsterdam News*, August 4, 1962.

107. MLK to JR, October 7, 1964, in Long, *First Class Citizenship*, 205–6.

108. Transcript of interview with Theodore Granik, "Youth Wants to Know," April 1967 television program, JRP, box 9, Manuscript Division, LOC, Washington, DC.

109. Jackie Robinson, "Home Plate," *New York Amsterdam News*, May 13, 1967.

110. Jackie Robinson, *I Never*, 214.

111. Jackie Robinson, "Home Plate," *New York Amsterdam News*, April 8, 1967.

112. Jackie Robinson, "Home Plate," *New York Amsterdam News*, January 29, 1966, 15.

113. JR to LBJ, April 18, 1967, in Long, *First Class Citizenship*, 252–53; quotations in that order.

114. Jackie Robinson, "Dr. Martin L. King," *New York Amsterdam News*, May 13, 1967; Long, *First Class Citizenship*, 256.

115. Sharon Robinson, *Stealing Home: An Intimate Family Portrait by the Daughter of Jackie Robinson* (New York: HarperPerennial, 1997), 147.

116. Jackie Robinson, "Home Plate," *New York Amsterdam News*, October 21, 1967, 17.

117. Jackie Robinson, *I Never*, 156.

118. Bill Francis, "National Tragedy Brought Baseball to a Halt for Two Days in 1968," National Baseball Hall of Fame, accessed October 13, 2021, https://baseball hall.org/discover/martin-luther-king-jrs-assassination-brought-baseball-to-a-halt -in-1968#:~:text=%E2%80%9CWe%20are%20doing%20this%20because,but%20 also%20with%20poor%20people.

119. Jackie Robinson, *I Never*, 216.

120. Jackie Robinson, "Home Plate," *New York Amsterdam News*, April 13, 1968, 21.

121. Jackie Robinson, "Church and the World," 10 (first quotation), 17 (second and third quotations).

122. Martin Luther King Jr., "The Ways of God in the Midst of Glaring Evil, Sermon Delivered at Dexter Avenue Baptist Church," January 13, 1957, in *The Papers of Martin Luther King, Jr.*, vol. 4, *Symbol of the Movement: January 1957–December 1958*, ed. Clayborne Carson et al. (Berkeley: University of California Press, 2000), 109.

123. Jackie Robinson, "Home Plate," *New York Amsterdam News*, April 13, 1968, 21.

124. Jackie Robinson, "Home Plate," *New York Amsterdam News*, June 13, 1968.

125. Francis, "National Tragedy Brought Baseball to a Halt for Two Days in 1968." On Clemente's social activism and legacy, see James Wagner, "For Many Latino Players, Roberto Clemente's Number Is Off Limits, Too," *New York Times*, April 16, 2019, https:// www.nytimes.com/2019/04/16/sports/roberto-clemente-number-retired.html. I am referring here to MLB postponing games, not canceling them because of strikes.

126. Jackie Robinson, *I Never*, 215.

127. Jackie Robinson, *I Never*, 127–28.

128. Samuel Haynes, "'High Point of My Career'—Jackie of Spingarn Award," *Baltimore Afro-American*, December 8, 1956, 3.

129. JR to MLK, February 11, 1957, in Long, *First Class Citizenship*, 24.

130. Jackie Robinson, "Home Plate," *New York Amsterdam News*, March 30, 1963.

131. JR to Kivie Kaplan, [1966], in Long, *First Class Citizenship*, 226. See also Jackie Robinson, "Home Plate," *New York Amsterdam News*, May 27, 1966, 15; and October 22, 1966, 7.

132. Jackie Robinson, "Home Plate," *New York Amsterdam News*, January 14, 1967, 13–14.

133. Wilkins to JR, February 8, 1967, in Long, *First Class Citizenship*, 246.

134. JR to Wilkins, February 15, 1967, in Long, *First Class Citizenship*, 246.

135. Jackie Robinson, *I Never*, 131.

136. JR to JFK, February 9, 1961, in Long, *First Class Citizenship*, 125.

137. Jackie Robinson, "Home Plate," *New York Amsterdam News*, May 5, 1962.

138. MLK to JR, May 14, 1962, 146; Abernathy to JR, June 7, 1962, in Long, *First Class Citizenship*, 147.

139. Jackie Robinson, "Home Plate," *New York Amsterdam News*, August 18, 1962.

140. Jackie Robinson, "Home Plate," *New York Amsterdam News*, August 11, 1962.

141. JR to JFK, May 7, 1963, in Long, *First Class Citizenship*, 168 (first quotation), 169 (remaining quotations). Robinson discussed these themes in *New York Amsterdam News*, May 18, 1963, 11.

142. John F. Kennedy, "Radio and Television Report to the American People on Civil Rights," American Presidency Project, June 11, 1963, https://www.presidency .ucsb.edu/documents/radio-and-television-report-the-american-people-civil-rights.

143. Jackie Robinson, "Home Plate," *New York Amsterdam News*, June 12, 1963.

144. Jackie Robinson, "Home Plate," *New York Amsterdam News*, November 30, 1963. Robinson often commended Johnson for his civil rights activism. For example, he wrote: "May God give you continued good health and wisdom." "No president could have affected the progress in our drive for human dignity as you have done" (JR to LBJ, February 4, 1965, in Long, *First Class Citizenship*, 213).

145. Jackie Robinson, "Church and the World," 14.

146. Jackie Robinson, "Home Plate," *New York Amsterdam News*, August 11, 1968.

147. JR to Nixon, January 22, 1969, in Long, *First Class Citizenship*, 291–92.

148. See "Robinson Cautions Nixon on Slum Aids," *New York Times*, January 30, 1969, 22.

149. JR to Nixon, December 1971, in Long, *First Class Citizenship*, 311.

150. JR to Nixon, March 21, 1972, in Long, *First Class Citizenship*, 313.

151. Justin Tinsley, "Jackie Robinson vs. Malcolm X," *Undefeated*, May 25, 2016, https://theundefeated.com/features/jackie-robinson-vs-malcolm-x/.

152. Jackie Robinson, "Home Plate," *New York Amsterdam News*, July 13, 1963.

153. Quoted in Tinsley, "Jackie Robinson vs. Malcolm X."

154. Tinsley, "Jackie Robinson vs. Malcolm X."

155. Malcolm X to JR, November 30, 1963, in Long, *First Class Citizenship*, 184 (first two quotations), 186 (remaining quotations).

156. Jackie Robinson, "Home Plate," *New York Amsterdam News*, December 14, 1963, 1, 53 (quotations).

157. Jackie Robinson, "Home Plate," *New York Amsterdam News*, November 16, 1963, 11, https://oac.cdlib.org/view?docId=hb9v19p4rt;NAAN=13030&doc.view= content&chunk.id=0&toc.depth=1&brand=oac4&anchor.id=0.

158. Alex Haley, "An Interview with Malcolm X," *Playboy*, May 1963, https://the facultyorganization.weebly.com/musings-of-a-black-man.

159. Jackie Robinson, "Home Plate," November 16, 1963, 11. See also Jackie Robinson, "Home Plate," *New York Amsterdam News*, March 30, 1963.

160. Jackie Robinson, "Malcolm X and the Destiny of the Negro," *Chicago Defender*, July 18, 1964, 8.

161. Jackie Robinson, "Martyr Malcolm," *Chicago Defender*, March 20, 1965, 8.

162. Jackie Robinson, *I Never*, 180 (first quotation), 182 (second quotation).

163. Falkner, *Great Time Coming*, 309–10.

164. Long, *First Class Citizenship*, 149.

165. Jackie Robinson, "Home Plate," *New York Amsterdam News*, April 20, 1963.

166. Jackie Robinson, "Home Plate," *New York Amsterdam News*, August 31, 1963, 11.

167. Jackie Robinson, "Home Plate," *New York Amsterdam News*, October 7, 1967, 15.

168. Steven Lawson, *Running for Freedom: Civil Rights and Black Politics in America Since 1941* (Philadelphia: Temple University Press, 1991), 117–18, 120–21.

169. Jackie Robinson, "Home Plate," *New York Amsterdam News*, July 30, 1966, 15.

170. Long, *Beyond Home Plate*, 116 (these are Long's words). See Homer Bigart, "Rap Brown Calls Riots 'Rehearsals for Revolution,'" *New York Times*, August 7, 1967, 1.

171. Jackie Robinson, "Home Plate," *New York Amsterdam News*, October 22, 1966. See also Adam Clayton Powell Jr., *Keep the Faith, Baby!* (New York: Simon & Schuster, 1967), 9–11, 16–17.

172. Jackie Robinson, *Baseball Has Done It*, 213.

173. Jackie Robinson, "Home Plate," *New York Amsterdam News*, August 12, 1967.

174. Jackie Robinson, "Cast the First Stone," 10 (first quotation), 11 (second quotation), 21 (third and fourth quotations). Robinson repeated this statement in his column in the *New York Amsterdam News*, October 7, 1967, 15. He made the same point in other opinion pieces, including *New York Post*, August 22, 1960, 48, and *New York Amsterdam News*, June 1, 1963, 11.

175. Jackie Robinson, *I Never*, 268–69.

176. Jackie Robinson, *I Never*, 270.

177. "Remarks of Mr. Jackie Robinson at SCLC Operation Breadbasket Saturday Morning Meeting," January 23, 1971, in Long, *First Class Citizenship*, 303.

178. JR to Calvin Morris, February 1971, in Long, ed., *First Class Citizenship*, 305.

179. Stephanie Christensen, "Operation PUSH (People United to Serve Humanity)," BlackPast, December 13, 2007, https://www.blackpast.org/african-american-history/operation-push-people-united-serve-humanity/.

180. Quoted in Chris Kaltenbach, "Jackie Robinson: At Bat for Equality," *Baltimore Sun*, February 15, 1995, https://www.baltimoresun.com/news/bs-xpm-1995-02-15-1995046149-story.html.

181. Williams, "After the Cheering Stopped, Jackie Robinson Played Harder Than Ever."

Chapter 7

1. Sharon Robinson, *Stealing Home: An Intimate Family Portrait by the Daughter of Jackie Robinson* (New York: HarperPerennial, 1997), 153.

2. Rachel Robinson with Lee Daniels, *Jackie Robinson: An Intimate Portrait* (New York: Abrams, 1996), 132, 135, 161 (quotations). See also "Our History," North Stamford Community Church, accessed October 20, 2021, https://www.northstamford church.org/our-history; Evan Simko-Bednarski, "Stamford Church Asks What's in a Name?," *Stamford (CT) Advocate*, February 22, 2016, https://www.stamfordadvocate .com/local/article/Iconic-Stamford-church-asks-whats-in-a-name-6844150.php; Jamal Powell, "North Stamford Congregational Church Remembers Jackie Robinson,"

Patch, February 13, 2012, https://patch.com/connecticut/stamford/north-stamford
-congregational-church-remembers-jackie-robinson.

3. Jackie Robinson, "Home Plate," *New York Amsterdam News*, December 2, 1967.

4. Jackie Robinson, "The G.O.P.: For White Men Only?," *Saturday Evening Post*, August 10–17, 1963, 10.

5. E.g., Rachel Robinson, *Jackie Robinson*, 179.

6. Jackie Robinson, "The Church and the World," May 3, 1968, JRP, box 8, folder 3, Manuscript Division, LOC, Washington, DC, 25 (first quotation), 25–26 (second quotation), 18 (third quotation).

7. Bob Wells, "Breathtaking: The Life and Times of the Rev. Gardner C. Taylor," *Faith & Leadership*, February 23, 2009, https://faithandleadership.com/breathtaking
-life-and-times-rev-gardner-c-taylor; Robert McFadden, "Rev. Gardner C. Taylor, Powerful Voice for Civil Rights, Dies at 96," *New York Times*, April 6, 2015, B19.

8. Jackie Robinson, "My Greatest Day," unpublished manuscript, n.d., but probably written in 1961, JRP, box 11, folder 12, Manuscript Division, LOC, Washington, DC. As another example of his religious activism, Robinson served in 1958 as the moderator of *Talk Back*, a television program jointly produced by the National Council of Churches and the Methodist church; each episode featured a dramatization and discussion of a moral problem. See Alison Leigh Cowan, "Archive Shows Robinson as Moderator on Morality," *New York Times*, December 24, 2010, https://www.nytimes
.com/2010/12/25/sports/baseball/25robinson.html; Linda Bloom, "Church TV Show and Jackie Robinson," *UM News*, February 28, 2011, https://www.umnews.org/en
/news/church-tv-show-and-jackie-robinson.

9. NR to JR, September 19, 1962, in Michael G. Long, ed., *First Class Citizenship: The Civil Rights Letters of Jackie Robinson* (New York: Holt, 2007), 152–53; quotations in that order. See Robinson, "Home Plate," *New York Amsterdam News*, September 22, 1962, 11; "Jackie Robinson," Georgia Historical Society, accessed October 20, 2021, https://georgiahistory.com/education-outreach/online-exhibits/featured-historical
-figures/jackie-robinson/robinson-and-the-civil-rights-movement/.

10. "Jackie Robinson, President," *Living Church* 147 (November 24, 1963): 13.

11. *United Church Herald* 6 (1963): 16.

12. Jackie Robinson, "Home Plate," *New York Amsterdam News*, July 27, 1963.

13. Jackie Robinson, "Address to the General Synod of the United Church of Christ," July 10, 1963, JRP, box 13, folder 3, Manuscript Division, LOC, Washington, DC, 1, 2 (quotation), 3.

14. Jackie Robinson, "Home Plate," *New York Amsterdam News*, January 26, 1963, 4.

15. *The Living Church* 147 (November 24, 1963): 13; Arnold Rampersad, *Jackie Robinson: A Biography* (New York: Knopf, 1997), 352.

16. JR to BR, received by BR on April 12, 1965, in Long, *First Class Citizenship*, 218. The LOC (box 8, folder 4) contains invitations for Robinson to speak in Lee, Massachusetts; Anchorage, Alaska; and Seattle. Robinson did give a lecture on the brotherhood of man at the First Congregational Church in Berkeley, California, on March 7, 1965.

17. See Leah Wright Rigueur, *The Loneliness of Black Republicans: Pragmatic Politics and the Pursuit of Power* (Princeton: Princeton University Press, 2015), and Timothy

Thurber, *Republicans and Race: The GOP's Frayed Relationship with African Americans, 1945-1974* (Lawrence: University of Kansas Press, 2013).

18. Jackie Robinson, "Home Plate," *New York Amsterdam News*, May 4, 1963.

19. Rampersad, *Jackie Robinson*, 371, 319.

20. Rampersad, *Jackie Robinson*, 319. See also Gerald Early, "The Dilemma of the Black Republican," in *42 Today: Jackie Robinson and His Legacy*, ed. Michael G. Long (New York: New York University Press, 2021), 100–112.

21. JR to NR, July 2, 1964, in Long, *First Class Citizenship*, 187.

22. Roger Kahn, "The Jackie Robinson I Remember," *Journal of Blacks in Higher Education* 14 (Winter 1996/1997): 92.

23. Quoted in Gene Seymour, "What the Jackie Robinson Film Leaves Out," *New Republic*, April 19, 2013, https://newrepublic.com/article/112953/jackie-robinson-and -42-conservative-politics.

24. JR to NR, February 1, 1965, in Long, *First Class Citizenship*, 212; JR to NR, February 22, 1965, in Long, 214 (quotation).

25. Jackie Robinson, "Home Plate," *New York Amsterdam News*, December 11, 1965, 34.

26. Clarence Taylor, *Black Religious Intellectuals: The Fight for Equality from Jim Crow to the Twenty-First Century* (New York: Routledge, 2002), 38–40.

27. JR to NR, December 7, 1961, in Long, *First Class Citizenship*, 135.

28. JR to Jacob Javits, November 22, 1965, in Long, *First Class Citizenship*, 224.

29. JR to NR, February 22, 1965, in Long, *First Class Citizenship*, 214.

30. JR to NR, January 12, 1966, in Long, *First Class Citizenship*, 226–27.

31. Jackie Robinson, *I Never Had It Made: Jackie Robinson, an Autobiography* (New York: HarperCollins, 1995), 166.

32. JR to NR, August 16, 1966, in Long, *First Class Citizenship*, 233.

33. JR to NR, [December 1966], in Long, *First Class Citizenship*, 240.

34. JR to NR, January 18, 1968, in Long, *First Class Citizenship*, 267.

35. Jackie Robinson, "Home Plate," *New York Amsterdam News*, January 20, 1968, 15.

36. JR to Hubert Humphrey, May 3, 1968, in Long, *First Class Citizenship*, 277.

37. Jackie Robinson, letter to the editor of the *New York Post*, March 18, 1971, in Long, *First Class Citizenship*, 307–8.

38. JR to NR, May 2, 1972, in Long, *First Class Citizenship*, 314.

39. Jackie Robinson, *I Never*, 136.

40. "Keeping Posted with Jackie," *Time*, April 11, 1960, 93.

41. Jackie Robinson, *I Never*, 135, 137.

42. JR to Nixon, March 19, 1957, in Long, *First Class Citizenship*, 26.

43. Jackie Robinson, *I Never*, 135; Holmes Alexander, "Kennedy Couldn't Look Me in the Eye," *Newark (NJ) Advocate*, October 6, 1960, 4.

44. Jackie Robinson, *New York Post*, May 23, 1960, 72.

45. Jackie Robinson, *I Never*, 137–38.

46. JFK to JR, July 1, 1960, in Long, *First Class Citizenship*, 107.

47. Quoted in Steven Levingston, "Before Trump vs. the NFL, There Was Jackie Robinson vs. JFK," *Washington Post*, September 24, 2017, https://www.washington post.com/news/retropolis/wp/2017/09/24/before-trump-vs-the-nfl-there-was -jackie-robinson-vs-jfk/.

48. Jackie Robinson, *New York Post*, July 15, 1960, 60.

49. Rachel Robinson, *Jackie Robinson*, 175.

50. "Rockefeller's Sermon Theme Race Equality," *Journal*, October 24, 1960, 18 (quotation); "Rocky Takes to Pulpit in Four Negro Churches," *Syracuse (NY) Post-Standard*, October 24, 1960, 2; "Rocky Preaches in Negro Churches," *Newsday*, October 24, 1960, 4. On Rockefeller's frequent use of this phrase, see "Born to Wealth but to the Wrong Party," *New York Times*, January 28, 1979, E2.

51. Jackie Robinson, *I Never*, 140.

52. This is Taylor Branch's assessment in Chris Kaltenbach, "Jackie Robinson: At Bat for Equality," *Baltimore Sun*, February 15, 1995, https://www.baltimoresun.com/news/bs-xpm-1995-02-15-1995046149-story.html.

53. Quoted in Jon Meacham, "Jackie Robinson's Inner Struggle," *New York Times*, July 20, 2020, https://www.nytimes.com/2020/07/20/books/review/jackie-robinson-inner-struggle.html. See also Jackie Robinson, "The G.O.P.," 10.

54. Jackie Robinson, *I Never*, 174.

55. Jackie Robinson, "Home Plate," *New York Amsterdam News*, August 29, 1964, 19.

56. Jackie Robinson, "Home Plate," *New York Amsterdam News*, July 4, 1964, 19.

57. Jackie Robinson, "Home Plate," *New York Amsterdam News*, September 22, 1967.

58. JR to NR, March 8, 1968, in Long, *First Class Citizenship*, 273–74.

59. Jackie Robinson, "Home Plate," *New York Amsterdam News*, August 17, 1968, 13. See also "Jackie Robinson Splits with G.O.P. over Nixon Choice," *New York Times*, August 12, 1968, 1.

60. Jackie Robinson, *I Never*, 236 (quotation), 237. On Robinson's relationship with Nixon, see Johnny Moore, "Robinson Agonistes: The Curious Bromance and Breakup of Jackie Robinson and Richard Nixon," in *The Cooperstown Symposium on Baseball and American Culture, 2017–2018*, ed. William Simons (Jefferson, NC: McFarland, 2019), 132–49.

61. Humphrey to JR, December 14, 1968, in Long, *First Class Citizenship*, 285.

62. Doc A. S. Young, "The Case of the Athletic Patsies," *Negro Digest* 12 (July 1963): 30–31.

63. William Buckley Jr., "Robinson Strikes Out," *New York Post*, August 15, 1968.

64. Robinson helped Lindsay win 43 percent of the African American vote to defeat Democrat Abraham Beame and Conservative William Buckley in the 1965 New York City mayoral race.

65. Seymour, "What the Jackie Robinson Film Leaves Out."

66. Michael G. Long, ed., *Beyond Home Plate: Jackie Robinson on Life after Baseball* (Syracuse, NY: Syracuse University Press, 2013), xv.

67. Rachel Robinson, *Jackie Robinson*, 190; Jackie Robinson, *I Never*, 184.

68. See Bethany Moreton, *To Serve God and Wal-Mart: The Making of Christian Free Enterprise* (Cambridge, MA: Harvard University Press, 2010); Kevin Kruse, *One Nation under God: How Corporate America Invented Christian America* (New York: Basic Books, 2015); Darren Grem, *The Blessings of Business: How Corporations Shaped Conservative Christianity* (New York: Oxford University Press, 2016); and Darren Dochuk, *Anointed with Oil: How Christianity and Crude Made Modern America* (New York: Basic Books, 2019).

69. April Joyner, "Jackie Robinson, Business Pioneer," *USA Today*, May 11, 2015, https://www.usatoday.com/story/money/business/2015/05/11/ozy-jackie-robinson -business-pioneer/27115531/.

70. Jackie Robinson, *I Never*, 167.

71. Quoted in Juan Williams, "After the Cheering Stopped, Jackie Robinson Played Harder Than Ever," *Washington Post*, April 12, 1987, https://www.washingtonpost .com/archive/lifestyle/magazine/1987/04/12/after-the-cheering-stopped-jackie -robinson-played-harder-than-ever-in-1947-he-broke-baseballs-color-line-then-un like-so-many-of-todays-star-athletes-he-used-fame-as-a-way-tohelp-his-people /a06b8ec8-8c04-420a-b0d4-dcd10f7bb715/.

72. Jackie Robinson, "My Greatest Day," 6.

73. Jackie Robinson, "Home Plate," *New York Amsterdam News*, January 2, 1965.

74. Hans Baer and Merrill Singer, *African-American Religion in the Twentieth Century: Varieties of Protest and Accommodation* (Knoxville: University of Tennessee Press, 1992), 101.

75. Jackie Robinson, *I Never*, 166.

76. Jackie Robinson, *New York Post*, July 6, 1959.

77. Jackie Robinson, "Cast the First Stone," October 15, 1967, JRP, box 8, folder 3, Manuscript Division, LOC, Washington, DC, 19.

78. Rachel Robinson, *Jackie Robinson*, 154; Jackie Robinson, *I Never*, 126 (quotation). See also Dan Burley, "Did Jackie Robinson Betray Baseball?," *Jet*, January 1957, 54.

79. Williams, "After the Cheering Stopped, Jackie Robinson Played Harder Than Ever."

80. Sam Ostrove, quoted in Joe Reichler, "He's Just as Touchy, Outspoken, Dedicated," *Asbury Park (NJ) Press*, February 18, 1962, 10.

81. Leonard Gross, "*Pageant* Listens to Jackie Robinson," *Pageant*, May 1957, 140.

82. Jackie Robinson, *I Never*, 103 (first and third quotations), JR to A. Philip Randolph, December 30, 1964, in Long, *First Class Citizenship*, 207 (second quotation), 184, 189; Pearce is quoted in Williams, "After the Cheering Stopped, Jackie Robinson Played Harder Than Ever."

83. Quoted in Williams, "After the Cheering Stopped, Jackie Robinson Played Harder Than Ever."

84. Jason Sokol, "Jackie Robinson's Life Was No Home Run for Racial Progress," *Time*, July 4, 2015, https://time.com/3942084/jackie-robinson-racial-progress/.

85. Kahn, "Jackie Robinson," 92.

86. Williams, "After the Cheering Stopped, Jackie Robinson Played Harder Than Ever."

87. JR to NR, February 26, 1969, in Long, *First Class Citizenship*, 293.

88. John Emmeus Davis, "Arc of Justice: The Rise, Fall and Rebirth of a Beloved Community," Arc of Justice, accessed October 20, 2021, https://static1.square space.com/static/574610bb20c647ad3c3c2daf/t/583c8c659de4bb595172a9b2 /1480363113503/AoJ_backstory_v4a.pdf.

89. "Jackie Robinson Tells OIC Students They're in 'Spring Training,'" *Philadelphia Tribune*, October 20, 1964.

90. Jackie Robinson, "Home Plate," *New York Amsterdam News*, October 31, 1964.

91. Michael G. Long and Chris Lamb, *Jackie Robinson: A Spiritual Biography; The Faith of a Boundary-Breaking Hero* (Louisville: Westminster John Knox, 2017), 138.

92. Jackie Robinson, *I Never*, 238–39. See, for example, JR to Nixon, February 9, 1970, in *I Never*, 239–40; and Paul Delaney, "Jackie Robinson Scored Nixon on Black Capitalism Problems," *New York Times*, January 21, 1970, 27.

93. Jackie Robinson, letter to the *New York Post*, March 18, 1971.

94. JR to BR, July 24, 1962, in Long, *First Class Citizenship*, 151.

95. Dave Anderson, "Jackie Robinson, First Black in Major Leagues, Dies," *New York Times*, October 25, 1972, 56; Jackie Robinson, *I Never*, xxii; quotations in that order.

96. Jackie Robinson, "Home Plate," *New York Amsterdam News*, December 18, 1965.

97. Jackie Robinson, *I Never*, 260.

98. Rachel Robinson, *Jackie Robinson*, 144.

99. Sharon Robinson, *Stealing Home*, 46.

100. Chris Lamb, "How Jackie Robinson's Wife, Rachel, Helped Him Break Baseball's Color Line," History News Network, January 30, 2019, https://historynewsnetwork.org/article/171107.

101. Quoted in Rampersad, *Jackie Robinson*, 421.

102. Sharon Robinson, *Stealing Home*, 182–83. Although Jackie frequently praised Rachel, extolled the political and social contributions of black women, and helped African American women in their sports careers, throughout his life, he "displayed a tension between a belief in traditional gender roles and a more progressive stance on women's autonomy and employment." He struggled for many years with Rachel's desire to have a professional career (Amira Rose Davis, "Supporting Black Women Athletes," in Long, *42 Today*, 179).

103. Jackie Robinson, "Home Plate," *New York Amsterdam News*, February 2, 1963.

104. Jackie Robinson, "Home Plate," *New York Amsterdam News*, February 9, 1963.

105. JR to Caroline Wallerstein, July 20, 1968, JRP, Manuscript Division, LOC, Washington, DC.

106. Sharon Robinson, *Stealing Home*, 153.

107. "Jackie Robinson Says," *Pittsburgh Courier*, March 27, 1948, 12.

108. J. K. Pollack, "A Family Named Robinson," *Parents Magazine*, in *The Jackie Robinson Reader: Perspectives on an American Hero*, ed. Jules Tygiel (New York: Penguin, 1997), 204.

109. Rachel Robinson, "I Live with a Hero," *McCall's*, March 1951, 112 (quotation), 114.

110. Pollack, "A Family Named Robinson," 209.

111. Rachel Robinson, *Jackie Robinson*, 60, 202; quotations in that order.

112. Sharon Robinson, *Stealing Home*, 46 (first quotation) 91 (remaining quotations).

113. Jackie Robinson, *I Never*, 89.

114. Sharon Robinson, *Stealing Home*, 86 (quotation), 87.

115. Reichler, "He's Just as Touchy," 10.

116. William Borders, "Jackie Robinson Jr. Is Arrested on Heroin Charge in Stamford," *New York Times*, March 5, 1968, 20.

117. Sharon Robinson, *Stealing Home*, 158.

118. Jackie Robinson, *I Never*, 153.

119. Sharon Robinson, *Stealing Home*, 87.

120. Jackie Robinson, *I Never*, 152.

121. Roger Kahn, *The Boys of Summer* (Evanston, IL: Holtzman, 1972), 399.

122. Jack Orr, "Jackie Robinson: Symbol of the Revolution," *Sport* 29 (March 1960): 54.

123. Sharon Robinson, *Stealing Home*, 92 (first quotation); Rachel Robinson, *Jackie Robinson*, 194 (second quotation), 200, 201 (third quotation).

124. Rachel Robinson, *Jackie Robinson*, 201.

125. Sharon Robinson, *Stealing Home*, 95.

126. Kahn, *The Boys of Summer*, 400.

127. Jackie Robinson, *I Never*, 218.

128. JR to Goldwater, March 26, 1968, in Long, *First Class Citizenship*, 274.

129. Jules Tygiel, introduction to Tygiel, *The Jackie Robinson Reader*, 12.

130. Jackie Jr.'s testimony before the US Senate Sub-Committee to Investigate Juvenile Delinquency, October 30, 1970, as quoted in Jackie Robinson, *I Never*, 233.

131. Sharon Robinson, *Stealing Home*, 173.

132. Jackie Robinson, *I Never*, 226.

133. Borders, "Jackie Robinson Jr.," 20.

134. JR to Wallerstein, July 20, 1968.

135. Cordell Thompson, "Jackie Robinson Joins War against Dope in the Ghettoes," *Jet*, September 10, 1970, 25 (first quotation), 28 (remaining quotations), 27.

136. Sharon Robinson, *Stealing Home*, 155 (first two quotations), 157 (third quotation).

137. Jackie Robinson, *I Never*, 253 (first quotation), 254 (remaining quotations).

138. Quoted in Anderson, "Jackie Robinson, First Black in Major Leagues, Dies."

139. Jackie Robinson, *I Never*, 248 (first quotation), 252 (second quotation), 249 (third and fourth quotations).

140. Sharon Robinson, *Stealing Home*, 180.

141. Nixon to JR, June 17, 1971, in Long, *First Class Citizenship*, 309–10.

142. Red Barber, "It Was Never a Game for Jackie," *New York Times*, November 12, 1972, https://timesmachine.nytimes.com/timesmachine/1972/11/12/91354522.pdf?pdf_redirect=true&ip=0.

143. Jackie Robinson, *I Never*, 254–55.

144. Sharon Robinson, *Stealing Home*, 179.

Conclusion

1. See Paul Putz, "Finally, Jackie Robinson's Faith Is Getting the Attention It Deserves," *Christianity Today*, June 29, 2017, https://www.christianitytoday.com/ct/2017/june-web-only/jackie-robinsons-faith-attention-deserves.html.

2. The Presbyterian Church (USA) became the United Presbyterian Church (USA) in 1958.

3. Michael Hout, Andrew Greeley, and Melissa J. Wilde, "The Demographic Im-

perative in Religious Change in the United States," *American Journal of Sociology* 107, no. 2 (September 2001), https://www.journals.uchicago.edu/doi/10.1086/324189.

4. Elesha Coffman, *The Christian Century and the Rise of Mainline Protestantism* (New York: Oxford University Press, 2013), 147.

5. E. Digby Baltzell, *The Protestant Establishment* (New York: Vintage Books, 1964), 9.

6. On mainline churches, see also Martin Marty, *The Public Church: Mainline, Evangelical, Catholic* (New York: Crossroad, 1981); Wade Clark Roof and William McKinney, *American Mainline Religion: Its Changing Shape and Future* (New Brunswick, NJ: Rutgers University Press, 1990); Jason Lantzer, *Mainline Christianity: The Past and Future of America's Majority Faith* (New York: New York University Press, 2012); Heidi Unruh, Jill Sinha, and John Belcher, "Mainline Protestants and Their Organizations," in *Comparing Strategies to Maintain Connections between Faith Communities and Organizations across Religions. Volume Two of the Report: Maintaining Vital Connections between Faith Communities and Their Nonprofits*, ed. Jo Anne Schneider and Isaac Morrison (College Park, MD: Faith and Organizations Project, 2010), 30–46.

7. See, for example, "Resistance Movement Grows in South," *Christian Century* 77 (March 16, 1960): 308–9.

8. "Race Relations: A Statement of the Lutheran Church in America, 1964." David S. Yeago, "Modern but Not Liberal," *First Things*, June 2012, https://www.firstthings.com/article/2012/06/modern-but-not-liberal.

9. Putz, "Finally, Jackie Robinson's Faith Is Getting the Attention It Deserves."

10. Michael Long, email to author, May 25, 2021.

11. Jackie Robinson, "Home Plate," *New York Amsterdam News*, April 13, 1968, 21.

12. Jackie Robinson, *Breakthrough to the Big League: The Story of Jackie Robinson* (New York: Harper & Row, 1965), 169.

13. Jackie Robinson, "My Greatest Day," unpublished manuscript, n.d., but probably written in 1961, JRP, box 11, folder 12, Manuscript Division, LOC, Washington, DC.

14. Jackie Robinson, *Breakthrough to the Big League*, 167.

15. Jackie Robinson, *Baseball Has Done It* (Brooklyn, NY: Ig, 2005), 42.

16. Jackie Robinson, "Untitled Speech," JRP, box 13, folder 3, Manuscript Division, LOC, Washington, DC. The second half of this quotation is Job 13:15.

17. Rachel Robinson with Lee Daniels, *Jackie Robinson: An Intimate Portrait* (New York: Abrams, 1996), 167.

18. Richard Stoll Armstrong, "My Reactions to '42,'" *Minding What Matters*, September 28, 2013, http://rsarm.blogspot.com/2013/09/my-reactions-to-42.html.

19. Michael G. Long, as quoted in Eric Scicchitano, "A Lasting Legacy: Robinson Led Way in Baseball, Civil Rights," *Sunbury (PA) Daily Item*, April 14, 2017, https://www.dailyitem.com/news/a-lasting-legacy-robinson-led-way-in-baseball-civil-rights/article_ff443bac-2106-11e7-9c91-07e76e967aee.html.

20. Jerome Ledoux, "Untold Part of Jackie Robinson Story Centers on Faith," *Daily World*, May 28, 2017, https://www.dailyworld.com/story/opinion/2017/05/28/untold-part-jackie-robinson-story-centers-faith/102097256/.

21. Arnold Rampersad, *Jackie Robinson: A Biography* (New York: Knopf, 1997), 222.

22. J. Cadou, "Jackie Robinson Writes Little Boy Who Wishes He Was White," *Pittsburgh Courier*, March 13, 1954, 1.

23. Rampersad, *Jackie Robinson*, 163–64, 212.

24. Rampersad, *Jackie Robinson*, 118.

25. JR to Ron Rabinowitz, n.d., in *Minneapolis Star and Tribune*, April 12, 1987.

26. Mary Caffrey, "Robinson Biography Puts Baseball Great in Context," *Princeton Weekly Bulletin*, September 15, 1997, https://pr.princeton.edu/pwb/97/0915/0915-rob inson.html.

27. "Jackie Robinson: This I Believe," NPR, March 25, 2008; this is from a 1952 episode for Edward R. Murrow's radio series and is available at https://www.npr.org /templates/story/story.php?storyId=89030535.

28. Michael G. Long and Chris Lamb, *Jackie Robinson: A Spiritual Biography; The Faith of a Boundary-Breaking Hero* (Louisville: Westminster John Knox, 2017), 131.

29. Jackie Robinson, "Home Plate," *New York Amsterdam News*, April 13, 1968, 21.

30. Long and Lamb, *Jackie Robinson*, 120.

31. "Jackie Robinson: This I Believe."

32. Jackie Robinson, *Jackie Robinson's Little League Book* (Englewood Cliffs, NJ: Prentice Hall, 1972), 135.

33. Jules Tygiel, *Baseball's Great Experiment: Jackie Robinson and His Legacy* (New York: Oxford University Press, 2008), 193.

34. Maury Allen, *Jackie Robinson: A Life Remembered* (New York: Franklin Watts, 1987), 170.

35. Tygiel, *Baseball's Great Experiment*, 59.

36. Roger Kahn, *The Boys of Summer* (Evanston, IL: Holtzman, 1972), 407.

37. Dave Anderson, "Jackie Robinson, First Black in Major Leagues, Dies," *New York Times*, October 25, 1972, 56.

38. Jackie Robinson, "Untitled Speech."

39. Jack Orr, "Jackie Robinson: Symbol of the Revolution," *Sport* 29 (March 1960): 56.

40. "Interview with Rachel Robinson," *Scholastic*, February 11, 1998, https://www .scholastic.com/teachers/articles/teaching-content/interview-rachel-robinson/.

41. Orr, "Jackie Robinson," 58.

42. Roger Kahn, "The Jackie Robinson I Remember," *Journal of Blacks in Higher Education* 14 (Winter 1996/1997): 88. On the other hand, Robinson argued that adults did "a great disservice to youth" if they did not teach them how to be good losers; learning how to "be a good loser is perhaps one of the most important lessons in life." "Jackie Robinson," *New York Post*, August 21, 1959, 48.

43. Allen, *Jackie Robinson*, 117–18; the Snider quote is from Baseball Almanac, ac- cessed October 20, 2021, https://www.baseball-almanac.com/quotes/quosnid.shtml.

44. Quoted in Patrick Henry, "Jackie Robinson: Athlete and American Par Excel- lence," *Virginia Quarterly Review* 73 (Spring 1997): 191.

45. Red Smith, "Death of an Unconquerable Man," *New York Times*, October 25, 1972, 53.

46. These articles appeared on January 11, 1950, and December 10, 1952, respectively.

47. Kahn, *The Boys of Summer*, 121.

48. Red Barber, "It Was Never a Game for Jackie," *New York Times*, November 12,

1972, https://timesmachine.nytimes.com/timesmachine/1972/11/12/91354522.pdf
?pdf_redirect=true&ip=0.

49. Rachel Robinson, *Jackie Robinson*, 86.

50. Jackie Robinson, "The Church and the World," May 3, 1968, JRP, box 8, folder 3, Manuscript Division, LOC, Washington, DC, 6.

51. Orr, "Jackie Robinson," 54.

52. Kahn, *The Boys of Summer*, 108.

53. Rampersad, *Jackie Robinson*, 218.

54. Jackie Robinson, *I Never Had It Made: Jackie Robinson, an Autobiography* (New York: HarperCollins, 1995), 79.

55. Jackie Robinson, "Now I Know Why They Boo Me!," *Look*, January 25, 1955, 24.

56. Editors of *Sport* magazine, "Hurray for Jackie Robinson," *Negro History Bulletin* 18 (January 1955): 93.

57. "Meet the Press," April 14, 1957, Library of Congress, https://www.loc.gov
/collections/jackie-robinson-baseball/articles-and-essays/baseball-the-color-line
-and-jackie-robinson/meet-the-press/.

58. Dave Anderson, "Jackie Robinson," 56.

59. Carl Erskine, "Greetings," in *Jackie Robinson: Race, Sports, and the American Dream*, ed. Joseph Dorinson and Joram Warmund (Armonk, NY: M. E. Sharp, 1999), 238.

60. Jonathan Eig, *Opening Day: The Story of Jackie Robinson's First Season* (New York: Simon & Schuster, 2007), 12.

61. Roger Kahn, "Another Viewpoint," *New York Herald Tribune*, August 29, 1954, B3.

62. Jackie Robinson, "Home Plate," *New York Amsterdam News*, January 12, 1962, 11.

63. E.g., Kahn, *The Boys of Summer*, 110–11, 120–21.

64. Robert Creamer, afterword to Jocko Conlan and Robert Creamer, *Jocko* (Lincoln: University of Nebraska Press, 1997), 151.

65. "Interview with Rachel Robinson."

66. Scott Simon, *Jackie Robinson and the Integration of Baseball* (Hoboken, NJ: Wiley & Sons, 2007), 7. Cf. Tygiel, *Baseball's Great Experiment*, 322.

67. Roger Kahn, *Rickey & Robinson: The True, Untold Story of the Integration of Baseball* (New York: Rodale, 2014), 274. See also Kahn, *The Boys of Summer*, 390.

68. Reichler to JR, February 17, 1958, JRP, Manuscript Division, LOC, Washington, DC.

69. Kahn, "Jackie Robinson," 88.

70. See Lyle Dorsett, *Billy Sunday and the Redemption of Urban America* (Grand Rapids: Eerdmans, 1991).

71. Donald McKim, "'Matty' and 'Ol' Pete': Divergent American Heroes," in *The Faith of 50 Million: Baseball, Religion, and American Culture*, ed. Christopher Evans and William Herzog II (Louisville: Westminster John Knox, 2002), 76.

72. Paul Putz and Art Remillard, "Ten Christian Athletes Who Were Tebowing before Tebow," *Christianity Today*, September 28, 2016, https://www.christianitytoday
.com/history/2016/september/ten-christian-athletes-who-were-tebowing-before
-tebow.html. See also Eric Rolfe Greenberg, *The Celebrant* (New York: Everest House, 1983); Ray Robinson, *Matty, an American Hero: Christy Mathewson of the New York Giants* (New York: Oxford University Press, 1993); and Bob Gaines, *Christy Mathewson,*

the Christian Gentleman: How One Man's Faith and Fastball Forever Changed Baseball (Lanham, MD: Rowman & Littlefield, 2014).

73. McKim, "'Matty' and 'Ol' Pete,'" 76.

74. Barry Lewis, "Pro Baseball: Popular Former Tulsa Coach Pepper Martin Joins Cards Hall of Fame," *Tulsa World*, August 26, 2017, https://tulsaworld.com/sports extra/drillers/pro-baseball-popular-former-tulsa-coach-pepper-martin-joins-cards -hall-of-fame/article_f1496d31-b199-597e-91f2-a9385f7daf19.html. See also Thomas Barthel, *Pepper Martin: A Baseball Biography* (Jefferson, NC: McFarland, 2003).

75. See "A Tribute to Jackie Robinson," John F. Kennedy Presidential Library and Museum, October 16, 2007, https://www.jfklibrary.org/events-and-awards/forums /past-forums/transcripts/a-tribute-to-jackie-robinson; Tom Oliphant, *Praying for Gil Hodges* (New York: St. Martin's, 2013).

76. Putz and Remillard, "Ten Christian Athletes Who Were Tebowing before Tebow." See also John Sickels, *Bob Feller: Ace of the Greatest Generation* (Lincoln: University of Nebraska Press, 2014).

77. On Alou, see Paul Putz, "The Pioneering Felipe Alou, Latino Christian Athlete," *Real Clear Religion*, July 18, 2017, https://www.realclearreligion.org/2017/07/18 /the_pioneering_felipe_alou_latino_christian_athlete_277945.html.

78. Hank Aaron, "Guidepost Classics: Hank Aaron on Sacrificing for Others," *Guideposts*, September 1973, https://www.guideposts.org/better-living/entertain ment/sports/guideposts-classics-hank-aaron-sacrifice-for-others.

79. Kenny Herzog, "Major League Baseball Has Hit a Christian Crossroads," *Inside Hook*, May 15, 2019, https://www.insidehook.com/article/sports/baseballs -christian-crossroads-evangelical-mlb. See Rob Maaddi, *Mike Schmidt: The Phillies' Legendary Slugger* (Chicago: Triumph Books, 2010).

80. Email to the author, September 12, 2017.

81. Lee Weeks, "Dave Dravecky's Fateful Pitch Glorifies Christ—30 Years Later," *Decision Magazine*, April 1, 2020, https://decisionmagazine.com/dave-draveckys-fate ful-pitch-glorifies-christ-30-years-later/.

82. Gary Scott Smith, *A History of Christianity in Pittsburgh* (Charleston, SC: History, 2019), 200–201.

83. Clayton Trutor, "10 of the Best Books on Sports and Christianity from the Past 10 Years," *Christianity Today*, December 30, 2020, https://www.christianitytoday .com/ct/2020/december-web-only/10-best-books-sports-christianity-past-10-years .html?utm.

84. Samuel Smith, "10 MLB Players You Didn't Know Were Christian," *Christian Post*, March 3, 2017, https://www.christianpost.com/news/10-mlb-players-you-didnt -know-were-christian.html?page=5.

85. Samuel Smith, "10 MLB Players You Didn't Know Were Christian."

86. See Megan Bailey, "Christian Baseball Athletes to Watch in the MLB Playoffs," beliefnet, accessed October 20, 2021, https://www.beliefnet.com/entertainment /sports/christian-baseball-athletes-to-watch-in-the-mlb-playoffs.aspx.

87. See Dave Zirin, "The Rockies Pitch Religion," *Nation*, June 2, 2006, https:// www.thenation.com/article/archive/rockies-pitch-religion/.

88. Steve Cady, "Jackie Goes Home to Brooklyn," *New York Times*, October 28,

1972, 25; "Thousands Mourn Jackie Robinson," *New York Amsterdam News*, November 4, 1972; Hamilton Bims, "Black America Says, 'Goodbye, Jackie,'" *Ebony*, December 1972, 174.

89. "Jack Roosevelt Robinson," *Ebony*, December 1972, 170.

90. Jesse Jackson, "Eulogy for Jackie Robinson," October 27, 1972, in *Jackie Robinson and Race in America: A Brief History with Documents*, ed. Thomas Zeiler (Boston: Bedford/St. Martin's, 2014).

91. George Vecsey, "For Baseball and the Country, Jackie Robinson Changed the Game," *New York Times*, January 31, 2019, https://www.nytimes.com/2019/01/31/sports/baseball-jackie-robinson-integration.html. For other athletes Robinson influenced both in their sports and civic engagement, see Peter Dreier, "The First Famous Jock for Justice," in *42 Today: Jackie Robinson and His Legacy*, ed. Michael G. Long (New York: New York University Press, 2021), 154–76, and Amira Rose Davis, "Supporting Black Women Athletes," in Long, *42 Today*, 177–88.

92. Eig, *Opening Day*, 77; Margalit Fox, "Gilbert Jonas, 76, N.A.A.C.P. Fund-Raiser, Dies," *New York Times*, September 27, 2006, https://www.nytimes.com/2006/09/27/obituaries/27jonas.html.

93. Hank Aaron, "When Baseball Mattered," *New York Times*, April 13, 1997, https://www.nytimes.com/1997/04/13/opinion/when-baseball-mattered.html.

94. Douglas Brinkley, "A Final Interview with Hank Aaron: 'I Recognized That I Had a Gift,'" *New York Times*, January 23, 2021, https://www.nytimes.com/2021/01/23/opinion/hank-aaron-interview.html.

95. Quoted in "The Big 10 with Jeff D'Alessio: Black History Month Heroes," *Champaign (IL) News-Gazette*, February 23, 2020, https://www.news-gazette.com/news/the-big-10-with-jeff-dalessio-black-history-month-heroes/article_7b06ffb8-6226-561f-b6ed-9cfc75830868.html.

96. Hank Aaron, introduction to *I Never Had It Made*, by Jackie Robinson, xv.

97. Aaron to Rachel Robinson, October 25, 1972, in Long, *First Class Citizenship*, 320.

98. Aaron, "When Baseball Mattered."

99. Dave Anderson, "Jackie Robinson," 56.

100. Kareem Abdul-Jabbar with Mignon McCarthy, *Kareem* (New York: Random House, 1990), 190.

101. Rafer Johnson, "Training to Win," *Christian Athlete*, September 1962, https://bayareafca.org/newpage. See also "Rafer Johnson: An Athlete Whose Faith Came First," by the editors of *Guidepost*, December 1958, https://www.guideposts.org/better-living/entertainment/sports/rafer-johnson-an-athlete-whose-faith-came-first; Rafer Johnson, *The Best That I Can Be* (New York: Doubleday, 1998), 18–19, 46–48, 83–86, 129, 191, 206; Bill Dwyre, "Appreciation: Rafer Johnson Was a Humble Champion Who Put Others in the Spotlight," *Los Angeles Times*, December 5, 2020, https://www.latimes.com/sports/story/2020-12-05/rafer-johnson-humble-olympic-champion; "Rafer Johnson, 86, Olympic Medalist, Champion for Equality and Exemplar of Bruin Values," *UCLA Newsroom*, December 2, 2020, https://newsroom.ucla.edu/stories/rafer-johnson-exemplar-bruin-values.

102. Quoted in David Falkner, *Great Time Coming: The Life of Jackie Robinson from Baseball to Birmingham* (New York: Simon & Schuster, 1995), 237.

103. Morris to JR, February 1, 1971, in Long, *First Class Citizenship*, 304.

104. Spike Lee, introduction to *Baseball Has Done It*, by Jackie Robinson, 9, 11.

105. "How Jackie Robinson Saved My Life by Vince Antonucci," Will Mancini, April 2013, https://www.willmancini.com/how-jackie-robinson-saved-my-life-by -vince-antonucci.

106. Claire Smith, "Jackie Robinson Showed Me How to Fight On, Not Fight Back," *New York Times*, January 31, 2019, https://www.nytimes.com/2019/01/31 /sports/jackie-robinson-women-color-barrier.html.

107. Aaron, "When Baseball Mattered."

108. "Hank Aaron Became America's Home Run King," accessed October 21, 2020, https://sports.jrank.org/pages/10/Aaron-Hank-Became-America-s-Home-Run -King.html; Angela Tuck, "Hank Aaron Wants to Be Remembered for More Than Home Runs," *Undefeated*, April 14, 2017, https://theundefeated.com/features/hank -aaron-remembered-for-more-than-home-runs/; Richard Goldstein, "Hank Aaron, Home Run King Who Defied Racism, Dies at 86," *New York Times*, January 22, 2021, https://www.nytimes.com/2021/01/22/sports/baseball/hank-aaron-dead.html; David Von Drehle, "Henry Aaron Did as Much as Anyone to Redeem the South," *Washington Post*, January 22, 2021, https://www.washingtonpost.com/opinions/hank-aaron -did-as-much-as-anyone-to-redeem-the-south/2021/01/22/6eeb8242-5cec-11eb-8b cf-3877871c819d_story.html; Howard Bryant, *Hank Aaron: Baseball's Last Hero* (New York: Pantheon Books, 2010).

109. See the following websites, http://davewinfieldhof.com/winfield-foundation/ and http://davewinfieldhof.com/.

110. Tygiel, *Baseball's Great Experiment*, 345.

111. Michael G. Long, "That Day," in Long, *42 Today*, 4.

112. The Snider quotation comes from IMDB, accessed October 21, 2020, https://m.imdb.com/name/nm0811128/quotes.

113. Craig Muder, "Jackie Robinson Left Lasting Legacy," National Baseball Hall of Fame, accessed October 21, 2021, https://baseballhall.org/discover/inside-pitch /jackie/robinson/legacy.

114. Quoted in Juan Williams, "After the Cheering Stopped, Jackie Robinson Played Harder Than Ever," *Washington Post*, April 12, 1987, https://www.washington post.com/archive/lifestyle/magazine/1987/04/12/after-the-cheering-stopped-jackie -robinson-played-harder-than-ever-in-1947-he-broke-baseballs-color-line-then-un like-so-many-of-todays-star-athletes-he-used-fame-as-a-way-tohelp-his-people /a06b8ec8-8c04-420a-b0d4-dcd10f7bb715/.

115. See Samuel Regalado, "Jackie Robinson and the Emancipation of Latin American Baseball Players," in Dorinson and Warmund, *Race, Sports, and the American Dream*, 157–64; Adrian Burgos, *Playing America's Game: Baseball, Latinos, and the Color Line* (Berkeley: University of California Press, 2007), 188, 197 (quotation).

116. Quoted in Henry, "Jackie Robinson," 202.

117. Henry, "Jackie Robinson," 198.

118. Rampersad, *Jackie Robinson*, 186–87.

119. Steven Norword and Harold Brackman, "Going to Bat for Jackie Robinson: The Jewish Role in Breaking Baseball's Color Line," *Journal of Sport History* 26 (Spring

1999): 127. See also Rebecca Alpert, "Jackie Robinson: Jewish Icon," *Shofar: An Interdisciplinary Journal of Jewish Studies* 26 (Winter 2008): 42, 48–51; Ivan Hametz, "A Ten-Year-Old Dodger Fan Welcomes Jackie Robinson to Brooklyn," in Dorinson and Warmund, *Race, Sports, and the American Dream,* 68; Peter Levine, "Father and Son at Ebbets Field," in Dorinson and Warmund, 63.

120. Mary Caffrey, "Robinson Biography Puts Baseball Great in Context," *Princeton Weekly Bulletin,* September 15, 1997, https://pr.princeton.edu/pwb/97/0915/0915 -robinson.html.

121. Tygiel, *Baseball's Great Experiment,* 346. This celebration largely ignored Latinos, prompting protests from many active and retired Latino players (Burgos, *Playing America's Game,* 196).

122. Alpert, "Jackie Robinson," 57.

123. Simon, *Jackie Robinson,* 151.

124. Kevin Nelson, comp., *Baseball's Greatest Quotes: The Wit, Wisdom, and Wisecracks of America's National Pastime* (New York: Simon & Schuster, 1982), 369.

125. A. S. Young, *Negro Firsts in Sports,* quoted in Hamilton Bims, "Black America Says, 'Goodbye, Jackie,'" *Ebony,* December 1972, 174.

126. Roy Wilkins, foreword to *Jackie Robinson,* by Rachel Robinson, 11.

127. "Jack Roosevelt Robinson," *Ebony,* December 1972, 170.

128. Quoted in Cady, "Jackie Goes Home," 25.

129. See David Naze, "On Retiring 42," in Long, *42 Today,* 71–80.

130. Robinson, "Home Plate," *New York Amsterdam News,* January 19, 1963, 11.

131. Jackie Robinson Foundation, https://www.jackierobinson.org/museum.

132. Michael Anderson, "Baseball in Black and White: Whoever Wants to Know the Heart and Mind of America Had Better Learn the Jackie Robinson Story," *New York Times,* October 19, 1997, https://archive.nytimes.com/www.nytimes.com/books/97 /10/19/reviews/971019.19anderst.html (first and second quotations); Rampersad, *Jackie Robinson,* 180 (third quotation).

133. Jon Meacham, "Jackie Robinson's Inner Struggle," *New York Times,* July 20, 2020, https://www.nytimes.com/2020/07/20/books/review/jackie-robinson-inner -struggle.html.

134. Tygiel, *Baseball's Great Experiment,* 320.

135. Mike Wise and the Undefeated, "'Jackie Robinson' Documentary Kills Myths of Civil Rights Legend," ESPN, April 11, 2016, https://www.espn.com/mlb/story /_/id/15183801/ken-burns-new-jackie-robinson-documentary-kills-myths-civil -rights-legend-mlb.

136. John Thorn, *Baseball in the Garden of Eden: The Secret History of the Early Game* (New York: Simon & Schuster, 2011), xi.

137. Phil Alden Robinson, *Field of Dreams* (Universal City, CA: MCA Home Video, 1989).

138. Randy Roberts, "Baseball Myths and American Realities," *Reviews in American History* 10 (March 1982): 141–45; 145 (first quotation), 142 (second quotation), 144 (third and fourth quotations).

139. Joseph Campbell with Bill Moyers, *The Power of Myth* (New York: Doubleday Dell, 1988); Michael Wood, *In Search of Myths and Heroes* (London: BBC Books, 2005);

Mark Goddard, "Mythology—What Purpose Do Myths Serve in Society and Culture?," HealthGuidance.org, updated January 29, 2020, https://www.healthguidance.org/en try/17778/1/mythology-what-purpose-do-myths-serve-in-society-and-culture.html.

140. Henry, "Jackie Robinson," 202 (quotation), 203.

141. John Kelly, "Integrating America: Jackie Robinson, Critical Events and Base-ball Black and White," *International Journal of the History of Sport* 22, no. 6 (2005): 1030.

142. Long and Lamb, *Jackie Robinson*, 95.

143. Red Barber with Robert Creamer, *Rhubarb in the Catbird Seat* (Garden City, NY: Doubleday, 1968), 272–73.

144. Eig, *Opening Day*, 275.

145. *Christian Science Monitor*, December 5, 1996, B4.

146. "Supporting the Pursuit of Excellence," https://jackierobinson.org/schol arship/; Peter Dreier, "In Ken Burns' New Documentary, Rachel Robinson Finally Gets Her Due," *Huffington Post*, April 8, 2016, https://www.huffpost.com/entry/in -ken-burns-new-document_b_9645502.

147. Peter J. Kaplan, "Rachel Robinson," Peter J. Kaplan, July 15, 2020, https:// petejkaplan.medium.com/rachel-robinson-edca2f4038ef.

148. Claire Smith, "Jackie Robinson Showed Me How to Fight On, Not Fight Back."

149. Kurt Streeter, "Sports Are Returning to Normal. So Is Their Role in Political Fights," *New York Times*, March 15, 2021, https://www.nytimes.com/2021/03/15/sports /transgender-sports-mcdermott-leonard.html.

150. Michael P. Jeffries, "Athletes Are Finished Playing America's Rigged Game," *New York Times*, August 28, 2020, https://www.nytimes.com/2020/08/28/opinion /NBA-boycott-history.html?campaign_id=2&emc=edit_th_20200829&instance_id =21739&nl=todaysheadlines&regi_id=22350591&segment_id=37150&user_id=5fd 181c059d04ab3e0b4910db10e7372.

151. Simon Henderson, *How American Sports Challenged the Black Freedom Struggle* (Lexington: University Press of Kentucky 2013); Charles Martin, *Benching Jim Crow: The Rise and Fall of the Color Line in Southern College Sports, 1890–1980* (Urbana: University of Illinois Press, 2010).

152. Frank Andre Guridy, *The Sports Revolution: How Texas Changed the Culture of American Athletics* (Austin: University of Texas Press, 2021), 85, 90 (first quotation), 94 (second quotation).

153. Michael Hurd, *Thursday Night Lights: The Story of Black High School Football in Texas* (Austin: University of Texas Press, 2017), 183.

154. Henderson, *How American Sports Challenged the Black Freedom Struggle*; Doug-las Kellner, "Sports, Media, Culture, and Race: Some Reflections on Michael Jordan," *Journal of Sociology of Sport* 13, no. 4 (1996): 462–65; Harry Edwards, *The Revolt of the Black Athlete* (New York: Free Press, 1969); Douglas Hartmann, *Race, Culture, and the Revolt of the Black Athlete* (Chicago: University of Chicago Press, 2003); Simon Hen-derson, "Crossing the Line: Sport and the Limits of Civil Rights Protest," *International Journal of the History of Sport* 26 (January 2009): 101–21.

155. Henderson, *How American Sports Challenged the Black Freedom Struggle*; John Hoberman, *Darwin's Athletes: How Sport Has Damaged Black America and Preserved the*

Myth of Race (New York: Houghton Mifflin, 1997); Dana Brooks and Ronald Althouse, "Fifty Years after Jackie Robinson: Equal Access but Unequal Outcome," in *Racism in College Athletics*, ed. Dana Brooks and Ronald Althouse (Morgantown, WV: Fitness Information Technology, 2000), 301–10; C. K. Pace, ed., *Race and Sport: The Struggle for Equality on and off the Field* (Jackson: University Press of Mississippi, 2004).

156. See, for example, Tyler Kepner, "The Hall of Fame Tries to Contextualize Baseball's Racist Past," *New York Times*, December 21, 2020, https://www.nytimes.com/2020/12/21/sports/baseball/hall-of-fame.html.

157. Barry Svrluga, "Baseball Is Finally Addressing Its Racist Past, but Its Work Can't End There," *Washington Post*, December 16, 2020, https://www.washingtonpost.com/sports/2020/12/16/mlb-josh-gibson-satchel-paige-negro-leagues/. For recent trends of African American and Latino players, see Burgos, *Playing America's Game*, and Rob Ruck, *Raceball: How the Major Leagues Colonized the Black and Latin Game* (Boston: Beacon, 2012). Sadly, during the 1950s, Latinos, like blacks, faced beanballs, bench jockeying, and taunts from fans who opposed integration.

158. In 2020 black major leaguers created the Players Alliance to increase the diversity in MLB. See "About Us," https://theplayersalliance.com/about/; Barry Svrluga, "After Summer Awakening, MLB players Are Taking Their Efforts to the Streets," *Washington Post*, December 4, 2020, https://www.washingtonpost.com/sports/2020/12/04/players-alliance-tour-covid/; Mark Feinsand, "MLB Commits up to $150M to Players Alliance," July 12, 2021, https://www.mlb.com/news/mlb-players-alliance-donation.

159. Julie Zauzmer, "The Bible Was Used to Justify Slavery. Then Africans Made It Their Path to Freedom," *Washington Post*, April 30, 2019, https://www.washingtonpost.com/local/the-bible-was-used-to-justify-slavery-then-africans-made-it-their-path-to-freedom/2019/04/29/34699e8e-6512-11e9-82ba-fcfeff232e8f_story.html.

160. Isaac Chotiner, "Bryan Stevenson on the Frustration behind the George Floyd Protests," *New Yorker*, June 1, 2020, https://www.newyorker.com/news/q-and-a/bryan-stevenson-on-the-frustration-behind-the-george-floyd-protests.

161. Timothy Dalrymple, "Justice Too Long Delayed," *Christianity Today*, June 10, 2020, https://www.christianitytoday.com/ct/2020/june-web-only/justice-too-long-delayed.html.

162. Robert Ellis, *The Games People Play: Theology, Religion, and Sports* (Eugene, OR: Wipf & Stock, 2014); quotation from Clayton Trutor, "10 of the Best Books on Sports and Christianity from the Past 10 Years," *Christianity Today*, December 30, 2020, https://www.christianitytoday.com/ct/2020/december-web-only/10-best-books-sports-christianity-past-10-years.html?utm.

163. Quoted in Christopher Klein, "Silent No Longer: The Outspoken Jackie Robinson," History.com, April 14, 2017, https://www.history.com/news/silent-no-longer-the-outspoken-jackie-robinson.

A Note on Sources

The Jackie Robinson Papers at the Library of Congress in Washington, DC, contain numerous materials about Robinson's religious beliefs and life, most importantly, his undated, unpublished manuscript "My Greatest Day." His papers also contain several of Robinson's addresses and letters he exchanged with Branch Rickey and others about religious matters. In addition, the collection contains letters written to Robinson that discuss religious themes. Also helpful for understanding Robinson's religious life is "Mrs. Robinson's Notes," an undated interview of Jackie's mother, Mallie, by journalist Carl Rowan.

Two other collections of personal papers shed light on Robinson's faith and the integration of baseball. The Branch Rickey Papers at the Library of Congress include many items that explain Robinson's religious convictions and activities as well as correspondence between the two men. The Wendell Smith Papers at the National Baseball Hall of Fame, Cooperstown, New York, detail the important role of the African American sportswriter in integrating Major League Baseball.

Jackie Robinson discusses his religious beliefs and practices in his four autobiographies: *Jackie Robinson: My Own Story* (New York: Greenburg, 1948); *Baseball Has Done It* (Brooklyn, NY: Ig, 2005 [1964]) (which includes statements by numerous other black major leaguers); *Breakthrough to the Big League: The Story of Jackie Robinson* (New York: Harper & Row, 1965);

and *I Never Had It Made: Jackie Robinson, an Autobiography* (New York: HarperCollins, 1995 [1972]).

Robinson also testifies to his faith in several articles and speeches, including "Trouble Ahead Needn't Bother You," *Guideposts*, August 1948, available under the headline "Guideposts Classics: Jackie Robinson on Facing Challenges," https://www.guideposts.org/better-living/entertainment/sports/guideposts-classics-jackie-robinson-on-facing-challenges; "Robinson Never Forgets Mother's Advice," *Washington Post*, August 23, 1949, 12–13; "Jackie Robinson: This I Believe," NPR, March 25, 2008; this is from a 1952 episode for Edward R. Murrow's radio series and is available at https://www.npr.org/templates/story/story.php?storyId=89030535; and his Hall of Fame speech, July 23, 1962, https://www.americanrhetoric.com/speeches/jackierobinsonbaseballhofinduction.htm.

In his "Jackie Robinson Says" columns in the *Pittsburgh Courier* written during the 1947 and 1948 MLB seasons, Robinson describes the challenges he faced in integrating the game. In 1959 and 1960, Robinson wrote three columns a week for the *New York Post*. From 1962 to 1968, he penned a weekly column for the *New York Amsterdam News* titled "Home Plate." These columns discuss Robinson's views on a wide variety of social, economic, political, and religious topics.

Books and articles by Jackie's wife, Rachel, and daughter, Sharon, also discuss his faith. The most important ones are Rachel Robinson, "I Live with a Hero," *McCall's*, March 1951, 39–40, 106, 111–16; Rachel Robinson with Lee Daniels, *Jackie Robinson: An Intimate Portrait* (New York: Abrams, 1996); Sharon Robinson, *Stealing Home: An Intimate Family Portrait by the Daughter of Jackie Robinson* (New York: HarperPerennial, 1997); "Interview with Rachel Robinson," *Scholastic*, February 11, 1998, https://www.scholastic.com/teachers/articles/teaching-content/interview-rachel-robinson/. Also helpful is Carl Erskine and Burton Rocks, *What I Learned from Jackie Robinson: A Teammate's Reflections on and off the Field* (New York: McGraw-Hill, 2005).

Robinson has been the subject of numerous biographies. Several sportswriters who knew Robinson personally and watched him play comment on his faith, including Bill Roeder, *Jackie Robinson* (New York: A. S. Barnes, 1950); Arthur Mann, *The Jackie Robinson Story* (New York: Grosset & Dunlop, 1951); Carl Rowan, *Wait Till Next Year: The Life Story of Jackie Robin-

son (New York: Random House, 1960); Roger Kahn, *The Boys of Summer* (Evanston, IL: Holtzman, 1972); and Maury Allen, *Jackie Robinson: A Life Remembered* (New York: Franklin Watts, 1987).

The best biography of Robinson is Arnold Rampersad, *Jackie Robinson: A Biography* (New York: Knopf, 1997), which pays significant attention to his religious life. Other helpful biographies are David Falkner, *Great Time Coming: The Life of Jackie Robinson from Baseball to Birmingham* (New York: Simon & Schuster, 1995), and Scott Simon, *Jackie Robinson and the Integration of Baseball* (Hoboken, NJ: Wiley & Sons, 2007). While analyzing broader themes, Jules Tygiel, *Baseball's Great Experiment: Jackie Robinson and His Legacy* (New York: Oxford University Press, 2008), discusses many aspects of Robinson's life.

Two biographies published in 2017—Michael G. Long and Chris Lamb, *Jackie Robinson: A Spiritual Biography; The Faith of a Boundary-Breaking Hero* (Louisville: Westminster John Knox), and Ed Henry, *42 Faith: The Rest of the Jackie Robinson Story* (Nashville: W Publishing)—highlight Robinson's religious convictions and the connection between his faith and activism.

Dozens of scholarly and popular articles insightfully analyze Robinson's character, convictions, MLB career, and postbaseball activities. Especially important are editors of *Sport* magazine, "Hurray for Jackie Robinson," *Negro History Bulletin* 18 (January 1955): 93; Jack Orr, "Jackie Robinson: Symbol of the Revolution," *Sport* 29 (March 1960): 52–59; Joe Reichler, "He's Just as Touchy, Outspoken, Dedicated," *Asbury Park (NJ) Press*, February 18, 1962, 10; A. S. Young, "The Black Athlete in the Golden Age of Sports: Branch Rickey Launched Negroes to Stardom with Signing of Jackie Robinson," *Ebony*, November 1968; Bill Weaver, "The Black Press and the Assault on Professional Baseball's Color Line, October 1945–April 1947," *Phylon* 40 (Winter 1979): 303–17; David Wiggins, "Wendell Smith, the Pittsburgh Courier-Journal and the Campaign to Include Blacks in Organized Baseball, 1933-1945," *Journal of Sport History* 10 (Summer 1983): 5–29; Chris Kaltenbach, "Jackie Robinson: At Bat for Equality," *Baltimore Sun*, February 15, 1995, https://www.baltimoresun.com/news/bs-xpm-1995-02-15-1995046149-story.html; Roger Kahn, "The Jackie Robinson I Remember," *Journal of Blacks in Higher Education* 14 (Winter 1996/1997): 88–93; Patrick Henry, "Jackie Robinson: Athlete and American Par Excellence," *Virginia Quarterly Review* 73 (Spring 1997): 189–203; Chris

Lamb, "'I Never Want to Take Another Trip like This One': Jackie Robinson's Journey to Integrate Baseball," *Journal of Sport History* 24 (Summer 1997): 177–91; Joseph Dorinson, "Paul Robeson and Jackie Robinson: Athletes and Activists at Armageddon," *Pennsylvania History* 66 (Winter 1999): 16–26; Steven Norword and Harold Brackman, "Going to Bat for Jackie Robinson: The Jewish Role in Breaking Baseball's Color Line," *Journal of Sport History* 26 (Spring 1999): 115–41; Larry Powell, "Jackie Robinson and Dixie Walker: Myths of the Southern Baseball Player," *Southern Cultures* 8 (Summer 2002): 56–70; John Kelly, "Integrating America: Jackie Robinson, Critical Events and Baseball Black and White," *International Journal of the History of Sport* 22, no. 6 (2005): 1011–35; Rebecca Alpert, "Jackie Robinson: Jewish Icon," *Shofar: An Interdisciplinary Journal of Jewish Studies* 26 (Winter 2008): 42–58; Jack Doyle, "Reese & Robbie, 1945–2005," Pop History Dig, June 29, 2011, https://www.pophistorydig.com/topics/pee -wee-and-jackie/; Brian Carroll, "This Is IT! The PR Campaign by Wendell Smith and Jackie Robinson," *Journalism History* 37, no. 3 (2011): 151–62; Peter Dreier, "The Real Story of Baseball's Integration That You Won't See in *42*," *Atlantic*, April 11, 2013, https://www.theatlantic.com/entertainment /archive/2013/04/the-real-story-of-baseballs-integration-that-you-wont -see-in-i-42-i/274886/; Gene Seymour, "What the Jackie Robinson Film Leaves Out," *New Republic*, April 18, 2013, https://newrepublic.com/arti cle/112953/jackie-robinson-and-42-conservative-politics; Abraham Khan, "Jackie Robinson, Civic Republicanism, and Black Political Culture," in *Sports and Identity: New Agendas in Communication,* ed. Barry Brummett (New York: Routledge, 2014), 83–105, available at https://www.academia .edu/15605045/Jackie_Robinson_Civic_Republicanism_and_Black_Po litical_Culture; David Prince, "The 'Ferocious Christian Gentleman' be-hind Jackie Robinson's Famous Moment," Prince on Preaching, April 15, 2015, https://www.davidprince.com/2015/04/15/the-ferocious-christian -gentleman-behind-jackie-robinsons-famous-moment-2/; William Nack, "The Breakthrough: Why May 1947 Was Crucial for Jackie Robinson," *Sports Illustrated*, April 15, 2015, https://www.si.com/mlb/2015/04/15 /jackie-robinson-day-william-nack-si-vault; Chris Lamb, "Breaking the Color Line: The Politics of Signing Jackie Robinson," *New Republic*, April 13, 2016, https://newrepublic.com/article/132646/breaking-color-line-politics -signing-jackie-robinson; Justin Tinsley, "Jackie Robinson vs. Malcolm X,"

Undefeated, May 25, 2016, https://theundefeated.com/features/jackie
-robinson-vs-malcolm-x/; Jerome Ledoux, "Untold Part of Jackie Robinson Story Centers on Faith," *Daily World*, May 28, 2017, https://www.daily
world.com/story/opinion/2017/05/28/untold-part-jackie-robinson-story
-centers-faith/102097256/; Steven Levingston, "Before Trump vs. the
NFL, There Was Jackie Robinson vs. JFK," *Washington Post*, September 24,
2017, https://www.washingtonpost.com/news/retropolis/wp/2017/09/24
/before-trump-vs-the-nfl-there-was-jackie-robinson-vs-jfk/; Clemente
Lisi, "Jackie Robinson's Forgotten Christianity: How Being a Devout Methodist Impacted His Life," *Religion Unplugged*, February 20, 2019, https://re
ligionunplugged.com/news/2019/2/19/jackie-robinson-and-christianity
-how-being-a-devout-methodist-impacted-his-life; Jon Meacham, "Jackie
Robinson's Inner Struggle," *New York Times*, July 20, 2020, https://www
.nytimes.com/2020/07/20/books/review/jackie-robinson-inner-struggle
.html; Paul Putz, "Who Was Karl Downs? Exploring the Life and Legacy
of Jackie Robinson's Mentor," *Faith & Sports*, March 12, 2021, https://blogs
.baylor.edu/faithsports/2021/03/12/who-was-karl-downs-exploring-the
-life-and-legacy-of-jackie-robinsons-mentor/#_edn1.

Three collections of essays about Robinson's life and legacy provide
astute analysis of his faith, MLB career, and civil rights activism: Jules Tygiel, ed., *The Jackie Robinson Reader: Perspectives on an American Hero* (New
York: Penguin, 1997); Joseph Dorinson and Joram Warmund, eds., *Jackie
Robinson: Race, Sports, and the American Dream* (Armonk, NY: M. E. Sharp,
1999); and Michael G. Long, ed., *42 Today: Jackie Robinson and His Legacy*
(New York: New York University Press, 2021).

Two articles discuss Robinson's work as a businessman: Leonard Gross,
"*Pageant* Listens to Jackie Robinson," *Pageant*, May 1957, 139–40, and April
Joyner, "Jackie Robinson, Business Pioneer," *USA Today*, May 11, 2015,
https://www.usatoday.com/story/money/business/2015/05/11/ozy-jackie
-robinson-business-pioneer/27115531/.

Robinson's civil rights activism is described in Juan Williams, "After
the Cheering Stopped, Jackie Robinson Played Harder Than Ever," *Washington Post*, April 12, 1987, https://www.washingtonpost.com/archive/life
style/magazine/1987/04/12/after-the-cheering-stopped-jackie-robinson
-played-harder-than-ever-in-1947-he-broke-baseballs-color-line-then
-unlike-so-many-of-todays-star-athletes-he-used-fame-as-a-way-tohelp

-his-people/a06b8ec8-8c04-420a-b0d4-dcd10f7bb715/; John Vernon, "Beyond the Box Score: Jackie Robinson, Civil Rights Crusader," *Negro History Bulletin* 58 (October-December 1995): 15–22; Michael G. Long, ed., *First Class Citizenship: The Civil Rights Letters of Jackie Robinson* (New York: Holt, 2007); Michael G. Long, ed., *Beyond Home Plate: Jackie Robinson on Life after Baseball* (Syracuse, NY: Syracuse University Press, 2013); Thomas Zeiler, ed., *Jackie Robinson and Race in America: A Brief History with Documents* (Boston: Bedford/St. Martin's, 2014); and Peter Dreier, "Jackie Robinson: A Legacy of Activism," *American Prospect*, January 31, 2019, https://prospect.org/civil-rights/jackie-robinson-legacy-activism.

Sources that provide a context for Robinson's civil rights activism include C. Vann Woodward, *The Strange Career of Jim Crow* (New York: Oxford University Press, 1974); Andrew Manis, *A Fire You Can't Put Out: The Civil Rights Life of Birmingham's Fred Shuttlesworth* (Boston: South End, 1980); Aldon Morris, *The Origins of the Civil Rights Movement: Black Communities Organizing for Change* (New York: Free Press, 1984); Steven Lawson, *Running for Freedom: Civil Rights and Black Politics in America Since 1941* (Philadelphia: Temple University Press, 1991); Gary Scott Smith, *The Search for Social Salvation: Social Christianity and America, 1880–1925* (Lanham, MD: Lexington Books, 2000); Clarence Taylor, *Black Religious Intellectuals: The Fight for Equality from Jim Crow to the Twenty-First Century* (New York: Routledge, 2002); David Chappell, "Religious Revivalism in the Civil Rights Movement," *African American Review* 36 (Winter 2002): 581–95; Barbara Ransby, *Ella Baker and the Black Freedom Movement: A Radical Democratic Vision* (Chapel Hill: University of North Carolina Press, 2003); Dennis Dickerson, *African American Preachers and Politics: The Careys of Chicago* (Jackson: University Press of Mississippi, 2010); Timothy Thurber, *Republicans and Race: The GOP's Frayed Relationship with African Americans, 1945–1974* (Lawrence: University of Kansas Press, 2013); Erik Gellman and Jarod Roll, *The Gospel of the Working Class: Labor's Southern Prophets in New Deal America* (Urbana: University of Illinois Press, 2016); Gary Dorrien, *The New Abolition: W. E. B. Du Bois and the Black Social Gospel* (New Haven: Yale University Press, 2016); and Jarod Roll, *Labor and Religion in the New Cotton South* (Urbana: University of Illinois Press, 2016).

A few sources explain how important Rachel was to Jackie's success, including Roger Wilkins, "Jack and Rachel Robinson," *Nation*, April 21, 1997,

4–5; Kostya Kennedy, "Rachel Robinson Reflects on Her Life with Jackie and the Movie 42," *Sports Illustrated*, April 11, 2013, https://www.si.com/mlb /2013/04/11/rachel-robinson-jackie-robinson-chadwick-boseman-42; Peter Dreier, "In Ken Burns' New Documentary, Rachel Robinson Finally Gets Her Due," *Huffington Post*, April 8, 2016, https://www.huffpost.com/entry /in-ken-burns-new-document_b_9645502; Chris Lamb, "How Jackie Robinson's Wife, Rachel, Helped Him Break Baseball's Color Line," History News Network, January 30, 2019, https://historynewsnetwork.org/arti cle/171107; and Peter J. Kaplan, "Rachel Robinson," Peter J. Kaplan, July 15, 2020, https://petejkaplan.medium.com/rachel-robinson-edca2f4038ef.

Several authors discuss Branch Rickey's personality, faith, and role in the integration of MLB: Arthur Mann, *Branch Rickey: American in Action* (Boston: Houghton Mifflin, 1957); Murray Polner, *Branch Rickey: A Biography* (New York: Athenaeum, 1982); John Chalberg, *Rickey and Robinson: The Preacher, the Player, and America's Game* (Wheeling, IL: Harlan Davidson, 2000); Lee Lowenfish, *Branch Rickey: Baseball's Ferocious Gentleman* (Lincoln: University of Nebraska Press, 2007); and Roger Kahn, *Rickey & Robinson: The True, Untold Story of the Integration of Baseball* (New York: Rodale, 2014).

Several engaging books analyze the relationship between baseball and Christianity, most notably Bart Giamatti, *Take Time for Paradise: Americans and Their Games* (New York: Summit Books, 1989); Christopher Evans and William Herzog II, eds., *The Faith of 50 Million: Baseball, Religion, and American Culture* (Louisville: Westminster John Knox, 2002); John Thorn, *Baseball in the Garden of Eden: The Secret History of the Early Game* (New York: Simon & Schuster, 2011); Mitchell Nathanson, *A People's History of Baseball* (Urbana: University of Illinois Press, 2012); John Sexton, *Baseball as a Road to God* (New York: Gotham, 2014); Robert Ellis, *The Games People Play: Theology, Religion, and Sports* (Eugene, OR: Wipf & Stock, 2014); and Rebecca Alpert and Arthur Remillard, eds., *Gods, Games, and Globalization: New Perspectives on Religion and Sport* (Macon, GA: Mercer University Press, 2019).

Other books assess the development and importance of baseball in American society, including Harold Seymour, *Baseball: The Early Years* (New York: Oxford University Press, 1960); Steven Riess, *Touching Base: Professional Baseball and American Culture in the Progressive Era* (Westport,

CT: Greenwood, 1980); David Voigt, *American Baseball*, 3 vols. (University Park: Pennsylvania State University Press, 1983); Peter Levine, *A. G. Spalding and the Rise of Baseball: The Promise of American Sport* (New York: Oxford University Press, 1985); Harold Seymour, *Baseball: The People's Game* (New York: Oxford University Press, 1990); and John Rossi, *The National Game: Baseball and American Culture* (Chicago: Ivan R. Dee, 2000).

Numerous scholars describe the participation of African Americans, Native Americans, and Latino Americans in professional baseball from the 1880s to the 1960s: John Holway, *Voices from the Great Black Baseball Leagues* (New York: Da Capo, 1975); Robert Peterson, *Only the Ball Was White: A History of Legendary Black Players and All-Black Professional Teams* (New York: Oxford University Press, 1992); Larry Moffi and James Kronstadt, *Crossing the Line: Black Major Leaguers, 1947–1959* (Jefferson, NC: McFarland, 1994); Donn Rogosin, *Invisible Men: Life in Baseball's Negro Leagues* (New York: Kodansha, 1995); Thomas Gilbert, *Baseball at War: World War II and the Fall of the Color Line* (New York: Grolier, 1997); Brad Snyder, *Beyond the Shadow of the Senators: The Untold Story of the Homestead Grays and the Integration of Baseball* (Chicago: Contemporary Books, 2003); Neil Lanctot, *Negro League Baseball: The Rise and Ruin of a Black Institution* (Philadelphia: University of Pennsylvania Press, 2004); Bill Kirwin, *Out of the Shadows: African American Baseball from the Cuban Giants to Jackie Robinson* (Lincoln: University of Nebraska Press, 2005); Adrian Burgos, *Playing America's Game: Baseball, Latinos, and the Color Line* (Berkeley: University of California Press, 2007); Tom Swift, *Chief Bender's Burden: The Silent Struggle of a Baseball Star* (Lincoln: University of Nebraska Press, 2008); Jeffrey Powers-Beck, *The American Indian Integration of Baseball* (Lincoln: University of Nebraska Press, 2009); Rob Ruck, *Raceball: How the Major Leagues Colonized the Black and Latin Game* (Boston: Beacon, 2012); and Paul Putz, "Black Christians Play a Crucial Role in Athlete Activism," *Christianity Today*, August 31, 2020, https://www.christianitytoday.com/ct/2020/august-web-only/nba-protests -christian-athletes-jacob-blake-fca-sports-mini.html.

Many books and articles assess the efforts of African American athletes and sportswriters, Jews, and other groups to combat discrimination in professional sports, including Harry Edwards, *The Revolt of the Black Athlete* (New York: Free Press, 1969); Renford Reese, "The Socio-Political Context of the Integration of Sport in America," *Journal of African American Men*

3 (Spring 1998): 5–22; Douglas Hartmann, *Race, Culture, and the Revolt of the Black Athlete* (Chicago: University of Chicago Press, 2003); C. K. Pace, ed., *Race and Sport: The Struggle for Equality on and off the Field* (Jackson: University Press of Mississippi, 2004); Rick Swayne, *Black Stars Who Made Baseball Whole: The Jackie Robinson Generation in the Major Leagues* (Jefferson, NC: McFarland, 2005); Steve Jacobson, *Carrying Jackie's Torch: The Players Who Integrated Baseball—and America* (New York: Lawrence Hill Books, 2007); Dave Zirin, *What's My Name, Fool? Sports and Resistance in the United States* (Sydney: Accessible Publishing System, 2010); Rebecca Alpert, *Out of Left Field: Jews and Black Baseball* (New York: Oxford University Press, 2011); Chris Lamb, *Conspiracy of Silence: Sportswriters and the Long Campaign to Desegregate Baseball* (Lincoln: University of Nebraska Press, 2012); Simon Henderson, *How American Sports Challenged the Black Freedom Struggle* (Lexington: University Press of Kentucky, 2013); Howard Bryant, *The Heritage: Black Athletes, a Divided America, and the Politics of Patriotism* (Boston: Beacon, 2018); and Frank Andre Guridy, *The Sports Revolution: How Texas Changed the Culture of American Athletics* (Austin: University of Texas Press, 2021).

Other authors discuss various aspects of Robinson's life or the Dodgers' history during his playing career: Red Barber, *1947: When All Hell Broke Loose in Baseball* (New York: Da Capo, 1984); Peter Golembock, *Bums: An Oral History of the Brooklyn Dodgers* (New York: Putnam, 1984); Carl Prince, *Brooklyn's Dodgers: The Bums, the Borough, and the Best of Baseball* (New York: Oxford University Press, 1996); William Marshall, *Baseball's Pivotal Era: 1945–1951* (Lexington: University Press of Kentucky, 1999); Chris Lamb, *Blackout: The Untold Story of Jackie Robinson's First Spring Training* (Lincoln: University of Nebraska Press, 2004); Rudy Marzano, *The Brooklyn Dodgers in the 1940s: How Robinson, MacPhail, Reiser, and Rickey Changed Baseball* (Jefferson, NC: McFarland, 2005); Jonathan Eig, *Opening Day: The Story of Jackie Robinson's First Season* (New York: Simon & Schuster, 2007); Roger Kahn, *The Era, 1947–1957: When the Yankees, the Giants, and the Dodgers Ruled the World* (New York: Diversion Books, 2012); and Michael Lee Lanning, *The Court-Martial of Jackie Robinson: The Baseball Legend's Battle for Civil Rights during World War II* (Lanham, MD: Stackpole Books, 2020).

For the religious context of the late 1940s and 1950s, see Will Herberg, *Protestant, Catholic, Jew: An Essay in American Religious Sociology* (Garden

City, NY: Doubleday, 1955); William Lee Miller, *Piety along the Potomac: Notes on Politics and Morals in the Fifties* (Boston: Houghton Mifflin, 1964); Patrick Allitt, *Religion in America Since 1945* (New York: Columbia University Press, 2003); Diane Kerby, ed., *Religion and the Cold War* (New York: Palgrave Macmillan, 2003); Jonathan Herzog, *The Spiritual-Industrial Complex* (New York: Oxford University Press, 2011); and George Marsden, *The Twilight of the American Enlightenment: The 1950s and the Crisis of Liberal Belief* (New York: Basic Books, 2014).

Two books provide a good overview of mid-twentieth-century American Methodism: Frederick Norwood, *The Story of American Methodism: A History of the United Methodists and Their Relations* (Nashville: Abingdon, 1974); and Russell E. Richey, Kenneth E. Rowe, and Jean Miller Schmidt, *The Methodist Experience in America*, vol. 2, *Sourcebook* (Nashville: Abingdon, 2000).

On other mainline Protestant denominations during this period, see E. Digby Baltzell, *The Protestant Establishment* (New York: Vintage Books, 1964); Martin Marty, *The Public Church: Mainline, Evangelical, Catholic* (New York: Crossroad, 1981); Wade Clark Roof and William McKinney, *American Mainline Religion: Its Changing Shape and Future* (New Brunswick, NJ: Rutgers University Press, 1990); Jason Lantzer, *Mainline Christianity: The Past and Future of America's Majority Faith* (New York: New York University Press, 2012); and Elesha Coffman, *The Christian Century and the Rise of Mainline Protestantism* (New York: Oxford University Press, 2013).

Several books provide a helpful analysis of African American religion from 1920 to 1970, including Harry Richardson, *Dark Glory: A Picture of the Church among Negroes in the Rural South* (New York: Friendship, 1947); Frank Loescher, *The Protestant Church and the Negro* (Westport, CT: Negro Universities Press, 1971); Gayraud Wilmore, *Black Religion and Black Radicalism* (Maryknoll, NY: Orbis, 1983); Hans Baer and Merrill Singer, *African-American Religion in the Twentieth Century: Varieties of Protest and Accommodation* (Knoxville: University of Tennessee Press, 1992); Charles Eric Lincoln and Lawrence Mamiya, *The Black Church in African American Experience* (Durham, NC: Duke University Press, 2005); Sylvester Johnson, *African American Religion, 1500–2000* (New York: Cambridge University Press, 2015); and Dennis Dickerson, *The African Methodist Church: A History* (New York: Cambridge University Press, 2020).

Index

Aaron, Hank, 53, 119, 137, 200–201, 203, 205, 207, 209, 212
Abdul-Jabbar, Kareem, 205
Abernathy, Ralph, 127, 156
Abyssinian Baptist Church in Harlem, 73, 127–28
African American Christianity, 7–8, 10, 126–28
African American churches and civil rights, 126–29, 264n131
African Methodist Episcopal Church, 8, 16, 29, 30, 126, 263n125
Alexander, Sadie, 127
Ali, Muhammad, 147, 159, 204
Anderson, Carl, 23
Andrews, William T., 44
Antonucci, Vince, 206
Armstrong, Richard Stoll, 7, 195

Baker, Ella, 127
Barber, Red, 70, 78, 80, 189, 197
Bartlett, Ray, 24
baseball: and African American players, 2, 4, 113, 114, 117, 145–46, 217, 287n158; and Asian Americans, 4; and black executives, managers, and coaches, 7, 138, 215; Christians in, 199–202; and civil rights, 130–33, 137–38; as a

cultural battleground, 10; impact of the integration of, on other sports, 130, 208; impact of the integration of, on the South, 131, 138; importance of, 1, 10–13, 208; interracial competition in, 4; and Latinos, 4–5, 47, 53, 113, 114, 138, 209, 212, 217, 287n157; as a microcosm of America, 11–12; and myths, 212–15; and Native Americans, 4; origins of, 11, 213; owners of teams as robber barons, 214; popularity of, 12–14, 208; racism in, after 1947, 14, 101–2, 129, 131, 137, 138; television and, 13, 93, 110; therapeutic aspect of, 13–14; and the use of performance-enhancing drugs, 210; values of, 11, 12, 14, 213
Baseball as a Road to God (Sexton), 11
Baseball Chapel, 200, 201, 202
Baseball Has Done It (Robinson), 137
Bender, Charles Albert, 4
Benswanger, William, 48
Berra, Yogi, 42, 116
Bethune, Mary McLeod, 3, 10, 69, 124
Black, William, 135, 159–60, 169, 179–80
Black Panthers, 136, 162, 163
Black Power Movement, 162

Titles published in the

LIBRARY OF RELIGIOUS BIOGRAPHY SERIES

The Kingdom Is Always but Coming: A Life of **Walter Rauschenbusch**
by Christopher H. Evans

Strength for the Fight: The Life and Faith of **Jackie Robinson**
by Gary Scott Smith

A Christian and a Democrat: A Religious Life of **Franklin D. Roosevelt**
by John F. Woolverton with James D. Bratt

Francis Schaeffer *and the Shaping of Evangelical America*
by Barry Hankins

Harriet Beecher Stowe: *A Spiritual Life*
by Nancy Koester

Billy Sunday *and the Redemption of Urban America*
by Lyle W. Dorsett

Howard Thurman *and the Disinherited: A Religious Biography*
by Paul Harvey

Assist Me to Proclaim: The Life and Hymns of **Charles Wesley**
by John R. Tyson

Prophetess of Health: A Study of **Ellen G. White**
by Ronald L. Numbers

George Whitefield: *Evangelist for God and Empire*
by Peter Y. Choi

The Divine Dramatist: **George Whitefield** *and
the Rise of Modern Evangelicalism*
by Harry S. Stout

Liberty of Conscience: **Roger Williams** *in America*
by Edwin S. Gaustad